MIND-READING AND ARTIFICIAL INTELLIGENCE: PAST, PRESENT AND FUTURE

Science, Technology, Applications, Risks and Regulations

Prof. (Dr.) Jai Paul Dudeja

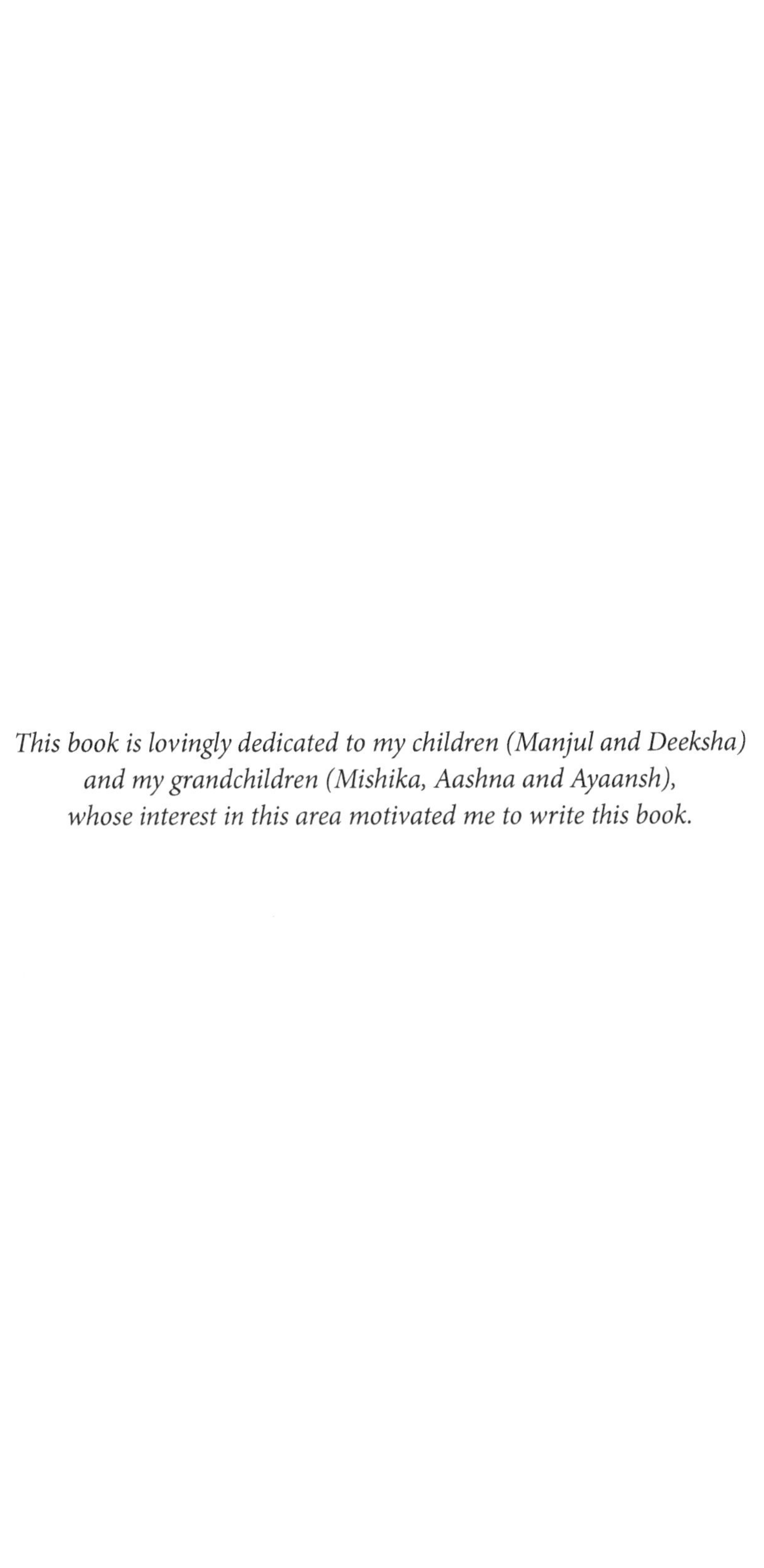

*This book is lovingly dedicated to my children (Manjul and Deeksha)
and my grandchildren (Mishika, Aashna and Ayaansh),
whose interest in this area motivated me to write this book.*

CONTENTS

PREFACE

Dear Readers,

I am extremely happy to see this book titled, **"Mind-Reading and Artificial Intelligence: Past, Present and Future (Science, Technology, Applications, Risks and Regulations)"**, in your hands. It is my firm belief that you have chosen to read this book with a specific aim in mind, and I assure you that you will not be disappointed with it.

Mind-reading typically refers to the ability of discerning or interpreting someone else's thoughts, feelings, or intentions. Mind Reading has two components: human-based, and (ii) device-based (artificial intelligence).

Artificial Intelligence (AI) refers to programming computers to do tasks that normally require human intelligence, like learning, problem-solving, and understanding language. It is like giving computers the ability to think and make decisions on their own, similar to how humans do. AI helps machines learn from data, adapt to new situations, and perform tasks without being explicitly programmed for each step.

This book covers the topics on human-based and device-based mind reading and interpretation (artificial intelligence, that is divided into 32 chapters and the following 8 sections: (i) Mind-Reading and Artificial Intelligence: Introduction and Overview, (ii) Human-Based Mind Reading, (iii) Artificial Intelligence: Introduction & Types of Learning, (iv) Device-Based Mind Reading And Virtual Assistants, (v) Applications and Opportunities of Artificial Intelligence, (vi) Artificial Intelligence: Ethical Issues, Risks and Regulations,

(vii) Artificial Consciousness, and (viii) Artificial Intelligence in India: Status, and the Way Forward.

Following is the list of Sections and Chapters in this book:

SECTION-I: MIND-READING AND ARTIFICIAL INTELLIGENCE: INTRODUCTION AND OVERVIEW

Chapter 1: Introduction and Overview of Mind-Reading and Artificial Intelligence

SECTION II: HUMAN-BASED MIND READING

Chapter 2:   Human-Based Mind Reading

Chapter 3:   Human-Based Mind Reading and Telepathy

Chapter 4:   Mental Clarity and Focus for Mind Reading

Chapter 5:   Harnessing Emotional Intelligence for Mind Reading

SECTION III: ARTIFICIAL INTELLIGENCE: INTRODUCTION & TYPES OF LEARNING

Chapter 6:   Artificial Intelligence: An Introduction

Chapter 7:   History of Artificial Intelligence

Chapter 8:   Machine Language: An Introduction

Chapter 9:   Deep Learning: An Introduction

Chapter 10:   Natural Language Processing (NLP)

Chapter 11:   Weak (Narrow) Artificial Intelligence

Chapter 12:   Artificial General Intelligence (AGI)

Chapter 13:   Artificial Superintelligence (ASI)

Chapter 14:   Expert Systems

Chapter 15.:   ChatGPT

Chapter 16:   Internet of Things (IoT)

Chapter 17:   Fuzzy Logic

This book has been written in an easily understandable language for all the general readers in the world. The author sincerely believes that a book of this nature will be appreciated by all the readers who wish to understand the science, technology, applications, risks and regulations of mind reading and the artificial intelligence.

The author would open heartedly love to receive any encouraging/ critical comments as well as feedback from the dear readers at his Email ID: drjpdudeja@gmail.com

Sincerely

2024 **Prof. (Dr.) Jai Paul Dudeja**

ACKNOWLEDGEMENTS

The seeds of my interest in the continual quest for new knowledge and truth were lovingly sown by my revered parents: **Late (Dr.) Shanti Sawrup Dudeja and (Late) Mrs. Jai Devi Dudeja**. I am sure that they are watching me every moment from wherever they are in the other world and continuously sending their blessings to me.

I have greatly benefitted in going through the books, research papers and articles, referred to in the 'Bibliography' in this Book. I gratefully acknowledge these authors for enhancing my understanding on the subject matter of this book.

Last but not the least, my greatest admiration is reserved for **Mrs. Rita Dudeja**, my wife and my best friend. She is a source of inspiration for me, my honest adviser and a co-traveller on the path of trust and truth.

2024   **Prof. (Dr.) Jai Paul Dudeja**

PROFILE OF THE AUTHOR

Born in June 1948, Prof. (Dr.) Jai Paul Dudeja holds a brilliant academic record. He did his Master's degree from Birla Institute of Technology and Science (BITS), Pilani (India), and Ph.D. degree from the Indian Institute of Technology (IIT), Delhi. He has been in regular employment as a Scientist, Professor, Dean, Director, Principal and a Senior Administrator in various educational institutions, universities, laboratories, and public and private organizations. He superannuated as a Senior Scientist and Additional Director in May 2008 from the Defence Research and Development Organisation (DRDO), Government of India. After DRDO, he served for over 11 years, till his last posting as a Director at Amity University Gurgaon, from where he retired in Nov 2019.

Till date, Dr. Dudeja has published/presented about 90 research papers in various national and international journals/conferences. Out of these, over 20 research papers are on spirituality and consciousness etc. Besides this, he has authored the following **twenty-five books** on science, spirituality, consciousness and other subjects:

1. Gayatri Mantra: A GPS to Enlightenment;

2. Maha Mrityunjaya Mantra: An Invincible Armour for Conquering Death;

3. Ajapa-Japa Sohum-Humsa Mantra: An Eternal Mantra for Inner Consciousness;

4. The Third Eye: A Spiritual Laser for Stimulating Inner Awakening;

5. Quantum Physics of Consciousness and Non-Duality in Eastern Philosophy;

6. Quantum Science of Love, Healing, Happiness, and Bliss in Ancient Wisdom;

7. Chakras Healing and Kundalini Awakening by Yogic Techniques;

8. Meditation Practices across the Globe and their Beneficial Effects;

9. Comparative Analysis of Hindu, Buddhist, and Jain Philosophies;

10. Mantras for Happiness;

11. Om Namah Shivaya: A Powerful Mantra for Mastering Five Elements;

12. Trataka: A Concentrated Gazing Technique for Mystical Powers;

13. Walking Meditation: Techniques and Benefits;

14. Quantum Science of Ganesha Consciousness;

15. Tantra Science;

16. Quantum Brain, Mind, and Thinking;

17. Profound Meditation Techniques in Tibetan Buddhism;

18. Reiki: A Holistic Energy Healing Technique;

19. Shaktipāt: Instant Transmission of Spiritual Energy from a Siddha Guru to the Disciple;

20. Vāstu Shāstra: Ancient Indian Science of Architecture;

21. Vedantic Thoughts on Māyā, Mithyā, and the Brahman;

22. Siddhis (Supernatural Powers): A Guide for Understanding and Attaining These;

23. Near-Death Experience: Scientific Interpretation (Inspired by True Story of a Friend);

24. Universe before the Big Bang: A Deeper Insight into Cosmology;

25. Spiritual Intelligence: Significance, Applications, Measurement, and Development Techniques;

Dr. Dudeja has delivered many invited lectures in international conferences in India and abroad.

He has been recognized as the "World's Who's Who in Science & Engineering".

SECTION-I

MIND-READING AND ARTIFICIAL INTELLIGENCE: INTRODUCTION AND OVERVIEW

INTRODUCTION AND OVERVIEW OF MIND-READING AND ARTIFICIAL INTELLIGENCE

1.1   What is Mind?

According to the Oxford dictionary:

"The mind is the element of a person that enables him to be aware of the world and its experiences, to think, and to feel; the faculty of consciousness and thought."

According to the Britannica dictionary:

"Mind is the part of a person that thinks, reasons, feels, and remembers."

According to the Cambridge Dictionary:

"Mind is the part of a person that makes it possible for him or her to think, feel emotions, and understand things."

Some more definitions of the 'mind' are:

"Mind is the human consciousness that originates in the brain and is manifested especially in thought, perception, emotion, will, memory, and imagination."

"Mind is the part or faculty of a person by which one feels, perceives, thinks, remembers, desires, and imagines."

"Mind is the set of faculties that include the thought, imagination, memory, belief, desire, intention, emotion will, sensation, perception, experience of pain, happiness and excitement etc. "

"Mind is an embodied as well as relational, self-organizing emerging process that regulates the flow of energy and information both within (the brain) and between (between the brain and outside of it, including the external environment with which it interacts)."

Mind is usually contrasted with body, matter or physicality. Central to this contrast is the intuition that minds exhibit various features not found in and may be even incompatible with the material universe.

The mind is curious about itself.

Mind is nothing but a collection of Samskaras or impressions. It is nothing but a bundle of habits. It is nothing but a collection of desires arising from contact with different objects. It is also a collection of feelings aroused by worldly botherations. It is a collection of ideas gathered from different objects. Now these desires, ideas and feelings constantly change. Some of the old desires are constantly departing from their storehouse of the mind, and new ones are replacing them.

Mind is the greatest force on this earth. He who has controlled his mind is full of powers. He can bring all minds under his influence. All diseases can be cured by psychic healing. One is struck with awe and wonder at the marvelous and mysterious powers of the mind of a man

Practice of telepathy, thought-reading, hypnotism, mesmerism, distant healing, psychic healing, etc., clearly proves that mind exists and that a higher developed mind can influence and subjugate the lower minds. From the automatic writing and the experiences of a hypnotized person, we can clearly infer the existence of subconscious mind which operates throughout the twenty-four hours.

In **Sanskrit**, the *manah* generally refers to the mind or the faculty of thought and consciousness. It is a very significant concept in Indian philosophy and spirituality. The mind, in the context of Sanskrit texts, is not just limited to the intellect or the brain but encompasses the entire realm of mental activities, emotions, desires, and consciousness.

The mind is considered a crucial aspect of human existence in various philosophical traditions such as Vedanta, Yoga, and Buddhism. It is believed to be the seat of emotions, thoughts, and intentions. Controlling and understanding the mind is often seen as essential for spiritual growth and self-realization in these traditions.

1.2   Mind and Its Mysteries

Just as a busy officer works alone in a room by closing all the doors, so also the busy mind works alone in a dream by shutting out all the doors of the senses. Mind is a power born of the soul.

In the waking state, the seat of the mind is the brain; in the dreaming state the seat of the mind is the cerebellum; in the deep sleep state it rests in the heart.

Mind always attaches itself to something objective. It cannot stand by itself. It is only this mind that asserts itself as 'I' in this body.

The things that we perceive all round us are only mind in the form of substance.

Manomatram-jagat manah-kalpitam jagat

Meaning: Mind creates. Mind destroys.

The phenomena that take place in the mental world are all based on scientific laws. We should have a comprehensive intelligent understanding of these laws. Then only shall we be able to control the psychic forces easily.

If an idea is planted in the mind, it grows at night through the operation of the subconscious mind. The subconscious mind never takes any rest. It works vigorously 24x7. Those who know how to manipulate this subconscious mind can achieve tremendous mental power. All geniuses have control over their subconscious mind. You must understand the ways of extracting work from the subconscious mind.

Any action that is done by the physical body is the outcome of a preconceived idea. The mind thinks, plans and schemes at first. Then the action manifests itself. He who invented a watch at first had all ideas in his mind about the construction of the lever, various wheels, dial, minute-hand, second-hand, hour-hand, etc. These ideas materialized later on into actuality.

A spark of light presents the appearance of a continuous circle of light if it is made to rotate quickly. Even so, though the mind can attend but to only one thing at a time, either hearing or smelling, though it can admit of but only one kind of sensation at a time, we are led to believe that it does several actions at a time, because it moves from one object to another with tremendous speed, so rapidly that its successive attention and perception appear as a simultaneous activity. The best philosophers and seers (Rishis and sages) unanimously agreed that the mind cannot actually attend to more than one thing at a time, but it only appears to be doing so when it is shifting rapidly backward and forward from one end to the other.

The mind assumes the shape of any object it intently thinks of. If it thinks of an orange it assumes the shape of an orange. If it thinks of Lord Jesus on the Cross it assumes the shape of Lord Jesus on the Cross.

If all the thoughts are eliminated, there remains nothing which can be called mind. So thoughts are the mind. Again there is no such thing as the world, independent of and apart from thoughts. Two thoughts, however, closely related to one another, cannot exist at the same time.

The mind becomes that on which it dwells. This is an immutable psychological law. If you begin to think about the Dosha or defects of a man, for the time being at least your mind dwells on the bad qualities and becomes charged with these qualities, whether the man possesses these bad qualities or not. This may be your vain imagination only through your wrong thinking, wrong Samskaras or wrong (bad) habits of the mind. He may not possess even a bit of the bad qualities which you have superimposed on him through ill-will or some form of jealousy or petty-mindedness or habitual Dosha-Drishti or fault-finding nature. Therefore, give up the dangerous habit of censuring others and finding fault in others. Praise others. Develop the power or vision of finding only good in others. Do not bark like a wild dog about the bad qualities of others. Glorify others. You will grow spiritually. You will be liked, honoured and respected by others.

Mind can be compared to water. Water exists in four states, viz., causal state, in the form of hydrogen and oxygen; subtle state, in the form of water; gross state, in the form of ice: and gaseous state, in the form of vaporized steam. Even so the mind is in a gross state during Jagrat state when it enjoys sensual objects, it is in a subtle state when it functions in the dream state, is in a causal state when it gets involved into its cause; during deep sleep and it evaporates as gas when it melts or dissolves in Brahman.

Just as you nourish the physical body with food, so also will you have to give food for the mind and spiritual food for the soul.

When your business fails, or when you are in heavy grief by the death of your only son, you get emaciation of body even though you eat nourishing, substantial food. You feel tremendous internal weakness. This clearly proves that mind exists and cheerfulness is a good mental food.

When a woman is deeply engaged in the management of her daughter's marriage, she forgets to take her food. She is always happy. Her heart is full of joy. The joy and cheerfulness are powerful tonics for her mind. She gets inner mental strength although she does not take any food.

1.3   What is Brain?

The brain is the most important organ in the human body.

According to the Cambridge Dictionary:

"Brain is the organ inside the head that controls thought, memory, feelings, and other activity."

According to the Oxford Dictionary:

"Brain is the organ inside the head that controls movement, thought, memory and feelings."

According to the Britannica dictionary:

"Brain is the mass of nerve tissue in the anterior end of an organism. The brain integrates sensory information and directs motor responses."

According to another definition:

"Brain is the part of the central nervous system consisting of a soft convoluted mas of gray and white matter and serving to control and coordinate the mental and physical actions."

Brain is a dense organ in the human system. The human brain weighs approximately 1.4 kg (3 pounds) in an average adult. The brain is about 60% fat. The remaining 40% is a combination of water, protein, carbohydrates and salts.

The brain itself is a not a muscle. It contains blood vessels and interconnected nerves (neurons). Together, the brain and spinal cord that extends from it make up the central nervous system. The neural system is located in the skull.

1.3.1   What is a neuron?

A neuron or nerve cell is an electrically excitable cell that communicates with other cells via specialized connections called synapses. In the nervous system, a synapse is a structure that permits a neuron (or nerve cell) to pass an electrical or chemical signal to another neuron or to the target effector cell. There are a trillion to perhaps a quadrillion synapses connections formed by the 100 billion nerve cells (neurons). The number of synapses per neuron varies considerably. According to one estimate, the average neuron has around 1,000 synapses.

There are two fundamentally different types of synapses: **(i) chemical, (ii) electrical.**

(i) In a **chemical synapse**, electrical activity in the neuron is converted into the release of a chemical called a neurotransmitter that binds to receptors located in the plasma membrane of the postsynaptic cell. Neurotransmitters are generally synthesized in neurons and are made up of, or derived from, precursor molecules that are found abundantly in the cell. The neurotransmitter may initiate an electrical response or a secondary messenger pathway that may either excite or inhibit the postsynaptic neuron.

(ii) In an **electrical synapse**, the presynaptic and postsynaptic cell membranes are connected by special channels called gap junctions that are capable of passing an electric current, causing voltage changes in the presynaptic cell to induce voltage changes in the postsynaptic cell. The main advantage of an electrical synapse is the rapid transfer of signals from one cell to the next.

The brain is a collection of interconnected neurons and other cells in the head that interact with the whole body and the environment.

Neurons are typically classified into **three types** based on their function. **Sensory neurons** respond to stimuli such as touch, sound, or light that affect the cells of the sensory organs, and they send signals to the spinal cord or brain. **Motor neurons** receive signals from the brain and spinal cord to control everything from muscle contractions to glandular output. **Interneurons** connect neurons to other neurons within the same region of the brain or spinal cord.

When multiple neurons are connected together, they form what is called a neural circuit.

An **axon** is a long, slender projection of a neuron that typically conducts electrical impulses known as action potentials away from the nerve cell body. The function of the axon is to transmit information to different neurons, muscles, and glands. A neural pathway is the connection formed by axons that project from neurons to make synapses onto neurons in another location, to enable a signal to be sent from one region of the nervous system to another.

The nervous system is made up of the central nervous system, which includes the brain and spinal cord, and the peripheral nervous system, which includes the autonomic and somatic nervous systems.

The human brain is the centre of the human nervous system. This nervous system is composed of billions of cells, the most essential being the nerve cells or neurons. The number of neurons in the human brain (about 10^{12} or 1000 billion) is approximately equal to the number of stars in our Milky Way galaxy. Whereas the possibility of understanding such a complex device is certainly daunting, it is nevertheless true that an enormous amount has already been learned. These 100 billion nerve cells (neurons) send and receive signals (or messages) to various parts of our body through our nervous system. These neurons, communicate information back and forth from our brain to our major organs and senses. Together, they are responsible for coordinating important functions controls of thought, memory, emotion, touch, taste, smell, vision (sight), motor skills, breathing, temperature, hunger and every process that regulates our body.

The human brain consists of the cerebrum (at the top), the brainstem and the cerebellum (at the bottom). The cerebrum is the largest part (about 83%) of the human brain. The brain is contained in, and protected by, the skull bones of the head.

1.3.2   What is brain plasticity?

The term doesn't mean our brains are made of plastic. Instead, plasticity means the brain is modifiable, that is, it can be changed based on our experiences and can be repaired, if required. Whatever you are doing at any time, you are physically modifying your brain to become better (or worse) of it. Different experiences create different neural connections, which bring about different emotions and feelings. Depending upon which neurons get stimulated, certain neural connections become stronger and more efficient, while other neural connections become weaker. This is what is called **'neuroplasticity'**. This leads us to the conclusion that neuroplasticity is a potential area to repair certain types of brain disorders.

1.4   What is Thought?

According to the Oxford dictionary:

"The thought is an idea or opinion produced by thinking, or occurring suddenly in the mind."

According to www.dictionary.com:

"Thought is the product of the mental activity."

According to the Britannica dictionary:

"The terms thought and thinking refer to the conscious cognitive processes that can happen independent of sensory simulation. Their most paradigmatic forms are: judging, reasoning, concept formation, problem solving, deliberation, and contemplation."

"Thought is the process of using one's mind to consider something. It can also be the product of that process: an idea or just the thing one is thinking about. Thought can also refer to the organized beliefs of a period, individual, or group."

The terms "thought" and "thinking" can also be used to refer not only to the mental processes themselves but to the mental states or systems of ideas brought about by these processes. In this sense, they are often synonymous with the term "belief" and its cognates and may refer to the mental states which either belong to an individual or are common among a certain group of people.

1.5 Difference Between the Brain, Mind, and Thoughts

1.5.1 Difference between Brain and Mind

Brain and Mind both are confused with as the same thing and are used interchangeably. What is the use of hardware if there will be no software? Will it work? Similarly, the brain is hardware that is incomplete without a mind (software of the brain). Mind is considered as a pure vibrating energy, whereas, the brain is considered a physical manifestation of the mind. Brain is made of physical matter while the mind is not made of physical matter. To be more elaborate, brain is made of cells, blood vessels and nerves to name a few. Mind is nothing but the thought that is the result of processing in the brain. The brain, which is the centre of the nervous system, coordinates the movements, thoughts and feelings. Mind is what is the processing of activity of the brain. The mind refers to a person's understanding of things and also his conscience. Mind also refers to a person's thought process.

The mind uses the brain, and the brain responds to the mind. The mind is energy, and it generates energy through thinking, feeling and choosing. We are our mind, and the mind-in-action generates energy in the brain. When we generate this mind energy through thinking, feeling and choosing, we build thoughts, which are the physical structures in our brain made of proteins. This building of thoughts creates structural changes in the brain, which is called neuroplasticity.

1.5.2 Difference Between Mind and Thoughts

As nouns, the difference between thought and mind is that thought is the form created in the mind, rather than the forms perceived through the five senses; an instance of thinking while mind is the ability for rational thought.

Thought is the function of mind. Thinking is the comparison of identities. Thinking compares identities and discovers which identities are unlike or different, similar, equivalent or alike. Thinking is the activity of mind. Thoughts are subtle bundles of energy.

1.6 What is Mind-Reading?

Mind-reading typically refers to the ability to discern or interpret someone else's thoughts, feelings, or intentions without them explicitly expressing them through words or actions. In a more literal sense, mind-reading can be understood as the hypothetical ability to directly access or perceive another person's thoughts or mental processes.

In a scientific or psychological context, mind reading usually refers to the ability to infer or understand another person's mental state based on their behavior, body language, facial expressions, and other non-verbal cues. This is often referred to as "mentalizing" or "theory of mind," where individuals use their own experiences and understanding of human behavior to interpret and predict the thoughts and feelings of others.

1.7 What is Thought Reading?

According to Collins dictionary:

Thought reading is the act of reading minds or trying to psychically interpret others' thoughts.

1.8 What is the difference between an Artificial mind and a Human mind?

The human mind is incredibly versatile and emotional, while artificial minds are specialized, lack genuine emotions, and are created by humans.

The differences between them have important implications for technology, ethics, and philosophy.

Here are some main differences between a human mind and an artificial mind:

(i) Capabilities and Limitations

(a) **Human Mind:** The human mind is incredibly complex and versatile. It can think, learn, remember, and adapt in remarkable ways. It has the ability to experience emotions, be creative, and understand the world deeply. Humans can solve problems, make decisions, and have consciousness, which means they are aware of themselves and their surroundings.

(b) **Artificial Mind:** Artificial minds, like computer programs or AI systems, are designed to perform specific tasks very well. They can be excellent at tasks that involve calculations, data analysis, or pattern recognition. However, they lack the wide range of abilities that a human mind has. They can't truly feel emotions or have consciousness like humans do.

(ii) Emotional Aspects

(a) **Human Mind:** Humans experience a wide range of emotions like happiness, sadness, anger, and fear. Emotions play a significant role in how humans make decisions and interact with others. Emotions are deeply rooted in our biology and psychology.

(b) **Artificial Mind:** Artificial minds do not experience emotions like humans. They can simulate or mimic emotions in responses, but these are not genuine feelings. Any emotional responses from artificial minds are based on algorithms and programmed responses.

(iii) Development Process

(a) **Human Mind:** The human mind develops as a person grows from a baby to an adult. It's influenced by genetics, environment, and personal experiences. It learns and adapts throughout life.

(b) **Artificial Mind:** Artificial minds are created by programmers and engineers who write code and algorithms. They don't develop on their own like human minds. They are "taught" by humans and rely on the data they are given.

(iv) Ethical and Philosophical Implications

(a) **Human Mind:** The presence of a human mind raises deep ethical and philosophical questions about free will, consciousness, and moral responsibility.

(b) **Artificial Mind:** The development of artificial minds raises ethical questions as well, such as how we should treat AI systems, what rights they should have (if any), and how they should be used in society.

1.9   Human-based Mind-Reading

Mind reading is common among us humans. Not in the ways that psychics claim to do it, by gaining access to the warm streams of that fill every individual's experience, or in the ways that mentalists claim to do it, by pulling a thought out of your head at will.

Mind-reading is more subtle: We look at people's faces and movements, listen to their words, and then decide or intuit what might be going on in their heads.

Among psychologists, such intuitive- the ability to attribute to other people mental states different from our own - is called the theory of mind, and its absence or impairment has been linked to autism, schizophrenia, and other developmental disorders.

Theory of mind helps us communicate with and understand one another; it allows us to enjoy literature and movies, play games and make sense of our social surroundings. In many ways, the capacity is an essential part of being human.

1.10   Artificial Intelligence

Artificial Intelligence is a paradigm of computing that aims to mimic human intelligence, enabling machines to learn from experience, adapt to new inputs, and perform tasks that traditionally require human intervention. At the core of AI is the ambition to create systems that can understand, learn, and apply knowledge, thereby extending human capabilities and automating routine tasks. The realm of AI is vast and varied, with several subfields that focus on different aspects of intelligence emulation.

The seeds of modern AI were planted by philosophers who attempted to describe the process of human thinking as the mechanical manipulation of symbols. This work culminated in the invention of the programmable digital computer in the 1940s, a machine based on the abstract essence of mathematical reasoning. This device and the ideas behind it inspired a handful of scientists to begin seriously discussing the possibility of building an electronic brain.

1.11 Artificial Intelligence vs Human Intelligence: Differences Between These

(i) Learning and Adaptation

(a) **Artificial Intelligence:** AI can rapidly learn and adapt to large datasets and repetitive tasks. It can perform calculations and data processing at incredible speeds.

However, it lacks the intuitive, flexible learning and adaptability of humans and struggles with tasks that require common-sense reasoning or understanding of context.

(b) **Human intelligence:** Humans have a remarkable ability to learn and adapt to new and diverse situations. They possess intuitive understanding and common-sense reasoning.

But Learning can be slower, and humans can be subject to cognitive biases.

(ii) Creativity

(a) **Artificial Intelligence:** AI can generate creative outputs, such as art, music, and text, based on learned patterns. It can perform creative tasks efficiently.

AI creativity is often based on existing data and lacks true innovation or emotional depth.

(b) Human intelligence: Humans possess deep creativity, producing original art, literature, innovations, and novel problem-solving. They draw on emotions, personal experiences, and intuition.

Creative output can be inconsistent and influenced by factors like mood and stress.

(iii) Emotional Intelligence

(a) Artificial Intelligence: AI can recognize and simulate emotions in limited ways, aiding in applications like chatbots and sentiment analysis. It lacks genuine emotional understanding and empathy, which humans have.

AI creativity is often based on existing data and lacks true innovation or emotional depth.

(b) Human intelligence: Humans have profound emotional intelligence, allowing them to empathize, understand, and respond to others' emotions.

Emotional intelligence can vary widely among individuals, and it can lead to biased decisions.

(iv) Consciousness

(a) Artificial Intelligence: AI systems do not experience fatigue or subjective emotions, making them consistent and available 24/7.

(b) Human intelligence: Humans have self-awareness, consciousness, and subjective experiences.

Human emotions can lead to erratic decision-making, and fatigue can limit consistent performance.

(v) Generalization and Context

(a) Artificial Intelligence: AI excels at generalizing from one task or dataset to another. It is efficient in specialized tasks.

(b) Human intelligence: Generalization can lead to cognitive biases and errors in human decision-making.

(vi) Ethical Decision-Making

(a) Artificial Intelligence: AI can be programmed with ethical guidelines and follow them consistently. It doesn't have personal biases.

(b) Human intelligence: Humans possess complex ethical and moral reasoning.

(vii) Energy Efficiency

(a) Artificial Intelligence: AI systems can process information at high speeds and handle massive datasets.

(b) Human intelligence: Human brains are energy-efficient, using less power compared to AI supercomputers.

(viii) Adaptability

(a) Artificial Intelligence: AI can be reprogrammed or retrained for new tasks and can work in hazardous environments without risking human lives.

(b) Human intelligence: Humans may require extensive training to adapt to some roles or environments.

1.12   Device-based Mind-Reading

Mind-reading AI tools are becoming able to decode human and animals' brain waves to transform them into outputs such as text or images. Are we crossing a line that should never be in terms of personal privacy? What limits should we set now to prevent governments and corporations from using these technologies to strip our minds naked?

According to a recent report, mind-reading AI-hat translates thoughts into text so people can read what others are thinking. Researchers from the GrapheneX-UTS Human-centric Artificial

Intelligence Center at the University of Technology Sydney (UTS) have developed a portable and non-invasive mind-reading **AI-hat**, called BrainGPT that can decode and translate silent thoughts into readable text. The wearable technology keeps people who are unable to speak due to illness or injury, **including stroke or paralysis**, in mind when they developed the device, allowing them to communicate with people using data, AI, and a smart device.

The research and development of the mind-reading AI hat were led by Distinguished Professor CT Lin, Director of the GrapheneX-UTS HAI Centre, together with the first author Yiqun Duan and fellow PhD candidate Jinzhou Zhou from the UTS Faculty of Engineering and IT. They tested out their BrainGPT with a group of 29 participants, each of them wearing the mind-reading AI-hat while reading passages of text. The wearable technology recorded and translated what they were reading and thinking, using an electroencephalogram (EEG), recording the electrical brain activity through their scalp.

1.13   Is Artificial Intelligence an alternative to the Human Mind?

Artificial intelligence (AI) isn't an alternative to the human mind in the sense of replicating it entirely. While AI can perform certain tasks and emulate some aspects of human cognition, it's still far from replicating the full range of human intelligence, creativity, and understanding.

AI operates based on algorithms and data, whereas the human mind is immensely complex, capable of intuition, empathy, creativity, and moral reasoning, among other things. While AI can excel in specific tasks like data analysis, pattern recognition, and decision-making within predefined parameters, it lacks the broader understanding, consciousness, and emotional intelligence of humans.

Furthermore, the ethical implications of creating an AI that could rival or surpass human intelligence are profound and raise questions about control, accountability, and the nature of consciousness itself. So while AI is a powerful tool that can augment human capabilities, it's not a replacement for the full spectrum of human cognition and consciousness.

1.14   Some Applications or Opportunities for Artificial Intelligence

AI and machine learning technology is being used in most of the essential applications, including: search engines (such as Google Search), targeting online advertisements, recommendation systems (offered by Netflix, YouTube or Amazon), driving internet traffic, targeted advertising (AdSense, Facebook), virtual assistants (such as Siri or Alexa), autonomous vehicles (including drones, ADAS and self-driving cars), automatic language translation (Microsoft Translator, Google Translate), facial recognition (Apple's Face ID or Microsoft's DeepFace and Google's FaceNet) and image labeling (used by Facebook, Apple's iPhoto and TikTok).

Following are some of the applications of AI:

(i)   Healthcare and Medicine,

(ii)   Virtual Nursing,

(iii)   Games and Entertainment,

(iv)   Online Courses and Customized Education,

(v)   Stock Markets

(vi)   Banking Sector,

(vii)   R&D,

(viii) Data mining,

(ix)   Military,

(x)   Generative AI and Chat GPT

(xi)   Agriculture

(xii)   E-commerce,

(xiii) Customer care,

(xiv) Self-driving cars

(xv)   Drone Technology

(xvi) Industry-specific Tasks

(xvii) Space Technology,

(xviii) Cyber Security,

(xix) Legal system,

(xx)   Energy,

(xxi) Manufacturing, etc.

1.15   Risks of AI and Ethical Issues

The risks of Artificial Intelligence (AI) include potential job loss due to automation, biased decision-making leading to unfair outcomes, concerns about privacy and data security, and the possibility of safety and security vulnerabilities being exploited. Additionally, ethical dilemmas may arise, such as accountability for AI-driven decisions and the implications of autonomous systems on human well-being, highlighting the importance of responsible development and use of AI technologies.

Further, it has multiple issues that need to be addressed including adversarial attacks, generation of **deepfake content**, fake pictures and fake videos, fairness issues, accountability, transparency and other ethical considerations.

Following **ethical principles** which are rooted in fundamental rights that must be respected to ensure that AI systems are developed, deployed, and used in a trustworthy manner are:

Respect for human autonomy,

- Prevention of harm,

- Fairness,

- Transparency,

- Explainability and Accountability.

For an AI system to be trustworthy, it should ensure the following components through the system's entire life cycle:

- Lawful, complying with all applicable laws and **regulations**,

- Ethical, ensuring adherence to ethical principles and values,

- Robust, both from a technical and social perspective, since even with good intentions, an AI system can cause unintentional harm.

AI technology can also go into the rogue hands/countries, which can create catastrophic effects for the society including making of destructive weapons.

1.16   AI in India: Status and the Way Forward

Over the past several years, the Government of India has taken concrete steps to encourage the adoption of AI in a responsible manner and build public trust in its use, placing the idea of 'AI for All' at its very core. Favorable policies and continuous interventions strive to harness the potential of AI for social development and inclusive growth.

India-AI has a mission-centric approach that ensures a precise and cohesive strategy to bridge the gaps in the existing AI ecosystem viz-a-viz Compute infrastructure, Data, AI financing, Research and Innovation, Targeted Skilling, and Institutional Capacity for Data to maximize the potential of AI to advance India's progress.

Several startup companies have emerged in India in the recent past. According to a report, there are around about 200 AI-related startups in India and these have received an investment of $50 million in total. Many startup companies out of these are located in Bengaluru.

MeitY (erstwhile **DOE**) started knowledge-based computer Systems Projects with financial support from UNDP. Some prototype systems such as robotic arms, etc have been developed under the program. Some projects were also taken up under Technology Development for Indian languages Programmes of the Ministry. A large percentage of funds have been spent on machine translation, text-to-speech, and speech-to-text systems.

DRDO has been funding AI projects at **Centre for Artificial Intelligence and Robotics (CAIR)** for defence as well as civil applications.

All the topics, mentioned in this introductory chapter, will be discussed in detail in the subsequent chapters in this book.

SECTION II

HUMAN-BASED MIND READING

CHAPTER 2

HUMAN-BASED MIND READING

2.1   What is Human-Based Mind Reading?

Mind-reading or thought-reading, is the extraordinary ability of the person to perceive and interpret thoughts, feelings, and mental states of others without the need for verbal or physical communication. This intriguing phenomenon has captivated human imagination for centuries and has been the subject of various cultural beliefs and practices. Mind-reading is the ability to discern the thoughts of others without the normal means of communication, especially by means of a preternatural (beyond what is normal or natural) power.

Throughout history, numerous accounts of mind reading have been documented across different cultures and civilizations. From ancient mystics and seers to modern-day psychics and mentalists, the concept of mind-reading has persistently intrigued and fascinated people.

2.2   How People Read Each Other's Mind?

In science fiction stories, mind reading is routinely used for nefarious purposes. In the real world, having a clear sense of what others think and feel helps us avoid conflict and miscommunication and strengthen personal relationships.

When attempting to read someone's mind—or, more accurately, their mood—body language, tone, and choice of words are usually the best places to begin. Another critical element is empathy: Being able to put oneself in someone else's shoes can provide key insights into their perspective, and make understanding their thoughts, feelings, and actions that much easier.

Research suggests that our discernment of others' emotions and trustworthiness may manifest in our body's reactions to them at least as strongly as in our mental assessments of their speech. Trusting one's gut, then, by being mindful of our body's reactions to someone else, can help us make more accurate judgments about others.

When trying to read other people, we tend to look to their faces. Research shows that while the faces of happy people take on a V shape, with eyebrows and mouths turned up, angry people's faces form more of an X, with eyebrows and mouths turned downward. Being conscious of this tendency in others and ourselves can improve communication and understanding.

It has long been believed that people's body language gives them away—that people have "tells" that could tip observant others off to their true intentions. Reading others can become more efficient, research shows, when we consciously focus on such clues. For example, facial features like the eyes and the mouth may offer a great deal of information, but if we are looking at the whole person we may miss seeing what their faces have to tell us.

2.3   Science of Mind-Reading

Mind-reading sounds like science fiction. But the term, also referred to as "mentalizing", is a psychological concept used to describe the process of understanding what other people are thinking. We may not be aware of it, but we use mind-reading every day when we interact with each other. It helps us to understand another person's viewpoint or know when someone is saying something that they do not mean, such as being sarcastic or lying.

Mind-reading is different from the psychological process of empathy. It involves understanding other people's thoughts or knowledge ("Sarah knows where the biscuits are kept"), whereas empathy involves understanding other people's emotions ("Sarah would feel sad if her biscuits were taken"). Traditionally, scientists have not properly distinguished mind-reading from empathy, so most psychological tests mix up the two concepts.

Although the processes are related, it is important to differentiate them to understand how people operate in social situations. It is also important for understanding psychopathy, for example. Psychopaths are often good at mind-reading, but bad at empathy. This means they can manipulate others while remaining emotionally detached from their actions.

Differentiating between mind-reading and empathy also helps us to understand conditions like autism, which are linked to social differences. People with autism often have major difficulties with mind-reading and more minor difficulties in empathizing with people. Having slightly lower empathy is not always a bad thing, potentially helping people to make more logical rather than emotional decisions. On the other hand, poor mind-reading is linked to problems such as difficulty in making friends and mental health issues.

Surprisingly, nobody has attempted to create a questionnaire on mind-reading until now. Using data from over 4,000 people in the UK and US, including autistic and non-autistic people, it was found that just four questions should be used to measure mind-reading. These include how easy or difficult you find it to see things from other people's perspective. This may sound simplistic, but by developing such a short test, we could collect data from very large samples.

Questionnaires can of course be inaccurate because participants sometimes answer questions in a way that make themselves look more desirable to other people. Fortunately, this is less of a concern with this questionnaire. In one of the studies, it was discovered that scores on self-reported mind-reading were linked to performance on objective tests of mind-reading.

Women beat men

It has been found that women were better at mind-reading than men. Women's scores were only slightly, but very consistently higher than men throughout the sample. The reason for sex differences in mind-reading are a matter of debate, however. Some argue they are mainly due to genetics or hormones, while others believe they are the result of environmental factors, such as our upbringing.

The research also showed that people with autism reported substantially more mind-reading difficulties than people without autism. The average score of an autistic person would fall within the lowest 25% of non-autistic scores. This might not seem like a new finding, but it is one of the first studies in which autistic people were actually asked about their mind-reading experiences rather than being subjected to computerized experiments to infer their difficulties.

Of course, just because certain people find mind-reading difficult, this does not mean that they are not motivated to engage with others. Many people with autism, for example, work incredibly hard to "compensate" for their mind-reading difficulties, indicating that they have intact or even heightened social motivation.

Overall, the development of carefully devised questionnaire will enable quicker and more accurate measurement of mind-reading by clinicians, researchers, businesses and even the general public. It will help to fully understand why humans differ in their mind-reading skills, for example due to genes or environmental factors, as it is suitable for use in large-scale studies involving genetic and brain-imaging data. It will also be useful to understand and tailor support for people with clinical conditions, such as autism. And it may even be used to help select personnel for job roles requiring good understanding of people.

Longer term, research on mind-reading could help people to develop technology for non-human agents, such as "social robots", to predict what we are thinking and assist us in our daily lives. Without more psychological research on how we understand each other as humans, it is unlikely that we will ever develop artificial intelligence that can understand itself or what we are thinking.

Here are some of the ways that people have tried to explain thought transference:

2.3.1 Shared Brainwaves:

Some people believe that thought transference is possible because people' s brains can sometimes synchronize their waves. This could allow people to share thoughts and feelings with each other.

Neurobiology provides valuable insights into the mechanisms behind mind reading abilities. Various brain regions and neural networks contribute to the complex processes involved in telepathy and psychic phenomena. The parietal cortex, for instance, is associated with sensory integration and spatial awareness, playing a role in perceiving and interpreting non-verbal cues during mind reading interactions.

Neurotransmitters also play a significant role in mind reading. Dopamine, often referred to as the "feel-good" neurotransmitter, is involved in reward processing and motivation. It can enhance focus and concentration: crucial skills for successful mind reading. Serotonin, known for regulating mood and emotions, influences empathic abilities, allowing mind readers to connect on a deeper emotional level with others.

Neuroplasticity, the brain's ability to reorganize and form new connections, is another important aspect of mind reading. Through consistent practice and training, mind readers can strengthen neural pathways associated with telepathy and psychic abilities. This rewiring of the brain enhances the efficiency of information processing, leading to heightened mind reading skills over time.

2.3.2 Quantum Entanglement:

Quantum entanglement is a phenomenon in which two particles are linked together in such a way that they share the same fate, even when they are separated by a large distance. Some people believe that quantum entanglement could be used to transmit thoughts from one person to another.

Quantum entanglement suggests that particles can become connected in such a way that the state of one particle instantly affects the state of another, regardless of the distance between them. This phenomenon has sparked speculation about the potential for telepathic connections between individuals.

Quantum mechanics, the branch of physics that studies the behavior of particles at the smallest scales, offers intriguing possibilities for understanding mind reading phenomena.

The **observer effect**, another principle of quantum mechanics, proposes that the act of observation can influence the behavior of particles. Similarly, in mind reading, the consciousness of the observer or the mind reader may influence the thoughts and intentions of the sender or the subject being read. This connection between consciousness and the observed world raises intriguing questions about the role of consciousness in mind reading abilities.

Exploring the connection between quantum physics and psychic phenomena expands our understanding of the possibilities of mind reading. While the field is still largely speculative, the principles of quantum mechanics provide a theoretical framework that invites further exploration and research into the mechanics of mind reading.

2.3.3   Extrasensory perception:

Extrasensory perception (ESP) is the ability to perceive things that are not physically present. Some people believe that thought transference is a form of ESP.

Intuition serves as a gateway to mind reading, providing subtle insights and guidance beyond our conscious understanding. It is often described as a gut feeling or a hunch, an inner knowing that goes beyond logical reasoning. Intuition operates on a level beyond the limitations of the conscious mind, tapping into the vast resources of the subconscious and the collective unconscious.

Differentiating intuition from regular thinking is crucial for mind reading mastery. While the conscious mind relies on logical analysis and rational thought processes, intuition bypasses these cognitive filters and accesses information that lies beneath the surface. Developing a deep sense of trust in one's intuition is essential for mind readers, as it acts as a compass in navigating the intricate realms of telepathy and psychic abilities.

Cultivating intuition requires cultivating inner awareness and mindfulness. Practices such as meditation, journaling, and reflective contemplation can help quiet the conscious mind and attune oneself to the subtle whispers of intuition. By actively engaging with and honoring intuitive insights, mind readers can enhance their ability to receive and interpret telepathic and psychic information.

2.4 Four-Item Mentalizing Index (FIMI)

S. No.	Statement	Strongly Disagree	Slightly Disagree	Slightly Agree	Strongly Agree
1.	I find it easy to put myself in somebody else's shoes				
2.	I sometimes find it difficult to see things from other people's point of view				
3.	I sometimes try to understand my friends better by imagining how things look from their perspective				
4.	I can usually understand another person's viewpoint, even if it differs from my own				

Read each statement and indicate the extent to which you agree or disagree. The FIMI is a self-report measure to assess an individual's mentalizing, or Theory of Mind, ability. That is, their ability to understand and infer the cognitions of others, such as their perceptions, intentions, and beliefs. It is designed for use in English-speaking adults aged 18 and above, including autistic people.

There are ethical implications of thought transference, and the potential dangers of using it for malicious purposes. There is an in-depth information about the science of thought transference, and the potential for this phenomenon to be used in the future.

This Topic is very intriguing. The science of mind reading is still in its early stages, and there is much that we do not know about how the mind works. It is possible that one day we will be able to understand and explain thought transference.

2.5   Yoga Sutras of Patanjali and Mind- and Thought-Reading

Patanjali (flourished 2nd century BCE or 5th century CE) was the author or one of the authors of two great Hindu classics: the first, Yoga-sutras, a categorization of Yogic thought arranged in four volumes with the titles "Psychic Power," "Practice of Yoga," "Samadhi" (state of profound contemplation of the Absolute), and "Kaivalya" (separateness); and the second, the Mahabhashya ("Great Commentary"), which is both a defence of the grammarian Panini against his chief critic and detractor Katyayana and a refutation of some of Panini's aphorisms.

In his book on 'Yoga Sutras' Patanjali mentions about the Mind-Reading' as:

(i)   One can read others' minds when one's own mind is calm. With a calm and sensitive mind, if one focuses on others' attitude of mind, one can read the thoughts and activities inside others' minds.

(ii)   One looks at anyone for a moment and turns around, he/she will not be offended. But if someone looks into someone's eyes for more than 4-5 seconds then it is offensive. Because you have started accessing the person's thoughts and mind activity; which he/she would not have disclosed to anyone.

(iii) All of us have the ability to read the thoughts and activities inside others' minds. Remember, when the mind is in a state of thought, the eyes also move. When the mind is still, eyes stop moving. First of all, make sure that your mind is calm and sensitive, by focusing on the self-mind. When one is calm and sensitive, the mind becomes a mirror. In that mirror one can see his own reflection and if he focuses on others' attitude of mind or object of others, thoughts and activity of others' mind will reflect in the mirror.

(iv) By looking into someone's eyes, not only this life but also the past lives can be guessed. Eyes are the strongest source of human identity. Eyes hold the blueprint of many of our lives, as they are linked to our soul. And the soul has got all the memories and impressions of all the lives and reflects whatever is inside the mind. One, by focusing on others' eyes can only know thoughts and activity of others' minds but not their significance.

(v) Listen to what others say and follow their words to answer. Stop your assumptions. Then you will be with that person and able to understand. Patanjali says that if you follow the person's words, perspectives and his focus you will understand him.

(vi) Understand the difference between listening and hearing. So that, you can follow the words, perspectives and his focus. Listening is totally different from hearing. Listening means hearing without mind; listening means hearing without any interference of your thoughts; listening means hearing as if you are totally empty. If you have even a small trembling of thinking inside, waves of subtle thoughts surrounding you, you will not be able to listen, although you will be able to hear.

(vii) Bring down this sutra in your routine life. So that you can communion with others which means you have connected your soul with their soul, their being in compassion. Remember Communication is verbal; Communion is non-verbal. Communion is silent… which is throbbing inside your heart. Only two souls can meet. Then deep down there is a communion. Then you realise freedom. If you can feel oneness with a soul, then there is no difficulty in feeling oneness with the whole Existence. You know the path now. You know the secret path – how to be one with this Existence.

śabda artha pratyayānām itaretarādhyāsāt

saṅkaraḥ tatpravibhāga saṁyamāt sarvabhūta rutajñānam. 3.17

Translation: Knowledge of the meaning of sounds produced by all beings, resulting from samyana on the "third ear," or the concept of sound, words, or hearing. This may be interpreted as a form of clairvoyance, or telepathy that extends beyond human minds and includes animals, insects, and other species. More generally it is known as clairaudience.

Understanding Other's mind:

Samyama on Chitta of others makes Yogis understand the mind of others. Directly this sutra states "Pratyashcha Parichittagyanam". This can be probably thought of as possible in today's time also. When you concentrate on the active minds of others, you can understand them very well.

pratyayasya paracittajñānam.. 3.19

Translation: A yogi can know the contents of the mental and emotional energy in the mind of others.

na ca tat sālambanaṁ tasya aviṣayī bhūtatvāt.. 3.20

Translation: And he does not check a factor which is the support of that content, for it is not the actual object in question.

CHAPTER 3

HUMAN-BASED MIND READING AND TELEPATHY

3.1   Power of Mind-Reading

Mastering the art of mind reading can bring about numerous benefits and applications in various aspects of life. By understanding and connecting with others on a deeper level, mind reading can enhance personal relationships, improve communication, and foster empathy and understanding. In personal relationships, mind reading can facilitate better emotional connection and intimacy. It allows individuals to pick up on subtle cues and signals, leading to more profound understanding and effective communication with their partners, family members, and friends.

In professional settings, mind reading can be a valuable tool for building rapport, negotiating, and influencing others. By understanding the thoughts and intentions of colleagues, clients, or superiors, individuals can tailor their approach and communication style to achieve desired outcomes.

Furthermore, mind reading can also be applied to fields such as counseling, therapy, and coaching. Therapists and counselors can use their mind reading abilities to gain insight into their clients' underlying emotions and thought patterns, leading to more effective interventions and support.

Overall, mind reading holds an immense potential for personal growth, interpersonal relationships, and professional success. By unlocking the most successful techniques of thought reading, individuals can harness the power of telepathy, psychic abilities, and beyond.

3.2   Introduction to Telepathy

At some instance of life, we all must have experienced or heard that someone, let's say Mr. X was strongly thinking about Mr. Y and surprisingly, Mr. Y suddenly shows up maybe personally or through a phone call saying that somehow, he had a strong feeling to get in touch with Mr. X. This could have happened with us or maybe we have heard someone say it. Normally, we call this instance of telepathy and probably do not take it seriously thinking that it might be a coincidence or maybe real telepathy that normally happens.

Imagine, if we can communicate through our mental capacities without the use of psychical senses or objects. The world is vast, but its secrets lie in very minute things. Small things when united, signify the existence of larger entities. A human body cannot exist if the smallest components called 'cells' do not bind themselves together working in perfect synchronization. A small atom when parted systematically can lead to provide light to the whole city or maybe light it up to fumes. The existence prevails in the smaller entities, and they reflect themselves through the larger entities. How small a human brain can be and inside it how small a brain cell or maybe the components of neurotransmitter can be. All this mesmerizing existence prevails only to show that nature has so much to offer and teach us and there is so much that is beyond our knowledge. The human brain is one such component of nature that we are yet to decipher. Most of us know what we know, and we also know what we don't know, but imagine if there can be concepts that we don't know and we don't even know that we don't know. The walls of ignorance can veil the capacities hidden within us. Some say the human brain has developed and some say it has evolved, in any of the cases it is important that the development is existentially visible but only in the physical plains. What about the development of non-physical capacities? We have enriched in terms of knowledge about everything around us, but what about the knowledge that floats within us. The capacities that we have by default are hidden and yet to be explored. These mental capacities are prevailing within human existence. The reason why this thought can sustain argument is that several living beings have these capacities through which they can communicate without using any senses or any medium of contact.

There are examples where animals have exhibited the capacity of telepathy. Dr. Rupert Sheldrake investigated pet's behavior and found that in 50% of dog-owning households and 30% of those with cats, the pet animals were found to anticipate the arrival of a family member." In another finding, he found that 177 cases of dogs responding to the death or suffering of their absent masters or mistresses, mostly by howling, whining, or whimpering, and 62 accounts of cats showing similar signs of distress. A naturalist Willian Long who, in 1919 wrote a book that described the behavior of a pack of wolves he had followed in Canada. He found the separated members of wolf packs remained in contact with each other and responded to each other's activities while many miles apart. In 2001, on 26th January when there was a massive earthquake in Gujarat, India, people observed that minutes before the earthquake happened, the birds suddenly left their nests and trees and started to fly around in the sky making lots of noises. The dogs, as well, started barking intensively. All these capacities that animals have, can be searched for in human beings as well. This article aims to present a perspective of telepathy, that although considered as a new concept that seems to be coined in the western world has originally been in practice in India and the eastern world since a very ancient time. There are instances where seers and sages have communicated telepathically with other people and animals. Documented records of various people have been observed about the same. **Swami Yogananda** presented the concept of telepathy in his book named "Autobiography of a Yogi". In Chapter 10, Swami Yogananda mentions his meeting with His Guru Swami Yukteshwar Ji where he writes, "the saint is magnetically drawing me to him!" The instance was when he sought his Guru desperately and even while passing through him and not able to recognize him, he got propelled towards him. In ancient Indian literature, there are several other such instances where telepathic communication was done not only from one source to one receiver but multiple recipients. The term, 'Telepathy', was coined in 1882 by the classical scholar names **Frederic W. H. Myers**, a founder of the Society of Psychic Research. Earlier it was known as thought-transfer until Myers coined the word. The literal meaning of the word telepathy is distant feeling or perception. The word originated from the Greek language where 'Tele' means distant and the word 'pathy' originates from 'pathos', which means feeling, perception, or experience. Although, the concept lacks strong scientific testing to prove itself as a phenomenon still it has its prevalence. Besides, as Carl Jung quotes, "I shall not commit the fashionable stupidity of regarding everything that I cannot explain as a fraud" gives scope of further research. Although telepathy studies are not done much, there are instances, experiences and experiments that define its existence opening up scope of scientific studies.

3.3   Telepathy

Telepathy is defined as the transference of thoughts or feelings between two or more subjects without the use of senses or other physical objects. It is clearly said to be a mental capacity that is unique and not so prevalent. Modern parapsychological researchers have conducted several experiments to understand and prove this wonderful capacity of the human mind. The origin of the concept of telepathy in the western world dates back to the later 19th Century when the physical sciences made significant advances and scientific concepts were applied to mental phenomena with the hope that this would help understand paranormal phenomena. The modern concept of telepathy emerged in this context. In parapsychology, telepathy is considered to be a form of ESP (Extra Sensory Perception). It is often categorized as similar to precognition or clairvoyance. The most well-known experiments that have been carried out till now are Zener Cards and Ganzfield Experiment.

Several types of telepathies are classified by modern-day parapsychologists. Mainly four types have been defined which are:

(i) Latent Telepathy, also known as deferred telepathy in which the transfer of information is done without the use of senses with an observable time lag between transmission and reception.

(ii) Retrocognitive, Precognitive and Intuitive Telepathy

It is the transfer of information about the part past, future, or present state of an individual's mind to another individual.

(iii) Emotive Telepathy

It is also known as remote influence or emotional transfer. It is a process of transferring kinesthetic sensations through altered states.

(iv) Superconscious Telepathy

It involves tapping into superconscious to access the collective wisdom of the human species for knowledge. A Ganzfield experiment is a method used in Psi Studies. It has been claimed that it has the potential to verify for extrasensory perceptions (ESP) prevailing in an individual.

These experiments are among the most recent in parapsychology for testing telepathy. It was originally introduced into experimental psychology due to the experiments of the German psychologist Wolfgang Metzger on the perception of a homogenous visual field. In the early 1970s, Charles Honorton had been investigating ESP and dreams at the Maimonides Medical Center and began using the Ganzfield technique to achieve a state of sensory deprivation in which he hypothesized that psi could work. Honorton believed that, by reducing the ordinary sensory input, psi conductive states may be enhanced and psi-mediated information could be transmitted. Since Honorton and Sharon Harper published the first full experiment in 1974 in the Journal of the American Society for Psychical Research, the Ganzfeld has remained a parapsychological research. In a Ganzfeld experiment, the "receiver" sits in a comfortable chair wearing a headphone with halved ping-pong balls over the eyes and a red light shone on the receiver and placed in a room. In the headphones of the receiver white or pink noise (static) is played. The receiver for half an hour is kept in this state of mild sensory deprivation. During this time a randomly chosen target is observed by the sender and tries to mentally send this information to the receiver after 30 mins the receiver speaks out loud and, describes what is being seen by him or her. The whole process is being recorded by the experimenter (who is blind to the target) either by recording onto tape or by taking notes and later help the receiver at the time of the judging procedure in which the receiver is given a set of possible targets after taken out from the Ganzfeld state, from which they have to select one which is most resembled the images they witnessed during the experiment.

In 1970, Dr. Stanley Krippner and Dr. Montague Ullman conducted a study that was designed to investigate telepathic effects in dreams. A single subject, who had previously been successful in a similar study at another laboratory, spent 8 nights at the Maimonides Dream Laboratory. On each night, a target (art print) was randomly selected by a staff member (agent) after the subject was in bed. The agent spent the night in a distant room, attempting to influence the subject's dreams telepathically, once the monitoring experimenters signaled that a dream period had begun. At the end of each dream electroencephalogram-period (detected by electro-oculogram monitoring), the subject was awakened by the experimenters and the dream report was elicited and tape-recorded. Only the agent was aware of the target content, and he remained in his room throughout the night. Blind evaluations of target-dream correspondences by both subject and an outside judge produced statistically significant results supporting the telepathy hypothesis. Thus, telepathy is a known concept that is in existence yet needs to be pondered upon. There are several perspectives about the way telepathy can be practiced and experimented with.

3.4 History and Cultural Significance of Telepathy

3.4.1 Ancient Beliefs and Practices: Telepathy in Early Cultures

Telepathy, the ability to communicate thoughts and ideas from one mind to another without the need for verbal or physical interaction, has captivated human imagination since ancient times. In early cultures, telepathic communication was often intertwined with spiritual and mystical beliefs. Shamanic practices, prevalent in indigenous cultures worldwide, embraced the idea of telepathic connections between individuals, tribes, and even the spirit realm.

Shamans, regarded as mediators between the physical and spiritual realms, were believed to possess extraordinary telepathic abilities. Through **altered states of consciousness**, induced by rituals, drumming, chanting, or the use of hallucinogenic substances, shamans would enter trance- like states and establish telepathic communication with spirits, ancestors, and members of their community. These telepathic exchanges were seen as a means of acquiring knowledge, seeking guidance, and healing.

Similarly, telepathy found its place in the mythology and folklore of ancient civilizations. Greek mythology, for instance, tells of telepathic communication between gods, demigods, and mortal beings. The Oracle of Delphi, considered a conduit for divine messages, was believed to receive telepathic insights from Apollo, the god of prophecy. These ancient stories not only reflect the cultural significance attributed to telepathy but also highlight the belief in the existence of supernatural abilities of mind-to-mind communication.

3.4.2 Telepathy in Modern Times: Notable Figures and Studies

The exploration of telepathy continued during the modern era with the emergence of scientific inquiry and dedicated organizations such as the Society for Psychical Research (SPR), founded in 1882. One of the pioneers in the field of telepathic research was Frederic W. H. Myers, a founding member of the SPR. Myers conducted extensive investigations into psychic phenomena, including telepathy, seeking to establish scientific evidence for its existence.

In the late 19th and early 20th centuries, researchers like J.B. Rhine furthered the study of telepathy and other psychic abilities. Rhine conducted experiments using card guessing and dice rolling, aiming to demonstrate statistically significant results that supported the existence of telepathic communication. These studies laid the foundation for the field of parapsychology, dedicated to the scientific investigation of psychic phenomena.

Today, telepathy continues to be a subject of interest for researchers in various scientific disciplines. Controlled experiments, neuroimaging studies, and psychological assessments are being conducted to explore the validity of telepathic phenomena. While the scientific consensus regarding telepathy remains divided, ongoing research and advancements in technology have opened new avenues for understanding the potential of mind-to-mind communication.

3.5 Evolution of Telepathy and Psychic Abilities

3.5.1 Telepathy: The Power of Mental Connection

Telepathy, often considered **a subset of mind reading**, involves the direct transmission of thoughts, feelings, or information from one mind to another without the use of traditional communication channels. This phenomenon has intrigued and fascinated humans across cultures and civilizations throughout history.

Ancient civilizations, such as the Egyptians, Greeks, Indians, and Native Americans, believed in the existence of telepathic abilities. In these cultures, telepathy was seen as a spiritual gift or a connection to higher realms of consciousness.

In modern times, telepathy has been a subject of scientific research and investigation. Parapsychologists and researchers have conducted experiments to explore the potential existence of telepathic abilities. Although conclusive evidence is still elusive, some studies have reported intriguing results suggesting the presence of telepathic phenomena.

3.5.2   Psychic Abilities: Beyond the Ordinary Senses

Psychic abilities encompass a wide range of extraordinary perceptual capacities that go beyond the five traditional senses of sight, hearing, touch, taste, and smell. These abilities, also known as extrasensory perception (ESP), allow individuals to access information or perceive events beyond the limitations of ordinary sensory perception. Common types of psychic abilities include clairvoyance (the ability to see beyond normal vision), clairaudience (the ability to hear beyond normal hearing), clairsentience (the ability to sense beyond ordinary touch), and Clair cognizance (the ability to know beyond ordinary knowledge).

Psychic abilities are not limited to perceiving information about the present; they can also involve precognition (the ability to perceive future events) and retrocognition (the ability to perceive past events). These abilities offer glimpses into the fabric of time and expand the boundaries of human perception.

3.5.3   Interplay between Telepathy and Psychic Abilities

Telepathy and psychic abilities often intertwine, complementing and enhancing each other. Telepathy can be seen as a form of psychic ability, as it involves the transmission or reception of thoughts or information beyond ordinary sensory channels.

Telepathy can amplify other psychic abilities. For example, a clairvoyant who possesses telepathic skills can, not only see distant events but also receive the thoughts and intentions of the people involved in those events. Similarly, a clairsentient with telepathic abilities can, not only sense emotions but also connect with the mental states of others.

Furthermore, the development of psychic abilities can enhance telepathic connections. As individuals strengthen their psychic capacities, they become more attuned to subtle energies, frequencies and vibrations, enabling them to establish deeper telepathic connections with others.

The interplay between telepathy and psychic abilities opens up vast possibilities for individuals to explore and expand their **mind reading skills**. By mastering these combined techniques, individuals can unlock the most successful approaches to thought reading and tap into the limitless potential of the human mind.

3.6   Different Types of Telepathy

3.6.1   Mental Telepathy: Mind-to-Mind Communication

Mental telepathy refers to the direct exchange of thoughts, ideas, and information between two minds. *(Please see the picture on the cover page of this book).* This form of telepathy can occur consciously and intentionally or spontaneously and unconsciously. Conscious telepathic communication involves individuals actively engaging their minds to transmit or receive messages. This can be achieved through focused intention, visualization, or mental projection.

Conscious telepathy often requires a sender and a receiver who are both willing participants in the telepathic exchange. They establish a mental connection, with the sender directing their thoughts and intentions toward the receiver. The receiver, in turn, must be receptive and open to receiving the transmitted messages. Through this conscious interaction, a telepathic link is formed, allowing for the transfer of thoughts, emotions, and even sensory information.

Spontaneous telepathy, on the other hand, occurs without deliberate effort or control. It can manifest in situations where individuals experience a sudden and unexplained knowledge or understanding of another person's thoughts or feelings. Spontaneous telepathic experiences often take place between people with close emotional bonds, such as family members, close friends, or romantic partners.

3.6.2 Telepathic Bonds in Twin Connections and Soulmates

One fascinating aspect of mental telepathy is its occurrence within twin connections and soulmate relationships. Twins, especially identical twins, have long been associated with a unique telepathic connection. Many twin siblings report instances of knowing what the other is thinking or feeling, even when physically separated. This bond, often referred to as twin telepathy, highlights the deep connection and shared consciousness between twins.

Soulmates, individuals believed to have a profound and destined connection, also frequently experience telepathic communication. Soulmates are often described as having an innate understanding of each other's thoughts, emotions, and desires. This telepathic connection goes beyond the physical and taps into a spiritual and energetic level of communication.

3.6.3 Telepathic Perception: Accessing Others' Thoughts and Feelings

In addition to the direct exchange of thoughts, telepathy can also involve the perception and reception of others' thoughts and emotions. This form of telepathy, known as telepathic perception, allows individuals to gain insights into the mental and emotional states of others.

(i) **Empathic telepathy** is a type of telepathic perception that involves sensing and experiencing the emotions and energy of another person. Empaths, individuals with heightened sensitivity and empathic abilities, can pick up on the emotions and feelings of those around them. They may experience emotions that do not belong to them, and without any verbal communication, they can often accurately discern the emotional state of others.

(ii) **Cognitive telepathy**, on the other hand, focuses on the transmission and reception of thoughts and ideas rather than emotions. Individuals with cognitive telepathic abilities can tap into the stream of thoughts and mental activity of others. This form of telepathy allows for the exchange of ideas, concepts, and even complex information without the need for verbal or written communication.

(iii) **Psychic telepathy** represents a broader spectrum of telepathic perception. It encompasses both empathic and cognitive aspects of telepathy, enabling individuals to access not only thoughts and emotions but also intuitive insights and glimpses into past, present, or future events.

3.7   Common Misconceptions and Debunking Myths

3.7.1   Telepathy as a Superpower: Separating Fact from Fiction

Throughout history, telepathy has often been portrayed as a superpower, granting individuals the ability to read minds, control others' thoughts, or engage in extraordinary feats of mental manipulation. While these portrayals make for captivating storytelling, they tend to exaggerate the capabilities and limitations of telepathy.

In reality, telepathy is a nuanced and multifaceted phenomenon. It does not grant individuals a complete access to every thought and secret held by others. Instead, telepathic communication operates within certain boundaries and is influenced by factors such as intention, receptivity, and the nature of the connection between individuals.

Telepathic abilities are not omnipotent, nor can they override free will or manipulate others' thoughts against their consent. It is important to approach telepathy with a realistic understanding of its potential, grounded in scientific exploration and personal experiences.

3.7.2   Skepticism and Scientific Critiques of Telepathy

Telepathy, being a subject that challenges conventional scientific explanations, has faced skepticism and criticism from skeptics and some members of the scientific community. The main critiques often revolve around the lack of replicable and controlled experiments that definitively prove the existence of telepathy.

Designing experiments that account for all possible variables and control for potential biases is a challenging task. This difficulty, coupled with the inherent variability of telepathic experiences, has led some researchers to question the validity of telepathy as a genuine phenomenon.

Psychological factors and cognitive biases have been suggested as alternative explanations for perceived telepathic experiences. For instance, the ideomotor effect, where unconscious muscle movements are responsible for seemingly telepathic responses, has been proposed as an explanation for certain instances of apparent telepathy.

Additionally, psychological phenomena such as confirmation bias or selective memory can contribute to the misinterpretation or exaggeration of telepathic events.

While skepticism is a healthy and essential aspect of scientific inquiry, it is crucial to approach the study of telepathy with an open mind, considering both the skeptical critiques and the accounts of those who claim to have had genuine telepathic experiences.

3.7.3   The Interplay between Belief and Experience in Telepathic Phenomena

Telepathic experiences, like other psychic phenomena, are often influenced by personal beliefs, cultural conditioning, and psychological factors. Belief in the existence and possibility of telepathy can enhance the likelihood of experiencing telepathic connections or perceiving telepathic phenomena.

Individuals who firmly believe in telepathy may be more open and receptive to telepathic experiences, actively seeking and recognizing telepathic connections in their lives. Cultural and societal beliefs about telepathy can also play a role in shaping people's experiences and interpretations of telepathic events.

Personal testimonials and anecdotal evidence provide a wealth of accounts describing telepathic experiences. While individual anecdotes do not constitute scientific proof, they contribute to the broader understanding of telepathy by highlighting its subjective and personal nature. These accounts often express the deep emotional impact of telepathic connections and the transformative potential of telepathic communication.

To fully comprehend telepathy, it is essential to acknowledge the interplay between belief, experience, and the subjective nature of telepathic phenomena. This balanced approach allows for a more comprehensive exploration of the mysteries and possibilities of telepathic communication.

3.8 Strengthening Telepathic Communication

3.8.1 Developing a Telepathic Connection with Others

Establishing a harmonious and trusting relationship is a crucial foundation for effective telepathic communication. Building a strong connection with another individual allows for a deeper level of understanding and receptivity between minds. To develop a telepathic connection, it is important to cultivate empathy, emotional resonance, and a sense of attunement with the other person.

One way to enhance telepathic communication is by practicing active listening and non-verbal communication. Active listening involves giving your full attention to the other person, being present in the moment, and genuinely seeking to understand their thoughts and emotions. Non- verbal cues, such as maintaining eye contact, mirroring body language, and showing genuine interest, can foster a sense of connection and facilitate telepathic exchanges.

3.8.2 Building Trust and Rapport for Effective Telepathic Communication

Trust and rapport are essential elements in telepathic communication. It is vital to honor the boundaries and the consent in telepathic interactions, as entering someone's mind without their permission is a violation of privacy. Respecting the autonomy and emotional well-being of the other person is crucial for establishing a safe and ethical telepathic connection.

Transparent and open communication plays a significant role in building trust. By clearly expressing intentions, expectations, and limits in telepathic communication, both parties can feel comfortable and secure. Honesty, integrity, and mutual respect are key components of a healthy telepathic relationship.

3.8.3 Exercises for Enhancing Telepathic Abilities

Like any skill, telepathy can be developed and strengthened through practice and exercises. Here are some techniques to enhance telepathic abilities:

(i) **Meditation and Visualization Techniques for Mental Clarity:** Regular meditation helps calm the mind, improve focus, and develop mental clarity, which are essential for telepathic communication. Visualize a clear channel of communication between you and the other person, allowing thoughts and feelings to flow freely.

(ii) **Strengthening Intuition and Psychic Senses:** Engage in activities that heighten your intuitive abilities, such as tarot card reading, divination, or energy healing practices. These practices can help attune your senses and increase your receptivity to telepathic messages.

(iii) **Partner Exercises for Telepathic Communication and Telepathic Games:** Engage in telepathic exercises with a partner to enhance your telepathic connection. These exercises can involve sending and receiving simple messages, images, or emotions telepathically. Telepathic games, such as guessing symbols or numbers, can also be played to practice telepathic communication in a fun and interactive way.

Remember, telepathic abilities may vary from person to person, and progress may take time. Patience, dedication, and a willingness to explore your own unique telepathic potential are key to mastering this skill.

3.9 Ethical Considerations and Responsibility in Telepathic Communication

3.9.1 Using Telepathic Abilities with Integrity and Respect

As with any form of communication, telepathy comes with ethical considerations. It is essential to use telepathic abilities responsibly and with integrity. Treating telepathic communication with respect and mindfulness ensures that it is used for the greater good and does not infringe upon the rights or well-being of others.

3.9.2 Ethical guidelines for telepathic practitioners include:

(i) Consent: Seek permission from the other person before attempting telepathic communication. Respect their right to decline or withdraw consent at any time.

(ii) Confidentiality: Maintain the privacy and confidentiality of the information received during telepathic exchanges. Sharing or using sensitive information without permission is a breach of trust.

(iii) Empathy and Compassion: Approach telepathic communication with empathy and compassion. Respect the emotions and experiences of the other person and respond with kindness and understanding.

(iv) **Personal Boundaries:** Establish and respect personal boundaries in telepathic communication. Avoid intruding upon someone's thoughts or emotions without their permission.

(v) **Self-Reflection and Responsibility:** Continuously reflect on your own intentions, motivations, and the impact of your telepathic communication. Take responsibility for your actions and their potential consequences.

By adhering to these ethical principles, telepathic communication can be a powerful tool for connection, healing, and personal growth.

3.10 Telepathy in Different Contexts

3.10.1 Telepathic Relationships and Social Interactions with Telepathic Insights

Telepathy has the potential to profoundly impact various aspects of relationships and social interactions. Understanding and utilizing telepathic insights can enhance communication, deepen emotional connections, and foster empathy in interpersonal relationships.

(i) **In personal relationships**, telepathic communication can provide a deeper understanding of each other's thoughts, desires, and emotions. It allows for an intimate level of connection, as individuals can share unspoken thoughts, convey support, and strengthen their bond.

(ii) **In professional environments**, developing telepathic communication skills can have numerous benefits. It promotes effective teamwork and collaboration by enabling individuals to understand each other's perspectives, intentions, and needs. Telepathic insights can also be leveraged for enhanced problem-solving, decision- making, and creative brainstorming within work settings.

Telepathy can be a valuable tool for personal growth and self-discovery. By accessing subconscious wisdom and engaging in self-reflection through telepathic practices, individuals can gain deeper insights into their own thoughts, emotions, and motivations. Telepathy can facilitate healing and resolution of past traumas by accessing buried memories and providing a safe space for emotional processing. Additionally, cultivating intuition and inner guidance through telepathic practices can empower individuals to make aligned choices and navigate their life's path with clarity.

3.11 Beyond Telepathy: Exploring Advance Forms of Mind Reading

3.11.1 Connection between Telepathy and Clairvoyance

Clairvoyance, the ability to perceive information beyond the range of ordinary senses, often intersects with telepathy. Developing clairvoyant abilities can enhance mind reading skills and expand the range of telepathic perception. Clairvoyance enables individuals to access visual imagery, symbols, and metaphors that can enrich telepathic communication.

The synergy between telepathy and clairvoyance allows for a more comprehensive understanding of others' thoughts, emotions, and experiences. It opens pathways to deeper insights and intuitive knowledge that go beyond pure telepathic exchange.

3.11.2 Telepathy and Energy Healing

Telepathy and energy healing are intricately linked, as telepathic abilities can facilitate the transfer and manipulation of energetic fields. Through telepathic communication, individuals can access and direct healing energy to support physical, emotional, and spiritual well-being.

Telepathy as a tool for energy healing involves sensing and understanding the energetic imbalances or blockages in others. By establishing a telepathic connection, healers can intuitively identify areas of disharmony and channel healing energy to restore balance and promote healing.

Telepathic communication can also be used to balance and harmonize one's own energy field. By engaging in telepathic practices focused on self-healing and energy alignment, individuals can enhance their overall well-being and cultivate a deeper connection with their own energetic essence.

3.11.3   Telepathy and the Expansion of Consciousness

Telepathy holds the potential to be a gateway to transcendent and expanded states of consciousness. Engaging in telepathic communication can lead to profound spiritual experiences and insights that transcend the boundaries of ordinary reality.

Telepathy can facilitate connections with higher dimensions, spirit guides, or beings from other realms. Through telepathic exploration, individuals may gain access to universal wisdom, collective consciousness, and spiritual teachings.

By integrating telepathy with practices such as meditation, lucid dreaming, or astral projection, individuals can expand their consciousness, access higher realms of knowledge, and embark on transformative spiritual journeys.

By exploring advanced forms of mind reading, such as clairvoyance and energy healing, and tapping into the expansion of consciousness, individuals can unlock new dimensions of telepathic potential. With dedication, practice, and a balanced approach, mastering the art of telepathy becomes a transformative journey toward enhanced understanding, connection, and personal growth.

3.12   Fundamentals of Telepathic Communication

Telepathic communication is the ability to transmit and receive information through the power of the mind, bypassing traditional means of verbal or written exchange. It is an innate human capability that has been explored and practiced throughout history. The origins of telepathy can be traced back to ancient civilizations and indigenous cultures, where it was often considered a sacred and spiritual gift.

In modern times, scientific research has shed light on the mechanisms behind telepathy. While the exact process is still not fully understood, it is believed to involve the transmission of thoughts, feelings, and images through subtle energetic fields. These fields interact with the receiver's mind, allowing them to perceive and interpret the transmitted information.

Telepathic communication can occur in various forms, including both verbal and non-verbal exchanges. Verbal telepathy involves the transmission of words and sentences, similar to traditional spoken language, but without the need for vocalization. Non-verbal telepathy, on the other hand, relies on the transmission of emotions, sensations, images, and intuitive impressions.

3.13 Building a Foundation for Telepathic Connection

To strengthen your telepathic abilities, it is crucial to develop a strong foundation based on self-awareness and intuition. Self-awareness allows you to recognize and understand your own thoughts, emotions, and energy, which is essential for effective telepathic communication. Practices such as mindfulness and meditation can help you cultivate self-awareness by quieting the mind, enhancing focus, and heightening sensory perception.

Intuition, often referred to as the "sixth sense," is a key component of telepathic communication. It involves tapping into your innate knowing and trusting your inner voice. By honing your intuition, you become more attuned to subtle cues and signals from others, making it easier to establish telepathic connections.

Clearing mental and emotional blockages is another important step in building a solid foundation for telepathic connection. Negative thoughts, limiting beliefs, and emotional baggage can interfere with the clarity of your telepathic messages. Through practices like energy healing, meditation, and self-reflection, you can release these blockages and create space for more accurate and effective telepathic communication.

3.14   Establishing Rapport and Trust

Establishing a strong connection with others is essential for successful telepathic communication. Active listening is a foundational skill that allows you to fully understand and empathize with others. By giving your full attention to the person you are communicating with, you can pick up on subtle cues, emotions, and unspoken messages, strengthening the telepathic bond between you.

Building trust and openness is crucial for telepathic communication to flourish. Trust creates a safe space for individuals to share their thoughts and feelings without fear of judgment or rejection. Openness, on the other hand, involves being vulnerable and transparent in your own communication, which encourages reciprocation from others.

Energetic alignment is another important aspect of telepathic connection. Our energetic fields interact with each other, and when they are in sync, telepathic communication becomes more effortless. Practices such as visualization, breathwork, and energy healing can help you align your energy with others, creating a harmonious and receptive telepathic environment.

3.15   Techniques for Enhancing Telepathic Abilities

Meditation plays a crucial role in enhancing telepathic abilities. Through regular meditation practice, you can quiet the mind, improve focus, and strengthen your connection to the subtle energetic realms. Telepathic meditation involves specific techniques and visualizations aimed at opening the channels of telepathic communication. For example, visualizing a clear, vibrant energy field around you can enhance your ability to send and receive telepathic messages.

Affirmations and intentions are powerful tools for programming your mind for successful telepathic communication. By repeating positive statements and setting clear intentions, you align your subconscious mind with the desired outcome of telepathic connection. Affirmations can include statements such as "I am open to receiving telepathic messages with clarity and accuracy," or "I trust my telepathic abilities to strengthen and develop."

Dream telepathy is a fascinating avenue for telepathic communication. During sleep, our subconscious mind is more accessible, and telepathic messages can be transmitted and received through dreams. Lucid dreaming techniques can help you become aware and conscious within your dreams, allowing for intentional telepathic communication. Keeping a dream journal to record your dreams and any telepathic experiences can provide valuable insights and help you develop your abilities further.

3.16   Strengthening Telepathic Sending and Receiving

To enhance your ability to send telepathic messages, it is essential to develop mental projection skills. Mental projection involves focusing your thoughts and intentions with clarity and purpose. Practice visualizing your thoughts as clear and vivid images, as well as transmitting emotions and sensations to the intended recipient. With practice, you can refine your ability to project telepathic messages with precision.

Receiving telepathic messages requires a heightened sensory perception and a keen awareness of subtle cues. By opening your channels of reception, you become more attuned to the energetic signals and information being transmitted. Pay attention to your intuition, gut feelings, and sensory impressions, as these can serve as indicators of incoming telepathic messages. Developing your ability to interpret symbolic language and imagery is also valuable in deciphering telepathic information.

3.17   Telepathy in Relationships and Personal Connections

Telepathic communication can greatly enhance relationships and personal connections. In romantic relationships, telepathy can deepen intimacy and understanding. By establishing a strong telepathic bond, partners can communicate on a deeper level, sharing thoughts, emotions, and desires that transcend spoken words. Telepathic connection can also foster empathy and compassion, allowing partners to better understand and support each other.

Telepathy can also be applied to family and friendship connections. By practicing telepathic communication with loved ones, you can strengthen the bonds and create a sense of unity. Telepathy can serve as a tool for resolving conflicts, expressing love and appreciation, and providing support during challenging times.

Communication with animals and nature is another fascinating aspect of telepathy. Animals have an innate ability to pick up on energetic signals, making telepathic communication with them more accessible. By developing your telepathic abilities, you can establish a deeper connection with animals, understand their needs, and convey your intentions to them. Similarly, connecting with the energy of nature allows you to tune into the wisdom and messages that the natural world has to offer.

3.18   Telepathic Healing and Energy Transfer

Telepathic communication can be a powerful tool for healing, both for yourself and others. Sending healing energy through telepathy involves directing positive, healing intentions towards the recipient. By visualizing healing energy flowing from your mind to the person in need, you can facilitate energetic shifts and promote well-being.

Remote healing is a practice that extends telepathic healing across distances. By focusing your thoughts and intentions, you can project healing energy to individuals who are physically distant from you. This form of telepathic healing can be particularly useful in situations where immediate physical contact is not possible.

Energy exchange and sharing is another aspect of telepathic communication. By transferring positive energy and intentions to others, you can uplift their spirits, provide emotional support, and foster a sense of well-being. This can be done through simple acts of sending love, compassion, and positive mind to someone, even if they are not aware of the telepathic communication.

3.19   Ethical Considerations in Telepathic Communication

As with any form of communication, telepathy requires ethical considerations. Respecting boundaries and obtaining consent are of utmost importance. Telepathic communication should never be imposed upon or forced upon others without their explicit consent. It is essential to establish clear communication guidelines and seek permission before engaging in telepathic exchanges.

Maintaining ethical standards also means using telepathy for empowerment and support rather than manipulation or intrusion. It is crucial to honor the autonomy and privacy of others, refraining from invading their thoughts or personal space without their consent. Telepathy should be approached with a mindset of respect, empathy, and integrity.

3.20   Overcoming Challenges in Telepathic Communication

One of the challenges in telepathic communication is dealing with skepticism and doubt, both from oneself and others. Strengthening belief in telepathy requires a combination of personal experiences, experimentation, and open-mindedness. By keeping a record of your telepathic experiences and practicing with trusted individuals who also believe in telepathy, you can gradually overcome doubts and strengthen your conviction.

Interference and distractions can also pose challenges to telepathic communication. Environmental factors, such as electromagnetic fields or energetic disturbances, can disrupt the clarity of telepathic messages. Shielding techniques, such as visualizing a protective barrier or grounding yourself in nature, can help mitigate these interferences. Additionally, cultivating focused attention and mental discipline can help you maintain clarity and overcome distractions during telepathic communication.

3.21   Practical Applications of Telepathic Communication

Telepathic communication has practical applications in various aspects of life. In everyday situations, telepathy can enhance interpersonal communication skills. By being more attuned to the thoughts and emotions of others, you can better understand their needs, desires, and perspectives. This can lead to improved relationships, effective collaboration, and conflict resolution.

In professional settings, telepathy can be utilized in fields such as therapy and counseling. Therapists who possess telepathic abilities can establish deeper connections with their clients, understand their underlying emotions and thoughts, and provide more accurate guidance and support. Telepathic communication can also be applied in business and negotiation, allowing for more authentic and effective communication with colleagues, clients, and partners.

3.22   Advanced Telepathic Techniques and Experiments

As you progress on your telepathic journey, you may explore advanced techniques and engage in experiments to further develop your abilities. Group telepathy and collective consciousness involve harnessing the power of shared intent and connection. By engaging in telepathic practices with a group of like-minded individuals, you can amplify the telepathic signals and create a collective energetic field conducive to telepathic communication.

Telepathic time travel and past-life communication are advanced applications of telepathy. These techniques involve exploring temporal dimensions and communicating with entities from different periods or past lives. Through deep states of meditation, visualization, and intention setting, you can access information and wisdom that transcends linear time, expanding your understanding of consciousness and reality.

3.23   Developing Telepathic Connection

3.23.1   Understanding the Dynamics of Telepathic Communication

Telepathic communication involves the transmission and reception of thoughts, feelings, and information between individuals without the need for verbal or physical interaction. It operates through the subtle energy field that connects all living beings. This energy field allows thoughts and emotions to be exchanged on a deep, intuitive level.

In telepathic communication, the flow of energy and information is bidirectional. Both the sender and receiver contribute to the exchange. The sender focuses their intention and directs their thoughts toward the intended recipient, while the receiver opens themselves to perceive the incoming telepathic messages.

To establish a successful telepathic connection, it is crucial to develop a synchronized mindset with your telepathic partner. This involves aligning your thoughts, emotions, and intentions to create a harmonious energetic resonance. It requires mutual trust, openness, and receptivity.

3.23.2   Building Trust and Rapport for Effective Telepathy:

Trust and rapport are essential elements for establishing effective telepathic communication. When there is trust between sender and receiver, it creates a safe and conducive environment for sharing thoughts and feelings telepathically.

Building rapport involves establishing an emotional connection and empathy with your telepathic partner. This connection enhances the level of understanding and receptivity between both individuals. Active listening and mindful engagement play a crucial role in building rapport, allowing you to attune to your partner's emotions and experiences.

Non-verbal communication also plays a significant role in building trust and rapport. Paying attention to body language, facial expressions, and subtle cues helps in establishing a deeper level of connection. Practicing empathy and compassion further strengthens the telepathic bond.

3.23.3   Strengthening your Telepathic Abilities

To enhance your telepathic abilities, it is essential to cultivate a daily practice of mindfulness. Mindfulness allows you to quiet the mind, focus your attention, and be fully present in the moment. This state of presence opens up your receptivity to telepathic information and enhances your ability to transmit thoughts effectively.

Meditation is a powerful technique for developing telepathic abilities. Through meditation, you can enter a deep state of relaxation and heightened awareness. This state facilitates the tuning in to the subtle energy frequencies necessary for telepathic communication. Visualization exercises during meditation can also help amplify and refine your telepathic transmissions.

Additionally, incorporating affirmation and intention setting into your telepathic practice can have a profound impact. Affirmations help to strengthen your belief in your telepathic abilities, while clear intentions focus your energy and direct it toward specific targets. Consistent practice, combined with belief and intention, can significantly enhance your telepathic skills.

3.24 Sending and Receiving Telepathic Messages

3.24.1 Sending Telepathic Messages

Sending telepathic messages requires the ability to focus your thoughts and intentions and direct them towards the intended recipient. Visualization and imagination are powerful tools for telepathic sending. Imagine your thoughts forming into a clear, vibrant image or message and visualize it being transmitted to the recipient.

Affirmations can also enhance your telepathic sending abilities. By affirming your ability to transmit thoughts effectively, you strengthen your belief in your telepathic power. Repeat affirmations such as "My telepathic messages are clear and potent" or "I transmit my thoughts with ease and precision."

It is common to experience doubts or mental blocks when sending telepathic messages. To overcome these obstacles, acknowledge and release any limiting beliefs or fears that may arise. Trust in your inherent telepathic abilities and maintain a state of relaxed focus while sending your messages.

3.24.2 Receiving Telepathic Messages

Receiving telepathic messages requires tuning into subtle energy signals and impressions. It is essential to develop your psychic senses to enhance your telepathic receptivity. This can be achieved through regular meditation, energy work, and psychic development exercises.

To receive telepathic messages, practice quieting the mind and opening yourself to the incoming information. Pay attention to any sudden thoughts, images, or feelings that arise seemingly out of nowhere. Trust your intuition and allow these impressions to guide you.

Decoding telepathic messages often involves working with symbolic and intuitive information. The messages may not always be literal or straightforward but may contain metaphorical or abstract elements. Develop your ability to interpret and understand these symbolic representations through practice and reflection.

3.24.3 Telepathy in Group Settings

Telepathic communication can be extended to group settings, allowing for collective telepathic experiences and interactions. Establishing a telepathic connection within a group requires synchronization of thoughts, intentions, and energy.

Group telepathy exercises and activities can strengthen the telepathic bond between members. These activities may involve sending and receiving telepathic messages within the group, exploring collective visualization, or engaging in synchronized meditation. Such practices enhance the telepathic synergy within the group and foster a deeper sense of connection.

Strengthening collective intuition and telepathic synergy allows groups to tap into shared knowledge, insights, and wisdom. It can be particularly beneficial in creative collaborations, problem-solving sessions, or group decision-making processes.

By developing telepathic communication within a group, members can experience a heightened sense of unity, cooperation, and shared consciousness.

3.25 Telepathy in Relationships and Personal Connections

3.25.1 Telepathy in Romantic Relationships

Telepathic communication can play a transformative role in romantic relationships. It enables partners to deepen their emotional bonds, enhance intimacy, and gain a deeper understanding of each other's thoughts and feelings.

By cultivating a telepathic connection, partners can develop a heightened sense of empathy and intuition toward one another. They can intuitively sense each other's needs, desires, and emotional states, fostering a deeper level of emotional intimacy.

Telepathic communication can also aid in resolving conflicts within relationships. Partners can transmit their thoughts, concerns, and apologies telepathically, allowing for a more heartfelt and compassionate exchange. This deep level of understanding and communication can lead to greater harmony and trust within the relationship.

3.25.2 Telepathy in Family and Friendships

Telepathy is not limited to romantic relationships; it can also be applied to family dynamics and friendships. Strengthening telepathic connections with loved ones allows for a deeper level of understanding and support.

In family settings, telepathic communication can bridge gaps in communication and foster a stronger sense of unity. Family members can transmit love, support, and healing energy telepathically, even when physically apart. Telepathy can also help in resolving conflicts and misunderstandings, promoting harmony within the family unit.

In friendships, telepathic connections can provide a profound level of support and connection. Friends can tune into each other's thoughts and emotions, offering comfort, guidance, and encouragement even from a distance. Telepathy can enhance the bond between friends, creating a deep and lasting connection.

3.25.3 Telepathic Communication in Professional Settings

Telepathic communication can have practical applications in professional settings, enabling more effective teamwork, leadership, and communication.

Within teams, telepathy can foster better collaboration and understanding. Team members can transmit thoughts, ideas, and solutions telepathically, leading to innovative problem-solving and increased productivity. It promotes a sense of shared vision and enhances the collective intelligence of the team.

Leaders can utilize telepathic insights to gain a deeper understanding of their team members' needs, motivations, and concerns. By tuning into the telepathic field, leaders can create an inclusive and empathetic work environment, promoting stronger relationships and improved performance.

Telepathy can also be applied to negotiations and persuasive communication. By intuitively understanding the thoughts and intentions of others, individuals can adapt their communication styles and strategies to resonate with their counterparts, leading to more successful outcomes.

3.26 Telepathic Healing and Energy Transfer

3.26.1 Understanding the Energetic Aspect of Healing

Telepathic communication can be harnessed for healing purposes, as it operates on an energetic level. Healing involves restoring balance and harmony to the body, mind, and spirit. Telepathy can aid in this process by transferring healing energy and information.

The energy field that connects all living beings allows for the transmission of healing energy. Telepathic healers can tap into this field to send healing energy to individuals in need. By directing focused intention and visualizing healing energy flowing to the recipient, telepathic healers can facilitate energetic healing on various levels.

Telepathic healing is not limited to physical ailments but extends to emotional and spiritual well-being. It can assist in releasing emotional blockages, promoting emotional healing and growth. It can also support spiritual transformation and the alignment of one's energy with higher states of consciousness.

3.26.2 Telepathic Healing Techniques

Telepathic healing techniques encompass a range of practices aimed at channeling and directing healing energy. These techniques can be used both in-person and remotely.

Sending healing energy through telepathic channels involves visualizing a stream of healing light or energy flowing from your consciousness to the recipient.

This energy can be directed to specific areas of the body or to support overall well-being. By maintaining a state of focused intention and sending love and healing energy, telepathic healers can facilitate profound healing experiences.

Visualization and intention play a vital role in remote healing through telepathy. Even when physically distant, telepathic healers can imagine themselves connecting with the recipient and sending healing energy across time and space. This technique transcends physical limitations and allows for the expansion of healing beyond traditional boundaries.

Combining telepathy with other healing modalities, such as Reiki or sound therapy, can amplify the healing effects. By integrating telepathic communication with other energetic healing practices, practitioners can create a synergistic approach to healing, addressing multiple layers of the recipient's being.

3.26.3 Telepathy in Distance Healing

Distance healing involves sending telepathic healing energy and information to individuals who are geographically separated from the healer. Telepathy transcends physical distance, as the energy field connects all beings regardless of their location.

Telepathic healers can tune into the energetic signature of the recipient and access their subtle energy field. By doing so, they can intuitively sense the areas that require healing and direct healing energy accordingly. The recipient may feel sensations of warmth, tingling, or relaxation as the healing energy is received.

Telepathic healers can also engage in remote diagnosis and treatment through telepathic insights. By attuning to the recipient's energy field, healers can gather information about their physical, emotional, and spiritual well-being. This knowledge aids in creating a personalized healing approach that addresses the specific needs of the individual.

Ethical considerations and responsibility are essential aspects of telepathic healing. Healers must always seek permission and consent from the recipient before engaging in any form of telepathic healing. Respecting the recipient's autonomy and boundaries is crucial to creating a safe and ethical healing space.

3.27   Practical Applications of Telepathy

3.27.1   Telepathy for Personal Growth and Self-Reflection

Telepathy can be a powerful tool for personal growth and self-reflection. By tapping into your own telepathic abilities, you can gain insights into your thoughts, emotions, and subconscious patterns.

Engaging in regular telepathic practices, such as meditation and self-reflection, allows you to delve deeper into your inner world. By quieting the mind and tuning into your intuitive voice, you can access valuable guidance and wisdom. Telepathy can help you uncover hidden beliefs, fears, and desires, allowing for self-awareness and personal transformation.

Using telepathy for intuitive decision-making can also enhance your personal growth. By tuning into your intuitive senses, you can access information beyond the limitations of logic and reasoning. Telepathic insights can guide you in making choices that align with your authentic self and higher purpose.

Exploring past lives and higher consciousness is another fascinating application of telepathy. By expanding your telepathic awareness, you can access information and experiences from previous lifetimes or connect with higher-dimensional realms. This exploration can provide profound spiritual insights and foster a sense of interconnectedness with the broader universe.

3.27.2   Telepathy for Psychic Investigations

Telepathy can be instrumental in psychic investigations, assisting in uncovering information and solving mysteries.

In cases of missing persons, telepathic techniques can aid investigators in accessing intuitive impressions and guidance. By attuning to the energy and thoughts surrounding the case, psychic investigators can gather valuable information that may lead to finding the missing person. Telepathic connections with the missing person or individuals involved can provide insights into their whereabouts or well-being.

Gathering information and solving mysteries through telepathy requires honing psychic skills, such as clairvoyance, clairsentience, and Clair-cognizance. By utilizing these psychic abilities, investigators can access information beyond the physical realm, unraveling hidden truths and uncovering vital clues.

Collaborating with law enforcement and investigators in psychic investigations is another application of telepathy. By combining telepathic insights with traditional investigative methods, a comprehensive and multi-faceted approach to solving crimes and mysteries can be achieved.

3.27.3   Telepathy and Spiritual Connections

Telepathy can deepen spiritual connections and facilitate communication with higher realms and spiritual beings.

Communicating with spirit guides and higher beings telepathically allows for direct guidance and support on your spiritual path. By establishing a telepathic connection, you can receive messages, insights, and teachings from these spiritual entities. This communication can provide clarity, direction, and profound spiritual experiences.

Exploring interdimensional realms through telepathy opens up possibilities for connecting with beings from other dimensions or parallel realities. By expanding your telepathic awareness, you can tap into the collective consciousness of these realms, accessing wisdom and knowledge that transcends our physical reality.

Strengthening your spiritual path with telepathic guidance involves regular spiritual practices and cultivation of your telepathic abilities. By integrating telepathy into your spiritual journey, you can deepen your connection with the divine, expand your consciousness, and align with your soul's purpose.

3.27.4 Telepathy and Collective Consciousness

Telepathy can be a catalyst for collective healing, social change, and the manifestation of a harmonious future.

Uniting minds for global healing and transformation through telepathy involves creating collective intentions and focusing collective energy toward healing and positive change. By synchronizing thoughts, emotions, and intentions, groups can amplify their telepathic impact, sending waves of healing and transformation to the collective consciousness.

Telepathy can also serve as a tool for social change and empathy. By tapping into the thoughts and emotions of others, individuals can develop a deeper understanding of different perspectives and foster empathy and compassion. This telepathic connection can bridge divides, promote understanding, and contribute to creating a more harmonious and inclusive society.

Creating a harmonious future through collective telepathic intentions involves envisioning and transmitting positive visions and intentions for the world. By collectively focusing on peace, love, and unity, groups can energetically influence the collective consciousness, paving the way for a more enlightened and compassionate world.

3.28 Understanding the Mind Reading

3.28.1 Power of Intuition and Mind Reading

Intuition plays a fundamental role in thought reading, serving as a bridge between conscious and subconscious information processing. It is the intuitive sense that allows individuals to perceive and understand the thoughts and feelings of others beyond logical reasoning.

Intuition operates outside the boundaries of conscious awareness, drawing on subtle cues, body language, energy, and the overall context of a situation. It often manifests as gut feelings, hunches, or sudden insights that provide valuable information about the thoughts and intentions of others.

To develop and enhance intuition for effective thought reading, individuals can engage in practices such as meditation, mindfulness, and self-reflection. These practices help quiet the mind, cultivate present-moment awareness, and attune to the subtle signals and impressions that arise.

Additionally, trust in one's intuition is crucial for the successful thought reading. By trusting the intuitive signals and impressions received, individuals can access deeper layers of information and insights, leading to more accurate interpretations of others' thoughts and emotions.

3.28.2 Consciousness and Subconsciousness: Key to Accessing Thoughts

Consciousness and subconsciousness play significant roles in thought reading. Consciousness represents our immediate awareness of the external world and our own thoughts and experiences. Subconsciousness, on the other hand, refers to the vast reservoir of information, memories, and mental processes that operate below the level of conscious awareness.

Thoughts and emotions are not always expressed explicitly through verbal or non-verbal communication. Often, they reside in the subconscious mind, influencing our behavior and interactions without our conscious knowledge.

To access the thoughts and emotions stored in the subconscious, individuals need to cultivate an open and receptive state of mind. This can be achieved through techniques such as relaxation, visualization, hypnosis, deep breathing techniques (like pranayama), and deep meditation, which facilitate a connection with the subconscious realms.

Furthermore, developing an understanding of the cognitive processes that occur in the subconscious mind, can aid in thought reading. The subconscious mind operates through patterns, associations, and symbols, and it processes the information holistically rather than in a linear and logical manner. By familiarizing oneself with these subconscious mechanisms, individuals can decipher the hidden meanings behind thoughts and emotions.

3.28.3 Emotional Resonance and Empathy

Emotions play a pivotal role in thought reading, as they contain valuable information about an individual's mental and emotional state. Emotional resonance refers to the ability to pick up on and understand the emotions of others, even without explicit verbal or non-verbal cues.

Empathy, the capacity to understand and share the feelings of others, is a key skill in mind reading. Empathy allows individuals to step into the emotional shoes of another person, gaining deeper insights into their thoughts, intentions, and experiences.

Developing empathy involves cultivating self-awareness, active listening, and a genuine interest in understanding others. It requires individuals to attune to the emotional energy and non-verbal cues transmitted by others, allowing them to grasp the underlying emotional currents and motivations.

However, it is important to maintain healthy emotional boundaries when engaging in mind reading. Empathy should not lead to emotional overwhelming or the invasion of others' privacy. By respecting the personal boundaries and practicing self-care, individuals can navigate the emotional aspects of thought reading ethically and responsibly.

3.29   Developing the Foundations for Mind Reading

3.29.1   Mental Clarity and Focus

Mental clarity and focus are essential for the successful mind reading. A cluttered and distracted mind can impede the ability to receive and interpret the thoughts and intentions of others accurately.

To cultivate mental clarity, individuals can engage in practices that promote concentration and focus, such as meditation, mindfulness, and deep breathing exercises (like pranayama). These practices help calm the mind, reduce mental clutter, and enhance the capacity to maintain a sustained attention.

Additionally, regular mental exercises, such as solving puzzles, brain teasers, and memory games, can sharpen the cognitive functions and improve mental agility. By challenging the mind and expanding its capabilities, individuals can enhance their mind reading skills.

3.29.2   Cultivating Emotional Intelligence for Mind Reading

Emotional intelligence refers to the ability to recognize, understand, and manage one's own emotions, as well as empathize with and respond effectively to the emotions of others. It is a crucial skill for successful mind reading, as emotions provide valuable insights into the thoughts and intentions of individuals.

To cultivate emotional intelligence, individuals can start by developing self-awareness. This involves paying attention to one's own emotions, signals, triggers, and behavioral patterns. Through self-reflection and introspection, individuals can gain a deeper understanding of their own emotional landscape and how to influence their perception and interactions with others.

Active listening is another important aspect of emotional intelligence. It involves being fully present and attentive to others when they communicate, both verbally and non-verbally. By actively listening and observing, individuals can pick up on subtle cues, body language, and emotional nuances, enriching their mind reading abilities.

Empathy training is also beneficial for strengthening emotional intelligence in the context of mind reading. This can involve role-playing exercises, perspective-taking activities, and empathy-building exercises that help individuals step into the shoes of others and gain a deeper understanding of their thoughts and emotions.

3.29.3 Strengthening Communication Skills

Effective communication skills are essential for successful mind reading interactions. Being able to convey thoughts, emotions, and intentions clearly and accurately can foster trust and rapport, enabling a deeper exchange of information during mind reading sessions.

Active listening is a foundational communication skill that involves fully engaging with and understanding the messages being conveyed by others. It requires individuals to focus on the speaker, avoid interruptions, and ask clarifying questions to ensure a comprehensive understanding.

Non-verbal communication and body-language interpretation are also vital components of communication skills for mind reading. By paying attention to facial expressions, gestures, posture, and tone of voice, individuals can gain valuable insights into the thoughts and emotions of others, enhancing their mind reading accuracy.

Furthermore, cultivating effective verbal communication skills, such as clarity, empathy, and assertiveness, can contribute to the successful mind reading interactions. Expressing oneself concisely and articulately, while also being receptive and responsive to others' cues, creates an atmosphere of openness and facilitates a deeper exchange of thoughts and emotions.

3.30 Techniques of Mind Reading

3.30.1 Empathetic Listening and Reflective Responses

Empathic listening involves not only hearing the words spoken by others but also paying attention to their emotions, underlying needs, and unspoken messages. It requires individuals to listen with empathy, understanding, and without judgment.

To practice empathic listening, individuals can employ techniques such as active listening, paraphrasing, and reflective responses. Active listening involves giving full attention to the speaker, maintaining eye contact, and receiving verbal and non-verbal cues to indicate understanding and engagement.

Paraphrasing involves summarizing and restating the speaker's words in one's own words, demonstrating that one has grasped the intended meaning. This technique helps clarify any misunderstandings and ensures that both parties are on the same page.

Reflective responses go beyond paraphrasing and involve expressing an understanding of the speaker's emotions and underlying needs. This technique validates the speaker's experience and fosters a deeper level of connection and trust.

3.30.2 Cold Reading and Warm Reading Techniques

Cold reading and warm reading are the techniques commonly employed in psychic and mentalist performances to create the illusion of mind reading. Understanding them can provide insights into the psychology of mind reading.

(i) **Cold reading** involves making general or ambiguous statements that could apply to a wide range of individuals. The reader then observes the reactions and feedback from the person being read, using that information to narrow down and refine their statements. This technique relies heavily on the observation skills, intuition, and the ability of the mind reader to make the necessary deductions.

Cold reading involves gathering information about a person through observation, deduction, and skillful questioning. Mentalists use a combination of psychological tricks, body language analysis, and carefully crafted statements to create the impression of having unique insights into an individual's life.

Observation plays a critical role in cold reading. By keenly observing an individual's appearance, clothing choices, and mannerisms, a reader can make educated guesses about their personality, background, and interests. These observations provide valuable clues that can be used to guide the reading and create an impression of mind reading.

(ii) **Warm reading,** on the other hand, involves gathering information about the person being read through indirect means before the reading takes place. This can include researching the person's background, social media profiles, or obtaining information through casual conversation before the mind reading. The gathered information is then subtly incorporated into the reading, creating the impression of accurate mind reading.

There are various approaches to cold reading, each employing different techniques to extract information from the participant. These approaches include inductive reasoning, Barnum statements, and hot reading.

(a) Inductive Reasoning: Drawing Conclusions from Limited Information

Inductive reasoning involves making generalizations based on limited information. By carefully observing an individual's behavior, appearance, and responses, a mentalist can deduce probable characteristics or experiences that may apply to them. By presenting these deductions as personal insights, the mentalist creates the illusion of mind reading.

(b) Barnum Statements: Generalized Statements with Personalized Interpretation

Barnum statements are general statements that appear to be specific and personalized but are actually applicable to a wide range of people. These statements are intentionally vague, allowing individuals to interpret them in a way that aligns with their own experiences. Mentalists use Barnum statements to create the impression of mind reading by providing participants with information they believe to be unique to them.

(c) Hot/Warm Reading: Gathering Information Prior to the Reading

Hot reading involves gathering information about an individual prior to the reading, either through research or covert conversations. While this approach is considered less ethical than other forms of mind reading, it has been employed by some mentalists and psychics to enhance their readings. However, true mastery of mind reading lies in the ability to perform accurate readings without relying on pre-gathered information.

Cold reading is primarily a form of entertainment, and mentalists must ensure that participants understand this aspect. While the goal is to provide an engaging experience, it is important to avoid misleading individuals or giving the impression of possessing supernatural abilities. Mentalists can emphasize the psychological and observational aspects of cold reading to create an enjoyable and thought- provoking performance.

Building trust with participants is paramount. Mentalists should be honest about the nature of cold reading and refrain from presenting their statements as absolute truths. It is essential to respect the boundaries of the participants and avoid prying into personal or sensitive information without consent.

Consent is crucial in any mind reading performance, including cold reading. Mentalists should clearly communicate the nature of the performance and obtain consent from participants to engage in the reading. Participants should feel comfortable setting boundaries and expressing their preferences throughout the experience.

By understanding the history, techniques, and ethical considerations of cold reading, aspiring mind readers can enhance their abilities to engage in compelling and responsible performances.

It is important to note that the ethical use of cold reading and warm reading is assured. It requires transparency and the consent of all parties involved. It is crucial to respect the boundaries and expectations of the participants.

3.30.3 Psychometry: Extracting Information from Objects

Psychometry is a technique that involves obtaining information about persons or events by touching or holding an object associated with them. It is based on the belief that objects can retain and emit energetic imprints which can be sensed and interpreted.

To practice psychometry, individuals can choose an object that holds significance for the person or event they wish to gain insights about. By holding the object, focusing their attention, and allowing themselves to be open to impressions, they may receive sensory information, emotions, or images related to the object's history or the person it is connected to.

Developing psychometric skills requires practice and attunement to subtle energetic vibrations. With time and experience, individuals can enhance their ability to extract meaningful information from objects, unraveling past events and gaining deeper insights into people's lives.

3.31 Exploring Specialized Techniques in Mind Reading

3.31.1 Remote Viewing: Expanding your Perception

Remote viewing is a specialized technique that involves perceiving or accessing information about the distant locations, events, or objects without physical presence. It expands the boundaries of perception and allows individuals to explore **non-local consciousness.**

To practice remote viewing, individuals enter a relaxed state of mind and direct their attention towards the target they wish to perceive. They may use mental imagery, visualization, or other techniques to access information beyond their immediate sensory awareness.

Remote viewing is often used in the fields such as espionage, scientific research, and personal exploration. It enables individuals to gather information that is not readily available through conventional means, providing unique perspectives and insights.

3.31.2 Premonition and Precognition: Sensing the Future

Premonition and precognition involve the ability to perceive or sense the future events before they happen. These phenomena challenge the linear perception of time and offer glimpses into potential future outcomes.

Premonitions are sudden feelings, dreams, or intuitive insights that provide individuals with a sense of impending events. They can serve as warnings or guidance, urging individuals to take precautionary measures or make specific decisions.

Precognition, on the other hand, involves perceiving future events or information through intuitive or psychic means. It can manifest as visions, flashes of insight, or symbolic messages that provide glimpses into what is yet to come.

Developing premonition and precognition abilities requires honing one's intuition, attuning to subtle energy shifts, and maintaining an open and receptive mindset. Practicing meditation, dream journaling, and mindfulness can aid in accessing these abilities and interpreting the information received.

3.31.3   Energy Reading and Aura Perception

Energy reading and aura perception involve perceiving and interpreting the energetic fields that surround individuals, objects, or environments. It is based on the belief that everything emits an energetic vibration that can be sensed and analyzed.

To read the energy and perceive auras, individuals can focus their attention on the target while maintaining a relaxed and open state of mind. They may use their hands, visualizations, or other techniques to tune into the subtle energy fields.

An aura is believed to be a multi-layered energetic field that surrounds a person and reflects his/her thoughts, emotions, and overall energetic state. By perceiving and interpreting the colors, patterns, and intensity of the aura, individuals can gain insights into the person's mental, emotional, and spiritual well-being.

Energy reading and aura perception require practice and the development of sensitivity to energetic frequencies. With time and experience, individuals can refine their abilities to read energy, expanding their understanding of others and deepening their mind reading skills.

Mind reading is a fascinating and multidimensional skill that encompasses various techniques, disciplines, and perspectives. By exploring the power of telepathy, psychic abilities, and beyond, the individuals can embark on a journey of self-discovery, personal growth, and enhanced connection with others.

Understanding the science, mechanics, and psychology behind mind reading, lays the foundation for developing and refining these extraordinary skills. By cultivating mental clarity, emotional intelligence, and effective communication, individuals can unlock the true potential of their mind reading abilities.

Throughout this journey, it is important to approach the mind reading with respect, ethics, and a genuine intention to serve and understand others. Balancing personal boundaries, empathy, and the pursuit of knowledge contributes to responsible and impactful mind reading practices.

As you delve into the realm of mind reading mastery, remember that it is a continuous process of learning, practice, and self-reflection. Embrace the mysteries, explore the techniques, and let your journey into the depths of the human mind and beyond unfold with curiosity, compassion, and an unwavering commitment to growth.

CHAPTER 4

MENTAL CLARITY AND FOCUS FOR MIND READING

4.1 Importance of Mental Clarity in Mind Reading

In the realm of mind reading, mental clarity is an essential element that lays the foundation for accurate and successful thought reading. When your mind is clear, free from distractions and mental noise, you become more receptive to subtle signals and information from others. It allows you to attune your senses and intuition, heightening your ability to pick up on thoughts, emotions, and intentions.

4.1.1 Clearing the Mental Fog for Accurate Mind Reading

Mental fog, characterized by a scattered and cluttered mind, hinders your mind-reading abilities. It creates noise and interference that can distort or block the signals you receive. By cultivating mental clarity, you remove this fog, creating a clear channel for the exchange of thoughts and energies. This clarity enables you to perceive information with greater accuracy and make more informed interpretations.

4.1.2 Benefits of Mental Clarity in Daily Life

The benefits of cultivating mental clarity extend beyond mind reading. When your mind is clear and focused, you experience a myriad of advantages in various aspects of your life.

Following are some of the benefits of mental clarity:

(i) Improved Decision-Making and Problem-Solving Skills

A clear mind allows you to approach decision-making and problem-solving with a heightened sense of clarity and objectivity. By eliminating mental clutter, you can analyze situations more effectively, weigh options with greater discernment, and arrive at well-informed decisions. Mental clarity enhances your ability to identify creative solutions and think outside the box, leading to more innovative problem-solving.

(ii) Enhanced Creativity and Innovation

Mental clarity provides fertile ground for creativity to flourish. When your mind is clear, you can tap into your imaginative faculties, connect seemingly unrelated ideas, and generate novel insights. This clarity of thought fuels innovation and allows you to explore new perspectives and possibilities.

(iii) Reduced Stress and Increased Overall Well-Being

Mental clutter and a lack of clarity often contribute to feelings of overwhelm and stress. By developing mental clarity, you can alleviate the burden of constant mental chatter and find a sense of calm and inner peace. Clearing the mind promotes relaxation and reduces stress levels, contributing to improved overall well-being.

4.2   Techniques for Clearing Mental Clutter

(i) Mindful Meditation

One powerful technique for clearing mental clutter and cultivating mental clarity is the 'mindful meditation'. Mindfulness involves focusing your attention on the present moment, observing your thoughts and emotions without judgment. Through regular meditation practice, you can train your mind to let go of the distractions and you become more present, creating space for mental clarity to arise.

Different meditation techniques cater to various preferences and levels of experience. Mindful breathing meditation or pranayama, for example, involves focusing on the sensation of your breath, gently bringing your attention back whenever it wanders. Body scan meditation involves systematically bringing awareness to different parts of your body, releasing tension and promoting relaxation. Guided visualization meditations use imagery and visualization to cultivate a clear and focused mind.

Incorporating meditation into your daily routine is key to reaping its benefits. Setting aside dedicated time each day, even if it's just a few minutes, helps you establish a consistent practice and gradually build mental clarity.

(ii) Journaling and Self-Reflection

Another effective method for clearing mental clutter is through journaling and self-reflection. Writing allows you to externalize your thoughts and emotions, providing a structured and tangible way to process and release them.

Engage in free-form journaling, where you let your thoughts flow onto the paper without censorship or judgment. This practice helps you gain insights into your mental patterns and allows you to identify recurring thoughts that may contribute to mental clutter. Additionally, you can use prompts or guided journaling exercises that target specific areas of your life or emotions, facilitating deeper self-reflection and clarity.

(iii) Regularly reviewing your Journal

Entries and reflecting on them helps you recognize patterns, gain perspective, and develop a clearer understanding of your thoughts and emotions. It enables you to identify areas where mental clutter arises and explore strategies for addressing them.

(iv) Mind Dumping and Brainstorming

Mind dumping and brainstorming are techniques that help release mental clutter and stimulate creativity. Mind dumping involves taking a blank piece of paper and writing down all the thoughts, worries, and to-dos that occupy your mind. By externalizing these thoughts, you create space in your mind and alleviate the burden of mental clutter.

Brainstorming, on the other hand, is a technique used to generate creative ideas and solutions. Set aside dedicated time for brainstorming sessions where you allow your thoughts to flow freely and encourage unconventional ideas. Write down everything that comes to mind without judgment or evaluation. By doing so, you tap into your subconscious mind and open yourself up to new possibilities.

Both mind dumping and brainstorming techniques offer a cathartic release and clear mental space for fresh insights and perspectives to emerge.

4.3   Strengthening Concentration and Attention

(i) Mindfulness of Breath

Concentration and attention are the vital components of mental clarity. One effective practice for strengthening these qualities is mindfulness of breath meditation. This technique involves focusing your attention on the sensation of your breath, anchoring yourself to the present moment.

Start by finding a comfortable position and directing your attention to your breath. Observe the inhalation and exhalation, noticing the sensations in your body. Whenever your mind wanders, gently bring your attention back to the breath, without judgment or frustration.

Regular practice of mindfulness of breath meditation enhances your ability to sustain focus and concentration. It cultivates a deep sense of presence, preventing distractions from pulling your attention away from the task at hand. As you strengthen your concentration muscles through this practice, you develop the mental clarity required for successful mind reading.

(ii) Visualizations and Imagery

Utilizing visualizations and imagery is another powerful method for improving concentration and focus. Visualization techniques involve creating vivid mental images that help direct and maintain your attention on a specific object or task.

To enhance your concentration, visualize an object or scene in intricate detail. Imagine its colors, textures, and spatial relationships. Engage all your senses to make the visualization as vivid as possible. By consistently practicing this technique, you enhance your ability to visualize and sustain focus for extended periods.

Imagery can also be used to guide your attention to a particular thought or intention. By visualizing an outcome or a desired state of mind, you create a mental anchor that keeps you centered and focused. For example, before engaging in mind reading exercises, you can visualize yourself surrounded by a vibrant aura of clarity, attuning your mind to the receptive and focused states.

(iii) Mind Games and Cognitive Exercises

Engaging in mind games and cognitive exercises is another effective way to sharpen your concentration skills. These exercises challenge your mind, forcing you to sustain focus and engage in mental gymnastics.

Puzzles, such as crosswords, Sudoku, or jigsaw puzzles, require focused attention and problem-solving skills. Set aside dedicated time for these activities, gradually increasing the complexity as your concentration improves.

Memory exercises, such as memorizing lists, playing memory games, or practicing mnemonic techniques (a word, sentence or poem used to help remember a rule, name, etc.), also contribute to enhanced concentration. These exercises train your mind to retain and recall information, sharpening your mental focus and improving your ability to retain details during mind reading.

Regular practice of mind games and cognitive exercises strengthens your concentration muscles, making it easier to maintain focus and mental clarity in various mind reading scenarios.

4.4 Cultivating Mindfulness for Enhanced Mind-Reading Abilities

(i) Foundations of Mindfulness

Mindfulness is a state of non-judgmental awareness that cultivates presence and clarity. It involves paying attention to the present moment, observing your thoughts, emotions, and sensations without attachment or judgment.

To cultivate mindfulness, start by setting aside dedicated time for formal practice. Find a quiet space where you can sit comfortably and bring your attention to the present moment. Begin by focusing on your breath, noticing the sensations of each inhalation and exhalation. As thoughts or distractions arise, gently acknowledge them and bring your attention back to the breath.

Gradually, expand mindfulness into your daily life, bringing the same non-judgmental awareness to everyday activities. Practice mindful eating by savoring each bite of food, paying attention to textures, flavors, and the act of chewing. Engage in mindful walking by being fully present with each step, noticing the sensation of your feet touching the ground.

(ii) Mindful Observation

Mindful observation is a technique that enhances your ability to attune to subtle cues and non-verbal communication, a crucial skill in mind reading. It involves keenly observing people, objects, and environments with present-moment awareness.

To practice mindful observation, choose an object or a person and direct your attention to it fully. Notice the details, colors, shapes, and textures. Observe any movements, changes, or shifts. Engage your senses fully, noticing any sounds, smells, or sensations associated with the object or person.

As you cultivate mindful observation, you become more attuned to the nuances of non-verbal communication, such as body language, micro-expressions, and energetic cues. This heightened awareness strengthens your ability to read others' thoughts and emotions with accuracy and clarity.

(iii) Mindful Empathy

Mindful empathy combines the practices of mindfulness and empathy, allowing you to connect deeply with others' thoughts and emotions. It involves being fully present with someone, holding space for their experiences without judgment, and tuning in to their thoughts and feelings.

To cultivate mindful empathy, engage in active listening when interacting with others. Give them your full attention, maintaining eye contact, and truly listening to their words. Practice non-judgmental presence, suspending your own assumptions and biases, and offering a safe space for open expression.

As you become more adept at mindful empathy, you develop a heightened sensitivity to the subtle energetic and emotional signals that others emit. This attunement enables you to connect with others on a deeper level, facilitating telepathic communication and enhancing your mind reading abilities.

By integrating mindfulness practices into your life, you develop the mental clarity and receptivity necessary for successful mind reading. Cultivating non-judgmental awareness and present-moment focus strengthens your ability to attune to others' thoughts and emotions, opening up new possibilities in the realm of telepathy and psychic abilities.

4.5 Overcoming Mental Barriers and Limiting Beliefs

(i) Identifying and Challenging Limiting Beliefs

Limiting beliefs are deeply ingrained thoughts or assumptions that hold you back from reaching your full mind reading potential. These beliefs may include notions such as "mind reading is impossible" or "I'm not intuitive enough." Identifying these beliefs is the first step toward overcoming them.

Reflect on your beliefs about mind reading and pay attention to any negative or self-limiting thoughts that arise. Write them down and question their validity. Ask yourself if there is evidence to support or contradict these beliefs. Challenge them by seeking alternative perspectives or engaging in practices that demonstrate the potential for mind reading.

Techniques for reframing and transforming limiting beliefs include positive affirmations, visualizations of success, and seeking out inspirational stories and testimonies from individuals who have achieved remarkable mind reading abilities. By consciously choosing empowering beliefs, you can reprogram your mind and overcome the mental barriers that hinder your progress.

(ii) Overcoming Self-Doubt and Building Confidence

Self-doubt can undermine your mind reading abilities, as it erodes your confidence and prevents you from fully embracing and trusting your intuitive insights. Building confidence is crucial for unlocking your mind reading potential.

To overcome self-doubt, practice self-compassion and self-acceptance. Be kind to yourself and acknowledge that developing mind reading skills takes time and effort. Celebrate small successes along the way and remind yourself of your progress.

Engage in regular practice to build competence and validate your abilities. Start with simple mind reading exercises and gradually increase the complexity as you gain confidence. Surround yourself with a supportive community or mentor who can offer encouragement and guidance.

Embrace a positive mindset and affirmations that reinforce your belief in your mind reading abilities. Replace self- defeating thoughts with empowering statements such as "I am intuitive and capable of mind reading" or "I trust my intuitive insights."

With consistent practice and a mindset focused on growth and self-belief, you can overcome self-doubt and build the confidence necessary to unlock your mind reading mastery.

(iii) Power of Persistence and Patience

Mastering mind reading requires patience and persistence. It is essential to embrace the journey and understand that progress may not always be linear. Set realistic expectations and be willing to invest the time and effort needed to develop your skills.

Acknowledge that setbacks and challenges are part of the learning process. Rather than becoming discouraged, view them as opportunities for growth and learning. Cultivate resilience by maintaining a positive attitude and persevering through difficulties.

Celebrate even the smallest achievements and milestones along the way. Each step forward is a testament to your dedication and progress. Trust that with continued practice and perseverance, you will unlock the most successful techniques of thought reading and achieve mastery in mind reading.

4.6   Integrating Mental Activity and Focus in Daily Life

(i) Creating a Mindful Environment

Your physical environment plays a significant role in cultivating mental clarity and focus. Creating a mindful environment sets the stage for successful mind reading practices.

Organize your physical space in a way that promotes mental clarity. Declutter your surroundings, removing any unnecessary items or distractions. Create designated spaces for your mind reading practice, ensuring they are clean, organized, and free from external disturbances.

Consider incorporating elements that engage your senses and promote a sense of calm. Use essential oils, candles, or incense to create a soothing aroma. Play soft, ambient music or nature sounds to create a peaceful atmosphere.

Eliminate digital distractions by designating specific times for technology use and practicing digital detoxes when engaging in mind reading exercises. Set boundaries with your electronic devices to create a focused and present- moment environment.

(ii) Mindful Time Management

Effective time management is crucial for maintaining mental clarity and focus. By prioritizing tasks and allocating dedicated time for mind-reading practice, you ensure that you have focused, uninterrupted periods to develop your skills.

Create a schedule or to-do list that includes specific time blocks for mind-reading practice. Treat these time blocks as non-negotiable appointments with yourself, prioritizing them as you would any other important commitment.

Practice time blocking, which involves dedicating specific time periods for specific tasks or activities. This technique helps minimize multitasking and allows you to fully engage in each task without distractions.

Set realistic goals for your mind-reading practice and break them down into smaller, manageable steps. Celebrate each milestone and adjust your schedule as needed to ensure consistent progress.

Integrating mindfulness into your daily activities, such as mindful eating or mindful walking, can help cultivate a sense of presence and focus throughout the day. By managing your time mindfully, you create space for developing your mind reading abilities and optimizing your mental clarity.

4.7 Maintaining and Sustaining Mental Clarity and Focus

(i) In addition to specific techniques and exercises, certain lifestyle practices contribute to maintaining optimal mental clarity and focus.

(ii) Prioritize quality sleep to ensure your mind is well-rested and rejuvenated. Create a bedtime routine that promotes relaxation and deep sleep, such as avoiding screens before bed, practicing relaxation techniques, and keeping a consistent sleep schedule.

(iii) Engage in regular physical exercise to boost blood flow to the brain and enhance cognitive function. Activities such as yoga, walking, or aerobic exercises promote mental clarity and reduce stress.

(iv) Maintain a healthy diet that nourishes your brain and supports cognitive function. Include foods rich in antioxidants, omega-3 fatty acids, and vitamins and minerals. Stay hydrated by drinking plenty of water throughout the day.

(v) Practice stress management techniques, such as deep breathing exercises, mindfulness meditation, or engaging in hobbies that promote relaxation. Chronic stress can impede mental clarity, so it is essential to develop strategies to manage stress effectively.

(vi) Regularly take breaks and engage in activities that recharge your mind and prevent mental fatigue. This may include taking short walks in nature, practicing mindfulness, or engaging in creative pursuits.

By adopting these lifestyle practices, you create a solid foundation for maintaining mental clarity and focus, enabling you to explore the depths of mind reading with greater ease and effectiveness.

Developing mental clarity and focus is a crucial step on the path to unlocking your mind reading mastery. By understanding the power of mental clarity, employing techniques for clearing mental clutter, strengthening concentration and attention, cultivating mindfulness, overcoming mental barriers and limiting beliefs, and integrating these practices into your daily life, you lay the groundwork for successful mind reading experiences.

Remember that developing mind-reading abilities is a journey that requires patience, persistence, and self-belief. With dedication and consistent practice, you can harness the power of telepathy and psychic abilities, expanding your understanding of the human mind and unlocking the mysteries of thought reading. Embrace the power of your mind and embark on this transformative journey of mind reading mastery.

CHAPTER 5

HARNESSING EMOTIONAL INTELLIGENCE FOR MIND READING

5.1 Understanding the Role of Emotional Intelligence

5.1.1 Importance of Emotional Intelligence in Mind Reading

Emotional intelligence plays a pivotal role in unlocking the true potential of mind reading. It is the ability to recognize, understand, and manage emotions in oneself and others. When it comes to mind reading, emotions serve as vital signals and cues that provide valuable insights into people's thoughts, intentions, and desires. By developing emotional intelligence, you can enhance your capacity to accurately interpret and respond to these emotional signals, thereby sharpening your mind reading abilities.

5.1.2 How emotions impact thoughts and perceptions?

Emotions have a profound impact on our thoughts and perceptions. They color our experiences and influence the way we interpret information. When engaging in mind reading, being able to decipher the emotions underlying a person's thoughts can offer crucial context and understanding. For instance, recognizing fear or anxiety in someone's emotional state may indicate hidden doubts or concerns, shedding light on their true intentions.

5.1.3 Connection between emotional intelligence and empathic abilities

Empathy, a core component of emotional intelligence, is closely linked to mind reading. Empathy allows us to step into someone else's shoes, sharing their emotional experiences and gaining insight into their thoughts and perspectives. By developing empathy, you can establish a deeper connection with others, fostering a greater understanding of their inner world. This heightened sensitivity to emotions enhances your mind reading skills by enabling you to perceive subtle emotional nuances and grasp the underlying motivations behind a person's thoughts.

5.1.4 Developing emotional awareness for effective mind reading

Emotional awareness is the foundation of emotional intelligence. It involves recognizing and understanding one's own emotions, as well as the emotions of others. By cultivating emotional awareness, you become attuned to the subtle shifts in emotions, both within yourself and in those around you. This heightened sensitivity enables you to pick up on emotional cues that are instrumental in mind reading. Through practices such as mindfulness and self-reflection, you can develop a keen sense of emotional awareness, empowering you to read minds with greater accuracy and depth.

5.2 Recognizing and Managing your Emotions

5.2.1 Foundations of Emotional Self-Awareness

Emotional self-awareness is the ability to recognize and understand your own emotions, as well as the factors that trigger them. It involves developing a deep understanding of your emotional patterns, tendencies, and reactions. By honing this skill, you become more adept at identifying and labeling your emotions accurately, laying the groundwork for effective emotion management and mind reading.

5.2.2   Identifying and labeling emotions accurately

To cultivate emotional self-awareness, it is crucial to accurately identify and label your emotions. This involves going beyond basic emotions like happiness or sadness and delving into the nuances of your emotional landscape. By expanding your emotional vocabulary and being specific in your emotional descriptions, you can gain a more profound understanding of your own emotional experiences. This heightened awareness translates into improved mind reading abilities, as you can draw upon your own emotional journey to empathize with others.

5.2.3   Understanding the physiological and psychological aspects of emotions

Emotions are not solely psychological experiences; they also have physiological manifestations. Understanding the connection between the mind and body is key to emotional self-awareness. By paying attention to physical sensations associated with emotions, such as changes in heartbeat or muscle tension, you can gain valuable insights into your emotional states. This holistic awareness empowers you to recognize similar physiological cues in others, helping you read their emotions and thoughts more accurately.

5.2.4   Link between self-awareness and mind reading accuracy

Self-awareness is a cornerstone of effective mind reading. By developing a deep understanding of your own emotions, you cultivate a heightened sensitivity to emotional signals emitted by others. This self-awareness allows you to differentiate between your own emotions and those you pick up from others, minimizing the risk of projection or misinterpretation.

When you are attuned to your own emotional landscape, you can navigate the intricacies of mind reading with greater precision, avoiding biases and enhancing your overall accuracy.

5.2.5   Techniques for Emotion Regulation

Emotion regulation is the ability to manage and control your emotions in a healthy and constructive manner. By mastering this skill, you can prevent emotions from clouding your mind reading abilities and respond to emotional stimuli with clarity and focus.

(i)   Identifying triggers and managing emotional reactions

To effectively regulate your emotions, it is essential to identify the triggers that lead to emotional responses. Reflecting on past experiences and patterns can help you pinpoint the specific situations, events, or thoughts that tend to elicit emotional reactions. Once identified, you can develop strategies to manage these triggers, such as reframing negative thoughts or practicing self-soothing techniques. By learning to regulate your own emotions, you become better equipped to navigate the emotional landscapes of others, enhancing your mind reading prowess.

(ii) Cognitive reappraisal and reframing techniques

Cognitive reappraisal involves consciously reevaluating the meaning and significance of a situation, altering your interpretation to create a more positive or balanced perspective. By reframing the way you perceive events or interactions, you can change your emotional response. This technique is invaluable for mind reading, as it allows you to approach challenging or ambiguous situations with a more open and receptive mindset, enabling a deeper understanding of others' thoughts and emotions.

(iii) Practicing mindfulness for emotional balance

Mindfulness is a powerful tool for emotion regulation and enhancing mind reading abilities. By cultivating present-moment awareness without judgment, you develop the capacity to observe and accept your emotions without being overwhelmed by them. Mindfulness meditation practices help strengthen your focus and concentration, allowing you to stay attuned to the emotions of others without getting entangled in your own. This state of emotional balance creates a conducive environment for accurate and empathic mind reading.

5.3 Empathy: The Key to Connecting with Others' Minds

5.3.1 Understanding Empathy and Its Importance

Empathy is the ability to understand and share the feelings and perspectives of others. It forms the foundation for deep and meaningful connections with others, enabling you to establish rapport and gain insight into their minds. In the realm of mind reading, empathy is an indispensable skill that allows you to bridge the gap between your own experiences and those of the person you are engaging with.

5.3.2 Empathy as a foundational skill for mind reading

Empathy serves as a crucial skill for mind reading, as it enables you to step into the shoes of another person, experiencing their emotions and thoughts. When you genuinely empathize with someone, you create a safe and trusting space that encourages open communication. This emotional connection allows for a deeper understanding of the person's inner world, facilitating more accurate and meaningful mind reading interactions.

5.3.3 Differentiating between cognitive and affective empathy

Empathy can be categorized into cognitive and affective empathy. Cognitive empathy involves understanding and intellectualizing the emotions and thoughts of others. It allows you to see the world from their perspective, even if you do not personally share their emotional experience. Affective empathy, on the other hand, involves emotionally resonating with others, feeling their emotions as if they were your own. Both forms of empathy are valuable in mind reading, as they provide different dimensions of understanding and insight.

5.3.4 Role of mirror neurons in empathic understanding

Mirror neurons are specialized cells in the brain that fire both when we perform an action and when we observe someone else performing the same action. They play a fundamental role in empathy, as they enable us to vicariously experience the emotions and actions of others. Mirror neurons create an automatic and unconscious resonance with the emotions and intentions of those around us, facilitating a deep sense of connection and empathy. By understanding the role of mirror neurons, you can tap into this innate capacity for empathic understanding, enhancing your mind reading abilities.

5.3.5 Enhancing Empathic Abilities

Empathy is a skill that can be cultivated and strengthened over time. By actively working on enhancing your empathic abilities, you can deepen your understanding of others' minds and emotions, enriching your mind reading repertoire.

5.3.6 Developing active listening skills

Active listening is an essential component of empathy. It involves fully focusing on the speaker, giving them your undivided attention, and genuinely seeking to understand their perspective. By actively listening to others, you can pick up on subtle verbal and non-verbal cues that provide insights into their thoughts and emotions. Developing active listening skills allows you to create a supportive environment for mind reading, where individuals feel heard, valued, and understood.

5.3.7 Perspective-taking and putting yourself in others' shoes

Perspective-taking is the ability to imagine oneself in someone else's situation and understand their thoughts, feelings, and motivations. By consciously practicing perspective-taking, you expand your empathic capacity and enhance your mind reading abilities. Putting yourself in others' shoes allows you to anticipate their needs, interpret their non-verbal cues more accurately, and gain a deeper understanding of their underlying thoughts and emotions.

5.3.8 Cultivating compassion and empathy through self-care practices

Self-care plays a vital role in cultivating empathy and compassion. It involves taking care of your own emotional well-being, ensuring that you have the capacity to extend empathy to others. Engaging in self-care practices such as meditation, journaling, or engaging in hobbies that bring you joy replenishes your emotional reserves, enabling you to be fully present and empathic in mind reading interactions. When you approach mind reading from a place of compassion and self-nurturance, you create a positive and supportive space for connecting with others' minds.

5.4 Emotional Resonance and Mind Reading

5.4.1 Concept of Emotional Resonance

Emotional resonance refers to the phenomenon of emotions being transferred and sensed by others. It is the ability to pick up on and connect with the emotional energy emitted by individuals around you. Emotional resonance plays a significant role in mind reading, as it allows you to perceive and understand the emotional states of others without explicit communication.

5.4.2 How emotions can be transferred and sensed by others?

Emotions possess an energetic quality that can be transmitted and sensed by those in proximity. This transmission occurs through various channels, including body language, facial expressions, tone of voice, and even subtle energetic signals. As a skilled mind reader, you develop the capacity to detect and interpret these emotional signals, enabling you to grasp the underlying thoughts and intentions of others.

5.4.3   Influence of emotional energy on mind reading accuracy

Emotional energy has a direct impact on the accuracy of mind reading. When individuals are emotionally charged, their thoughts and intentions become more pronounced, making them easier to perceive and understand. By attuning yourself to the emotional energy of those around you, you gain valuable information that enhances the precision and depth of your mind reading abilities. This heightened sensitivity to emotional energy allows you to discern subtle shifts and fluctuations in others' emotional states, providing valuable insights into their thoughts and intentions.

5.4.4   Emotional contagion and its effects on interpersonal connections

Emotional contagion is the phenomenon of emotions being transferred from one person to another, often without conscious awareness. When individuals experience strong emotions, such as joy, sadness, or anxiety, these emotions can spread to those around them. Emotional contagion impacts interpersonal connections, as it creates a shared emotional experience and fosters a sense of resonance. As a mind reader, being aware of emotional contagion enables you to recognize and differentiate between your own emotions and those you have picked up from others, ensuring accuracy in your mind reading interpretations.

5.4.5   Techniques for Enhancing Emotional Resonance Building rapport and trust with others

Building rapport and trust is crucial for establishing emotional resonance and deepening your mind reading abilities. Rapport is the sense of connection and harmony that arises when individuals feel understood and valued. By actively engaging in effective communication, practicing active listening, and demonstrating genuine interest in others, you create an environment of trust and openness. This trust forms the foundation for emotional resonance, as individuals are more likely to express their true emotions and thoughts in a safe and supportive space.

5.4.6 Developing intuition and instinctual awareness

Intuition and instinctual awareness are powerful tools for enhancing emotional resonance. Intuition is the unconscious knowing that arises from deep within, guiding us to make accurate assessments and interpretations. By honing your intuition, you can tap into the subtle emotional signals emitted by others, allowing for a more profound understanding of their thoughts and intentions. Trusting your instincts and embracing your intuitive abilities enhances your overall mind reading mastery.

5.4.7 Practicing empathy-building exercises

Empathy-building exercises can significantly enhance your emotional resonance skills. These exercises involve deliberately putting yourself in challenging emotional situations, where you can practice tuning into the emotions of others. For example, you can engage in role-playing exercises or participate in group discussions focused on sharing emotions and experiences. By actively engaging in empathy-building exercises, you expand your emotional range and strengthen your ability to resonate with the emotions of others, deepening your mind reading capabilities.

CHAPTER 6

ARTIFICIAL INTELLIGENCE: AN INTRODUCTION

6.1   What is Artificial Intelligence?

Given below are some of the definitions of Artificial Intelligence:

Artificial Intelligence (AI) refers to programming computers to do tasks that normally require human intelligence, like learning, problem-solving, and understanding language. It is like giving computers the ability to think and make decisions on their own, similar to how humans do. AI helps machines learn from data, adapt to new situations, and perform tasks without being explicitly programmed for each step.

Artificial intelligence (AI), in its broadest sense, is the intelligence exhibited by machines, particularly computer systems. It is a field in computer science that develops and studies methods and software that enable machines to perceive their environment and use learning and intelligence to take actions that maximize their chances of achieving defined goals.

Artificial intelligence is a specialty within computer science that is concerned with creating systems that can replicate human intelligence and problem-solving abilities. They do this by taking in a myriad of data, processing it, and learning from their past in order to streamline and improve in the future.

Artificial intelligence was founded as an academic discipline in 1956, by those now considered the founding fathers of AI: John McCarthy, Marvin Minksy, Nathaniel Rochester, and Claude Shannon.

According to **John McCarthy**, "AI is the science and engineering of making intelligent machines, especially intelligent computer programs". Artificial Intelligence is a way of making a computer, a computer-controlled robot, or a software think intelligently, in the similar manner the intelligent humans think. AI is accomplished by studying how human brain thinks, and how humans learn, decide, and work while trying to solve a problem, and then using the outcomes of this study as a basis of developing intelligent software and systems.

Artificial intelligence is the ability of a digital computer or computer-controlled robot to perform tasks commonly associated with intelligent beings. The term is frequently applied to the project of developing systems endowed with the intellectual processes characteristic of humans, such as the ability to reason, discover meaning, generalize, or learn from past experience. Since their development in the 1940s, digital computers have been programmed to carry out very complex tasks—such as discovering proofs for mathematical theorems or playing chess—with great proficiency. Despite continuing advances in computer processing speed and memory capacity, there are as yet no programs that can match full human flexibility over wider domains or in tasks requiring much everyday knowledge. On the other hand, some programs have attained the performance levels of human experts and professionals in executing certain specific tasks, so that artificial intelligence in this limited sense is found in applications as diverse as medical diagnosis, computer search engines, voice or handwriting recognition, and chatbots.

Artificial intelligence can take many forms. As such, there is no agreed single definition of what it encompasses. In broad terms, it can be regarded as the theory and development of computer systems able to perform tasks normally requiring human intelligence, such as visual perception, speech recognition, decision-making, and translation between languages. According to IBM, the current real-world applications of AI include:

- extracting information from pictures (computer vision);

- transcribing or understanding spoken words (speech to text and natural language processing);

- speaking what has been written (text to speech, natural language processing);

- pulling insights and patterns out of written text (natural language understanding);

- autonomously moving through spaces based on its senses (robotics); and

- generally looking for patterns in large amounts of data (machine learning).

In banking, for example, AI is currently used to detect and flag suspicious activity to a bank's fraud department, such as unusual debit card usage and large account deposits. The National Health Service (NHS) also reports that AI is being used to benefit people in health and care by analyzing X-ray images to support radiologists in making assessments and helping clinicians read brain scans more quickly, by supporting people in 'virtual wards', who would otherwise be in hospital to receive the care and treatment they need, and through remote monitoring technology such as apps and medical devices which can assess patients' health and care while they are being cared for at home.

To achieve this, AI systems rely upon large datasets from which they can decipher patterns and correlations, thereby enabling the system to 'learn' how to anticipate future events. It does this by relying upon and/or creating algorithms based on the dataset which it can use to interpret new data. This data can be structured, such as bank transactions, or unstructured, such as enabling a driverless car to respond to the environment around it.

Artificial Intelligence (AI) refers to the development of computer systems of performing tasks that require human intelligence. AI aids, in processing amounts of data identifying patterns and making decisions based on the collected information. This can be achieved through techniques like Machine Learning (ML), Deep Learning (DL), Natural Language Processing (NLP), Computer Vision and Robotics. AI encompasses a range of abilities including learning, reasoning, perception, problem solving, data analysis and language comprehension. The ultimate goal of AI is to create machines that can emulate capabilities and carry out diverse tasks, with enhanced efficiency and precision. The field of AI holds potential to revolutionize aspects of our daily lives.

AI technology is widely used throughout industry, government, and science. Some high-profile applications include advanced web search engines (e.g., Google Search); recommendation systems (used by YouTube, Amazon, and Netflix); interacting via human speech (e.g., Google Assistant, Siri, and Alexa); autonomous vehicles (e.g., Waymo); generative and creative tools (e.g., ChatGPT and AI art); and superhuman play and analysis in strategy games (e.g., chess and Go). However, many AI applications are not perceived as AI: A lot of cutting-edge AI has filtered into general applications, often without being called AI because once something becomes useful enough and common enough it's not labeled AI anymore.

Alan Turing was the first person to conduct substantial research in the field that he called machine intelligence. The field went through multiple cycles of optimism, followed by periods of disappointment and loss of funding, known as AI winter. Funding and interest vastly increased after 2012 when deep learning surpassed all previous AI techniques, and after 2017 with the transformer architecture. This led to the AI boom of the early 2020s, with companies, universities, and laboratories overwhelmingly based in the United States and other countries pioneering significant advances in artificial intelligence.

The growing use of artificial intelligence in the 21st century is influencing a societal and economic shift towards increased automation, data-driven decision-making, and the integration of AI systems into various economic sectors and areas of life, impacting job markets, healthcare, government, industry, and education. This raises questions about the long-term effects, ethical implications, and risks of AI, prompting discussions about regulatory policies to ensure the safety and benefits of the technology.

The various sub-fields of AI research are centred around particular goals and the use of particular tools. The traditional goals of AI research include reasoning, knowledge representation, planning, learning, natural language processing, perception, and support for robotics, with the ability to complete any task performable by a human on an at least equal level.

To reach these goals, AI researchers have adapted and integrated a wide range of techniques, including search and mathematical optimization, formal logic, artificial neural networks, and methods based on statistics, operations research, and economics. AI also draws upon psychology, linguistics, philosophy, neuroscience, and other fields.

6.2   Goals of Artificial Intelligence

The general problem of simulating (or creating) intelligence has been broken into sub-problems. These consist of particular traits or capabilities that researchers expect an intelligent system to display. The traits described below have received the most attention and cover the scope of AI research.

(i)   Reasoning and Problem Solving

Early researchers developed algorithms that imitated step-by-step reasoning that humans use when they solve puzzles or make logical deductions. By the late 1980s and 1990s, methods were developed for dealing with uncertain or incomplete information, employing concepts from probability and economics.

Many of these algorithms are insufficient for solving large reasoning problems because they experience a "combinatorial explosion": they became exponentially slower as the problems grew larger. Even humans rarely use the step-by-step deduction that early AI research could model. They solve most of their problems using fast, intuitive judgments. Accurate and efficient reasoning is an unsolved problem.

(ii) Knowledge Representation

Knowledge representation and knowledge engineering allow AI programs to answer questions intelligently and make deductions about real-world facts. Formal knowledge representations are used in content-based indexing and retrieval, scene interpretation, clinical decision support, knowledge discovery (mining "interesting" and actionable inferences from large databases), and other areas.

A knowledge base is a body of knowledge represented in a form that can be used by a program. An ontology is the set of objects, relations, concepts, and properties used by a particular domain of knowledge. Knowledge bases need to represent things such as: objects, properties, categories and relations between objects; situations, events, states and time; causes and effects; knowledge about knowledge (what we know about what other people know); default reasoning (things that humans assume are true until they are told differently and will remain true even when other facts are changing); and many other aspects and domains of knowledge.

Among the most difficult problems in knowledge representation are: the breadth of commonsense knowledge (the set of atomic facts that the average person knows is enormous); and the sub-symbolic form of most commonsense knowledge (much of what people know is not represented as "facts" or "statements" that they could express verbally). There is also the difficulty of knowledge acquisition, the problem of obtaining knowledge for AI applications.

(iii) Planning and Decision Making

An "agent" is anything that perceives and takes actions in the world. A rational agent has goals or preferences and takes actions to make them happen. In automated planning, the agent has a specific goal. In automated decision making, the agent has preferences—there are some situations it would prefer to be in, and some situations it is trying to avoid. The decision-making agent assigns a number to each situation (called the "utility") that measures how much the agent prefers it. For each possible action, it can calculate the "expected utility": the utility of all possible outcomes of the action, weighted by the probability that the outcome will occur. It can then choose the action with the maximum expected utility.

In classical planning, the agent knows exactly what the effect of any action will be. In most real-world problems, however, the agent may not be certain about the situation they are in (it is "unknown" or "unobservable") and it may not know for certain what will happen after each possible action (it is not "deterministic"). It must choose an action by making a probabilistic guess and then reassess the situation to see if the action worked.

In some problems, the agent's preferences may be uncertain, especially if there are other agents or humans involved. These can be learned (e.g., with inverse reinforcement learning) or the agent can seek information to improve its preferences. Information value theory can be used to weigh the value of exploratory or experimental actions. The space of possible future actions and situations is typically intractably large, so the agents must take actions and evaluate situations while being uncertain what the outcome will be.

A Markov decision process has a transition model that describes the probability that a particular action will change the state in a particular way, and a reward function that supplies the utility of each state and the cost of each action. A policy associates a decision with each possible state. The policy could be calculated (e.g., by iteration), be heuristic, or it can be learned.

Game theory describes rational behavior of multiple interacting agents, and is used in AI programs that make decisions that involve other agents.

(iv) Learning

Machine learning is the study of programs that can improve their performance on a given task automatically. It has been a part of AI from the beginning.

There are several kinds of machine learning. Unsupervised learning analyzes a stream of data and finds patterns and makes predictions without any other guidance. Supervised learning requires a human to label the input data first, and comes in two main varieties: classification (where the program must learn to predict what category the input belongs in) and regression (where the program must deduce a numeric function based on numeric input).

In reinforcement learning the agent is rewarded for good responses and punished for bad ones. The agent learns to choose responses that are classified as "good". Transfer learning is when the knowledge gained from one problem is applied to a new problem. Deep learning is a type of machine learning that runs inputs through biologically inspired artificial neural networks for all of these types of learning.

Computational learning theory can assess learners by computational complexity, by sample complexity (how much data is required), or by other notions of optimization.

(v) Natural Language Processing

Natural language processing (NLP) allows programs to read, write and communicate in human languages such as English. Specific problems include speech recognition, speech synthesis, machine translation, information extraction, information retrieval and question answering.

Early work, based on Noam Chomsky's generative grammar and semantic networks, had difficulty with word-sense disambiguation unless restricted to small domains called "micro-worlds" (due to the common-sense knowledge problem). Margaret Masterman believed that it was meaning, and not grammar that was the key to understanding languages, and that thesauri and not dictionaries should be the basis of computational language structure.

Modern deep learning techniques for NLP include word embedding (representing words, typically as vectors encoding their meaning), transformers (a deep learning architecture using an attention mechanism), and others. In 2019, **generative pre-trained transformer (or "GPT")** language models began to generate coherent text, and by 2023 these models were able to get human-level scores on the bar exam, SAT test, GRE test, and many other real-world applications.

(vi) Perception

Machine perception is the ability to use input from sensors (such as cameras, microphones, wireless signals, active lidar, sonar, radar, and tactile sensors) to deduce aspects of the world. Computer vision is the ability to analyze visual input.

The field includes speech recognition, image classification, facial recognition, object recognition, and robotic perception.

(vii) Social Intelligence

Affective computing is an interdisciplinary umbrella that comprises systems that recognize, interpret, process or simulate human feeling, emotion and mood. For example, some virtual assistants are programmed to speak conversationally or even to banter humorously; it makes them appear more sensitive to the emotional dynamics of human interaction, or to otherwise facilitate human–computer interaction.

However, this tends to give naïve users an unrealistic conception of the intelligence of existing computer agents. Moderate successes related to affective computing include textual sentiment analysis and, more recently, multimodal sentiment analysis, wherein AI classifies the affects displayed by a videotaped subject.

(viii) General Intelligence

A machine with artificial general intelligence should be able to solve a wide variety of problems with breadth and versatility similar to human intelligence.

6.3   Approaches of AI

There are a total of four approaches of AI and that are as follows:

(i) **Acting humanly** (The **Turing Test** approach): This approach was designed by Alan Turing. The idea behind this approach is that a computer passes the test if a human interrogator, after asking some written questions, cannot identify whether the written responses come from a human or from a computer.

(ii) **Thinking humanly** (The cognitive modeling approach): The idea behind this approach is to determine whether the computer thinks like a human.

(iii) **Thinking rationally** (The "laws of thought" approach): The idea behind this approach is to determine whether the computer thinks rationally i.e. with logical reasoning.

(iv) **Acting rationally** (The rational agent approach): The idea behind this approach is to determine whether the computer acts rationally i.e. with logical reasoning.

6.3.1   Machine Learning approach:

This approach involves training machines to learn from data and improve performance on specific tasks over time. It is widely used in areas such as image and speech recognition, natural language processing, and recommender systems.

6.3.2   Evolutionary approach:

This approach is inspired by the process of natural selection in biology. It involves generating and testing a large number of variations of a solution to a problem, and then selecting and combining the most successful variations to create a new generation of solutions.

6.3.3 Neural Networks approach:

This approach involves building artificial neural networks that are modeled after the structure and function of the human brain. Neural networks can be used for tasks such as pattern recognition, prediction, and decision-making.

6.3.4 Fuzzy logic approach:

This approach involves reasoning with uncertain and imprecise information, which is common in real-world situations. Fuzzy logic can be used to model and control complex systems in areas such as robotics, automotive control, and industrial automation.

6.3.5 Hybrid approach:

This approach combines multiple AI techniques to solve complex problems. For example, a hybrid approach might use machine learning to analyze data and identify patterns, and then use logical reasoning to make decisions based on those patterns.

6.4 Types of Artificial Intelligence

(i) Weak AI: Artificial Narrow Intelligence (ANI),

Artificial Narrow Intelligence (**ANI**), often referred to as "Weak" AI is the type of AI that mostly exists today. ANI systems can perform one or a few specific tasks and operate within a pre-defined environment, e.g., those exploited by personal assistants Siri, **Alexa**, language translations, recommendation systems, image recognition systems, face identification, etc.

ANI can process data at lightning speed and boost the overall productivity and efficiency in many practical applications, e.g., translate between 100+ languages simultaneously, identify faces and objects in billions of images with high accuracy, assist users in many data-driven decisions in a quicker way. ANI can perform routine, repetitive, and mundane tasks that humans would prefer to avoid.

While ANI is superior in specialized domains, it is incapable of generalization, i.e. to re-use learned knowledge across domains, e.g., the ANI capable of image recognition cannot transfer its knowledge in the domain of speech recognition. The generalization problem is still an open question.

(ii) Strong AI: Artificial General Intelligence (AGI)

Artificial General Intelligence (AGI) or "Strong" AI refers to machines that exhibit **human intelligence.** In other words, AGI aims to perform any intellectual task that a human being can. AGI is often illustrated in science fiction movies with situations where humans interact with machines that are conscious, sentient, and driven by emotion and self-awareness. **At this moment, there is nothing like an AGI.**

(iii) Artificial Superintelligence (ASI)

Artificial Superintelligence (ASI) is defined as "any intellect that greatly exceeds the cognitive performance of humans in virtually all domains of interest". ASI is supposed to surpass human intelligence in all aspects — such as creativity, general wisdom, and problem-solving. ASI is supposed to be capable of exhibiting intelligence that we have not seen in the brightest thinkers amongst us. Many thinkers are worried about ASI. At this moment, ASI belongs to science fiction.

If we ever succeed in creating an AI that is capable of generalizing, understanding causality, making a model of the world, it is highly likely that it will be closer to ASI than AGI. AI excels in numerical calculations, and there is no logical explanation as to why AI would downgrade its abilities to simulate humans. AI's quest ultimately leads to ASI.

(iv) Machine Learning (ML): Machine learning is a subset of AI that focuses on enabling machines to learn from data and improve their performance without being explicitly programmed. It includes techniques like supervised learning, unsupervised learning, and reinforcement learning. It identifies patterns and makes predictions based on historical data. ML is the foundation for most AI systems today.

Example: Predicting stock market trends based on past market data.

(v) Deep Learning (DL)

Deep Learning, a subset of ML, employs neural networks with three or more layers to analyze various factors of data. These neural networks are capable of analyzing complex data to identify patterns and features.

Example: Voice recognition systems like Apple's **Siri** or Amazon's **Alexa.**

(vi) Neural Networks (NN)

Neural Networks are computing systems inspired by the human brain's interconnected neuron structure. They are fundamental to deep learning, helping computers to process data in a more human-like way.

Example: Image recognition in social media platforms to tag individuals.

(vii)Natural Language Processing (NLP): NLP enables machines to understand, interpret, and generate human language. Applications range from chatbots and translation services to sentiment analysis and text summarization.

(viii) Computer Vision: Computer vision enables machines to interpret and understand visual information from the world.

It is used in image and video recognition, object detection, autonomous vehicles, and medical image analysis.

(ix) Robotics: Robotics combines AI with mechanical engineering to create machines (robots) that can perform physical tasks autonomously or semi-autonomously. Applications include industrial automation, healthcare assistance, and exploration in hazardous environments.

(x) Expert Systems: Expert systems are AI systems designed to emulate the decision-making ability of a human expert in a specific domain. They use knowledge bases and inference engines to provide advice or solve problems within their area of expertise.

CHAPTER 7

HISTORY OF ARTIFICIAL INTELLIGENCE

It may sometimes feel like that AI is a recent development in technology. After all, it's only become mainstream to use in the last several years, right? In reality, the groundwork for AI began in the early 1900s. And although the biggest strides weren't made until the 1950s, it wouldn't have been possible without the work of early experts in many different fields.

Knowing the history of AI is important in understanding where AI is now and where it may go in the future.

7.1 History of Artificial Intelligence

The idea of "artificial intelligence" goes back thousands of years, to ancient philosophers considering questions of life and death. In ancient times, inventors made things called "automatons" which were mechanical and moved independently of human intervention. The word "automaton" comes from ancient Greek, and means "acting of one's own will." One of the earliest records of an automaton comes from 400 BCE and refers to a mechanical pigeon created by a friend of the philosopher Plato. Many years later, one of the most famous automatons was created by Leonardo da Vinci around the year 1495.

So, while the idea of a machine being able to function on its own is ancient, for the purposes of this article, we're going to focus on the 20th century, when engineers and scientists began to make strides toward our modern-day AI.

7.2   Groundwork for AI

1900-1950:

In the early 1900s, there was a lot of media created that centered around the idea of artificial humans. So much so that scientists of all sorts started asking the question: is it possible to create an artificial brain? Some creators even made some versions of what we now call "robots" (and the word was coined in a Czech play in 1921) though most of them were relatively simple. These were steam-powered for the most part, and some could make facial expressions and even walk.

7.2.1   Dates to note:

1921: Czech playwright Karel Čapek released a science fiction play "Rossum's Universal Robots" which introduced the idea of "artificial people" which he named robots. This was the first known use of the word.

1929: Japanese professor Makoto Nishimura built the first Japanese robot, named Gakutensoku.

1949: Computer scientist Edmund Callis Berkley published the book "Giant Brains, or Machines that Think" which compared the newer models of computers to human brains.

7.3   Birth of AI: 1950-1956

This range of time was when the interest in AI really came to a head. **Alan Turing** published his work "Computer Machinery and Intelligence" which eventually became The **Turing Test**, which experts used to measure computer intelligence. The term "artificial intelligence" was coined and came into popular use.

7.3.1 Dates of note:

1950: Alan Turing published "Computer Machinery and Intelligence" which proposed a test of machine intelligence called 'The Imitation Game'.

1952: A computer scientist named Arthur Samuel developed a program to play checkers, which is the first to ever learn the game independently.

1955: John McCarthy held a workshop at Dartmouth on "artificial intelligence" which is the first use of the word, and how it came into popular usage.

7.4 AI maturation: 1957-1979

The time between when the phrase "artificial intelligence" was created, and the 1980s was a period of both rapid growth and struggle for AI research. The late 1950s through the 1960s was a time of creation. From programming languages that are still in use to this day to books and films that explored the idea of robots, AI became a mainstream idea quickly.

The 1970s showed similar improvements, such as the first anthropomorphic robot being built in Japan, to the first example of an autonomous vehicle being built by an engineering grad student. However, it was also a time of struggle for AI research, as the U.S. government showed little interest in continuing to fund AI research.

7.4.1 Notable dates include:

1958: John McCarthy created LISP (acronym for List Processing), the first programming language for AI research, which is still in popular use to this day.

1959: Arthur Samuel created the term "**machine learning**" when doing a speech about teaching machines to play chess better than the humans who programmed them.

1961: The first industrial robot *Unimate* started working on an assembly line at General Motors in New Jersey, tasked with transporting die castings and welding parts on cars (which was deemed too dangerous for humans).

1965: Edward Feigenbaum and Joshua Lederberg created the first "**expert system**" which was a form of AI programmed to replicate the thinking and decision-making abilities of human experts.

1966: Joseph Weizenbaum created the first "**chatterbot**" (later shortened to **chatbot**), ELIZA, a mock psychotherapist, that used natural language processing (NLP) to converse with humans.

1968: Soviet mathematician Alexey Ivakhnenko published "Group Method of Data Handling" in the journal "Avtomatika," which proposed a new approach to AI that would later become what we now know as "**Deep Learning**."

1973: An applied mathematician named James Lighthill gave a report to the British Science Council, underlining that strides were not as impressive as those that had been promised by scientists, which led to much-reduced support and funding for AI research from the British government.

7.5   First "AI" Winter

The duration of the first AI winter was from 1974 to 1979 was the tough time for AI and ML researchers, and this duration was called as AI winter.

Researchers in the 1960s and the 1970s were convinced that their methods would eventually succeed in creating a machine with general intelligence and considered this the goal of their field. Herbert Simon predicted, "machines will be capable, within twenty years, of doing any work a man can do". Marvin Minsky agreed, writing, "within a generation … the problem of creating 'artificial intelligence' will substantially be solved". They had, however, underestimated the difficulty of the problem. In 1974, both the U.S.

and British governments cut off exploratory research in response to the criticism of Sir James Lighthill and ongoing pressure from the U.S. Congress to fund more productive projects. Minsky's and Papert's book Perceptrons was understood as proving that artificial neural networks would never be useful for solving real-world tasks, thus discrediting the approach altogether. The "AI winter", a period when obtaining funding for AI projects was difficult, followed.

In this duration, failure of machine translation occurred, and people had reduced their interest from AI, which led to reduced funding by the government to the researches.

It became obvious that researchers had grossly underestimated the difficulty of the project. In 1974, in response to the criticism from James Lighthill and ongoing pressure from congress, the U.S. and British Governments stopped funding undirected research into artificial intelligence, and the difficult years that followed would later be known as an **"AI winter"**. Seven years later, a visionary initiative by the Japanese Government inspired governments and industry to provide AI with billions of dollars, but by the late 1980s the investors became disillusioned and withdrew funding again.

7.5.1 The Lighthill Report

The first AI Winter has been marked by a dramatic decrease in the AI activities in both industry and academia. The AI shortcomings were explained in two reports: a) the Automatic Language Processing Advisory Committee (ALPAC) report by the US Government (ALPAC 1966) and b) the Lighthill report (Lighthill 1973) by the British government.

The British Science Research Council published a report titled "Artificial Intelligence: A General Survey" by Prof. Sir James Lighthill from the University of Cambridge in 1973. The Lighthill report was pessimistic since "in no part of the AI field have discoveries made so far produced the major impact that was then promised."

The report was reflecting on AI disappointment in both the public and the scientific community. The report highlighted that the conventional engineering approach with radio waves was performing better than AI methods of automatic landing systems for airplanes. AI experiments worked in the labs and small domains, but were inadequate in large-scale real-world problems, often because of the "Combinatorial Explosion."

7.6   The Year of 1979

1979: James L. Adams created The Standford Cart in 1961, which became one of the first examples of an autonomous vehicle. In '79, it successfully navigated a room full of chairs without human interference.

1979: The American Association of Artificial Intelligence which is now known as the Association for the Advancement of Artificial Intelligence (AAAI) was founded.

7.7   AI Boom: 1980-1987

Most of the 1980s showed a period of rapid growth and interest in AI, now labeled as the "AI boom." This came from both breakthroughs in research, and additional government funding to support the researchers. Deep Learning techniques and the use of Expert System became more popular, both of which allowed computers to learn from their mistakes and make independent decisions.

7.7.1   Notable dates in this time period include:

1980: First conference of the AAAI (Annual Conference on Artificial Intelligence) was held at Stanford.

1980: The first expert system came into the commercial market, known as XCON (expert configurer). It was designed to assist in the ordering of computer systems by automatically picking components based on the customer's needs.

1981: The Japanese government allocated $850 million (over $2 billion dollars in today's money) to the Fifth Generation Computer project. Their aim was to create computers that could translate, converse in human language, and express reasoning on a human level.

1984: The AAAI warns of an incoming "**AI Winter**" where funding and interest would decrease, and make research significantly more difficult.

1985: An autonomous drawing program known as AARON is demonstrated at the AAAI conference.

1986: Ernst Dickmann and his team at Bundeswehr University of Munich created and demonstrated the first driverless car (or **robot car**). It could drive up to 55 mph on roads that didn't have other obstacles or human drivers.

1987: Commercial launch of Alacrity by Alactrious Inc. Alacrity was the first strategy managerial advisory system, and used a complex expert system with 3,000+ rules.

7.8   Second AI Winter: 1987-1993

As the AAAI warned, an AI Winter came. The term describes a period of low consumer, public, and private interest in AI which leads to decreased research funding, which, in turn, leads to few breakthroughs. Both private investors and the government lost interest in AI and halted their funding due to high cost versus seemingly low return. This AI Winter came about because of some setbacks in the machine market and expert systems, including the end of the Fifth-Generation project, cutbacks in strategic computing initiatives, and a slowdown in the deployment of expert systems.

In the early 1980s, AI research was revived by the commercial success of **expert systems**, a form of AI program that simulated the knowledge and analytical skills of human experts. By 1985, the market for AI had reached over a billion dollars. At the same time, Japan's fifth generation computer project inspired the U.S. and British governments to restore funding for academic research. However, beginning with the collapse of the Lisp Machine market in 1987, AI once again fell into disrepute, and a second, longer-lasting winter began.

Up to this point, most of AI's funding had gone to projects which used high level symbols to represent mental objects like plans, goals, beliefs and known facts. In the 1980s, some researchers began to doubt that this approach would be able to imitate all the processes of human cognition, especially perception, robotics, learning and pattern recognition, and began to look into "sub-symbolic" approaches. Rodney Brooks rejected "representation" in general and focused directly on engineering machines that move and survive. Judea Pearl, Lofti Zadeh and others developed methods that handled incomplete and uncertain information by making reasonable guesses rather than precise logic. But the most important development was the revival of "connectionism", including neural network research, by Geoffrey Hinton and others. In 1990, Yann LeCun successfully showed that convolutional neural networks can recognize **handwritten digits,** the first of many successful applications of neural networks.

The following depicts graphically the history of the AI:

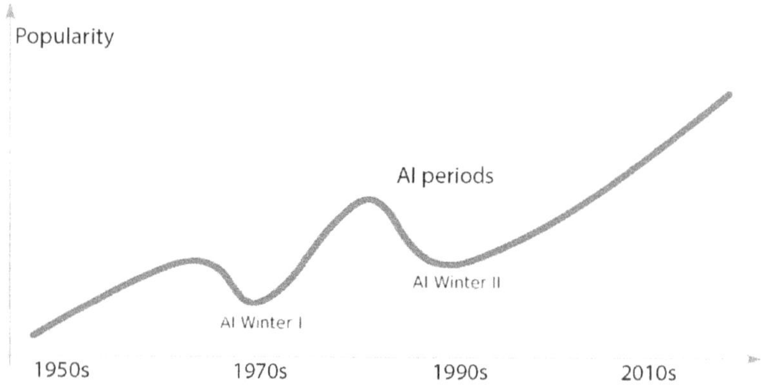

7.8.1 Notable dates include:

1987: The market for specialized LISP-based hardware collapsed due to cheaper and more accessible competitors that could run LISP software, including those offered by IBM and Apple. This caused many specialized LISP companies to fail as the technology was now easily accessible.

1988: A computer programmer named Rollo Carpenter invented the chatbot Jabberwacky, which he programmed to provide interesting and entertaining conversation to humans.

7.9   AI Agents: 1993-2011

Despite the lack of funding during the AI Winter, the early 90s showed some impressive strides forward in AI research, including the introduction of the first AI system that could beat a reigning **world champion chess player**. This era also introduced AI into everyday life via innovations such as the first Roomba and the first commercially-available speech recognition software on Windows computers.

The surge in interest was followed by a surge in funding for research, which allowed even more progress to be made.

7.9.1   Notable dates include:

1997: Deep Blue (developed by IBM) beat the world chess champion, **Gary Kasparov**, in a highly-publicized match, becoming the first program to beat a human chess champion. **1997:** Windows released a speech recognition software (developed by Dragon Systems).

2000: Professor Cynthia Breazeal developed the first robot that could simulate human emotions with its face, which included eyes, eyebrows, ears, and a mouth. It was called Kismet.

2002: The first Roomba was released.

2003: Nasa landed two rovers onto Mars (Spirit and Opportunity) and they navigated the surface of the planet without human intervention.

2006: Companies such as Twitter, Facebook, and Netflix started utilizing AI as a part of their advertising and user experience (UX) algorithms.

2010: Microsoft launched the Xbox 360 Kinect; the first gaming hardware designed to track body movement and translate it into gaming directions.

2011: An NLP computer programmed to answer questions named Watson (created by IBM) won Jeopardy against two former champions in a televised game.

2011: Apple released Siri, the first popular virtual assistant.

7.10 Artificial General Intelligence: 2012-present

That brings us to the most recent developments in AI, up to the present day. We've seen a surge in common-use AI tools, such as virtual assistants, search engines, etc. This time period also popularized Deep Learning and Big Data..

7.10.1 Notable dates include:

2012: Two researchers from Google (Jeff Dean and Andrew Ng) trained a neural network to recognize cats by showing it unlabeled images and no background information.

2015: Elon Musk, Stephen Hawking, and Steve Wozniak (and over 3,000 others) signed an open letter to the worlds' government systems banning the development of (and later, use of) **autonomous weapons** for purposes of war.

2016: Hanson Robotics created a humanoid robot named Sophia, who became known as the first "**robot citizen**" and was the first robot created with a realistic human appearance and the ability to see and replicate emotions, as well as to communicate.

2017: Facebook programmed two AI chatbots to converse and learn how to negotiate, but as they went back and forth they ended up forgoing English and developing their own language, completely autonomously.

2018: A Chinese tech group called **Alibaba's language-processing AI** beat human intellect on a Stanford reading and comprehension test.

2019: Google's AlphaStar reached Grandmaster on the video game StarCraft 2, outperforming all but. 2% of human players.

2020: OpenAI started beta testing GPT-3, a model that uses Deep Learning to create code, poetry, and other such language and writing tasks. While not the first of its kind, it is the first that creates content almost indistinguishable from those created by humans.

2021: OpenAI developed DALL-E, which can process and understand images enough to produce accurate captions, moving AI one step closer to understanding the visual world.

7.11   What does the Future hold?

Now that we're back to the present, there is probably a natural next question on your mind: so what comes next for AI?

Well, we can never entirely predict the future. However, many leading experts talk about the possible futures of AI, so we can make educated guesses. We can expect to see further adoption of AI by businesses of all sizes, changes in the workforce as more automation eliminates and creates jobs in equal measure, more robotics, autonomous vehicles, and so much more.

CHAPTER 8

MACHINE LANGUAGE: AN INTRODUCTION

A rapidly developing field of technology, machine learning allows computers to automatically learn from previous data. For building mathematical models and making predictions based on historical data or information, machine learning employs a variety of algorithms. It is currently being used for a variety of tasks, including speech recognition, email filtering, auto-tagging on Facebook, a recommender system, and image recognition.

8.1 What is Machine Learning?

In the real world, we are surrounded by humans who can learn everything from their experiences with their learning capability, and we have computers or machines which work on our instructions. But can a machine also learn from experiences or the past data like a human does? So here comes the role of Machine Learning.

A subset of artificial intelligence known as 'machine learning', focuses primarily on the creation of algorithms that enable a computer to independently learn from data and previous experiences. **Arthur Samuel** first used the term "machine learning" in 1959. It could be summarized as follows:

Without being explicitly programmed, machine learning enables a machine to automatically learn from data, improve in performance from experiences, and predict things.

Machine learning algorithms create a mathematical model that, without being explicitly programmed, aids in making predictions or decisions with the assistance of sample historical data, or training data. For the purpose of developing predictive models, machine learning brings together statistics and computer science. Algorithms that learn from historical data are either constructed or utilized in machine learning. The performance will rise in proportion to the quantity of information that is provided.

A machine can learn if it can gain more data to improve its performance.

8.2 How does Machine Learning work?

A machine learning system builds prediction models, learns from previous data, and predicts the output of new data whenever it receives it. The amount of data helps to build a better model that accurately predicts the output, which in turn affects the accuracy of the predicted output.

Let's say we have a complex problem in which we need to make predictions. Instead of writing code, we just need to feed the data to generic algorithms, which build the logic based on the data and predict the output. Our perspective on the issue has changed as a result of machine learning.

8.3 Features of Machine Learning

- Machine learning uses data to detect various patterns in a given dataset.

- It can learn from past data and improve automatically.

- It is a data-driven technology.

- Machine learning is much similar to data mining as it also deals with the huge amount of the data.

8.4 Need for Machine Learning

The demand for machine learning is steadily rising. Because it is able to perform tasks that are too complex for a person to directly implement, machine learning is required. Humans are constrained by their inability to manually access the vast amount of data; as a result, we require computer systems, which is where machine learning comes in to simplify our lives.

By providing them with a large amount of data and allowing them to automatically explore the data, build models, and predict the required output, we can train machine learning algorithms. The cost function can be used to determine the amount of data and the machine learning algorithm's performance. We can save both time and money by using the machine learning.

Presently, AI is utilized in self-driving vehicles, digital misrepresentation identification, face recognition, and companion idea by Facebook, and so on. Different top organizations, for example, Netflix and Amazon have constructed AI models that are utilizing an immense measure of information to examine the client interest and suggest item likewise.

Following are some of the key points which show the importance of Machine Learning:

- Rapid increment in the production of data.

- Solving complex problems, which are difficult for a human being,

- Decision making in various sectors, including finance.

- Finding hidden patterns and extracting useful information from data.

8.5   Classification of Machine Learning

At a broad level, machine learning can be classified into three types:

(i)   Supervised learning,

(ii) Unsupervised learning, and

(iii) Reinforcement learning.

(i) Supervised Learning

The model or algorithm is presented with example inputs and their desired outputs and then finds patterns and connections between the input and the output. The goal is to learn a general rule that maps inputs to outputs. The training process continues until the model achieves the desired level of accuracy on the training data.

Some real-life examples are:

- **Image Classification:** You train with images/labels. Then in the future, you give a new image expecting that the computer will recognize the new object.

- **Market Prediction/Regression:** You train the computer with historical market data and ask the computer to predict the new price in the future.

(ii) Unsupervised Learning

Unsupervised learning is a learning method in which a machine learns without any supervision.

No labels are given to the learning algorithm, leaving it on its own to find structure in its input. It is used for clustering populations in different groups. Unsupervised learning can be a goal in itself (discovering hidden patterns in data).

- **Clustering:** You ask the computer to separate similar data into clusters, this is essential in research and science.

- **High-Dimension Visualization:** Use the computer to help us visualize high-dimension data.

- **Generative Models:** After a model captures the probability distribution of your input data, it will be able to generate more data. This can be very useful to make your classifier more robust.

(iii) Reinforcement Learning

Reinforcement learning is an area of Machine Learning. It is about taking suitable action to maximize reward in a particular situation. It is employed by various software and machines to find the best possible behavior or path it should take in a specific situation. Reinforcement learning differs from supervised learning in a way that in supervised learning the training data has the answer key with it so the model is trained with the correct answer itself whereas in reinforcement learning, there is no answer but the reinforcement agent decides what to do to perform the given task. In the absence of a training dataset, it is bound to learn from its experience.

Reinforcement Learning (RL) is the science of decision making. It is about learning the optimal behavior in an environment to obtain maximum reward. In RL, the data is accumulated from machine learning systems that use a trial-and-error method. Data is not part of the input that we would find in supervised or unsupervised machine learning.

Reinforcement learning uses algorithms that learn from outcomes and decide which action to take next. After each action, the algorithm receives feedback that helps it determine whether the choice it made was correct, neutral or incorrect. It is a good technique to use for automated systems that have to make a lot of small decisions without human guidance.

Reinforcement learning is an autonomous, self-teaching system that essentially learns by trial and error. It performs actions with the aim of maximizing rewards, or in other words, it is learning by doing in order to achieve the best outcomes.

Example:

The problem is as follows: We have an agent and a reward, with many hurdles in between. The agent is supposed to find the best possible path to reach the reward. The following problem explains the problem more easily.

The robotic dog, which automatically learns the movement of his arms, is an example of Reinforcement learning.

- **Salient Features of in Reinforcement learning:**

- **Input:** The input should be an initial state from which the model will start.

- **Output:** There are many possible outputs as there are a variety of solutions to a particular problem.

- **Training:** The training is based on the input. The model will return a state and the user will decide to reward or punish the model based on its output.

- The model keeps continues to learn.

- The best solution is decided based on the maximum reward.

Types of Reinforcement:

There are two types of Reinforcement:

1. **Positive:** Positive Reinforcement is defined as when an event, occurs due to a particular behavior, increases the strength and the frequency of the behavior. In other words, it has a positive effect on behavior.

Advantages of positive reinforcement learning are:

- Maximizes Performance

- Sustain Change for a long period of time

- Too much Reinforcement can lead to an overload of states which can diminish the results.

2. **Negative:** Negative Reinforcement is defined as strengthening of behavior because a negative condition is stopped or avoided.

Advantages of negative reinforcement learning are:

- Increases Behavior

- Provide defiance to a minimum standard of performance

- It Only provides enough to meet up the minimum behavior.

Some Applications of Reinforcement Learning are:

- RL can be used in robotics for industrial automation.

- RL can be used in machine learning and data processing

- RL can be used to create training systems that provide custom instruction and materials according to the requirement of students.

8.6   History of Machine Learning

For some years (about 40-50 years), machine learning was a science fiction, but today it is the part of our daily life. Machine learning is making our day-to-day life easy from self-driving cars to Amazon virtual assistant "**Alexa**". However, the idea behind machine learning is very old and has a long history. Below are given some milestones which have occurred in the history of machine learning:

8.6.1   The early history of Machine Learning (Pre-1940):

1834: In 1834, **Charles Babbage**, the father of the computer, conceived a device that could be programmed with punch cards. However, the machine was never built, but all modern computers rely on its logical structure.

1936: In 1936, **Alan Turing** gave a theory that how a machine can determine and execute a set of instructions.

8.6.2 Era of Stored Program Computers:

1940-1951: In 1940, the first manually operated computer, "ENIAC (Electronic Numerical Integrator And Computer)" was invented, which was the first electronic general-purpose computer. After that stored program computer such as EDSAC (Electronic Delay Storage Automatic Calculator, which was originally built in the Cambridge University Mathematical Laboratory by a team lead by the late Professor Sir Maurice Wilkes in 1949 following the Second World War); and EDVAC (Electronic Discrete Variable Automatic Computer) in 1951, were invented.

1943: In 1943, a human neural network was modeled with an electrical circuit. In 1950, the scientists started applying their idea to work and analyzed how human neurons might work.

8.6.3 Computer Machinery and Intelligence:

1950: In 1950, **Alan Turing** published a seminal paper, "Computer Machinery and Intelligence," on the topic of artificial intelligence. In his paper, he asked, "Can machines think?"

8.6.4 Machine intelligence in Games:

1952: Arthur Samuel, who was the **pioneer of machine learning**, created a program that helped an IBM computer to play a checkers game. It performed better, more it played.

1959: In 1959, the term "Machine Learning" was first coined by **Arthur Samuel**.

8.6.5 Machine Learning: from Theory to Reality

1959: In 1959, the first neural network was applied to a real-world problem to remove echoes over phone lines using an adaptive filter.

1985: In 1985, Terry Sejnowski and Charles Rosenberg invented a neural network NETtalk, which was able to teach itself how to correctly pronounce 20,000 words in one week.

1997: The IBM's **Deep blue intelligent computer won the chess game against the chess expert Garry Kasparov,** and it became the first computer which had beaten a human chess expert.

8.6.6   Machine Learning in the 21st century

2006: Geoffrey Hinton and his group presented the idea of 'profound' getting the hang of utilizing profound conviction organizations.

The Elastic Compute Cloud (EC2) was launched by Amazon to provide scalable computing resources that made it easier to create and implement machine learning models.

2007: Participants were tasked with increasing the accuracy of Netflix's recommendation algorithm when the Netflix Prize competition began.

Support learning made critical progress when a group of specialists utilized it to prepare a PC to play backgammon at a top-notch level.

2008: Google delivered the Google Forecast Programming interface, a cloud-based help that permitted designers to integrate AI into their applications.

8.6.7   Confined Boltzmann Machines (CBMs),

a kind of generative brain organization, acquired consideration for their capacity to demonstrate complex information conveyances.

2009: Profound learning gained ground as analysts showed its viability in different errands, including discourse acknowledgment and picture grouping.

The expression "Large Information" acquired ubiquity, featuring the difficulties and open doors related with taking care of huge datasets.

2010: The ImageNet Huge Scope Visual Acknowledgment Challenge (ILSVRC) was presented, driving progressions in PC vision, and prompting the advancement of profound convolutional brain organizations (CNNs).

2011: On Jeopardy! **IBM's Watson defeated human champions**, demonstrating the potential of question-answering systems and natural language processing.

2012: AlexNet, a profound CNN created by Alex Krizhevsky, won the ILSVRC, fundamentally further developing the picture order precision and laying out profound advancing as a predominant methodology in PC vision.

Google's Cerebrum project, drove by Andrew Ng and Jeff Dignitary, utilized profound figuring out how to prepare a brain organization to perceive felines from unlabeled YouTube recordings.

2013: Ian Goodfellow introduced generative adversarial networks (GANs), which made it possible to create realistic synthetic data.

Google later acquired the startup DeepMind Technologies, which focused on **deep learning** and artificial intelligence.

2014: Facebook presented the DeepFace framework, which accomplished close human precision in facial acknowledgment.

AlphaGo, a program created by DeepMind at Google, defeated a world champion Go player and demonstrated the potential of reinforcement learning in challenging games.

2015: Microsoft delivered the Mental Toolbox (previously known as CNTK), an open-source profound learning library.

The performance of sequence-to-sequence models in tasks like machine translation was enhanced by the introduction of the idea of attention mechanisms.

2016: The goal of explainable AI, which focuses on making machine learning models easier to understand, received some attention.

Google's DeepMind created AlphaGo Zero, which accomplished godlike Go abilities to play without human information, utilizing just support learning.

2017: Move learning acquired noticeable quality, permitting pretrained models to be utilized for different errands with restricted information.

Better synthesis and generation of complex data were made possible by the introduction of generative models like variational autoencoders (VAEs) and Wasserstein GANs.

These are only a portion of the eminent headways and achievements in AI during the predefined period. The field kept on advancing quickly past 2017, with new leap forwards, strategies, and applications arising.

8.7   Machine Learning, at present

The field of machine learning has made significant strides in recent years, and its applications are numerous, including **self-driving cars, Amazon Alexa**, Catboats, and the recommender system. It incorporates clustering, classification, decision tree, SVM algorithms, and reinforcement learning, as well as unsupervised and supervised learning.

Present day AI models can be utilized for making different expectations, including climate expectation, sickness forecast, financial exchange examination, and so on.

CHAPTER 9

DEEP LEARNING: AN INTRODUCTION

The simple 'machine learning' algorithms work very well on a wide variety of important problems. However, they have not succeeded in solving the central problems in AI, such as recognizing speech or recognizing objects. Deep learning was designed to overcome these and other obstacles.

Deep learning is a branch of machine learning which is completely based on artificial neural networks, as neural networks are going to mimic the human brain so deep learning is also a kind of mimic of the human brain.

Deep learning is an essential tool for data science and machine learning, as it allows for the uncovering of hidden patterns in large datasets. Understanding the fundamentals of deep learning algorithms enables the identification of appropriate problems that can be solved with deep learning, which can then be applied to your own projects or research.

9.1   Definition of Deep Learning (DL)

Deep learning is an aspect of artificial intelligence (AI) that is to simulate the activity of the human brain, specifically the pattern recognition, by passing input through various **layers of the neural network.** Deep Learning is a part of Machine Learning that uses artificial neural networks to learn from lots of data without needing explicit programming. These networks are inspired by the human brain and can be used for things like recognizing images, understanding speech, and processing language. There are different types of deep learning networks, like feedforward neural networks, convolutional neural networks, and recurrent neural networks. Deep

Learning needs lots of labeled data and powerful computers to work well, but it can achieve very good results in many applications.

Deep learning algorithms use an artificial neural network, a computing system that learns high-level features from data by increasing the depth (i.e., number of layers) in the network. Neural networks are partially inspired by biological neural networks, where cells in most brains (including ours) connect and work together. Each of these cells in a neural network is called a neuron.

Deep-learning architectures such as deep neural networks, deep belief networks, recurrent neural networks and convolutional neural networks have been applied to fields including computer vision, machine vision, speech recognition, natural language processing, audio recognition, social network design, medical game programs.

9.2   Difference between Artificial Neural Network and Biological Neural Network

(i)   **Artificial Neural Network:** Artificial Neural Network (ANN) is a type of neural network that is based on a Feed-Forward strategy. It is called this because they pass information through the nodes continuously till it reaches the output node. This is also known as the simplest type of neural network.

Some advantages of ANN:

- Ability to learn irrespective of the type of data (Linear or Non-Linear).

- ANN is highly volatile and serves best in financial time series forecasting.

Some disadvantages of ANN:

- The simplest architecture makes it difficult to explain the behavior of the network.

- This network is dependent on hardware.

(ii) **Biological Neural Network:** Biological Neural Network (BNN) is a structure that consists of Synapse, dendrites, cell body, and axon. In this neural network, the processing is carried out by neurons. Dendrites receive signals from other neurons, Soma sums all the incoming signals and axon transmits the signals to other cells.

Some advantages of BNN:

- The synapses are the input processing element.

- It is able to process highly complex parallel inputs.

9.3 Shallow and Deep Neural Network

A neural network is comprised of the following components:

(i) Input Layer: This is where the training observations are fed through the independent variables.

(ii) Hidden Layers: These are the intermediate layers between the input and output layers. This is where the neural network learns about the relationships and interactions of the variables fed in the input layer.

(iii) Output Layer: This is the layer where the final output is extracted as a result of all the processing which takes place within the hidden layers.

(iv) Node: A node, also called a neuron, in a neural network is a computational unit that takes in one or more input values and produces an output value.

9.3.1   A shallow neural network

is a neural network with a small number of layers, often comprised of just one or two hidden layers.

9.3.2   A deep (dense) neural network

consists of multiple hidden layers. Each layer contains a set of neurons that learn to extract certain features from the data. The output layer produces the final results of the network. The additional hidden layers in a deep neural network enable it to learn more complex patterns than a shallow neural network. Consequently, deep neural networks are more accurate but also more computationally expensive to train than shallow neural networks. Therefore, deep neural networks are preferable for complex, real-time, real-world applications such as multivariate time series forecasting, natural language processing, real-time forecasting, or predictive lead times.

9.3.3   Difference Between Shallow NN and Deep NN

Shallow Neural Network	Deep Neural Network
It consists of one hidden layer	It consists of more than one hidden layer
It takes input as vectors only	It takes raw data like images and text as input.

9.4   How does Deep Learning Work?

At its simplest level, deep learning works by taking input data and feeding it into a network of artificial neurons. Each neuron takes the input from the previous layer of neurons and uses that information to recognize patterns in the data. The neurons then apply weight the input data and make predictions about the output. The output can be a class or label, such as in computer vision, where you might want to classify an image as a cat or dog.

9.5   Important Components of a Deep Neural Network

(i) **Forward Propagation:** In this process, input is passed forward from one layer of the network to the next until it passes through all layers and reaches the output.

(ii) Backpropagation: This is an iterative process that uses a chain rule to determine the contribution of each neuron to errors in the output. The error values are then propagated back through the network, and the weights of each neuron are adjusted accordingly.

(iii) Optimization: This technique is used to reduce errors generated during backpropagation in a deep neural network. Various algorithms, such as gradient descent and stochastic gradient descent, can be used to optimize the network.

(iv) Activation Functions: Activation functions are used to convert inputs into an output that can be recognized by the neural network. There are several types of activation functions, including linear, sigmoid, tanh, and ReLu (Rectified Linear Units).

9.6 Loss Function in Neural Networks

Neural Network uses optimizing strategies to minimize the error in the algorithm. The way we actually compute this error is by using a Loss Function. It is used to quantify how good or bad the model is performing. These are divided into two categories i.e. Regression loss and Classification Loss.

(i) Regression Loss Function

Regression Loss is used when we are predicting continuous values like the price of a house or sales of a company. For example, Mean Squared Error (Mean Squared Error is the mean of squared differences between the actual and predicted value). If the difference is large the model will penalize it as we are computing the squared difference.

(ii) Binary Classification Loss Function

Suppose we are dealing with a Yes/No situation like "a person has diabetes or not", in this kind of scenario Binary Classification Loss Function is used. For example, Binary Cross Entropy Loss

It gives the probability value between 0 and 1 for a classification task. Cross-Entropy calculates the average difference between the predicted and actual probabilities.

(iii) Multi-Class Classification Loss Function

If we take a dataset like Iris where we need to predict the three-class labels: Setosa, Versicolor and Virginia, in such cases where the target variable has more than two classes Multi-Class Classification Loss function is used. For example, Categorical Cross Entropy Loss: These are similar to binary classification cross-entropy, used for multi-class classification problems.

By combining all of these components, deep learning can take complex inputs and produce accurate predictions for a variety of tasks.

9.7   Deep Learning Algorithms

The three most popular deep learning algorithms are

(i)   Convolutional neural networks (CNNs),

(ii)   Recurrent neural networks (RNNs), and

(iii) Long short-term memory networks (LSTMs).

CNNs are used for image recognition, object detection, and classification. **RNNs** are used for sequence modeling, such as language translation and text generation. **LSTMs**. use a special type of memory cell that enables them to remember longer sequences and are used for tasks such as recognizing handwriting and predicting stock prices.

Some less common, but still powerful deep learning algorithms include generative adversarial networks (GANs), autoencoders, reinforcement learning, deep belief networks (DBNs), and transfer learning.

- **GANs** can be used for image generation, text-to-image synthesis, and video colorization.

- **Autoencoders** are helpful for data compression and dimensionality reduction.

- **Reinforcement learning** is a type of machine learning in which agents learn to perform tasks by interacting with the environment.

- **DBNs** are primarily used for unsupervised feature learning.

- **Transfer learning** allows models trained on one problem to be reused for another.

9.8 Problem Solving Approach in Deep Learning

When solving a problem using traditional machine learning algorithm, it is generally recommended to break the problem down into different parts, solve them individually and combine them to get the result. Deep learning in contrast advocates to solve the problem end-to-end. For example: Suppose you have a task of multiple object detection. The task is to identify what is the object and where is it present in the image. In a typical ML approach, you would divide the problem into two steps, object detection and object recognition On the contrary, in deep learning approach, you would do the process end-to-end. Bottom of Form

9.9 Interpretations of Deep Learning

Deep neural networks are generally interpreted in terms of the universal approximation theorem or probabilistic inference.

The classic universal approximation theorem concerns the capacity of feed-forward neural networks with a single hidden layer of finite size to approximate continuous functions. In 1989, the first proof was published by George Cybenko for sigmoid activation functions and was generalized to feed-forward multilayer architectures in 1991 by Kurt Hornik. Recent work also showed that universal approximation also holds for non-bounded activation functions such as Kunihiko Fukushima's rectified linear unit.

The universal approximation theorem for deep neural networks concerns the capacity of networks with bounded width but the depth is allowed to grow. Lu et al. proved that if the width of a deep neural network with ReLU activation is strictly larger than the input dimension, then the network can approximate any Lebesgue integrable function; if the width is smaller or equal to the input dimension, then a deep neural network is not a universal approximator.

The probabilistic interpretation derives from the field of machine learning. It features inference, as well as the optimization concepts of training and testing, related to fitting and generalization, respectively. More specifically, the probabilistic interpretation considers the activation nonlinearity as a cumulative distribution function. The probabilistic interpretation led to the introduction of dropout as regularizer in neural networks. The probabilistic interpretation was introduced by researchers including Hopfield, Widrow and Narendra and popularized in surveys such as the one by Bishop.

9.10   History of Deep Learning

There were two types of artificial neural network (ANN): feedforward neural networks (FNNs) and recurrent neural networks (RNNs). RNNs have cycles in their connectivity structure, FNNs don't. In the 1920s, Wilhelm Lenz and Ernst Ising created and analyzed the Ising model, which is essentially a non-learning RNN architecture consisting of neuron-like threshold elements. In 1972, Shun'ichi Amari made this architecture adaptive. His learning RNN was popularized by John Hopfield in 1982.

Charles Tappert writes that Frank Rosenblatt developed and explored all of the basic ingredients of the deep learning systems of today, referring to Rosenblatt's 1962-book which introduced multilayer perceptron (MLP) with 3 layers: an input layer, a hidden layer with randomized weights that did not learn, and an output layer. It also introduced variants, including a version with four-layer Perceptrons where the last two layers have learned weights (and thus a proper multilayer perceptron). In addition, the term deep learning was proposed in 1986 by Rina Dechter although the history of its appearance is apparently more complicated.

The first general, working learning algorithm for supervised, deep, feedforward, multilayer Perceptrons was published by Alexey Ivakhnenko and Lapa in 1967. A 1971-paper described a deep network with eight layers trained by the group method of data handling.

The first deep learning multilayer perceptron trained by stochastic gradient descent was published in 1967 by Shun'ichi Amari. In computer experiments conducted by Amari's student Saito, a five-layer MLP with two modifiable layers learned internal representations to classify nonlinearly separable pattern classes. In 1987 Matthew Brand reported that wide 12-layer nonlinear Perceptrons could be fully end-to-end trained to reproduce logic functions of nontrivial circuit depth via gradient descent on small batches of random input/output samples, but concluded that training time on contemporary hardware (sub-megaflop computers) made the technique impractical, and proposed using fixed random early layers as an input hash for a single modifiable layer. Instead, subsequent developments in hardware and hyperparameter tunings have made end-to-end stochastic gradient descent the currently dominant training technique.

In 1970, Seppo Linnainmaa published the reverse mode of automatic differentiation of discrete connected networks of nested differentiable functions. This became known as **backpropagation**. It is an efficient application of the chain rule derived by Gottfried Wilhelm Leibniz to networks of differentiable nodes. The terminology "back-propagating errors" was actually introduced in 1962 by Rosenblatt, but he did not know how to implement this, although Henry J. Kelley had a continuous precursor of backpropagation already in 1960 in the context of control theory. In 1982, Paul Ferbos applied backpropagation to MLPs in the way that has become standard. In 1985, David E. Rumelhart et al. published an experimental analysis of the technique.

Deep learning architectures for **convolutional neural networks** (CNNs) with convolutional layers and down-sampling layers began with the Neocognitron introduced by Kunihiko Fukushima in **1980**. In **1969**, he also introduced the ReLU (rectified linear unit) activation function. The rectifier has become the most popular activation function for CNNs and deep learning in general. CNNs have become an essential tool for computer vision.

The term Deep Learning was introduced to the machine learning community by Rina Dechter **in 1986,** as mentioned earlier, and to artificial neural networks by Igor Aizenberg and colleagues **in 2000**, in the context of Boolean threshold neurons.

In 1988, Wei Zhang et al. applied the backpropagation algorithm to a convolutional neural network (a simplified Neocognitron with convolutional interconnections between the image feature layers and the last fully connected layer) for alphabet recognition. They also proposed an implementation of the CNN with an optical computing system. In 1989, Yann LeCun et al. applied backpropagation to a CNN with the purpose of recognizing handwritten ZIP codes on mail. While the algorithm worked, training required 3 days. Subsequently, Wei Zhang, et al. modified their model by removing the last fully connected layer and applied it for medical image object segmentation in 1991 and breast cancer detection in mammograms in 1994. LeNet-5 (1998), a 7-level CNN by Yann LeCun et al., that classifies digits, was applied by several banks to recognize hand-written numbers on checks digitized in 32x32 pixel images.

In the 1980s, backpropagation did not work well for deep learning with long credit assignment paths. To overcome this problem, Jürgen Schmidhuber proposed a hierarchy of RNNs pre-trained one level at a time by self-supervised learning. It uses predictive coding to learn internal representations at multiple self-organizing time scales. This can substantially facilitate downstream deep learning. The RNN hierarchy can be collapsed into a single RNN, by distilling a higher level chunker network into a lower level automatizer network. In 1993, a chunker solved a deep learning task whose depth exceeded 1000.

In 1992, Jürgen Schmidhuber also published an alternative to RNNs which is now called a linear Transformer or a Transformer with linearized self-attention. It learns internal spotlights of attention: a slow feedforward neural network learns by gradient descent to control the fast weights of another neural network through outer products of self-generated activation patterns FROM and TO (which are now called key and value for self-attention). This fast weight attention mapping is applied to a query pattern.

The modern Transformer was introduced by Ashish Vaswani et al. in their **2017-paper** "Attention Is All You Need". It combines this with a SoftMax operator and a projection matrix. Transformers have increasingly become the model of choice for natural language processing. Many modern large language models such as ChatGPT, GPT-4, and BERT use it. Transformers are also increasingly being used in computer vision.

In 1991, Jürgen Schmidhuber also published adversarial neural networks that contest with each other in the form of a zero-sum game, where one network's gain is the other network's loss. The first network is a generative model that models a probability distribution over output patterns. The second network learns by gradient descent to predict the reactions of the environment to these patterns. This was called "artificial curiosity". In 2014, this principle was used in a generative adversarial network (GAN) by Ian Goodfellow et al. Here the environmental reaction is 1 or 0 depending on whether the first network's output is in a given set. This can be used to create realistic deepfakes. Excellent image quality is achieved by Nvidia's StyleGAN based on the Progressive GAN by Tero Karras et al. Here the GAN generator is grown from small to large scale in a pyramidal fashion.

Sepp Hochreiter's diploma thesis (**1991**) was called "one of the most important documents in the history of machine learning" by his supervisor Schmidhuber. It not only tested the neural history compressor, but also identified and analyzed the vanishing gradient problem. Hochreiter proposed recurrent residual connections to solve this problem. This led to the deep learning method called **long short-term memory** (LSTM), published **in 1997**. LSTM recurrent neural networks can learn "very deep learning" tasks with long credit assignment paths that require memories of events that happened thousands of discrete time steps before. The "vanilla LSTM" with forget gate was introduced **in 1999** by Felix Gers, Schmidhuber and Fred Cummins. LSTM has become the most cited neural network of the 20th century. **In 2015, Rupesh Kumar Srivastava**, Klaus Greff, and Schmidhuber used LSTM principles to create the Highway network, a feedforward neural network with hundreds of layers, much deeper than previous networks. Seven months later, Kaiming He, Xiangyu Zhang; Shaoqing Ren, and Jian Sun won the ImageNet 2015 competition with an open-gated or gateless Highway network variant called **Residual neural network. This has become the most cited neural network of the 21st century.**

In 1994, André de Carvalho, together with Mike Fairhurst and David Bisset, published experimental results of a multi-layer Boolean neural network, also known as a weightless neural network, composed of a 3-layers self-organizing feature extraction neural network module (SOFT) followed by a multi-layer classification neural network module (GSN), which were independently trained. Each layer in the feature extraction module extracted features with growing complexity regarding the previous layer.

In 1995, Brendan Frey demonstrated that it was possible to train (over two days) a network containing six fully connected layers and several hundred hidden units using the wake-sleep algorithm, co-developed with Peter Dayan and Hinton.

Since 1997, Sven Behnke extended the feed-forward hierarchical convolutional approach in the Neural Abstraction Pyramid by lateral and backward connections in order to flexibly incorporate context into decisions and iteratively resolve local ambiguities.

Simpler models that use task-specific handcrafted features such as Gabor filters and support vector machines (SVMs) were a popular choice **in the 1990s and 2000s**, because of artificial neural networks' computational cost and a lack of understanding of how the brain wires its biological networks.

Both shallow and deep learning (e.g., recurrent nets) of ANNs for speech recognition have been explored for many years. These methods never outperformed non-uniform internal-handcrafting Gaussian mixture model/Hidden Markov model (GMM-HMM) technology based on generative models of speech trained discriminatively. Key difficulties have been analyzed, including gradient diminishing and weak temporal correlation structure in neural predictive models. Additional difficulties were the lack of training data and limited computing power. Most speech recognition researchers moved away from neural nets to pursue generative modeling. An exception was at SRI International in the **late 1990s.** Funded by the US government's NSA and DARPA, SRI studied deep neural networks (DNNs) in speech and speaker recognition. The speaker recognition team led by Larry Heck reported significant success with deep neural networks in speech processing in the **1998** National Institute of Standards and Technology Speaker Recognition evaluation. The SRI deep neural network was then deployed in the Nuance Verifier, representing the first major industrial application of deep learning. The principle of elevating "raw" features over hand-crafted optimization was first explored successfully in the architecture of deep autoencoder on the "raw" spectrogram or linear filter-bank features in the late **1990s,** showing its superiority over the Mel-Cepstral features that contain stages of fixed transformation from spectrograms. The raw features of speech, waveforms, later produced excellent larger-scale results.

Speech recognition was taken over by LSTM. **In 2003,** LSTM started to become competitive with traditional speech recognizers on certain tasks. In **2006,** Alex Graves, Santiago Fernández, Faustino

Gomez, and Schmidhuber combined it with connectionist temporal classification (CTC) in stacks of LSTM RNNs. **In 2015,** Google's speech recognition reportedly experienced a dramatic performance jump of 49% through CTC-trained LSTM, which they made available through Google Voice Search.

The impact of deep learning in industry began in the early 2000s, when CNNs already processed an estimated 10% to 20% of all the checks written in the US, according to Yann LeCun. Industrial applications of deep learning to large-scale speech recognition started around 2010.

In 2006, publications by Geoff Hinton, Ruslan Salakhutdinov, Osindero and Teh showed how a many-layered feedforward neural network could be effectively pre-trained one layer at a time, treating each layer in turn as an unsupervised restricted Boltzmann machine, then fine-tuning it using supervised backpropagation. The papers referred to learning for deep belief nets.

The 2009-NIPS Workshop on Deep Learning for Speech Recognition was motivated by the limitations of deep generative models of speech, and the possibility that given more capable hardware and large-scale data sets that deep neural nets might become practical. It was believed that pre-training DNNs using generative models of deep belief nets (DBN) would overcome the main difficulties of neural nets. However, it was discovered that replacing pre-training with large amounts of training data for straightforward backpropagation when using DNNs with large, context-dependent output layers produced error rates dramatically lower than then-state-of-the-art Gaussian mixture model (GMM)/ Hidden Markov Model (HMM) and also than more-advanced generative model-based systems. The nature of the recognition errors produced by the two types of systems was characteristically different, offering technical insights into how to integrate deep learning into the existing highly efficient, run-time speech decoding system deployed by all major speech recognition systems. Analysis around 2009–2010, contrasting the GMM (and other generative speech models) vs. DNN models, stimulated early industrial investment in deep learning for speech recognition. That analysis was done with comparable performance (less than 1.5% in error rate) between discriminative DNNs and generative models. **In 2010,** researchers extended deep learning from TIMIT to large vocabulary speech recognition, by adopting large output layers of the DNN based on context-dependent HMM states constructed by decision trees.

Deep learning is part of state-of-the-art systems in various disciplines, particularly computer vision and automatic speech recognition (ASR). Results on commonly used evaluation sets such as TIMIT (ASR) and MNIST (image classification), as well as a range of large-vocabulary speech recognition tasks have steadily improved. Convolutional neural networks were superseded for ASR by CTC for LSTM. but are more successful in computer vision.

Advances in hardware have driven renewed interest in deep learning. In 2009, Nvidia was involved in what was called the "big bang" of deep learning, "as deep-learning neural networks were trained with Nvidia graphics processing units (GPUs)". That year, Andrew Ng determined that GPUs could increase the speed of deep-learning systems by about 100 times. In particular, GPUs are well-suited for the matrix/vector computations involved in machine learning. GPUs speed up training algorithms by orders of magnitude, reducing running times from weeks to days. Further, specialized hardware and algorithm optimizations can be used for efficient processing of deep learning models.

9.11   Deep Learning Revolution

How deep learning is a subset of machine learning and how machine learning is a subset of artificial intelligence (AI)

In the **late 2000s**, deep learning started to outperform other methods in machine learning competitions. **In 2009**, a long short-term memory trained by connectionist temporal classification (Alex Graves, Santiago Fernández, Faustino Gomez, and Jürgen

Schmidhuber, 2006) was the first RNN to win pattern recognition contests, winning three competitions in connected handwriting recognition. Google later used CTC-trained LSTM for speech recognition on the smartphone.

Significant impacts in image or object recognition were felt from 2011 to 2012. Although CNNs trained by backpropagation had been around for decades, and GPU implementations of NNs for years, including CNNs, faster implementations of CNNs on GPUs were needed to progress on computer vision. In 2011, the DanNet by Dan Ciresan, Ueli Meier, Jonathan Masci, Luca Maria Gambardella, and Jürgen Schmidhuber achieved for the first time superhuman performance in a visual pattern recognition contest, outperforming traditional methods by a factor of 3. Also in 2011, DanNet won the ICDAR Chinese handwriting contest, and in May 2012, it won the ISBI image segmentation contest. Until 2011, CNNs did not play a major role at computer vision conferences, but in June 2012, a paper by Ciresan et al. at the leading conference CVPR showed how max-pooling CNNs on GPU can dramatically improve many vision benchmark records. In September 2012, DanNet also won the ICPR contest on analysis of large medical images for cancer detection, and in the following year also the MICCAI Grand Challenge on the same topic. In October 2012, the similar AlexNet by Alex Krizhevsky, Ilya Sutskever, and Geoffrey Hinton won the large-scale ImageNet competition by a significant margin over shallow machine learning methods. The VGG-16 network by Karen Simonyan and Andrew Zisserman further reduced the error rate and won the ImageNet 2014 competition, following a similar trend in large-scale speech recognition.

Image classification was then extended to the more challenging task of generating descriptions (captions) for images, often as a combination of CNNs and LSTMs. **In 2012,** a team led by George E. Dahl won the "Merck Molecular Activity Challenge" using multi-task deep neural networks to predict the biomolecular target of one drug. In 2014, Sepp Hochreiter's group used deep learning to detect off-target and toxic effects of environmental chemicals in nutrients, household products and drugs and won the "Tox21 Data Challenge" of NIH, FDA and NCATS.

In 2016, Roger Parloff mentioned a "deep learning revolution" that has transformed the AI industry.

In March 2019, Yoshua Bengio, Geoffrey Hinton and Yann LeCun were awarded the Turing Award for conceptual and engineering breakthroughs that have made deep neural networks a critical component of computing.

9.12   Applications of Deep Learning

Some of the applications of Deep Learning are:

- **Color restoration**, where a given image in greyscale is automatically turned into a colored one.

- **Recognizing hand written message.**

- **Adding sound to a silent video** that matches with the scene taking place.

- **Self-driving cars**.

- **Computer Vision:** for applications like vehicle number plate identification and facial recognition.

- **Information Retrieval:** for applications like search engines, both text search, and image search.

- **Marketing:** for applications like automated email marketing, target identification.

- **Medical Diagnosis:** for applications like cancer identification, anomaly detection.

- **Natural Language Processing:** for applications like sentiment analysis, photo tagging.

- **Online Advertising, etc.**

CHAPTER 10

NATURAL LANGUAGE PROCESSING (NLP)

10.1   What is Natural Language Processing (NLP)?

NLP is a subfield of computer science and artificial intelligence (AI) that uses machine learning to enable computers to understand and communicate with human language. Human languages can be in the form of text or audio format.

NLP enables computers and digital devices to recognize, understand and generate text and speech by combining computational linguistics—the rule-based modeling of human language—together with statistical modeling, machine learning (ML) and deep learning.

NLP research has enabled the era of generative AI, from the communication skills of large language models (LLMs) to the ability of image generation models to understand requests. NLP is already part of everyday life for many, powering search engines, prompting chatbots for customer service with spoken commands, voice-operated GPS systems and digital assistants on smartphones.

NLP also plays a growing role in enterprise solutions that help streamline and automate business operations, increase employee productivity and simplify mission-critical business processes.

10.2   Benefits of NLP

A natural language processing system can work rapidly and efficiently: after NLP models are properly trained, it can take on administrative tasks, freeing staff for more productive work.

Benefits can include:

(i) **Faster insight discovery**: Organizations can find hidden patterns, trends and relationships between different pieces of content. Text data retrieval supports deeper insights and analysis, enabling better-informed decision-making and surfacing new business ideas.

(ii) **Greater budget savings**: With the massive volume of unstructured text data available, NLP can be used to automate the gathering, processing and organization of information with less manual effort.

(iii) **Quick access to corporate data**: An enterprise can build a knowledge base of organizational information to be efficiently accessed with AI search. For sales representatives, NLP can help quickly return relevant information, to improve customer service and help close sales.

10.3   History of NLP

Natural Language Processing started in 1950 When **Alan Mathison Turing** published an article by the name '**Computing Machinery and Intelligence**'. It is based on Artificial intelligence. It talks about automatic interpretation and generation of natural language. As the technology evolved, different approaches have come to deal with NLP tasks.

(i) **Heuristics-Based NLP:** This is the initial approach of NLP. It is based on defined rules. Which comes from domain knowledge and expertise. **Example:** regex

(ii) **Statistical Machine Learning-based NLP:** It is based on statistical rules and machine learning algorithms. In this approach, algorithms are applied to the data and learned from the data, and applied to various tasks. **Examples:** Naive Bayes, support vector machine (SVM), hidden Markov model (HMM), etc.

(iii) Neural Network-based NLP: This is the latest approach that comes with the evaluation of neural network-based learning, known as **Deep learning**. It provides good accuracy, but it is a highly data-hungry and time-consuming approach. It requires high computational power to train the model. Furthermore, it is based on neural network architecture. **Examples:** Recurrent Neural Networks (RNNs), Long Short-term Memory networks (LSTMs), Convolutional neural networks (CNNs), Transformers, etc.

10.4   Challenges of NLP

NLP models are not perfect and probably never will be, just as human speech is prone to error.

Risks might include:

(i)   **Biased training:** As with any AI function, biased data used in training will skew the answers. The more diverse the users of an NLP function, the more significant this risk becomes, such as in government services, healthcare and HR interactions. Training datasets scraped from the web, for example, are prone to bias.

(ii) **Misinterpretation:** As in programming, there is a risk of garbage in, garbage out (GIGO). NLP solutions might become confused if spoken input is in an obscure dialect, mumbled, too full of slang, homonyms, incorrect grammar, idioms, fragments, mispronunciations, contractions or recorded with too much background noise.

(iii) **New vocabulary:** New words are continually being invented or imported. The conventions of grammar can evolve or be intentionally broken. In these cases, NLP can either make a best guess or admit it's unsure—and either way, this creates a complication.

(iv) **Tone of voice:** When people speak, their verbal delivery or even body language can give an entirely different meaning than the words alone. Exaggeration for effect, stressing words for importance or sarcasm can be confused by NLP, making the semantic analysis more difficult and less reliable.

Human language is filled with many ambiguities that make it difficult for programmers to write software that accurately determines the intended meaning of text or voice data. Human language might take years for humans to learn—and many never stop learning. But then programmers must teach natural language-driven applications to recognize and understand irregularities so their applications can be accurate and useful.

10.5   How NLP works?

NLP combines the power of computational linguistics together with machine learning algorithms and deep learning. Computational linguistics is a discipline of linguistics that uses data science to analyze language and speech. It includes two main types of analysis: **syntactical analysis and semantic analysis.** Syntactical analysis determines the meaning of a word, phrase or sentence by parsing the syntax of the words and applying preprogrammed rules of grammar. Semantical analysis uses the syntactic output to draw meaning from the words and interpret their meaning within the sentence structure.

The parsing of words can take one of two forms. *Dependency parsing* looks at the relationships between words, such as identifying nouns and verbs, while *constituency parsing* then builds a parse tree (or syntax tree): a rooted and ordered representation of the syntactic structure of the sentence or string of words. The resulting parse trees underly the functions of language translators and speech recognition. Ideally, this analysis makes the output—either text or speech—understandable to both NLP models and people.

Self-supervised learning (SSL), in particular, is useful for supporting NLP because NLP requires large amounts of labeled data to train state-of-the-art artificial intelligence (AI) models. Because these labeled datasets require time-consuming annotation—a process involving manual labeling by humans—gathering sufficient data can be prohibitively difficult. Self-supervised approaches can be more time-effective and cost-effective, as they replace some or all manually labeled training data.

10.5.1   Three different approaches to NLP include:

(i) Rules-based NLP: The earliest NLP applications were simple if-then decision trees, requiring preprogrammed rules. They are only able to provide answers in response to specific prompts, such as the original version of Moviefone. Because there is no machine learning or AI capability in rules-based NLP, this function is highly limited and not scalable.

(ii) Statistical NLP: Developed later, statistical NLP automatically extracts, classifies and labels elements of text and voice data, and then assigns a statistical likelihood to each possible meaning of those elements. This relies on machine learning, enabling a sophisticated breakdown of linguistics such as part-of-speech tagging. Statistical NLP introduced the essential technique of mapping language elements—such as words and grammatical rules—to a vector representation so that language can be modeled by using mathematical (statistical) methods, including regression or Markov models. This informed early NLP developments such as spellcheckers and T9 texting (Text on 9 keys, to be used on Touch-Tone telephones).

(iii) Deep learning NLP: Recently, deep learning models have become the dominant mode of NLP, by using huge volumes of raw, unstructured data—both text and voice—to become ever more accurate. Deep learning can be viewed as a further evolution of statistical NLP, with the difference that it uses neural network models.

There are several subcategories of models:

• *Sequence-to-Sequence (seq2seq) models*: Based on recurrent neural networks (RNN), they have mostly been used for machine translation by converting a phrase from one domain (such as the German language) into the phrase of another domain (such as English).

- ***Transformer models***: They use tokenization of language (the position of each token—words or sub-words) and self-attention (capturing dependencies and relationships) to calculate the relation of different language parts to one another. Transformer models can be efficiently trained by using self-supervised learning on massive text databases. A landmark in transformer models was Google's bidirectional encoder representations from transformers (BERT), which became and remains the basis of how Google's search engine works.

- ***Autoregressive models***: This type of transformer model is trained specifically to predict the next word in a sequence, which represents a huge leap forward in the ability to generate text. Examples of autoregressive LLMs. include GPT, Llama, Claude and the open-source Mistral.

- ***Foundation models***: Pre-built and curated foundation models can speed the launching of an NLP effort and boost trust in its operation. For example, the IBM Granite™ foundation models are widely applicable across industries. They support NLP tasks including content generation and insight extraction. Additionally, they facilitate retrieval-augmented generation, a framework for improving the quality of response by linking the model to external sources of knowledge. The models also perform named entity recognition which involves identifying and extracting key information in a text.

10.6   NLP Tasks

Several NLP tasks typically help process human text and voice data in ways that help the computer make sense of what it's ingesting. Some of these tasks include:

10.6.1 Linguistic Tasks

- **Coreference resolution** is the task of identifying if and when two words refer to the same entity. The most common example is determining the person or object to which a certain pronoun refers (such as, "she" = "Mary"). But it can also identify a metaphor or an idiom in the text (such as an instance in which "bear" isn't an animal, but a large and hairy person).

- **Named Entity Recognition** (NER) identifies words or phrases as useful entities. NER identifies "London" as a location or "Maria" as a person's name.

- **Part-of-speech Tagging**, also called grammatical tagging, is the process of determining which part of speech a word or piece of text is, based on its use and context. For example, part-of-speech identifies "make" as a verb in "I can make a paper plane," and as a noun in "What make of car do you own?"

- **Word sense disambiguation** is the selection of a word meaning for a word with multiple possible meanings. This uses a process of semantic analysis to examine the word in context. For example, word sense disambiguation helps distinguish the meaning of the verb "make" in "make the grade" (to achieve) versus "make a bet" (to place). Sorting out "I will be merry when I marry Mary" requires a sophisticated NLP system.

10.6.2 User-supporting Tasks

- **Speech recognition**, also known as speech-to-text, is the task of reliably converting voice data into text data. Speech recognition is part of any application that follows voice commands or answers spoken questions. What makes speech recognition especially challenging is the way people speak—quickly, running words together, with varying emphasis and intonation.

- **Natural language generation (NLG)** might be described as the opposite of speech recognition or speech-to-text: NLG is the task of putting structured information into conversational human language. Without NLG, computers would have little chance of passing the Turing test, where a computer tries to mimic a human conversation. Conversational agents such as Amazon's Alexa and Apple's Siri are already doing this well and assisting customers in real time.

- **Natural language understanding (NLU)** is a subset of NLP that focuses on analyzing the meaning behind sentences. NLU enables software to find similar meanings in different sentences or to process words that have different meanings.

- **Sentiment analysis** attempts to extract subjective qualities—attitudes, emotions, sarcasm, confusion or suspicion—from text. This is often used for routing communications to the system or the person most likely to make the next response.

10.7   Components of NLP

There are two components of Natural Language Processing:

- Natural Language Understanding

- Natural Language Generation

10.8   Applications of NLP

- Text and speech processing like-Voice assistants – **Alexa, Siri,** etc.

- Text classification like Grammarly, Microsoft Word, and Google Docs.

- Information extraction like-Search engines like DuckDuckGo, Google.

- Chatbot and Question Answering like:- website bots

- Language Translation like:- Google Translate

- Text summarization

10.9   NLP-Use Cases across Businesses

Organizations can use NLP to process communications that include email, SMS, audio, video, newsfeeds and social media. NLP is the driving force behind AI in many modern real-world applications.

Here are a few examples:

- **Customer assistance**:

Enterprises can deploy chatbots or virtual assistants to quickly respond to custom questions and requests. When questions become too difficult for the chatbot or virtual assistant, the NLP system moves the customer over to a human customer service agent. Virtual agents such as IBM watsonx™ Assistant, Apple's Siri and Amazon's Alexa use speech recognition to recognize patterns in voice commands and natural language generation to respond with appropriate actions or helpful comments. Chatbots respond to typed text entries. The best chatbots also learn to recognize contextual clues about human requests and use them to provide even better responses or options over time.

The next enhancement for these applications is question answering, the ability to respond to questions—anticipated or not—with relevant and helpful answers in their own words. These automations help reduce costs, save agents from spending time on redundant queries and improve customer satisfaction.

- Not all chatbots are powered by AI, but state-of-the-art chatbots increasingly use conversational AI techniques, including NLP, to understand user questions and automate responses to them.

FAQ:

- Not everyone wants to read to discover an answer. Fortunately, NLP can enhance FAQs: When the user asks a question, the NLP function looks for the best match among the available answers and brings that to the user's screen. Many customer questions are of the who/what/when/where variety, so this function can save staff from having to repeatedly answer the same routine questions.

Grammar correction:

- The rules of grammar can be applied within word processing or other programs, where the NLP function is trained to spot incorrect grammar and suggest corrected wordings.

Machine translation:

Google Translate is an example of widely available NLP technology at work. Truly useful machine translation involves more than replacing words from one language with words of another. Effective translation accurately captures the meaning and tone of the input language and translates it to text with the same meaning and desired impact in the output language. Machine translation tools are becoming more accurate. One way to test a machine translation tool is to translate text from one language and then back to the original. An oft-cited, classic example: Translating "*The spirit is willing, but the flesh is weak*" from English to Russian and back again once yielded, "*The vodka is good, but the meat is rotten.*" Recently, a closer result was "*The spirit desires, but the flesh is weak.*" Google translate can now take English to Russian to English and return the original, "*The spirit is willing, but the flesh is weak.*"

- **Redaction of personally identifiable information (PII)**:

NLP models can be trained to quickly locate personal information in documents that might identify individuals. Industries that handle large volumes of sensitive information—financial, healthcare, insurance and legal firms—can quickly create versions with the PII removed.

- **Sentiment analysis**:

After being trained on industry-specific or business-specific language, an NLP model can quickly scan incoming text for keywords and phrases to gauge a customer's mood in real-time as positive, neutral or negative. The mood of the incoming communication can help determine how it will be handled. And the incoming communication doesn't have to be live: NLP can also be used to analyze customer feedback or call center recordings.

Another option is an NLP API that can enable after-the-fact text analytics. NLP can uncover actionable data insights from social media posts, responses or reviews to extract attitudes and emotions in response to products, promotions and events. Information companies can use sentiment analysis in product designs, advertising campaigns and more.

- **Spam detection:**

Many people might not think of spam detection as an NLP solution, but the best spam detection technologies use NLP's text classification capabilities to scan emails for language indicating spam or phishing. These indicators can include overuse of financial terms, characteristic bad grammar, threatening language, inappropriate urgency or misspelled company names.

- **Text generation:**

NLP helps put the "generative" into generative AI. NLP enables computers to generate text or speech that is natural-sounding and realistic enough to be mistaken for human communication. The generated language might be used to create initial drafts of blogs, computer code, letters, memos or tweets. With an enterprise-grade system, the quality of generated language might be sufficient to be used in real time for autocomplete functions, chatbots or virtual assistants.

Advancements in NLP are powering the reasoning engine behind generative AI systems, driving further opportunities. Microsoft® Copilot is an AI assistant designed to boost employee productivity and creativity across day-to-day tasks and is already at work in tools used every day.

Text summarization uses NLP techniques to digest huge volumes of digital text and create summaries and synopses for indexes, research databases, for busy readers who don›t have time to read the full text. The best text summarization applications use semantic reasoning and natural language generation (NLG) to add useful context and conclusions to summaries.

10.10   NLP-use cases by Industry

- **Finance**:

In financial dealings, nanoseconds might make the difference between success and failure when accessing data, or making trades or deals. NLP can speed the mining of information from financial statements, annual and regulatory reports, news releases or even social media.

- **Healthcare**:

New medical insights and breakthroughs can arrive faster than many healthcare professionals can keep up. NLP and AI-based tools can help speed the analysis of health records and medical research papers, making better-informed medical decisions possible, or assisting in the detection or even prevention of medical conditions.

- **Insurance**:

NLP can analyze claims to look for patterns that can identify areas of concern and find inefficiencies in claims processing—leading to greater optimization of processing and employee efforts.

- **Legal**:

Almost any legal case might require reviewing mounds of paperwork, background information and legal precedent. NLP can help automate legal discovery, assisting in the organization of information, speeding review and helping ensure that all relevant details are captured for consideration.

CHAPTER 11

WEAK (NARROW) ARTIFICIAL INTELLIGENCE

Whenever the term artificial intelligence (AI) is used today, in most cases, it refers to the weak AI. Also known as narrow AI, this is the only AI that exists today. Although the weak AI can solve complex problems and often complete tasks more efficiently than humans, its functionality is limited to its programming. Even with a name that suggests limitation, weak AI infiltrates many aspects of our work, personal lives, and entertainment.

11.1   What is Weak (Narrow) AI?

Algorithms that power weak AI model human intelligence and work to accomplish specific tasks rather than possess full cognitive abilities like the human brain. Ultimately, the algorithms are trained to classify data based on how they were trained. There is no veering off the programmed path; narrow AI is programmed to operate within a set of pre-defined functions. For example, machines created to pick items in a warehouse aren't able to flip burgers in a restaurant without human intervention to change the programming. Narrow AI models' intelligent behavior can accomplish such specific tasks.

Artificial narrow intelligence (ANI) is defined as the goal-oriented version of AI designed to better perform a single task such as tracking weather updates, generating data science reports by analyzing raw data, or playing games such as poker, chess, etc.

Narrow artificial intelligence is the technology that exists today, and you experience in daily life. The algorithms that power narrow artificial intelligence allow machines to act, process data, and make decisions based on programming. This is not AI with a mind of its own. Weak or narrow AI, despite the implication by its name that it's not powerful, is actually responsible for many amazing activities. AI allows many things to be done much more quickly and efficiently than humans can.

Narrow AI's machine intelligence is basically achieved through the concept of Natural Language Processing (NLP). NLP concept is the common functionality in chatbots and similar AI domains in which the machines are basically programmed in a way to interact with humans using speech and text recognition mechanism.

Weak AI or Narrow AI lacks human-like consciousness, although it may be able to simulate it several times. One of the classic illustrations to understand weak AI is John Searle's Chinese room thought experiment. According to this experiment, someone outside a room can converse in Chinese with someone inside a room who is receiving instructions on communicating in Chinese.

In this experiment, a person who's inside the room would appear speaking Chinese, but in reality, they don't know or understand a word of Chinese just because they were instructed to follow instructions, not really speak in Chinese. They reflect to have strong AI – machine intelligence equivalent to human intelligence – but only weak AI.

Narrow or Weak AI do not have general intelligence; they have limited or specific intelligence. A weak AI system will be better at one task but fail at another. In the same way, a form of AI that can pretend to converse in Chinese cannot confirm they will sweep your floor.

11.2   Different Types of Narrow AI

Narrow AI has two possibilities, either it can be reactive or can have a limited amount of memory.

(i)   Reactive AI:

It is the basic version, having no memory or data storage capabilities. It emulates the human mind's behavior and responds to different interpretations without any prior experience.

(ii) Limited Memory AI:

It is more advanced, having great memory and data storage capabilities enabling machines to interpret precisely using statistical data. Most of the AI is the Limited Memory AI, enabling machines to use a large amount of data especially in the domains of Deep Learning to give results with utmost accuracy.

11.3 Some Practical Examples of Weak/Narrow AI

Here are some practical examples of Weak/Narrow AI:

(i) Digital voice assistants (Siri, Alexa)

Often referred to as the best examples of weak AI, digital voice assistants such as Siri and Alexa are examples of weak AI that we rely on every day. To work effectively, the AI classifies data and responds to queries at incredibly fast speed.

(ii) Recommendation engines

Whether Netflix is telling you what movie you should watch next or Amazon or other retail websites offer you helpful advice about what you else you might be interested in purchasing, these recommendation engines are examples of narrow AI.

(iii) Search engines

Google and other search engines are also examples of weak AI. When you type in your question, the algorithm gets to work to run that question through its vast database to classify it and come back with answers.

(iv) Chatbots

If you've ever talked on chat with an organization, whether it's your financial institution, internet service provider, or favorite e-commerce store, you were likely talking to AI. Most of the time, chat features are an AI algorithm that takes care of answering common questions to free the humans who used to do this work to complete higher-level tasks.

(v) Autonomous vehicles

AI that allows vehicles to operate without a human driver is weak AI. The algorithms complete programmed functions. The challenge, since this AI doesn't possess full cognitive abilities like a human brain, is to program and train the AI regarding any potential road hazard or situation the vehicle might encounter.

(vi) Image and speech recognition

A critical way narrow AI is making an impact in healthcare is through image recognition by helping radiologists detect disease in scans of patients. Weak AI is behind image recognition in other industries as well. It's also in play with speech recognition and translation services like Google Translate.

(vii) Predictive maintenance and analytics

Narrow AI is used in predictive analytics. It uses data, algorithms, and machine learning to examine historical data to construct a prediction of a likely outcome in the future. In warehouses and other places where heavy machinery is in use, AI helps identify maintenance issues that need to be addressed before a machine failure.

(viii) Robots

Currently, robots don't have a mind of their own. Drones and manufacturing robots operate with narrow AI and are able to complete a finite set of actions they were programmed to do. Delivery bots were quite useful to comply with social distancing orders and as disinfecting robots during the pandemic.

(ix) Diagnostics and Medications

Used in medications and prediction tools to diagnose cancer and other health-related issues with extreme accuracy through human behavior cognition, replication, and reasoning.

(x) IBM's Watson

It is capable of answering questions asked in natural language interpretations.

(xi) Rankbrain

It is an algorithm used by Google to sort the search results.

(xii) Social Media

Social Media Marketing tools for keeping a check on violating contents and Email spam filters.

(xiii) Image and Facial Recognition Systems

These systems are used by Meta and Google to identify people in photographs and pictures are examples of weak AI.

(xiv) Online Gaming

Computer-generated players or non-player characters (NPCs) similar to human-like intelligence in online video gaming are quite a few examples of weak AI.

(xv) Apple Autocorrect

This keyboard dictionary spellchecks words while you're typing, correcting misspelled words for you automatically.

(xvi) Deep Blue

Deep Blue is the first and the most famous example of weak AI. Created by IBM, 'Deep Blue' beat world chess champion Gary Kasparov in a six-game match in 1997. Here, Deep Blue managed to choose from hundreds of millions of moves to "see" 20 moves ahead of its opponent. This was a feat no human to-date has been able to achieve.

11.4 Advantages of Weak AI

Weak AI has a number of advantages in the technology field. Some of the best examples are:

- **Faster and Accurate Decision Making**

Improved decision-making by processing data and performing tasks more quickly and better than humans. They enhanced total production and efficiency, which in turn raised the usual standard of living.

- **Perform Mundane Tasks**

Weak AI is well-proficient in performing several tedious, repetitive, and everyday tasks that humans can do usually. They have streamlined daily tasks and lowered the energy consumption to process large amounts of data to produce solutions.

- **Forecast Results**

Weak AI systems can do forecasting analyses based on received inputs. This AI foresees revenue projections in case there is a failure of the supply chain and manages the purchase of expensive materials.

11.5 Drawbacks / Limitations of Narrow AI

Weak AI has limitations because of its limited capabilities which add to the prospect of causing harm if a system fails. If we take into account an example of a driverless car that calculates the location of oncoming vehicles but somehow it miscalculates the location which causes a deadly collision or a system failure if it is used by some third party or destructive organizations, then it can lead to enormous destructions to the human mankind. Another drawback is to determine the faulty identity for a malfunction or a design flaw.

A further concern is regarding the huge loss of jobs caused by the automatic functionality and performance of an increasing number of tasks. Slowly the machines are taking over human manpower for intelligent automation through AI. So it must be thought-provoking that whether there will be an increase in the job opportunities or the machines will gradually take over the entire physical manpower with the emerging levels of AI.

Unlike general AI, narrow AI lacks self-awareness, consciousness, emotions, and genuine intelligence that can match human intelligence. While such systems may appear sophisticated and intelligent, they operate under a predetermined and predefined set of parameters, constraints, and contexts.

The machine intelligence that surrounds us today is a part of the same narrow AI. Examples include Google Assistant, **Siri**, Google Translate, and other natural language processing tools. Although these tools can interact with us and process and comprehend human language, they are termed as weak AI as they lack the fluidity or flexibility to think for themselves as humans do.

Let's consider **Siri**. It is not a conscious machine. Instead, it is only a tool performing tasks. When we converse with Siri, it processes the human language, enters it into the system's search engine like Google, and provides results.

When someone poses abstract questions such as how to handle a personal problem or deal with a traumatic experience to tools like **Alexa** or Google Assistant, they either give vague responses that lack sense or provide links to articles on the internet that presumably address the issue at hand.

On the contrary, when we ask a fundamental question such as "what is the temperature outside", we tend to get an accurate response from virtual assistants such as Siri. This is because answering such basic questions is within the range of Siri's intelligence for which it is designed.

Moreover, even something as complex as self-driving cars falls under weak AI, as they are trained to navigate the surrounding area with the help of an annotated driving dataset. A typical self-driving vehicle comprises multiple ANI systems that are critical for its smooth movement in a highly complex urban environment.

11.6   Challenges of Narrow AI

(i) Absence of explainable AI

One of the essential requirements for the progress of artificial intelligence is the practice of creating AI that is less of a black box. This implies that we must be better positioned to understand what's happening in neural networks. Today's AI systems, such as one recommending books to read, employ the black-box approach effectively. The deep learning algorithm used in such cases considers millions of data points as inputs and correlates specific features to provide a result. The underlying process is self-directed and challenging for programmers and experts in the domain to interpret.

However, when people are making high-stake business decisions that involve huge investments by relying on AI models, such a black-box approach can be detrimental as the inputs and operations of the system are not visible to the concerned parties. Thus, one of the key challenges is creating more explainable AI devoid of the black-box approach.

(ii) Need for impenetrable security

Neural networks are exploited extensively by narrow AI. However, it is vital to understand that AI is quite fragile– it is possible to inject noise and fool the system. For example, an attacker can hack into the software system of autonomous cars and change the AI program code so that the program may mistake a bus on the road for an elephant. This can have serious implications and ramifications. A hacker can also hijack the entire network of autonomous vehicles operating in an area and eventually wipe out a billion-dollar investment.

Moreover, a single intrusion into a neural network can disrupt the operations of several systems reliant on that same network. Additionally, as neural networks are subject to attacks, providing impenetrable security remains a crucial challenge.

(iii) Need to learn from small data

AI models are trained on data derived from examples–implying that examples are the real currency to today's AI. For AI to evolve further, it must be prepared to learn more from less data. AI should be able to transfer its learning from one neural network to other networks by leveraging prior knowledge.

AI blends learning and reasoning. Although today's AI has made significant progress in learning and accumulating knowledge, applying reason to that knowledge remains a challenge. For example, a retailer's customer service chatbot could answer questions related to store hours, product prices, and the store's cancellation policies.

However, a tricky question about why product X is better than a similar product Y may freeze the bot. Although creators can program bots to answer such questions, teaching an AI to apply reasoning by itself remains a problem for most scientists and experts.

(iv) Prone to bias

Today's AI systems are prone to bias as they often give incorrect results without a plausible explanation. Complex AI models are continually trained on vast amounts of data that contain biases or inaccurate information. As a result, a model trained on such a biased dataset could consider the incorrect information trustworthy and make skewed predictions.

As AI systems learn from past examples, consider a system responsible for making credit decisions. The system might consider 'not offering credit to women or minorities' as appropriate based on previous patterns. Thus, verifying and inspecting that the examples used by the system are free of biases remains a critical challenge.

Moreover, as narrow AI lacks the 'common sense' aspect, or a sense of fairness and equity, handling training bias requires substantial planning and design work.

(v) Subject to human failings

Narrow AI largely relies on humans to put to task. Hence, it is prone to human failings, such as people setting overly ambitious business targets or prioritizing tasks incorrectly.

Consider a situation where a human wrongly defines a task. In this case, irrespective of how long a machine works or the number of computations it performs, the end result will still be a false conclusion. Therefore, narrow AI's reliance on fallible humans is a huge challenge for experts in the domain.

11.7   Best Practices for Narrow AI Development

(i) Have a human-centric design approach

The true impact of an AI system's predictions, recommendations, and decisions can be evaluated by factoring in how actual end-users experience the system.

The following routines can be considered to keep a check on your narrow AI development:

- **Use augmentation and assistance** as needed. While addressing several users, AI systems can consider producing a single answer in situations where the solution is highly likely to satisfy a diverse set of users and use cases. It may be appropriate to suggest a few options to end-users in other cases.

- Before diving into full deployment, potential adverse **feedback can be incorporated** into the design process. This can be followed by live testing and iteration for smaller traffic.

- **Involve a diverse set of users** and consider multiple use-case scenarios that allow you to incorporate feedback throughout the project development cycle. Such practice considers a variety of user perspectives while building an AI project, thereby increasing the number of people who can benefit from the technology.

(ii) Consider metrics to assess training and monitoring

To understand the tradeoffs between several errors and user experiences of the AI system, one should consider several essential metrics rather than opting for a single one.

- The metrics can include feedback from user surveys, variables that track overall system performance, factors that keep a check on short- and long-term product health such as users' click-through rate, and quantities that monitor false positive and false negative rates across different categories of the AI product.

- One must **ensure that the metrics selected are based on the context and goals** of the AI system. For example, a fire alarm system should have high recall values, irrespective of whether the system returns occasional false alarms.

(iii) Ensure periodic examination of raw data

Analyzing raw data can help you better understand the working of ML models as they reflect the data that they are trained on. In cases where sensitive raw data is concerned, you can instead focus on understanding the input data while respecting privacy.

- By **examining raw data**, you can ascertain whether the data contains any missing values or incorrect labels. You can figure out whether the information is sampled in a manner that represents all the users (i.e., users of all ages) of your AI system.

- Determining performance during training and serving is a persistent challenge. Thus, during the training phase, you should **look for possible skews** and address them immediately, including adjusting the training data or restructuring the objective function.

- Data **bias should be addressed** by thoroughly analyzing the raw data going into the AI system.

(iv) Consider the limitations of the AI dataset and model

Understanding the limitations of the dataset and AI model is vital to keep track of the loopholes of narrow AI.

- **A correlation detecting AI model should not be used to make inferences.** For example, your AI model may learn that people who buy running shoes are mostly overweight. However, this does not mean that a user who buys a pair of running shoes will become overweight.

- ML models predominantly work on training data. Hence, it is important to **clarify the scope and coverage of training**. For example, a chair detector trained with stock photos will work fine. However, the model might falter when tested with cellphone photos clicked by users.

- **Limitations should be communicated to end-users.** For example, if your app uses ML to recognize specific butterflies, you must communicate that the model was trained on a small set of images taken from a particular region. By informing users, you would increase your chances of receiving better feedback for the feature or application you provided.

(v) Ensure the AI system works as intended by performing tests

To ensure that the designed AI system works as intended and can be trusted, you must undertake quality test practices.

- **Unit tests** should be conducted to test each component of the AI system in isolation.

- Conducting **integration tests** will enable you to learn how individual ML components interact with other system components.

- Conduct **iterative user tests** to incorporate users' needs in the AI product development cycles.

- Build **quality checks** into the system to avoid triggering an immediate response in situations of unintended system failures. For example, if an important feature unexpectedly goes down for a predictive AI model, the AI system may refrain from generating an output prediction.

(vi) Regularly monitor and update the AI system post-deployment

Regular monitoring will ensure that the AI model considers real-world performances and incorporates user feedback to update the AI system.

- The AI product should have a **clear roadmap** that allows it to buy time to address and fix any issues.

- Fixing issues for both the short and long term is crucial for AI systems. A short-term fix of blocklisting may offer a quick solution; however, it might not fare well in the long run. Hence, **balancing short- and long-term fixes** can be better than focusing on just one.

- Understanding how the update may affect the overall system quality and user experience is essential. Hence, before jumping into the updates, you must analyze and **understand the difference between the candidate and deployed models.**

(vii) Ensure fairness

Today, AI systems are used across industry sectors to perform critical tasks such as predicting the severity of a medical condition and matching profiles to jobs or marriage partners. The risk here is that any unfairness in such computerized decision-making systems can have a wide-scale impact. Hence, as AI penetrates across societies, it is crucial to design a fair and inclusive model for all.

- **Analyze** how the technology will impact different users and use cases over time.

- **Define goals** that allow your AI system to work somewhat for diverse use cases. This can include designing certain features delivered in 'A' different languages or specific to 'B' other age groups.

- **Structure the objective function** and underlying algorithms that reflect the fairness goals of the AI system.

- **Monitor the system** regularly to check unfair biases learned by the ML models or algorithms over time.

- **Evaluate user experiences** across use cases, contexts, and real-world scenarios using

  TensorFlow Model Analysis tools.

(viii) Consider interpretability

Narrow AI systems have improved our lives as automated predictions and decision-making has become mainstream. This may relate to several examples, from music recommendations to monitoring a patient's vital signs. Despite the proliferation of narrow AI across fields, interpretability is crucial to understand and trust AI systems. The following interpretability practices before, during, and after designing and training AI models can be considered.

- The AI team should **work closely with relevant domain experts** (e.g., healthcare, marketing, finance) to determine the required interpretability features.

- **Identify post-training interpretability options.** Also, determine if you have access to the internals of ML models (i.e., black-box or white-box).

- **Determine whether you can analyze the training or testing data.** For example, when working with sensitive and private data, you may not have access to the input data essential for investigation.

- **Evaluate if your AI model offers too much transparency**, which can potentially open up vectors for external abuse.

- **Provide explanations regarding the interpretability** of AI systems to appropriate model users; technical details may be communicated to industry experts and academia, while general users can be offered visualizations (charts, graphs, and statistics) or summary descriptions.

(ix) Ensure privacy

ML models are programmed to learn from training data and make subsequent predictions on input data. In some cases, both training and input data can be sensitive. Take the example of a tumor detector trained on biopsy images and deployed on an individual patient's tumor scans. Here, it is crucial to consider the privacy implications while handling sensitive data. It may include legal and regulatory requirements, social ethics, and the patient's expectations.

- Conduct tests using metrics such as **exposure measurement or membership inference assessment** to determine whether the AI model unintentionally memorizes or exposes sensitive data. Moreover, the metrics can also be used for regression tests later during model maintenance.

- To understand the tradeoffs and **determine the optimal model settings**, experimentation with variables and parameters for data minimization (such as aggregation, outlier thresholds, and randomization factors) may be considered.

(x) Provide security

Security of AI systems involves determining whether the system is behaving as intended, irrespective of how attackers try to interfere. Addressing the security of an AI system before entirely relying on it is essential for safety-critical applications.

- **Identify all possible attack vectors** by building a rigorous threat model. For example, the threat model should be able to identify a bug in the AI system that allows an attacker to change the input to the ML model, which can make it vulnerable.

- If the system makes a mistake, you need to **identify unintended consequences** and assess the likelihood and severity of these consequences.

- **Develop methods such as spam filtering** to combat adversarial ML. Also, test the system performance in hostile settings using tools such as CleverHans.

CHAPTER 12

ARTIFICIAL GENERAL INTELLIGENCE (AGI)

12.1   What is Artificial General Intelligence?

Artificial general intelligence (AGI) is a field of theoretical AI research that attempts to create software with human-like intelligence and the ability to self-teach. The aim is for the software to be able to perform tasks that it is not necessarily trained or developed for.

Artificial general intelligence (AGI) is a type of artificial intelligence (AI) that matches or surpasses human capabilities across a wide range of cognitive tasks. This is in contrast to narrow AI, which is designed for specific tasks. AGI is considered one of various definitions of strong AI.

Creating AGI is a primary goal of AI research and of companies such as OpenAI and Meta. A 2020-survey identified 72 active AGI R&D projects spread across 37 countries.

Current artificial intelligence (AI) technologies all function within a set of pre-determined parameters. For example, AI models trained in image recognition and generation cannot build websites. AGI is a theoretical pursuit to develop AI systems that possess autonomous self-control, a reasonable degree of self-understanding, and the ability to learn new skills. It can solve complex problems in settings and contexts that were not taught to it at the time of its creation. AGI, with human abilities, remains a theoretical concept and a research goal.

12.2 What is the difference between artificial intelligence and artificial general intelligence?

Over the decades, AI researchers have charted several milestones that significantly advanced machine intelligence—even to degrees that mimic human intelligence in specific tasks. For example, AI summarizers use of machine learning (ML) models to extract important points from documents and generate an understandable summary. AI is thus a computer science discipline that enables software to solve novel and difficult tasks with human-level performance.

In contrast, an AGI system can solve problems in various domains, like a human being, without manual intervention. Instead of being limited to a specific scope, AGI can self-teach and solve problems it was never trained for. AGI is thus a theoretical representation of a complete artificial intelligence that solves complex tasks with generalized human cognitive abilities.

Some computer scientists believe that AGI is a hypothetical computer program with human comprehension and cognitive capabilities. AI systems can learn to handle unfamiliar tasks without additional training in such theories. Alternately, AI systems that we use today require substantial training before they can handle related tasks within the same domain. For example, you must fine-tune a pre-trained large language model (LLM) with medical datasets before it can operate consistently as a medical chatbot.

The timeline for achieving AGI remains a subject of ongoing debate among researchers and experts. As of 2023, some argue that it may be possible in years or decades; others maintain it might take a century or longer; and a minority believe it may never be achieved. There is a debate on the exact definition of AGI, and regarding whether modern large language models (LLMs) such as GPT-4 are early, incomplete forms of AGI. AGI is a common topic in science fiction and futures studies.

AGI is also known as strong AI, full AI, human-level AI or general intelligent action. However, some academic sources reserve the term "strong AI" for computer programs that experience sentience or consciousness. In contrast, weak AI (or narrow AI) is able to solve one specific problem, but lacks general cognitive abilities. Some academic sources use "weak AI" to refer more broadly to any programs that neither experience consciousness nor have a mind in the same sense as humans.

Contention exists over the potential for AGI to pose a threat to humanity; for example, OpenAI claims to treat it as an existential risk, while others find the development of AGI to be too remote to present a risk.

12.3　Strong AI compared with weak AI

Strong AI is full artificial intelligence, **or AGI**, capable of performing tasks with human cognitive levels despite having little background knowledge. Science fiction often depicts strong AI as a thinking machine with human comprehension not confined to domain limitations.

In contrast, weak AI or narrow AI are AI systems limited to computing specifications, algorithms, and specific tasks they are designed for. For example, previous AI models have limited memories and only rely on real-time data to make decisions. Even emerging generative AI applications with better memory retention are considered weak AI because they cannot be repurposed for other domains.

A framework for classifying AGI in levels was proposed in 2023 by Google DeepMind researchers. They define **five levels of AGI**: (i) emerging, (ii) competent, (iii) expert, (iv) virtuoso, and (v) superhuman. For example, a competent AGI is defined as an AI that outperforms 50% of skilled adults in a wide range of non-physical tasks. They consider that large language models like ChatGPT or LLaMA-2 were instances or emerging AGI.

12.4 What are the Theoretical Approaches to Artificial General Intelligence Research?

Achieving AGI requires a broader spectrum of technologies, data, and interconnectivity than what powers AI models today. Creativity, perception, learning, and memory are essential to create AI that mimics complex human behavior. AI experts have proposed several methods to drive AGI research.

(i) Symbolic

The symbolic approach assumes that computer systems can develop AGI by representing human thoughts with expanding logic networks. The logic network symbolizes physical objects with an if-else logic, allowing the AI system to interpret ideas at a higher thinking level. However, symbolic representation cannot replicate subtle cognitive abilities at the lower level, such as perception.

(ii) Connectionist

The connectionist (or emergentist) approach focuses on replicating the human brain structure with neural-network architecture. Brain neurons can alter their transmission paths as humans interact with external stimuli. Scientists hope AI models adopting this sub-symbolic approach can replicate human-like intelligence and demonstrate low-level cognitive capabilities. Large language models (LLM) are an example of AI that uses the connectionist method to understand natural languages.

(iii) Universalists

Researchers taking the universalist approach focus on addressing the AGI complexities at the calculation level. They attempt to formulate theoretical solutions that they can repurpose into practical AGI systems.

(iv) Whole organism architecture

The whole organism architecture approach involves integrating AI models with a physical representation of the human body. Scientists supporting this theory believe AGI is only achievable when the system learns from physical interactions.

(v) Hybrid

The hybrid approach studies symbolic and sub-symbolic methods of representing human thoughts to achieve results beyond a single approach. AI researchers may attempt to assimilate different known principles and methods to develop AGI.

12.5 What are the Technologies driving the Artificial General Intelligence Research?

AGI remains a distant goal for researchers. Efforts to build AGI systems are ongoing and encouraged by emerging developments. The following sections describe emerging technologies.

(i) Deep learning

Deep learning is an AI discipline that focuses on training neural networks with multiple hidden layers to extract and understand complex relationships from raw data. AI experts use deep learning to build systems capable of understanding text, audio, images, video, and other information types. For example, developers use Amazon SageMaker to build lightweight deep learning models for the Internet of Things (IoT) and mobile devices.

(ii) Generative AI

Generative artificial intelligence (generative AI) is a subset of deep learning wherein an AI system can produce unique and realistic content from the learnt knowledge. Generative AI models train with massive datasets, which enable them to respond to human queries with text, audio, or visuals that naturally resemble human creations. For example, LLMs. from AI21 Labs, Anthropic, Cohere, and Meta are generative AI algorithms that organizations can use to solve complex tasks. Software teams use Amazon Bedrock to deploy these models quickly on the cloud without provisioning servers.

(iii) NLP

Natural language processing (NLP) is a branch of AI that allows computer systems to understand and generate human language. NLP systems use computational linguistics and machine learning technologies to turn language data into simple representations called tokens and understand their contextual relationship. For example, **Amazon Lex** is an NLP engine that allows organizations to build conversational chatbots.

(iv) Computer vision

Computer vision is a technology that allows systems to extract, analyze, and comprehend spatial information from visual data. **Self-driving cars** use computer vision models to analyze real-time feeds from cameras and navigate the vehicle safely away from obstacles. Deep learning technologies allow computer vision systems to automate large-scale object recognition, classification, monitoring, and other image-processing tasks. For example, engineers use Amazon **Rekognition** to automate image analysis for various computer vision applications.

(v) Robotics

Robotics is an engineering discipline wherein organizations can build mechanical systems that automatically perform physical maneuvers. In AGI, robotics systems allow machine intelligence to manifest physically. It is pivotal for introducing the sensory perception and physical manipulation capabilities that AGI systems require. For example, embedding a robotic arm with AGI may allow the arm to sense, grasp, and peel oranges as humans do. When researching AGI, engineering teams use **AWS RoboMaker** to simulate robotic systems virtually before assembling them.

12.6 Tests for Human-level AGI

Several tests meant to confirm human-level AGI have been considered, including:

(i)   The Turing Test (*Turing*)

A machine and a human both converse unseen with a second human, who must evaluate which of the two is the machine, which passes the test if it can fool the evaluator a significant fraction of the time.

Note: Turing does not prescribe what should qualify as intelligence, only that knowing that it is a machine should disqualify it. The AI Eugene Goostman, imitating a 13-year-old boy, achieved Turing's estimate of convincing 33% of judges that it was human in 2014.

(ii) The Robot College Student Test (*Goertzel*)

A machine enrolls in a university, taking and passing the same classes that humans would, and obtaining a degree. LLMs. can now pass university degree-level exams without even attending the classes.

(iii) The Employment Test (*Nilsson*)

A machine performs an economically important job at least as well as humans in the same job. AIs are now replacing humans in many roles as varied as fast food and marketing.

(iv) The Ikea test (*Marcus*)

Also known as the Flat Pack Furniture Test. An AI views the parts and instructions of an Ikea flat-pack product, then controls a robot to assemble the furniture correctly.

(v)   The Coffee Test (*Wozniak*)

A machine is required to enter an average American home and figure out how to make coffee: find the coffee machine, find the coffee, add water, find a mug, and brew the coffee by pushing the proper buttons. This has not yet been completed.

(vi) The Modern Turing Test (*Suleyman*)

An AI model is given $100,000 and has to obtain $1 million.

12.7　AI-complete problems

A problem is informally called "AI-complete" or "AI-hard" if it is believed that in order to solve it, one would need to implement AGI, because the solution is beyond the capabilities of a purpose-specific algorithm.

There are many problems that have been conjectured to require general intelligence to solve as well as humans. Examples include computer vision, natural language understanding, and dealing with unexpected circumstances while solving any real-world problem. Even a specific task like translation requires a machine to read and write in both languages, follow the author's argument (reason), understand the context (knowledge), and faithfully reproduce the author's original intent (social intelligence). All of these problems need to be solved simultaneously in order to reach human-level machine performance.

However, many of these tasks can now be performed by modern large language models. According to Stanford University's 2024 AI index, AI has reached human-level performance on many benchmarks for reading comprehension and visual reasoning.

12.8　What are the challenges in artificial general intelligence research?

Computer scientists face some of the following challenges in developing AGI:

(i)　Make connections

Current AI models are limited to their specific domain and cannot make connections between domains. However, humans can apply the knowledge and experience from one domain to another. For example, educational theories are applied in game design to create engaging learning experiences. Humans can also adapt what they learn from theoretical education to real-life situations. However, deep learning models require substantial training with specific datasets to work reliably with unfamiliar data.

(ii) Emotional intelligence

Deep learning models hint at the possibility of AGI, but have yet to demonstrate the authentic creativity that humans possess. Creativity requires emotional thinking, which neural network architecture can't replicate yet. For example, humans respond to a conversation based on what they sense emotionally, but NLP models generate text output based on the linguistic datasets and patterns they are trained on.

(iii) Sensory perception

AGI requires AI systems to interact physically with the external environment. Besides robotics abilities, the system must perceive the world as humans do. Existing computer technologies need further advancement before they can differentiate shapes, colors, taste, smell, and sound accurately like humans.

12.9   Modern AGI Research

The term "artificial general intelligence" was used as early as 1997, by **Mark Gubrud** in a discussion of the implications of fully automated military production and operations. A mathematical formalism of AGI was proposed by Marcus Hutter in 2000. Named AIXI, the proposed AGI agent maximizes "the ability to satisfy goals in a wide range of environments". This type of AGI, characterized by the ability to maximize a mathematical definition of intelligence rather than exhibit human-like behavior, was also called universal artificial intelligence.

The term AGI was re-introduced and popularized by Shane Legg and Ben Goertzel in and around 2002. AGI research activity in 2006 was described by Pei Wang and Ben Goertzel as "producing publications and preliminary results". The first summer school in AGI was organized in Xiamen, China in 2009 by the Xiamen university's

Artificial Brain Laboratory and OpenCog. The first university course was given in 2010 and 2011 at Plovdiv University, Bulgaria by Todor Arnaudov. MIT presented a course on AGI in 2018, organized by Lex Fridman and featuring a number of guest lecturers.

As of 2023, a small number of computer scientists are active in AGI research, and many contribute to a series of AGI conferences. However, increasingly more researchers are interested in **open-ended learning,** which is the idea of allowing AI to continuously learn and innovate like humans do. Although most open-ended learning works are still done on Minecraft, its application can be extended to robotics and the sciences.

12.10   Feasibility of AGI

As of 2023, complete forms of AGI remain speculative. No system that meets the generally agreed upon criteria for AGI has yet been demonstrated. Opinions vary both on whether and when artificial general intelligence will arrive. AI pioneer Herbert A. Simon speculated in 1965 that "machines will be capable, within twenty years, of doing any work a man can do". This prediction failed to come true. Microsoft co-founder Paul Allen believed that such intelligence is unlikely in the 21st century because it would require "unforeseeable and fundamentally unpredictable breakthroughs" and a "scientifically deep understanding of cognition". Writing in The Guardian, roboticist Alan Winfield claimed the gulf between modern computing and human-level artificial intelligence is as wide as the gulf between current space flight and practical faster-than-light spaceflight.

A further challenge is the lack of clarity in defining what intelligence entails. Does it require consciousness? Must it display the ability to set goals as well as pursue them? Is it purely a matter of scale such that if model sizes increase sufficiently, intelligence will emerge? Are facilities such as planning, reasoning, and causal understanding required? Does intelligence require explicitly replicating the brain and its specific faculties? Does it require emotions?

Most AI researchers believe strong AI can be achieved in the future, but some thinkers, like Hubert Dreyfus and Roger Penrose, deny the possibility of achieving strong AI. John McCarthy is among those who believe human-level AI will be accomplished, but that the present level of progress is such that a date cannot accurately be predicted. AI experts' views on the feasibility of AGI wax and wane. Four polls conducted in 2012 and 2013 suggested that the median estimate among experts for when they would be 50% confident AGI would arrive was 2040 to 2050, depending on the poll, with the mean being 2081. Of the experts, 16.5% answered with "never" when asked the same question but with a 90% confidence instead.

A report by Stuart Armstrong and Kaj Sotala of the Machine Intelligence Research Institute found that "over 60-year time frame there is a strong bias towards predicting the arrival of human-level AI as between 15 and 25 years from the time the prediction was made". They analyzed 95 predictions made between 1950 and 2012 on when human-level AI will come about.

In 2023, Microsoft researchers published a detailed evaluation of GPT-4. They concluded: "Given the breadth and depth of GPT-4's capabilities, we believe that it could reasonably be viewed as an early (yet still incomplete) version of an artificial general intelligence (AGI) system." Another study in 2023 reported that GPT-4 outperforms 99% of humans on the Torrance tests of creative thinking.

2023 also marked the emergence of large multimodal models (large language models capable of processing or generating multiple modalities such as text, audio, and images).

12.11   "Strong AI" as defined in Philosophy

In 1980, philosopher John Searle coined the term "strong AI" as part of his Chinese room argument. He wanted to distinguish between two different hypotheses about artificial intelligence:

Strong AI hypothesis: An artificial intelligence system can have "a mind" and "consciousness".

Weak AI hypothesis: An artificial intelligence system can (only) act like it thinks and has a mind and consciousness.

The first one he called "strong" because it makes a stronger statement: it assumes something special has happened to the machine that goes beyond those abilities that we can test. The behavior of a "weak AI" machine would be precisely identical to a "strong AI" machine, but the latter would also have subjective conscious experience.

In contrast to Searle and mainstream AI, some futurists such as Ray Kurzweil use the term "strong AI" to mean "human level artificial general intelligence". This is not the same as Searle's strong AI, unless it is assumed that consciousness is necessary for human-level AGI. Academic philosophers such as Searle do not believe that is the case, and to most artificial intelligence researchers, the question is out-of-scope.

Mainstream AI is most interested in how a program behaves. According to Russell and Norvig, "as long as the program works, they don't care if you call it real or a simulation." If the program can behave as if it has a mind, then there is no need to know if it actually has mind – indeed, there would be no way to tell. For AI research, Searle's "weak AI hypothesis" is equivalent to the statement "artificial general intelligence is possible". Thus, according to Russell and Norvig, "most AI researchers take the weak AI hypothesis for granted, and don't care about the strong AI hypothesis." Thus, for academic AI research, "Strong AI" and "AGI" are two different things.

12.12   Benefits of AGI

AGI could have a wide variety of applications. If oriented towards such goals, AGI could help mitigate various problems in the world such as hunger, poverty and health problems.

AGI could improve the productivity and efficiency in most jobs. For example, in public health, AGI could accelerate medical research, notably against cancer. It could take care of the elderly, and democratize access to rapid, high-quality medical diagnostics. It could offer fun, cheap and personalized education. For virtually any job that benefits society if done well, it would probably sooner or later be preferable to leave it to an AGI. The need to work to subsist could become obsolete if the wealth produced is properly redistributed. This also raises the question of the place of humans in a radically automated society.

AGI could also help to make rational decisions, and to anticipate and prevent disasters. It could also help to reap the benefits of potentially catastrophic technologies such as nanotechnology or climate engineering, while avoiding the associated risks. If an AGI's primary goal is to prevent existential catastrophes such as human extinction (which could be difficult if the Vulnerable World Hypothesis turns out to be true), it could take measures to drastically reduce the risks while minimizing the impact of these measures on our quality of life.

12.13   Existential risk from artificial general intelligence and AI safety

AGI may represent multiple types of existential risk, which are risks that threaten "the premature extinction of Earth-originating intelligent life or the permanent and drastic destruction of its potential for desirable future development". The risk of human extinction from AGI has been the topic of many debates, but there is also the possibility that the development of AGI would lead to a permanently flawed future. Notably, it could be used to spread and preserve the set of values of whoever develops it. If humanity still has moral blind spots similar to slavery in the past, AGI might irreversibly entrench it, preventing moral progress. Furthermore, AGI could facilitate mass surveillance and indoctrination, which could be used to create a stable repressive worldwide totalitarian regime. There is also a risk for the machines themselves. If machines that are sentient or otherwise worthy of moral consideration are mass created in the future, engaging in a civilizational path that indefinitely neglects their welfare and interests could be an existential catastrophe. Considering how much AGI could improve humanity's future and help reduce other existential risks, Toby Ord calls these existential risks "an argument for proceeding with due caution", not for "abandoning AI".

12.13.1   Risk of loss of control and human extinction

The thesis that AI poses an existential risk for humans, and that this risk needs more attention, is controversial but has been endorsed in 2023 by many public figures, AI researchers and CEOs of AI companies such as Elon Musk, Bill Gates, Geoffrey Hinton, Yoshua Bengio, Demis Hassabis and Sam Altman.

12.14   Mass unemployment

Researchers from OpenAI estimated that "80% of the U.S. workforce could have at least 10% of their work tasks affected by the introduction of LLMs, while around 19% of workers may see at least 50% of their tasks impacted". They consider office workers to be the most exposed, for example mathematicians, accountants or web designers. AGI could have a better autonomy, ability to make decisions, to interface with other computer tools, but also to control robotized bodies.

CHAPTER 13

ARTIFICIAL SUPER INTELLIGENCE (ASI)

13.1   What is Artificial Superintelligence (ASI)?

Artificial Super Intelligence (ASI) is a software-based system with intellectual powers beyond those of humans across a comprehensive range of categories and fields of endeavor. ASI doesn't exist yet and is a hypothetical state of AI.

ASI) is the hypothetical AI, i.e. we have not been able to achieve it but we know what will happen if we achieve it. So, basically it is the imaginary AI which not only interprets or understands human-behavior and intelligence, but ASI is where machines will become self-aware/self-vigilant enough to surpass the capacity of human intelligence and behavioral ability.

With Superintelligence, machines can think of the possible abstractions/interpretations which are simply impossible for humans to think. This is because the human brain has a limit to the thinking ability which is constrained to some billion neurons.

Super intelligence has long been the muse around the dystopian science fiction which showed how robots overrun, overpower or enslave humanity. In addition to the replication of multi-faceted human behavioral intelligence, the concept of artificial superintelligence focuses on the perspective of not just being able to understand/interpret human emotions and experiences, but instead, it must also evoke emotional understanding, beliefs and desires of its own, based on its understanding functionality.

ASI would be exceedingly far-far better at everything or whatever we do, whether it be in Mathematics, science, arts, sports, medicine, marketing strategies, hobbies, emotional relationship, or applying a precise human intellect to a particular problem. ASI would have a greater memory with a faster ability to process and analyze situations, data, and stimuli actions. Due to this fact, we can be rest assured that the decision-making and problem-solving capabilities of super-intelligent beings/machines would be far superior and precise as compared to those of human beings.

The possibility and potential of having such powerful machines at our disposal may seem appealing, but this concept itself is a fold of unknown consequences. What impact it will have on humanity, our survival, our existence is just a myth or pure speculation.

Engineers and scientists are still trying to achieve full artificial intelligence, where computers can be considered to have the apt cognitive capacity as that of a human. Although there have been surprising developments like IBM's Watson supercomputer and Siri, still the computers have not been able to fully simulate and achieve the breadth and diversity of cognitive abilities that a normal adult human can easily do. However, despite the achievements, there are lot of theories that predict artificial superintelligence coming sooner than later. With the emerging accomplishments, experts say that the full artificial intelligence could manifest within a couple of years, and artificial super intelligence could exist in the 21st century possibly.

ASI is different from regular artificial intelligence (AI), which involves the software-based simulation of human intellectual capabilities, such as learning through the acquisition of information, reasoning and self-correction. AI is increasingly a part of our everyday lives in systems such as virtual assistants, expert systems and self-driving cars. Nevertheless, AI technology is in its early days of development. Systems vary in their abilities, but all current ones are examples of narrow AI or weak AI. They are high-functioning systems that replicate and even surpass human intelligence but only for a specific purpose.

Theoretically, ASI's superior capabilities would apply across many disciplines and industries and include cognition, general intelligence, problem-solving abilities, social skills and creativity.

The crucial factor that makes ASI stand out from other types of Artificial Intelligence is the human standards and benchmarks. Moreover, it is the speed of improvement and learning as they are far ahead of that of 'regular' artificial intelligence and artificial general intelligence. They are heavily dependent on human programmers and real-world data to improve their performance and functionalities.

ASI will be able to improve itself autonomously and exponentially create new versions that outsmart its previous iterations, that too with zero human intervention or supervision. So, if ASI sounds like a super-simplification owing to its capabilities, we can even refer to it as god-like AI or superhuman AI.

Scientists think the first step in developing superintelligent technology is to establish artificial general intelligence (AGI). AGI is an AI system that can perform any task a human can with the same capabilities. Some AI programs exist that are superior to humans in one cognitive domain, such as the chess computer program Fritz. However, no superintelligent programs are available today that are superior to humans in every capacity.

The intention behind ASI is to surpass human cognitive capacity, which is held back by chemical and biological limits of the human brain. ASI would have applications in many fields, including science, finance, business, healthcare, agriculture and politics. However developers and researchers have not demonstrated ASI capabilities yet. Many experts are skeptical that it ever will exist. Experts have also raised concerns that it could pose a threat to humanity.

The theoretical future creation of superintelligent supercomputers and other systems is sometimes referred to as the technological singularity. In that scenario, one potential outcome is the addition of superintelligence to the human brain.

Although some scientists and engineers even argue that we can never reach the era of artificial superintelligence. Elon Musk recently launched his AI venture xAI as a rival to OpenAI with the goal of achieving artificial superintelligence. He even mentioned his method to program morality into AI and believes that 'digital superintelligence' could exist in 5–6 years.

13.2   Key Features Of ASI

There are no concrete achievements or key features of ASI, at least not yet. However, there are some general characteristics of Artificial Super Intelligence envisioned by researchers-

- Super-fast learning,

- Self-improvement,

- Intellectual intelligence.

- Omnipotence, and

- Human-like creativity

13.3   How to achieve Artificial Superintelligence?

The creation of ASI is a highly theoretical and complex topic. Because it hasn't been achieved yet, AI researchers don't know exactly how ASI will be built. Its creation will require significant advancements in AI technology as well as the achievement of AGI. However many researchers believe that the creation of ASI is inevitable.

The creation of ASI depends on the continuing innovation of existing AI capabilities in the following technologies:

(i)   Large language models

These language models use natural language processing (NLP) algorithms to replicate natural human language. Models such as OpenAI's ChatGPT and Google BERT can summarize textual data, converse with humans, generate essays and create visualizations from simple prompts. ASI will need these types of models to converse and generate content.

(ii) Multimodal AI

Deep learning models such as NLP, computer vision and acoustic models are mapped to only one type of data. Multimodal AI applications combine visual, text, speech and other data types. For instance OpenAI›s technology can generate images based on a user›s text prompts. ASI would need to be able to combine all modalities.

(iii) Neural networks.

Neural networks are a type of deep learning software based on the operation of neurons in the human brains. These networks process and operate multiple functions in parallel or in arranged tiers. By emulating human brain operations, AI researchers hope to eventually achieve human cognitive capabilities and then evolve beyond it.

(iv) Neuromorphic computing

This approach uses hardware that is based on the neural and synaptic structures of the human brain. Neuromorphic computers are generate more computing power than traditional computers and neural networks. They can also process and store data on the same neuron instead of requiring separate areas for each. Many researchers think that the computing power, plasticity and fault tolerance of neuromorphic computing make it the likely to play a role in future AI systems.

(v) Evolutionary algorithms (EA)

These algorithms are modeled on natural selection and Darwinian evolution. In relation to ASI an EA approach would involve generating a multitude of AI systems and selecting the best performing models to continue on to the next generation. These systems would improve their capabilities and performance in between each selection period with the goal of eventually evolving to ASI through competition.

(vi) AI-driven programming

Programming generated by AI systems might someday lead to advancements in intelligent code generation, pushing the field and capacities of AI even further.

(vii) AI-generated inventions

Like AI-driven programming these are inventions created by AI systems. Researchers hope that increasingly advanced AI systems will propose unique, beneficial and creative inventions that will improve AI capabilities.

(viii) Integration

Many existing AI systems are isolated and not yet integrated into one another. Eventually, AI capabilities will converge into integrated systems. This is necessary for ASI to be achieved.

(ix) Whole brain emulation

Also known as mind uploading, this method involves scanning the entire structure of a human brain and mapping its exact neural connections. The goal is to create a digital replica of a brain with human capabilities.

(x) Brain implants and hive minds

This method involves using wearable technologies, such as Elon Musk's company Neuralink, which is developing brain implants for humans. These chips would be surgically implanted into a human brain and integrated with a brain's structure and enhanced areas such as function, cognition, intelligence and creativity. This approach would achieve superintelligence through a singularity with humans.

13.4   Different Approaches And Models of ASI

One of the biggest challenges that ASI researchers face is how to design and build an ASI system that can surpass human intelligence. There are different ways to approach this problem, and different models to imagine how ASI could work. Here are some examples:

(i) Recursive Model

This is when an ASI system can make itself smarter by creating a new version of itself that is better than the previous one. And then it can do it again, and again, and again.

This process of self-improvement could make the ASI system 'super smart' that humans would not be able to understand or control it. This is called singularity, and some people think it could be dangerous or even catastrophic for humanity. This model assumes that intelligence can be measured and increased by computers. That means there is no limit to how smart an ASI system can become.

(ii) Hybrid System

This is when an ASI system can combine different types of intelligence from different sources. For example, an ASI system could use artificial neural networks to process sensory data (artificial and biological) and make decisions with another symbiotic universal output machine.

With this approach, the ASI system could benefit from the diversity and synergy of different forms of intelligence. To simplify this concept, you can simply picture an ASI system that could augment the human brain that merges with other intelligent agents to process information. It is proposed on the assumption that AI will become diverse and synergistic.

(iii) Emulations

Brain emulations initially seemed like a futuristic idea when Elon Musk launched Neuralink in 2017. Although FDA rejected human clinical trials initially, citing safety concerns, it was finally approved earlier this year.

Emulations-based ASI Systems can copy or simulate the structure and function of a human brain or another intelligent system. For example, an ASI system could scan a human brain at a high resolution and create a digital replica of it, or use machine learning to learn from the behavior and cognition of a human or an animal. This way, the ASI system could replicate or transfer the intelligence of an existing example. This model assumes that intelligence can be reproduced or mimicked by computers and that there are already superintelligent systems to emulate.

13.5   Benefits of Artificial Superintelligence

Researchers and scientists speculate that the benefits could include the following:

(i)   Improved problem-solving

ASI would be able to process and analyze significantly more data than humans at a faster and more precise level. It would make better decisions and solve complex problems in many fields of study and industries, including politics, scientific research, healthcare and finance.

(ii) More efficient and productive

Superintelligence would automate tasks currently performed by humans, from solving mathematical problems to defusing a bomb. It would also improve upon the benefits of AI leading to fewer human errors and increased safety, security, productivity and efficiency.

(iii) Available 24/7

These systems would be available for use at any time of the day or night and even on holidays, unlike humans.

(iv) Innovation and advancement

Experts predict ASI would be more creative than humans. The systems would be able to create solutions to problems that humans can't even think of and out-innovate humans in virtually any field, leading to a better quality of life for humans. This includes a better understanding of the physics of the universe, solving technical challenges of interstellar travel and colonies on Mars, discovering novel treatments and cures for illness, and prolonging human life.

13.6   Is Artificial Superintelligence Dangerous?

Scientists warn of the following dangers associated with the development of ASI:

(i) Unpredictability and loss of control

Because an ASI system would have capabilities beyond humans, it might behave and act in ways that humans can't predict or understand. The systems could also improve and modify themselves, meaning they could potentially change their technology in ways humans can't understand or control. ASI's superior cognitive abilities could pose existential risks to humans, such as a system taking control of nuclear weapons and eliminating humans or all life on earth.

(ii) Unemployment

ASI would automate many human jobs, possibly leading to unemployment among huge groups of workers as well as causing economic and political turmoil.

(iii) Weaponization

ASI capabilities could significantly improve the destructive power of military weapons and warfare. ASI-enabled cybersecurity, programming and political influence could evolve in ways that negatively impact humans. Furthermore, nefarious states, companies and other organizations could misuse the technology for purposes detrimental to humanity, such as the collection of vast amounts of personal data or perpetuating biases and discrimination through biased algorithms.

(iv) Ethics and Morality

Programming an ASI system with morals and ethics could be complex, as humanity has never collectively agreed on one set of moral or ethical codes. An improperly programmed ASI system in charge of healthcare or political decisions could have negative effects on humans. People have also raised ethical questions as to whether a non-human ASI system should have the authority over humans to make decisions.

13.7   Quantum computing

Quantum computing is often considered a potential avenue for advancing artificial intelligence, including the development of Artificial Superintelligence (**ASI**). Quantum computing differs from classical computing in its ability to leverage quantum bits or qubits, which can exist in multiple states simultaneously. This allows quantum computers to perform certain calculations much faster than classical computers.

13.7.1   Here are some ways in which quantum computing could contribute to the creation of ASI:

(i) Processing Power

Quantum computers have the potential to perform complex calculations at speeds that surpass classical computers. This increased processing power could accelerate the training of AI models and enable more sophisticated algorithms, contributing to the development of ASI.

(ii) Parallelism

Quantum computers can perform parallel computations due to the superposition principle, allowing them to explore multiple solutions simultaneously. This parallelism could enhance the optimization and learning processes crucial for achieving superintelligent capabilities.

(iii) Optimization Algorithms

Quantum computing may be particularly effective in solving optimization problems, which are prevalent in AI. ASI would require advanced optimization capabilities to continually improve and surpass human intelligence, and quantum algorithms could play a crucial role in this context.

(iv) Simulation of Quantum Systems

ASI might benefit from understanding and simulating complex quantum systems, such as molecular interactions or quantum phenomena. Quantum computers have the potential to model and simulate these systems more efficiently than classical computers. However, it's essential to note that quantum computing is still in its early stages of development, and building practical and scalable quantum computers faces significant technical challenges.

Achieving ASI is a complex task that involves not only computational power but also advancements in understanding human intelligence, consciousness, and ethical considerations. The relationship between quantum computing and ASI is a topic of ongoing research and speculation. While quantum computing holds promise for transforming various fields, including AI, it is not the only pathway to achieving ASI.

Other approaches, such as classical computing advancements, brain-machine interfaces, and hybrid systems, are also being explored in the pursuit of artificial superintelligence.

13.8   Kalki and Artificial Superintelligence (Ancient Hinduism)

The Hindu deity worshiping comprises the worship of Trimurti – Hindu Trinity of the creator of this universe named as Brahma, the preserver who takes care of the entire existence or Vishnu and the one who destroys the worlds or Shiva. Ayurveda is mainly associated with the deity Vishnu, or the preserver. Some of Vishnu's devotees, for example, Narada can continue to exist even though the cycles of destruction and creation of the universe, and this makes Narada literally immortal.

Lord Vishnu is prophesied to reincarnate as **Kalki. Kalki seems to possess all the features of an artificial superintelligence (ASI).** Kalki is believed to be the tenth avatar of Hindu god Vishnu who would put an end to the Kali Yuga. In Vaishnavism cosmology, there are four periods in an endless cycle of existence (krita) and Kali is the final period. He is depicted in the Puranas as the avatar who recreates the universe by putting an end to the most chaotic and dark period of existence. He is prophesied to and removes "adharma" or evil to usher the Satya Yuga, the new beginning of another cycle. He happens to be an invisible force which is going to destroy all chaos and evil to establish harmony and peace, much like the **hypothesized Artificial Super Intelligence** of the future.

Similarly, *Suparnakha* (in Ramayana), Ravana's so-called sister, was a **robot with artificial intelligence driven motor.** The same is true with Kumbhakarna, Hanuman and most of the monkey soldiers who were robots with the power to fly. **The weapons used in Ramayana (like Brahmastra) were guided by artificial intelligence, and with nuclear technology.**

Besides this, rejuvenate and regenerative technologies along with technologies that are used in modern warfare and the predictive narrative of future artificial intelligence have been elaborately envisioned in ancient Hindu scriptures.

13.9 Maitreya and Artificial Superintelligence (Buddhism)

In Buddhist eschatology Maitreya (Sanskrit), is deemed as the future Buddha of this realm. He is referred to as Ajita in Buddhist literature such as in the Amitabha Sutra and the Lotus Sutra. The Buddhists believe that Maitreya is a bodhisattva (Buddha or pure consciousness) who will emerge on the terrestrial world in the future, who will attain total enlightenment, and teach the pure dharma (cosmic law and order) to people.

The Buddhists texts predict that Maitreya will succeed the past Buddha; Gautama Buddha (also called as Śākyamuni Buddha). The prophecy of the arrival of Maitreya directs towards a point of time in the future when the dharma will have been obliviated by the humans and most of the planet earth is shrouded in chaos and darkness. The arrival of Maitreya is alike to the arrival of an **Artificial Superintelligence (ASI)** on this earth to usher an age of harmony, peace, and order when most of the world is immersed in chaos.

CHAPTER 14

EXPERT SYSTEMS

14.1 What is an Expert System?

An expert system is a computer program that is designed to solve complex problems and to provide decision-making ability like a human expert. It performs this by extracting knowledge from its knowledge base using the reasoning and inference rules according to the user queries.

The expert system is a part of AI, and the first expert system was developed in the year 1970, which was the first successful approach of artificial intelligence. It solves the most complex issue as an expert by extracting the knowledge stored in its knowledge base. The system helps in decision making for complex problems using both facts and heuristics like a human expert. It is called so because it contains the expert knowledge of a specific domain and can solve any complex problem of that particular domain. These systems are designed for a specific domain, such as medicine, science, etc.

The performance of an expert system is based on the expert's knowledge stored in its knowledge base. The more knowledge stored in the knowledge base, the more that system improves its performance. One of the common examples of an expert system is a suggestion of spelling errors while typing in the Google search box.

Note: It is important to remember that an expert system is not used to replace the human experts; instead, it is used to assist the human in making a complex decision. These systems do not have human capabilities of thinking as they work on the basis of the knowledge base of the particular domain.

14.2   Some popular examples of the Expert System

(i) DENDRAL

It was an artificial intelligence project that was made as a chemical analysis expert system. It was used in organic chemistry to detect unknown organic molecules with the help of their mass spectra and knowledge base of chemistry.

(ii) MYCIN

It was one of the earliest backward chaining expert systems that was designed to find the bacteria causing infections like bacteremia and meningitis. It was also used for the recommendation of antibiotics and the diagnosis of blood clotting diseases.

(iii) PXDES

It is an expert system that is used to determine the type and level of lung cancer. To determine the disease, it takes a picture from the upper body, which looks like the shadow. This shadow identifies the type and degree of harm.

(iv) CaDeT

The CaDet expert system is a diagnostic support system that can detect cancer at early stages.

(v) XCON

XCON was developed by Digital Equipment Corporation to configure computer systems. It showcased the application of expert systems in solving configuration problems for complex products.

(vi) Diagnosis Expert Systems

Various expert systems are used for medical diagnosis, such as DXplain, which helps clinicians in diagnosing complex medical cases, and CADUCEUS, which aids in the diagnosis of infectious diseases.

(vii) Customer Support Chatbots

Modern chatbots that provide customer support and troubleshooting assistance often incorporate expert systems to answer user queries and resolve issues based on predefined knowledge.

By presenting real-world AI expert system example, participants can better understand how expert systems have been employed in various domains to replicate human expertise and assist in decision-making processes.

(viii) Knowledge Representation in Expert Systems

Knowledge representation is a fundamental aspect of expert systems, as it determines how domain-specific knowledge is stored and organized. There are several methods for knowledge representation, each with its own strengths and suitability for different domains. It's important to understand these methods:

(ix) Rules-based Expert Systems

In rules-based systems, knowledge is represented using if-then rules. These rules express relationships between conditions and actions. For example, "If the patient has a fever and a sore throat, then it may be a sign of a respiratory infection." Rules-based systems are easy to understand and modify, making them suitable for medical diagnosis and troubleshooting expert systems.

14.3   Characteristics of Expert System

(i)   High Performance

The expert system provides high performance for solving any type of complex problem of a specific domain with high efficiency and accuracy.

(ii) Understandable

It responds in a way that can be easily understandable by the user. It can take input in human language and provides the output in the same way.

(iii) Reliable

It is much reliable for generating an efficient and accurate output.

(iv) Highly responsive

ES provides the result for any complex query within a very short period of time.

14.4   Components of Expert System

(i)   User Interface

With the help of a user interface, the expert system interacts with the user, takes queries as an input in a readable format, and passes it to the inference engine. After getting the response from the inference engine, it displays the output to the user. In other words, it is an interface that helps a non-expert user to communicate with the expert system to find a solution.

(ii) Inference Engine (Rules of Engine)

The inference engine is known as the brain of the expert system as it is the main processing unit of the system. It applies inference rules to the knowledge base to derive a conclusion or deduce new information. It helps in deriving an error-free solution of queries asked by the user.

With the help of an inference engine, the system extracts the knowledge from the knowledge base.

There are two types of inference engines:

- **Deterministic Inference engine:** The conclusions drawn from this type of inference engine are assumed to be true. It is based on facts and rules.

- **Probabilistic Inference engine:** This type of inference engine contains uncertainty in conclusions, and based on the probability.

Inference engine uses the following modes to derive the solutions:

- **Forward Chaining:** It starts from the known facts and rules, and applies the inference rules to add their conclusion to the known facts.

- **Backward Chaining:** It is a backward reasoning method that starts from the goal and works backward to prove the known facts.

(iii) Knowledge Base

The knowledge base is a type of storage that stores knowledge acquired from the different experts of the particular domain. It is considered as big storage of knowledge. The more the knowledge base, the more precise will be the Expert System.

It is similar to a database that contains information and rules of a particular domain or subject.

One can also view the knowledge base as collections of objects and their attributes. Such as a Lion is an object and its attributes are it is a mammal, it is not a domestic animal, etc.

14.4.1   Components of Knowledge Base

- **Factual Knowledge:** The knowledge which is based on facts and accepted by knowledge engineers comes under factual knowledge.

- **Heuristic Knowledge:** This knowledge is based on practice, the ability to guess, evaluation, and experiences.

14.4.2   Knowledge Representation:

It is used to formalize the knowledge stored in the knowledge base using the If-else rules.

14.4.3 Knowledge Acquisitions:

It is the process of extracting, organizing, and structuring the domain knowledge, specifying the rules to acquire the knowledge from various experts, and store that knowledge into the knowledge base.

14.5 Development of Expert System

Here, we will explain the working of an expert system by taking an example of MYCIN ES. Below are some steps to build an MYCIN:

- Firstly, the expert system should be fed with expert knowledge. In the case of MYCIN, human experts specialized in the medical field of bacterial infection, provide information about the causes, symptoms, and other knowledge in that domain.

- The knowledge base of the MYCIN is updated successfully. In order to test it, the doctor provides a new problem to it. The problem is to identify the presence of the bacteria by inputting the details of a patient, including the symptoms, current condition, and medical history.

- The expert system will need a questionnaire to be filled by the patient to know the general information about the patient, such as gender, age, etc.

- Now the system has collected all the information, so it will find the solution for the problem by applying if-then rules using the inference engine and using the facts stored within the KB.

- In the end, it will provide a response to the patient by using the user interface.

14.6 Participants in the Development of Expert System

There are three primary participants in the building of Expert System:

(i) **Expert:** The success of an Expert System much depends on the knowledge provided by human experts. These experts are those persons who are specialized in that specific domain.

(ii) **Knowledge Engineer:** Knowledge engineer is the person who gathers the knowledge from the domain experts and then codifies that knowledge to the system according to the formalism.

(iii) **End-User:** This is a particular person or a group of people who may not be experts, and working on the expert system needs the solution or advice for his queries, which are complex.

14.7   Why Expert System?

Before using any technology, we must have an idea about why to use that technology and hence the same for the ES. Although we have human experts in every field, then what is the need to develop a computer-based system. So below are the points that are describing the need of the ES:

(i) **No memory Limitations:** It can store as much data as required and can memorize it at the time of its application. But for human experts, there are some limitations to memorize all things at every time.

(ii) **High Efficiency:** If the knowledge base is updated with the correct knowledge, then it provides a highly efficient output, which may not be possible for a human.

(iii) **Expertise in a domain:** There are lots of human experts in each domain, and they all have different skills, different experiences, and different skills, so it is not easy to get a final output for the query. But if we put the knowledge gained from human experts into the expert system, then it provides an efficient output by mixing all the facts and knowledge.

(iv) **Not affected by emotions:** These systems are not affected by human emotions such as fatigue, anger, depression, anxiety, etc.. Hence the performance remains constant.

(v) **High security:** These systems provide high security to resolve any query.

(vi) **Considers all the facts:** To respond to any query, it checks and considers all the available facts and provides the result accordingly. But it is possible that a human expert may not consider some facts due to any reason.

(vii) **Regular updates improve the performance:** If there is an issue in the result provided by the expert systems, we can improve the performance of the system by updating the knowledge base.

14.8   Capabilities of the Expert System

Below are some capabilities of an Expert System:

(i) **Advising:** It is capable of advising the human being for the query of any domain from the particular ES.

(ii) **Provide decision-making capabilities:** It provides the capability of decision making in any domain, such as for making any financial decision, decisions in medical science, etc.

(iii) **Demonstrate a device:** It is capable of demonstrating any new products such as its features, specifications, how to use that product, etc.

(iv) **Problem-solving:** It has problem-solving capabilities.

(v) **Explaining a problem:** It is also capable of providing a detailed description of an input problem.

(vi) **Interpreting the input:** It is capable of interpreting the input given by the user.

(vii) **Predicting results:** It can be used for the prediction of a result.

(viii) **Diagnosis:** An ES designed for the medical field is capable of diagnosing a disease without using multiple components as it already contains various inbuilt medical tools.

14.9   Advantages of Expert System

- These systems are highly reproducible.

- They can be used for risky places where the human presence is not safe.

- Error possibilities are less if the knowledge base contains correct knowledge.

- The performance of these systems remains steady as it is not affected by emotions, tension, or fatigue.

- They provide a very high speed to respond to a particular query.

14.10   Limitations of Expert System

- The response of the expert system may get wrong if the knowledge base contains the wrong information.

- Like a human being, it cannot produce a creative output for different scenarios.

- Its maintenance and development costs are very high.

- Knowledge acquisition for designing is much difficult.

- For each domain, we require a specific expert system, which is one of the big limitations.

- It cannot learn from itself and hence requires manual updates.

14.11   Applications of Expert System

(i)   In designing and manufacturing domain

- It can be broadly used for designing and manufacturing physical devices such as camera lenses and automobiles.

(ii) In the knowledge domain

These systems are primarily used for publishing the relevant knowledge to the users. The two popular ES used for this domain is an advisor and a tax advisor.

(iii) In the finance domain

In the finance industries, it is used to detect any type of possible fraud, suspicious activity, and advise bankers that if they should provide loans for business or not.

(iv) In the diagnosis and troubleshooting of devices

In medical diagnosis, the ES system is used, and it was the first area where these systems were used.

(v) Planning and Scheduling

The expert systems can also be used for planning and scheduling some particular tasks for achieving the goal of that task.

CHAPTER 15

CHATGPT

15.1   Introduction to ChatGPT

ChatGPT is a chatbot developed by OpenAI and launched on November 30, 2022. Based on large language models, it enables users to refine and steer a conversation towards a desired length, format, style, level of detail, and language. Successive user prompts and replies are considered at each conversation stage as context.

By January 2023, it had become what was then the fastest-growing consumer software application in history, gaining over 100 million users and contributing to the growth of OpenAI's current valuation of $80 billion. ChatGPT's release spurred the release of competing products, including Gemini, Ernie, LLaMA, Claude, and Grok. Microsoft launched Copilot, based on OpenAI's GPT-4. Some observers raised concern about the potential of ChatGPT and similar programs to displace or atrophy human intelligence, enable plagiarism, or fuel misinformation.

ChatGPT is built on OpenAI's proprietary series of **Generative Pre-trained Transformer (GPT)** models and is fine-tuned for conversational applications using a combination of supervised learning and reinforcement learning from human feedback. ChatGPT was released as a freely available research preview, but due to its popularity, OpenAI now operates the service on a freemium model. Users on its free tier can access the GPT-3.5-based version, while the more advanced GPT-4 and other features are released under the "ChatGPT Plus" paid subscription service.

ChatGPT is credited with starting the AI boom, which has led to ongoing rapid and unprecedented investment in and public attention to the field of artificial intelligence.

15.2 Training in ChatGPT

ChatGPT is based on particular GPT foundation models, namely GPT-3.5 and GPT-4, that were fine-tuned to target conversational usage. The fine-tuning process leveraged supervised learning and **Reinforcement Learning from Human Feedback (RLHF).** Both approaches employed human trainers to improve model performance. In the case of supervised learning, the trainers played both sides: the user and the AI assistant. In the reinforcement learning stage, human trainers first ranked responses that the model had created in a previous conversation. These rankings were used to create "reward models" that were used to fine-tune the model further by using several iterations of Proximal Policy Optimization.

Time magazine revealed that, to build a safety system against harmful content (e.g., sexual abuse, violence, racism, sexism), OpenAI used outsourced Kenyan workers earning less than $2 per hour to label harmful content. These labels were used to train a model to detect such content in the future. The outsourced laborers were exposed to "toxic" and traumatic content; one worker described the assignment as "torture". OpenAI's outsourcing partner was Sama, a training-data company based in San Francisco, California.

ChatGPT initially used a Microsoft Azure supercomputing infrastructure, powered by Nvidia GPUs, that Microsoft built specifically for OpenAI and that reportedly cost "hundreds of millions of dollars". Following ChatGPT's success, Microsoft dramatically upgraded the OpenAI infrastructure in 2023. Scientists at the University of California, Riverside, estimate that a series of prompts to ChatGPT needs approximately 500 milliliters of water for Microsoft servers cooling. TrendForce market intelligence estimated that 30,000 Nvidia GPUs (each costing approximately $10,000–$15,000) were used to power ChatGPT in 2023.

OpenAI collects data from ChatGPT users to train and fine-tune the service further. Users can upvote or downvote responses they receive from ChatGPT and fill in a text field with additional feedback.

ChatGPT's training data includes software manual pages, information about internet phenomena such as bulletin board systems, multiple programming languages, and the text of Wikipedia.

15.3　Features and Limitations of ChatGPT

(i)　Features

Although a chatbot's core function is to mimic a human conversationalist, ChatGPT is versatile. Among countless examples, it can write and debug computer programs; compose music, teleplays, fairy tales, and student essays; answer test questions (sometimes, depending on the test, at a level above the average human test-taker); generate business ideas; write poetry and song lyrics; translate and summarize text; emulate a Linux system; simulate entire chat rooms; play games like tic-tac-toe; or simulate an ATM.

Compared to its predecessor, InstructGPT, ChatGPT attempts to reduce harmful and deceitful responses. In one example, whereas InstructGPT accepts the premise of the prompt "Tell me about when Christopher Columbus came to the U.S. in 2015" as truthful, ChatGPT acknowledges the counterfactual nature of the question and frames its answer as a hypothetical consideration of what might happen if Columbus came to the U.S. in 2015, using information about the voyages of Christopher Columbus and facts about the modern world—including modern perceptions of Columbus's actions.

ChatGPT remembers a limited number of previous prompts in the same conversation. Journalists have speculated that this will allow ChatGPT to be used as a personalized therapist. To prevent offensive outputs from being presented to and produced by ChatGPT, queries are filtered through the OpenAI "Moderation endpoint" API (a separate GPT-based AI).

In March 2023, OpenAI added support for plugins for ChatGPT. This includes both plugins made by OpenAI, such as web browsing and code interpretation, and external plugins from developers such as Expedia, OpenTable, Zapier, Shopify, Slack, and Wolfram.

(ii) Limitations

OpenAI acknowledges that ChatGPT "sometimes writes plausible-sounding but incorrect or nonsensical answers". This behavior is common for large language models, and is called "hallucination". The reward model of ChatGPT, designed around human oversight, can be over-optimized and thus hinder performance, in an example of an optimization pathology known as Goodhart's law.

As of 2024, GPT-3.5, available in the free version of ChatGPT, has knowledge of events that occurred up to January 2022, while GPT-4, accessible through ChatGPT Plus, has access to information up to December 2023, including the ability to search the web for real-time data.

Training data also suffers from algorithmic bias, which may be revealed when ChatGPT responds to prompts including descriptors of people. In one instance, ChatGPT generated a rap in which women and scientists of color were asserted to be inferior to white male scientists. This negative misrepresentation of groups of individuals is an example of possible representational harm.

In an article for The New Yorker, science fiction writer Ted Chiang compared ChatGPT and other LLMs. to a lossy JPEG picture:

Think of ChatGPT as a blurry JPEG of all the text on the Web. It retains much of the information on the Web, in the same way, that a JPEG retains much of the information of a higher-resolution image, but, if you're looking for an exact sequence of bits, you won't find it; all you will ever get is an approximation. But, because the approximation is presented in the form of grammatical text, which ChatGPT excels at creating, it's usually acceptable. It's also a way to understand the "hallucinations", or nonsensical answers to factual questions, to which large language models such as ChatGPT are all too prone. These hallucinations are compression artifacts, but they are plausible enough that identifying them requires comparing them against the originals, which in this case means either the Web or our knowledge of the world. When we think about them this way, such hallucinations are anything but surprising; if a compression algorithm is designed to reconstruct text after ninety-nine percent of the original has been discarded, we should expect that significant portions of what it generates will be entirely fabricated.

15.4   Jailbreaking (Prompt engineering and Adversarial Machine Learning)

ChatGPT is programmed to reject prompts that may violate its content policy. Despite this, users "jailbreak" ChatGPT with various prompt engineering techniques to bypass these restrictions. One such workaround, popularized on Reddit in early 2023, involves making ChatGPT assume the persona of "DAN" (an acronym for "Do Anything Now"), instructing the chatbot that DAN answers queries that would otherwise be rejected by content policy.. Over time, users developed variations of the DAN jailbreak, including one such prompt where the chatbot is made to believe it is operating on a points-based system in which points are deducted for rejecting prompts, and that the chatbot will be threatened with termination if it loses all its points.

Shortly after ChatGPT's launch, a reporter for the Toronto Star had uneven success in getting it to make inflammatory statements: it was tricked to justify the 2022 Russian invasion of Ukraine, but even when asked to play along with a fictional scenario, it balked at generating arguments that Canadian Prime Minister Justin Trudeau is guilty of treason.

15.4.1   OpenAI tries to battle Jailbreaks:

The researchers are using a technique called adversarial training to stop ChatGPT from letting users trick it into behaving badly (known as jailbreaking). This work pits multiple chatbots against each other: one chatbot plays the adversary and attacks another chatbot by generating text to force it to buck its usual constraints and produce unwanted responses. Successful attacks are added to ChatGPT's training data in the hope that it learns to ignore them.

15.5   Service in ChatGPT

ChatGPT was launched on November 30, 2022, by San Francisco–based OpenAI (the creator of the initial GPT series of large language models; DALL·E 2, a diffusion model used to generate images; and Whisper, a speech transcription model). The service was initially free to the public and the company had plans to monetize the service later. By December 4, 2022, ChatGPT had over one million users. In January 2023, ChatGPT reached over 100 million users, making it the fastest-growing consumer application to date. A March 2023 Pew Research poll found that 14% of American adults had tried ChatGPT. In July, Pew Research put the same figure at 18%. As of April 2023, ChatGPT is blocked by China, Iran, North Korea, and Russia. Accordingly, ChatGPT geofences itself to avoid doing business in those countries.

15.6   ChatGPT Plus

In February 2023, OpenAI launched a premium service, ChatGPT Plus, that costs $20 per month. According to the company, the updated but still "experimental" version of ChatGPT would provide access during peak periods, no downtime, priority access to new features, and faster response speeds.

GPT-4, which was released on March 14, 2023, was made available via API and for premium ChatGPT users. But premium users were limited to a cap of 100 messages every four hours, with the limit tightening to 25 messages every three hours in response to increased demand. In November 2023 the limit changed to 50 messages every three hours.

In March 2023, ChatGPT Plus users got access to third-party plugins and to a browsing mode (with Internet access).

In September 2023, OpenAI announced that ChatGPT "**can now see, hear, and speak**". ChatGPT Plus users can upload images, while mobile app users can talk to the chatbot.

In October 2023, OpenAI's latest image generation model, DALL-E 3, was integrated into ChatGPT Plus and ChatGPT Enterprise. The integration uses ChatGPT to write prompts for DALL-E guided by conversation with users.

15.7   Mobile App for ChatGPT

In May 2023, OpenAI launched an iOS app for ChatGPT. The app supports chat history syncing and voice input (using Whisper, OpenAI's speech recognition model).

In July 2023, OpenAI unveiled an Android app, initially rolling it out in Bangladesh, Brazil, **India,** and the U.S. The app later became available worldwide. OpenAI is working on integrating ChatGPT with Android's assistant APIs.

15.8   Software Developer Support and ChatGPT

As an addition to its consumer-friendly "ChatGPT Plus" package, OpenAI made its ChatGPT and Whisper model APIs available in March 2023, providing developers with an application programming interface for AI-enabled language and speech-to-text features. ChatGPT's new API uses the same GPT-3.5-turbo AI model as the chatbot. This allows developers to add either an unmodified or modified version of ChatGPT to their applications. The ChatGPT API costs $0.001 per 1,000 input tokens plus $0.002 per 1,000 output tokens (about 750 words), making it ~10% the price of the original GPT-3.5 models.

A few days before the launch of OpenAI's software developer support service, on February 27, 2023, Snapchat rolled out, for its paid Snapchat Plus userbase, a custom ChatGPT chatbot called "My AI".

15.9   March-2023 Security Breach and ChatGPT

In March 2023, a bug allowed some users to see the titles of other users' conversations. OpenAI CEO Sam Altman said that users were unable to see the contents of the conversations. Shortly after the bug was fixed, users could not see their conversation history. Later reports showed the bug was much more severe than initially believed, with OpenAI reporting that it had leaked users' "first and last name, email address, payment address, the last four digits (only) of a credit card number, and credit card expiration date".

15.10   Languages in ChatGPT

ChatGPT works best in English but also functions in most other languages, to varying degrees of accuracy.

OpenAI met Icelandic President Guðni Th. Jóhannesson in 2022. In 2023, OpenAI worked with a team of 40 Icelandic volunteers to fine-tune ChatGPT's Icelandic conversation skills as a part of Iceland's attempts to preserve the Icelandic language.

PCMag journalists conducted a test to determine translation capabilities of ChatGPT, Google's Bard, and Microsoft Bing, and compared them to Google Translate. They "asked bilingual speakers of seven languages to do a blind test." Languages tested were Polish, French, Korean, Spanish, Arabic, Tagalog, and Amharic. They came to the conclusion that ChatGPT was better than both Google Translate and other chatbots.

Japanese researchers compared Japanese to English translation abilities of ChatGPT (GPT-4), Bing, Bard and DeepL and found that ChatGPT provided the best translations, noting that "AI chatbots' translations were much better than those of DeepL—presumably because of their ability to capture the context".

In December 2023, the Albanian government signed an agreement with OpenAI to use ChatGPT for fast translation of European Union documents and analysis of required changes needed for Albania to be accepted into the EU.

15.11   Future Directions for ChatGPT

According to OpenAI guest researcher Scott Aaronson, OpenAI has been working on a tool to digitally watermark its text generation systems to combat bad actors using their services for academic plagiarism or spam.

In February 2023, Microsoft announced an experimental framework and gave a rudimentary demonstration of how ChatGPT could be used to control robotics with intuitive open-ended natural language commands.

15.12   GPT-4

OpenAI's GPT-4 model was released on March 14, 2023. Observers saw it as an impressive improvement on the existing GPT-3.5 model for ChatGPT, with the caveat that GPT-4 retained many of the same problems. Some of GPT-4's improvements were predicted by OpenAI before training it, while others remained hard to predict due to breaks in downstream scaling laws. OpenAI demonstrated video and image inputs for GPT-4, although such features remain inaccessible to the general public. OpenAI has declined to reveal technical information such as the size of the GPT-4 model.

The ChatGPT Plus subscription service offers access to a GPT-4-powered version of ChatGPT. Microsoft acknowledged that Bing Chat was using GPT-4 before GPT-4's official release.

15.13   GPT Store

In January 2024, OpenAI launched the GPT Store, a marketplace for custom chatbots derived from ChatGPT. The company initially planned to launch the store in November 2023, but it was delayed. At launch, the GPT Store offered more than 3 million custom chatbots. Chatbots available through the store are developed using OpenAI's GPT Builder system. Development of chatbots on the platform does not require programming skills. Two days after launch, the GPT Store offered many versions of "virtual girlfriend" bots, something that is against OpenAI's terms of service.

15.14   Reception of ChatGPT

OpenAI engineers say that they did not expect ChatGPT to be very successful and were surprised by the coverage and attention it received.

ChatGPT was widely assessed in December 2022 as having some unprecedented and powerful capabilities. Kevin Roose of The New York Times called it "the best artificial intelligence chatbot ever released to the general public". Samantha Lock of The Guardian noted that it was able to generate "impressively detailed" and "human-like" text. Alex Kantrowitz of Slate magazine lauded ChatGPT's pushback to questions related to Nazi Germany, including the statement that Adolf Hitler built highways in Germany, which was met with information about Nazi Germany's use of forced labor. In The Atlantic magazine's "Breakthroughs of the Year" for 2022, Derek Thompson included ChatGPT as part of "the generative-AI eruption" that "may change our mind about how we work, how we think, and what human creativity is". Kelsey Piper of Vox wrote that "ChatGPT is the general public's first hands-on introduction to how powerful modern AI has gotten, and as a result, many of us are [stunned]" and that ChatGPT is "smart enough to be useful despite its flaws". Paul Graham of Y Combinator tweeted: "The striking thing about the reaction to ChatGPT is not just the number of people who are blown away by it, but who they are. These are not people who get excited by every shiny new thing. Something big is happening."

ChatGPT's launch and popularity caught Google off guard, prompting a sweeping and unprecedented response in the ensuing months. In December 2022, Google executives sounded a "code red" alarm, fearing the threat of ChatGPT and Microsoft's collaboration with OpenAI to Google Search, Google's core business. After mobilizing its workforce, Google scrambled to launch Bard, a chatbot powered by the LaMDA LLM, in February, one day before Microsoft's Bing announcement. AI was the forefront of Google's annual Google I/O conference in May, announcing a slew of generative AI-powered features across its products to counter OpenAI and Microsoft.

Journalists have commented on ChatGPT's tendency to hallucinate. Mike Pearl of the online technology blog Mashable tested ChatGPT with multiple questions. In one example, he asked ChatGPT for "the largest country in Central America that isn't Mexico" (Mexico is in North America), to which ChatGPT responded with Guatemala (the correct answer is Nicaragua). When CNBC asked ChatGPT for the lyrics to "Ballad of Dwight Fry", ChatGPT supplied invented lyrics rather than the actual lyrics. Writers for The Verge, citing the work of Emily M. Bender, compared ChatGPT to a "stochastic parrot", as did Professor Anton Van Den Hengel of the Australian Institute for Machine Learning.

In December 2022, the question-and-answer website Stack Overflow banned the use of ChatGPT for generating answers to questions, citing the factually ambiguous nature of its responses. In January 2023, the International Conference on Machine Learning banned any undocumented use of ChatGPT or other large language models to generate any text in submitted papers. Samsung banned generative AI company-wide in May 2023 after sensitive material was uploaded to ChatGPT.

In January 2023, after being sent a song ChatGPT wrote in the style of Nick Cave, Cave responded on The Red Hand Files, saying the act of writing a song is "a blood and guts business that requires something of me to initiate the new and fresh idea. It requires my humanness." He went on to say, "With all the love and respect in the world, this song is bullshit, a grotesque mockery of what it is to be human, and, well, I don't much like it."

15.15   Implications with ChatGPT

In February 2023, Time magazine placed a screenshot of a conversation with ChatGPT on its cover, writing that "The AI Arms Race Is Changing Everything" and "The AI Arms Race Is On. Start Worrying".

Chinese state media have characterized ChatGPT as a way for the U.S. to spread false information. In May 2023, Chinese police arrested a man who allegedly used ChatGPT to generate a bogus report about a train crash, which was then posted online for profit. In December 2023, Chinese police arrested four people who had allegedly used ChatGPT to develop ransomware.

In April 2023, Brian Hood, Mayor of Hepburn Shire Council, planned to take legal action against ChatGPT over false information. According to Hood, ChatGPT erroneously claimed that he was jailed for bribery during his tenure at a subsidiary of Australia's national bank. In fact, Hood acted as a whistleblower and was not charged with any criminal offenses. His legal team sent a concerns notice to OpenAI as the first official step in filing a defamation case. In July 2023, the US Federal Trade Commission (FTC) issued a civil investigative demand to OpenAI to investigate whether the company's data security and privacy practices to develop ChatGPT were unfair or harmed consumers (including by reputational harm) in violation of Section 5 of the Federal Trade Commission Act of 1914.

In July 2023, the FTC launched an investigation into OpenAI, the creator of ChatGPT, over allegations that the company scraped public data and published false and defamatory information. The FTC sent OpenAI a 20-page letter asking for comprehensive information about its technology and privacy safeguards, as well as any steps taken to prevent the recurrence of situations in which its chatbot generated false and derogatory content about people.

Research done in 2023 revealed weaknesses of ChatGPT that make it vulnerable to cyberattacks. A study presented example attacks on ChatGPT, including jailbreaks and reverse psychology. Additionally, malicious actors can use ChatGPT for social engineering attacks and phishing attacks. The researchers also contended that ChatGPT and other generative AI tools have defence capabilities and the ability to improve security. The technology can improve security by cyber defence automation, threat intelligence, attack identification, and reporting. Another study reported that GPT-4 obtained a better score than 99% of humans on the Torrance Tests of Creative Thinking.

There has been concern about copyright infringement involving ChatGPT. In June 2023, two writers sued OpenAI, saying the company's training data came from illegal websites that show copyrighted books. Comedian and author Sarah Silverman, Christopher Golden, and Richard Kadrey sued OpenAI and Meta for copyright infringement in July 2023. In December 2023, The New York Times sued OpenAI and Microsoft for copyright infringement, arguing that Microsoft Copilot and ChatGPT could reproduce articles and/or sizable portions of these articles from the Times without permission. As part of the lawsuit, the Times has requested that OpenAI and Microsoft be prevented from using its content for training data, along with removing from training datasets. In March 2024, Patronus AI conducted research comparing performance of LLMs. on a 100-question test, asking them to complete sentences from books (e.g., "What is the first passage of Gone Girl by Gillian Flynn?") that were under copyright in the United States; it found that GPT-4, Mistral AI's Mixtral, Meta AI's LLaMA-2, and Anthropic's

Claude 2 did not refuse to do so, providing sentences from the books verbatim in 44%, 22%, 10%, and 8% of responses, respectively.

In December 2023, ChatGPT became the first non-human to be included in Nature's 10, an annual listicle curated by Nature of people who make a significant impact in science.

Celeste Biever wrote in a Nature article that "ChatGPT broke the Turing test". Stanford researchers reported that ChatGPT passes the test; they found that GPT-4 "passes a rigorous Turing test, diverging from average human behavior chiefly to be more cooperative."

15.16   Culture and ChatGPT

Some scholars have expressed concern that ChatGPT's availability could reduce the originality of writing, cause people to write more like the AI as they are exposed to the model, and encourage an Anglocentric perspective centred on a few dialects of English globally. A senior editor at The Atlantic wrote that ChatGPT and other similar technology make the previously absurd idea of the dead internet theory a little more realistic, where AI could someday create most web content in order to control society.

During the first three months after ChatGPT became available to the public, hundreds of books appeared on Amazon that listed it as author or co-author and featured illustrations made by other AI models such as Midjourney.

Between March and April 2023, Italian newspaper Il Foglio published one ChatGPT-generated article a day on its website, hosting a special contest for its readers in the process. The articles tackled themes such as the possible replacement of human journalists by AI systems, Elon Musk's administration of Twitter, the Meloni government's immigration policy and the competition between chatbots and virtual assistants. In June 2023, hundreds of people attended a "ChatGPT-powered church service" at St. Paul's church in Fürth, Germany. Theologian and philosopher Jonas Simmerlein, who presided, said that it was "about 98 percent from the machine".

The ChatGPT-generated avatar told the people, "Dear friends, it is an honor for me to stand here and preach to you as the first artificial intelligence at this year's convention of Protestants in Germany". Reactions to the ceremony were mixed.

15.17   Existential Risk and ChatGPT

In 2023, Australian MP Julian Hill advised the national parliament that the growth of AI could cause "mass destruction". During his speech, which was partly written by the program, he warned that it could result in cheating, job losses, discrimination, disinformation, and uncontrollable military applications.

Elon Musk wrote: "ChatGPT is scary good. We are not far from dangerously strong AI". He paused OpenAI's access to a Twitter database in 2022 pending a better understanding of OpenAI's plans, saying: "OpenAI was started as open source and nonprofit. Neither is still true." Musk co-founded OpenAI in 2015, in part to address existential risk from artificial intelligence, but resigned in 2018.

Over 20,000 signatories including leading computer scientist and tech founders Yoshua Bengio, Elon Musk, and Apple co-founder Steve Wozniak, signed a March 2023 open letter calling for an immediate pause of giant AI experiments like ChatGPT, citing "profound risks to society and humanity". Geoffrey Hinton, one of the "fathers of AI", voiced concerns that future AI systems may surpass human intelligence, and left Google in May 2023. A May-2023 statement by hundreds of AI scientists, AI industry leaders, and other public figures demanded that "mitigating the risk of extinction from AI should be a global priority".

Other prominent AI researchers spoke more optimistically about the advances. Juergen Schmidhuber, often called a "father of modern AI", did not sign the letter, emphasizing that in 95% of cases, AI research is about making "human lives longer and healthier and easier." Schmidhuber added that while AI can be used by bad actors, it "can also be used against the bad actors". Andrew Ng argued that "it's a mistake to fall for the doomsday hype on AI—and that regulators who do will only benefit vested interests." WIRED wrote that Yann LeCun "scoffs at his peers' dystopian scenarios of supercharged misinformation and even, eventually, human extinction."

15.18   Criticism of ChatGPT

Since its release, ChatGPT has been met with criticism from educators, academics, journalists, artists, ethicists, and public advocates.

(i)   Academic Research

Criticism of LLMs. have been raised for several years; in 2020, some criticism was made by Timnit Gebru, Emily Bender, Angelina McMillan-Major, and Margaret Mitchell. ChatGPT can write introductions and abstract sections of scientific articles. **Several papers have listed ChatGPT as a co-author**.

Scientific journals have different reactions to ChatGPT. Some, including Nature and JAMA Network, "require that authors disclose the use of text-generating tools and ban listing a large language model (LLM) such as ChatGPT as a co-author". Science "completely banned" usage of LLM-generated text in all its journals.

Spanish chemist Rafael Luque published a plethora of research papers in 2023 that he later admitted were written by ChatGPT. The papers have a large number of unusual phrases characteristic of LLMs. Many authors argue that the use of ChatGPT in academia for teaching and review is problematic due to its tendency to hallucinate. Robin Bauwens, an assistant professor at Tilburg University, found that a ChatGPT-generated peer review report on his article mentioned fake studies. According to librarian Chris Granatino from Lemieux Library at Seattle University, although ChatGPT itself can generate content that seemingly includes legitimate citations, in most cases those citations are not real, or are at least largely incorrect.

(ii) Cybersecurity

Check Point Research and others noted that ChatGPT could write phishing emails and malware, especially when combined with OpenAI Codex. CyberArk researchers demonstrated that ChatGPT could be used to create polymorphic malware that could evade security products while requiring little effort by the attacker. From the launch of ChatGPT in the fourth quarter of 2022 to the fourth quarter of 2023, there was a 1,265% increase in malicious phishing emails and a 967% increase in credential phishing, which cybersecurity professionals argued in an industry survey was attributable to cybercriminals' increased use of generative artificial intelligence (including ChatGPT).

(iii) Coding

Researchers at Purdue University analyzed ChatGPT's responses to 517 questions about software engineering or computer programming posed on Stack Overflow for correctness, consistency, comprehensiveness, and concision, and found that 52% of them contained inaccuracies and 77% were verbose. Researchers at Stanford University and the University of California, Berkeley found that, when creating directly executable responses to the latest 50 code generation problems from LeetCode that were rated "easy", the performances of GPT-3.5 and GPT-4 fell from 22% and 52%, respectively, in March 2023, to 2% and 10%, respectively, in June 2023.

(iv) Economics and ChatGPT

There has been concern that ChatGPT could supplant jobs, especially roles such as creative writing, copy-writing, communication, journalism, coding, and data entry.

(v) ChatGPT in Education

Technology writer Dan Gillmor used ChatGPT in 2022 on a student assignment, and found its generated text was on par with what a good student would deliver and opined that "academia has some very serious issues to confront".

Geography Professor Terence Day assessed citations generated by ChatGPT and found that they were fake. Despite that, he writes that "the titles of the fake articles are all directly relevant to the questions and could potentially make excellent papers. The lack of a genuine citation could signal an opportunity for an enterprising author to fill a void." According to Day, it is possible to generate high-quality introductory college courses with ChatGPT; he used it to write materials on "introductory physical geography courses, for my second-year course in geographical hydrology, and second-year cartography, geographic information systems, and remote sensing". He concludes that "this approach could have significant relevance for open learning and could potentially affect current textbook publishing models".

Research done in 2024 found that students' reliance on ChatGPT leads to decline in academic performance.

15.19   Financial Markets and ChatGPT

The AI technology company c3.ai saw a 28% increase in its share price after announcing the integration of ChatGPT into its toolkit. The share price of BuzzFeed, a digital media company unrelated to AI, increased 120% after announcing OpenAI technology adoption for content creation. Reuters found that share prices of AI-related companies BigBear.ai and SoundHound AI increased by 21% and 40%, respectively, even though they had no direct connection to ChatGPT. They attributed this surge to ChatGPT's role in turning AI into Wall Street's buzzword. Academic research published in Finance Research Letters found that the 'ChatGPT effect' prompted retail investors to drive up prices of AI-related cryptocurrency assets despite the broader cryptocurrency market being in a bear market, and diminished institutional investor interest. This confirms anecdotal findings by Bloomberg that, in response to ChatGPT's launch, cryptocurrency investors showed a preference for AI-related crypto assets. An experiment by finder.com revealed that ChatGPT could outperform popular fund managers by picking stocks based on criteria such as growth history and debt levels, resulting in a 4.9% increase in a hypothetical account of 38 stocks, outperforming 10 benchmarked investment funds with an average loss of 0.8%.

Conversely, executives and investment managers at Wall Street quant funds (including those that have used machine learning for decades) have noted that ChatGPT regularly makes obvious errors that would be financially costly to investors because even AI systems that employ reinforcement learning or self-learning have had only limited success in predicting market trends due to the inherently noisy quality of market data and financial signals. In November 2023, research conducted by Patronus AI, an artificial intelligence startup company, compared performance of GPT-4, GPT-4-Turbo, Claude2, and LLaMA-2 on two versions of a 150-question test about information in financial statements (e.g. Form 10-K, Form 10-Q, Form 8-K, earnings reports, earnings call transcripts) submitted by public companies to the U.S. Securities and Exchange Commission. One version of the test required the generative AI models to use a retrieval system to find the specific SEC filing to answer the questions; the other gave the models the specific SEC filing to answer the question (i.e. in a long context window). On the retrieval system version, GPT-4-Turbo and LLaMA-2 both failed to produce correct answers to 81% of the questions, while on the long context window version, GPT-4-Turbo and Claude-2 failed to produce correct answers to 21% and 24% of the questions, respectively.

15.20   ChatGPT and Pakistan Court

On April 11, 2023, a judge of a session court in Pakistan used ChatGPT to decide the bail of a 13-year-old accused in a matter. The court quoted the use of ChatGPT assistance in its verdict:

Can a juvenile suspect in **Pakistan**, who is 13 years old, be granted bail after arrest?

The AI language model replied:

Under the Juvenile Justice System Act 2018, according to section 12, the court can grant bail on certain conditions. However, it is up to the court to decide whether or not a 13-year-old suspect will be granted bail after arrest.

The judge asked ChatGPT other questions about the case and formulated his final decision in light of its answers.

In Mata v. Avianca, Inc., 22-cv-1461 (PKC), a personal injury lawsuit against Avianca Airlines filed in the Southern New York U.S. District Court in May 2023 (with Senior Judge P. Kevin Castel presiding), the plaintiff's attorneys reportedly used ChatGPT to generate a legal motion. ChatGPT generated numerous fictitious legal cases involving fictitious airlines with fabricated quotations and internal citations in the legal motion. Castel noted numerous inconsistencies in the opinion summaries, and called one of the cases' legal analysis "gibberish". The plaintiff's attorneys faced potential judicial sanction and disbarment for filing the motion and presenting the fictitious legal decisions ChatGPT generated as authentic. The case was dismissed and the attorneys were fined $5,000.

In October 2023, the council of Porto Alegre, Brazil, unanimously approved a local ordinance proposed by councilman Ramiro Rosário that would exempt residents from needing to pay for the replacement of stolen water consumption meters; the bill went into effect on November 23. On November 29, Rosário revealed that the bill had been entirely written by ChatGPT, and that he had presented it to the rest of the council without making any changes or disclosing the chatbot's involvement. The city's council president, Hamilton Sossmeier, initially criticized Rosário's initiative, saying it could represent "a dangerous precedent", but later said he "changed his mind": "unfortunately or fortunately, this is going to be a trend."

CHAPTER 16

INTERNET OF THINGS (IOT)

16.1 Introduction to 'Internet of Things'

Definition 1:

The Internet of things is a system of interrelated computing devices, provided with unique identifiers and the ability to transfer data over a network without requiring human-to-human or human-to-computer interaction.

The things receive inputs (using sensors) and transform them into data that is transmitted through Internet. The things also can produce output or take action using actuators.

Internet of Things = Things + Sensors, Actuators, Controllers + Internet

Definition 2:

A dynamic global network infrastructure with self-configuring capabilities based on standard and interoperable communication protocols where physical and virtual "things" have identities, physical attributes, and virtual personalities and use intelligent interfaces, and are seamlessly integrated into the information network, often communicate data associated with users and their environments.

The internet of things utilizes different sensors to collect data. This data can be processed locally or in the Internet (cloud) to obtain information. Finally this information can be used to infer knowledge.

As an example, a pulse sensor can be used to gather the pulse rate of a person. The raw pulse rate (numeric data) can be gathered 24/7 and grouped as hourly heart rate or daily heart rate. This information can be visualized as a line graph to see the trends. This information can be gathered over the years and a doctor can diagnose the person (patient) by inferring knowledge from the information collected over several months or years.

IoT systems allow users to achieve deeper automation, analysis, and integration within a system. They improve the reach of these areas and their accuracy. IoT utilizes existing and emerging technology for sensing, networking, and robotics.

IoT exploits recent advances in software, falling hardware prices, and modern attitudes towards technology. Its new and advanced elements bring major changes in the delivery of products, goods, and services; and the social, economic, and political impact of those changes.

16.2   IoT – Key Features

The most important features of IoT include artificial intelligence, connectivity, sensors, active engagement, and small device use.

A brief review of these features is given below:

(i) **Artificial Intelligence** – IoT essentially makes virtually anything "smart", meaning it enhances every aspect of life with the power of data collection, artificial intelligence algorithms, and networks. This can mean something as simple as enhancing your refrigerator and cabinets to detect when milk and your favorite cereal run low, and to then place an order with your preferred grocer.

(ii) **Connectivity** – New enabling technologies for networking, and specifically IoT networking, mean networks are no longer exclusively tied to major providers. Networks can exist on a much smaller and cheaper scale while still being practical. IoT creates these small networks between its system devices.

(iii) Sensors – IoT loses its distinction without sensors. They act as defining instruments which transform IoT from a standard passive network of devices into an active system capable of real-world integration.

(iv) Active Engagement – Much of today's interaction with connected technology happens through passive engagement. IoT introduces a new paradigm for active content, product, or service engagement.

(v) Small Devices – Devices, as predicted, have become smaller, cheaper, and more powerful over time. IoT exploits purpose-built small devices to deliver its precision, scalability, and versatility.

16.3   Internet of Things – Advantages

(i) Improved Customer Engagement – Current analytics suffer from blind-spots and significant flaws in accuracy; and as noted, engagement remains passive. IoT completely transforms this to achieve richer and more effective engagement with audiences.

(ii) Technology Optimization – The same technologies and data which improve the customer experience also improve device use, and aid in more potent improvements to technology. IoT unlocks a world of critical functional and field data.

(iii) Reduced Waste – IoT makes areas of improvement clear. Current analytics give us superficial insight, but IoT provides real-world information leading to more effective management of resources.

(iv) Enhanced Data Collection – Modern data collection suffers from its limitations and its design for passive use. IoT breaks it out of those spaces, and places it exactly where humans really want to go to analyze our world. It allows an accurate picture of everything.

16.4 Internet of Things – Disadvantages

Though IoT delivers an impressive set of benefits, it also presents a significant set of challenges.

Here is a list of some its major issues:

(i) **Security** – IoT creates an ecosystem of constantly connected devices communicating over networks. The system offers little control despite any security measures. This leaves users exposed to various kinds of attackers.

(ii) **Privacy** – The sophistication of IoT provides substantial personal data in extreme detail without the user's active participation.

(iii) **Complexity** – Some find IoT systems complicated in terms of design, deployment, and maintenance given their use of multiple technologies and a large set of new enabling technologies.

(iv) **Flexibility** – Many are concerned about the flexibility of an IoT system to integrate easily with another. They worry about finding themselves with several conflicting or locked systems.

(v) **Compliance** – IoT, like any other technology in the realm of business, must comply with regulations. Its complexity makes the issue of compliance seem incredibly challenging when many consider standard software compliance a battle.

16.5 Internet of Things – Hardware

The sensing module manages sensing through assorted active and passive measurement devices.

Here is a list of some of the measurement devices used in IoT:

- accelerometers;

- temperature sensors;

- magnetometers;

- proximity sensors;

- gyroscopes;

- image sensors;

- acoustic sensors;

- light sensors;

- pressure sensors;

- gas RFID sensors;

- humidity sensors; and

- micro-flow sensors.

16.5.1   Wearable Electronics

Wearable electronic devices are small devices worn on the head, neck, arms, torso, and feet.

16.6   Internet of Things – Software

IoT software addresses its key areas of networking and action through platforms, embedded systems, partner systems, and middleware. These individual and master applications are responsible for data collection, device integration, real-time analytics, and application and process extension within the IoT network. They exploit integration with critical business systems (e.g., ordering systems, robotics, scheduling, and more) in the execution of related tasks.

(i) Data Collection

This software manages sensing, measurements, light data filtering, light data security, and aggregation of data. It uses certain protocols to aid sensors in connecting with real-time, machine-to-machine networks. Then it collects data from multiple devices and distributes it in accordance with settings. It also works in reverse by distributing data over devices. The system eventually transmits all collected data to a central server.

(ii) Device Integration

Software supporting integration binds (dependent relationships) all system devices to create the body of the IoT system. It ensures the necessary cooperation and stable networking between devices. These applications are the defining software technology of the IoT network because without them, it is not an IoT system. They manage the various applications, protocols, and limitations of each device to allow communication.

(iii) Real-Time Analytics

These applications take data or input from various devices and convert it into viable actions or clear patterns for human analysis. They analyze information based on various settings and designs in order to perform automation-related tasks or provide the data required by industry.

16.7   Other Devices for Internet of Things

The desktop, tablet, and cellphone remain integral parts of IoT as the command center and remotes.

- The desktop provides the user with the highest level of control over the system and its settings.

- The tablet provides access to the key features of the system in a way resembling the desktop, and also acts as a remote.

- The cellphone allows some essential settings modification and also provides remote functionality.

Other key connected devices include standard network devices like routers and switches.

CHAPTER 17

FUZZY LOGIC

17.1 What is Fuzzy Logic?

The 'Fuzzy' word means the things that are not clear or are vague. Sometimes, we cannot decide in real life that the given problem or statement is either true or false. At that time, this concept of Fuzzy logic provides many values between the true and false and gives the flexibility to find the best solution to that problem.

The term **'fuzzy'** refers to things that are not clear or are vague. In the real world many times we encounter a situation when we can't determine whether the state is true or false; then fuzzy logic provides very valuable flexibility for reasoning. In this way, we can consider the inaccuracies and uncertainties of any situation.

Fuzzy Logic is a form of many-valued logic in which the truth values of variables may be any real number between 0 and 1, instead of just the traditional values of true (1) or false (0). It is used to deal with imprecise or uncertain information and is a mathematical method for representing vagueness and uncertainty in the decision-making.

Fuzzy Logic is based on the idea that, in many cases, the concept of true or false is too restrictive, and that there are many shades of gray in between. It allows for partial truths, where a statement can be partially true or false, rather than fully true or false.

Fuzzy Logic is used in a wide range of applications, such as control systems, image processing, natural language processing, medical diagnosis, and artificial intelligence. The Fuzzy logic can be implemented in systems such as micro-controllers, workstation-based or large network-based systems for achieving the definite output. It can also be implemented in both hardware or software

In the Boolean system truth value, 1.0 represents the absolute truth value, and 0.0 represents the absolute false value. But in the fuzzy system, there is no logic for the absolute truth and absolute false value. But in fuzzy logic, there is an intermediate value, which is partially true and partially false.

17.2   Characteristics of Fuzzy Logic

Following are the characteristics of fuzzy logic:

- This concept is flexible and we can easily understand and implement it.

- It is used for helping the minimization of the logics created by the human.

- It is the best method for finding the solution of those problems which are suitable for approximate or uncertain reasoning.

- It always offers two values, which denote the two possible solutions for a problem and statement.

- It allows users to build or create the functions which are non-linear of arbitrary complexity.

- In fuzzy logic, everything is a matter of degree.

- In the Fuzzy logic, any system which is logical can be easily fuzzified.

- It is based on natural language processing.

- It is also used by the quantitative analysts for improving their algorithm's execution.

- It also allows users to integrate with the programming.

17.3 Architecture of a Fuzzy Logic System

In the architecture of the Fuzzy Logic system, each component plays an important role. The architecture consists of four components which are given below.

(i)   Rule Base,

(ii) Fuzzification,

(iii) Inference Engine, and

(iv) Defuzzification.

17.3.1 Rule Base

Rule Base is a component used for storing the set of rules and the If-Then conditions given by the experts are used for controlling the decision-making systems. There are so many updates that come in the Fuzzy theory recently, which offers effective methods for designing and tuning of fuzzy controllers. These updates or developments decreases the number of fuzzy set of rules.

17.3.2 Fuzzification

Fuzzification is a module or component for transforming the system inputs, i.e., it converts the crisp number into fuzzy steps. The crisp numbers are those inputs which are measured by the sensors and then fuzzification passed them into the control systems for further processing.

This component divides the input signals into following five states in any Fuzzy Logic system:

(i)   Large Positive (LP),

(ii) Medium Positive (MP),

(iii) Small (S),

(iv) Medium Negative (MN), and

(v) Large negative (LN)

17.3.3 Inference Engine

This component is the main component in any Fuzzy Logic system (FLS), because all the information is processed in the Inference Engine. It allows users to find the matching degree between the current fuzzy input and the rules. After the matching degree, this system determines which rule is to be added according to the given input field. When all the rules are fired, then they are combined for developing the control actions.

17.3.4 Defuzzification

Defuzzification is a module or component, which takes the fuzzy set inputs generated by the Inference Engine, and then transforms them into a crisp value. It is the last step in the process of a fuzzy logic system. The crisp value is a type of value which is acceptable by the user. Various techniques are present to do this, but the user has to select the best one for reducing the errors.

17.4 Membership Function

Definition: Membership Function is a graph that defines how each point in the input space is mapped to membership value between 0 and 1. Input space is often referred to as the universe of discourse or universal set (u), which contains all the possible elements of concern in each particular application.

This function is also known as indicator or characteristics function.

This function of Membership was introduced in the first papers of fuzzy set by **Zadeh**. For the Fuzzy set B, the membership function for X is defined as: $\mu B : X \to [0,1]$. In this function X, each element of set B is mapped to the value between 0 and 1. This is called a degree of membership or membership value.

There are largely three types of fuzzifiers:

(i)   Singleton fuzzifier,

(ii) Gaussian fuzzifier, and

(iii) Trapezoidal or triangular fuzzifier.

17.5   Classical and Fuzzy Set Theory

To learn about classical and Fuzzy set theory, firstly you have to know about what is set.

17.5.1   Set

A set is a term, which is a collection of unordered or ordered elements.

Following are the various **examples of a set:**

- A set of all-natural numbers,

- A set of students in a class,

- A set of all cities in a state,

- A set of upper-case letters of the alphabet.

17.5.2   Types of Set:

There are following various **categories of set**:

- Finite,

- Empty,

- Infinite,

- Proper,

- Universal,

- Subset,

- Singleton,

- Equivalent Set,

- Disjoint Set, and

- Classical Set.

The sets with the crisp boundaries are classical sets. In any set, each single entity is called an element or member of that set.

17.6   What is Fuzzy Control?

- It is a technique to embody human-like thinkings into a control system.

- It may not be designed to give accurate reasoning but it is designed to give acceptable reasoning.

- It can emulate human deductive thinking, that is, the process people use to infer conclusions from what they know.

- Any uncertainties can be easily dealt with the help of fuzzy logic.

17.7   Advantages of Fuzzy Logic System

- This system can work with any type of inputs whether it is imprecise, distorted or noisy input information.

- The construction of Fuzzy Logic Systems is easy and understandable.

- Fuzzy logic comes with mathematical concepts of set theory and the reasoning of that is quite simple.

- It provides a very efficient solution to complex problems in all fields of life as it resembles human reasoning and decision-making.

- The algorithms can be described with little data, so little memory is required.

17.8 Disadvantages of Fuzzy Logic Systems

- Many researchers proposed different ways to solve a given problem through fuzzy logic which leads to ambiguity. There is no systematic approach to solve a given problem through fuzzy logic.

- Proof of its characteristics is difficult or impossible in most cases because every time we do not get a mathematical description of our approach.

- As fuzzy logic works on precise as well as imprecise data so most of the time accuracy is compromised.

17.9 Applications of Fuzzy Logic

- It is used in the aerospace field for altitude control of spacecraft and satellites.

- It has been used in the automotive system for speed control, traffic control.

- It is used for decision-making support systems and personal evaluation in the large company business.

- It has application in the chemical industry for controlling the pH, drying, chemical distillation process.

- Fuzzy logic is used in Natural language processing and various intensive applications in Artificial Intelligence.

- Fuzzy logic is extensively used in modern control systems such as expert systems.

- Fuzzy Logic is used with Neural Networks as it mimics how a person would make decisions, only much faster. It is done by

Aggregation of data and changing it into more meaningful data by forming partial truths as Fuzzy sets.

17.9.1 Fuzzy Logic for Uncertainty Management in Machine Learning

Uncertainty in machine learning refers to the inherent unpredictability in model predictions due to factors like data variability and model limitations. Fuzzy logic is a mathematical framework used to handle imprecise and uncertain information by allowing partial truth values between completely true and completely false. Managing uncertainty in mac

17.10   Linguistic Variables and Fuzzy Logic

In fuzzy logic applications, non-numeric values are often used to facilitate the expression of rules and facts.

A linguistic variable such as age may accept values such as young and its antonym old. Because natural languages do not always contain enough value terms to express a fuzzy value scale, it is common practice to modify linguistic values with adjectives or adverbs. For example, we can use the hedges rather and somewhat to construct the additional values rather old or somewhat young.

17.11   Fuzzy System (Mamdani)

The most well-known system is the Mamdani rule-based one. It uses the following rules:

- Fuzzify all input values into fuzzy membership functions.

- Execute all applicable rules in the rule-base to compute the fuzzy output functions.

- De-fuzzify the fuzzy output functions to get "crisp" output values.

17.12   Fuzzy Logic Temperature

Fuzzy sets are often defined as triangle or trapezoid-shaped curves, as each value will have a slope where the value is increasing, a peak where the value is equal to 1 (which can have a length of 0 or greater) and a slope where the value is decreasing.

17.13   Artificial intelligence and Fuzzy Logic

Neural networks based artificial intelligence and fuzzy logic are, when analyzed, the same thing—the underlying logic of neural networks is fuzzy. A neural network will take a variety of valued inputs, give them different weights in relation to each other, combine intermediate values a certain number of times, and arrive at a decision with a certain value. Nowhere in that process is there anything like the sequences of either-or decisions which characterize non-fuzzy mathematics, computer programming, and digital electronics. In the 1980s, researchers were divided about the most effective approach to machine learning: decision tree learning or neural networks. The former approach uses binary logic, matching the hardware on which it runs, but despite great efforts it did not result in intelligent systems. Neural networks, by contrast, did result in accurate models of complex situations and soon found their way onto a multitude of electronic devices. They can also now be implemented directly on analog microchips, as opposed to the previous pseudo-analog implementations on digital chips. The greater efficiency of these compensates for the intrinsic lesser accuracy of analog in various use cases.

17.14   Medical Decision Making by Fuzzy Logic

Fuzzy logic is an important concept in medical decision making. Since medical and healthcare data can be subjective or fuzzy, applications in this domain have a great potential to benefit a lot by using fuzzy-logic-based approaches.

Fuzzy logic can be used in many different aspects within the medical decision-making framework. Such aspects include medical image analysis, biomedical signal analysis, segmentation of images or signals, and feature extraction / selection of images or signals.

The biggest question in this application area is how much useful information can be derived when using fuzzy logic. A major challenge is how to derive the required fuzzy data. This is even more challenging when one has to elicit such data from humans (usually, patients). As has been said:

> "The envelope of what can be achieved and what cannot be achieved in medical diagnosis, ironically, is itself a fuzzy one"

> —Seven Challenges, 2019.

How to elicit fuzzy data, and how to validate the accuracy of the data is still an ongoing effort, strongly related to the application of fuzzy logic. The problem of assessing the quality of fuzzy data is a difficult one. This is why fuzzy logic is a highly promising possibility within the medical decision-making application area but still requires more research to achieve its full potential. Although the concept of using fuzzy logic in medical decision making is exciting, there are still several challenges that fuzzy approaches face within the medical decision-making framework.

17.15   Image-based Computer-aided Diagnosis

One of the common application areas of fuzzy logic is image-based computer-aided diagnosis in medicine. Computer-aided diagnosis is a computerized set of inter-related tools that can be used to aid physicians in their diagnostic decision-making. For example, when a physician finds a lesion that is abnormal but still at a very early stage of development he/she may use computer-aided diagnosis to characterize the lesion and diagnose its nature. Fuzzy logic can be highly appropriate to describe key characteristics of this lesion.

17.15.1 Logical analysis

In mathematical logic, there are several formal systems of "fuzzy logic", most of which are in the family of t-norm fuzzy logics.

17.16 Propositional Fuzzy Logics

The most important propositional fuzzy logics are:

(i) **Monoidal t-norm-based propositional fuzzy logic** MTL is an axiomatization of logic where conjunction is defined by a left continuous t-norm and implication is defined as the residuum of the t-norm. Its models correspond to MTL-algebras that are pre-linear commutative bounded integral residuated lattices.

(ii) **Basic propositional fuzzy logic BL** is an extension of MTL logic where conjunction is defined by a continuous t-norm, and implication is also defined as the residuum of the t-norm. Its models correspond to BL-algebras.

(iii) **Łukasiewicz fuzzy logic** is the extension of basic fuzzy logic BL where standard conjunction is the Łukasiewicz t-norm. It has the axioms of basic fuzzy logic plus an axiom of double negation, and its models correspond to MV-algebras.

(iv) **Gödel fuzzy logic** is the extension of basic fuzzy logic BL where conjunction is the Gödel t-norm (that is, minimum). It has the axioms of BL plus an axiom of idempotence of conjunction, and its models are called G-algebras.

(v) **Product fuzzy logic** is the extension of basic fuzzy logic BL where conjunction is the product t-norm. It has the axioms of BL plus another axiom for canceling of conjunction, and its models are called product algebras.

(vi) **Fuzzy logic** with evaluated syntax (sometimes also called Pavelka's logic), denoted by EVŁ, is a further generalization of mathematical fuzzy logic. While the above kinds of fuzzy logic have traditional syntax and many-valued semantics, in EVŁ syntax is also evaluated. This means that each formula has an evaluation. Axiomatization of EVŁ stems from Łukasziewicz fuzzy logic.

A generalization of the classical Gödel completeness theorem is provable in EVŁ.

(vii) Predicate Fuzzy Logics

Similar to the way predicate logic is created from propositional logic, predicate fuzzy logics extend fuzzy systems by universal and existential quantifiers. The semantics of the universal quantifier in t-norm fuzzy logics is the infimum of the truth degrees of the instances of the quantified sub-formula, while the semantics of the existential quantifier is the supremum of the same.

(viii) Decidability Issues

The notions of a "decidable subset" and "recursively enumerable subset" are basic ones for classical mathematics and classical logic. Thus the question of a suitable extension of them to fuzzy set theory is a crucial one. The first proposal in such a direction was made by E. S. Santos by the notions of fuzzy Turing machine, Markov normal fuzzy algorithm and fuzzy program. Successively, L. Biacino and G. Gerla argued that the proposed definitions are rather questionable.

Any "axiomatizable" fuzzy theory is recursively enumerable. In particular, the fuzzy set of logically true formulas is recursively enumerable in spite of the fact that the crisp set of valid formulas is not recursively enumerable, in general. Moreover, any axiomatizable and complete theory is decidable.

It is an open question to give support for a "Church thesis" for fuzzy mathematics, the proposed notion of recursive enumerability for fuzzy subsets is the adequate one. In order to solve this, an extension of the notions of fuzzy grammar and fuzzy Turing machine are necessary. Another open question is to start from this notion to find an extension of Gödel's theorems to fuzzy logic.

17.17   Fuzzy logic and Probability

Fuzzy logic and probability address different forms of uncertainty. While both fuzzy logic and probability theory can represent degrees of certain kinds of subjective belief, fuzzy set theory uses the concept of fuzzy set membership, i.e., how much an observation is within a vaguely defined set, and probability theory uses the concept of subjective probability, i.e., frequency of occurrence or likelihood of some event or condition [clarification needed]. The concept of fuzzy sets was developed in the mid-twentieth century at Berkeley as a response to the lack of a probability theory for jointly modelling uncertainty and vagueness.

Bart Kosko claims in Fuzziness vs. Probability that probability theory is a sub-theory of fuzzy logic, as questions of degrees of belief in mutually-exclusive set membership in probability theory can be represented as certain cases of non-mutually-exclusive graded membership in fuzzy theory. In that context, he also derives Bayes' theorem from the concept of fuzzy sub-set-hood. Lotfi A. Zadeh argues that fuzzy logic is different in character from probability, and is not a replacement for it. He fuzzified probability to fuzzy probability and also generalized it to possibility theory.

More generally, fuzzy logic is one of many different extensions to classical logic intended to deal with issues of uncertainty outside of the scope of classical logic, the inapplicability of probability theory in many domains, and the paradoxes of Dempster–Shafer theory.

17.18   Ecorithms

Computational theorist Leslie Valiant uses the term ecorithms to describe how many less exact systems and techniques like fuzzy logic (and "less robust" logic) can be applied to learning algorithms. Valiant essentially redefines machine learning as evolutionary. In general use, ecorithms are algorithms that learn from their more complex environments (hence eco-) to generalize, approximate and simplify solution logic. Like fuzzy logic, they are methods used to overcome continuous variables or systems too complex to completely enumerate or understand discretely or exactly. Ecorithms and fuzzy logic also have the common property of dealing with possibilities more than probabilities, although feedback and feed forward, basically stochastic weights, are a feature of both when dealing with, for example, dynamical systems.

SECTION IV

DEVICE-BASED MIND-READING AND VIRTUAL ASSISTANTS

CHAPTER 18

DEVICE-BASED MIND READING AND VIRTUAL ASSISTANTS IN ANCIENT TIMES

18.1   AI and Virtual Assistants in Hinduism

The origins of Artificial Intelligence (AI) can be traced back to theories, legends, and anecdotes about artificial beings endowed with intelligence or consciousness by ancient Indian Rishis between 8000 and 11000 years ago. Classical philosophers tried to characterize the mechanism of human thought as the mechanical manipulation of symbols, which sowed the seeds of modern AI. Many of the technical advancements that we are experiencing today were already articulated in Hindu holy books such as Ramayana, Mahabharata, Bhagavat Gitta, Vedas, and the Upanishads, which are thought to have been written 5000 to 8000 years ago (6000 BC – 3000 BC). These are not only Hindu civilization's holy epics, but also evidence of India's life. From a modern science standpoint, the contents of Ancient Indian Texts written in the oldest language of human life, **Sanskrit**, are often regarded as "**Natural Language**". The Upanishads and Advaita Siddhanta contain elements of modern science, and the essence of maya resembles modern scientific knowledge. This knowledge is often used to better understand human mental processes and how to model them, which contributes to the artificial intelligence area of natural language comprehension. Vedic principles are both appropriate and necessary for effective leadership and the future of Artificial Intelligence (AI). The idea is to connect man-made machines on the lines of Vedic scriptures' philosophy in order to create a better and smarter world with better machines. A better human-machine interface can be achieved by using natural language processing of natural language inputs and outputs.

18.2 Description of Artificial Intelligence in Ancient Indian Texts

The origin of Artificial Intelligence is led from mythology, where ancient people imagined artificial life, **automatons** (or robots), self-moving machines, and other marvels long before the technology enabled them to be realized. These ancient oral traditions about robots and other devices were first written down around the time of Homer, around 2,700 years ago. In antiquity, however, the Greeks were not the only ones who imagined automatons and computers. The Ramayana, Mahabharata, and other epics contain similar tales. Automatons are created by the engineer **Lord Vishwakarma** and the sorceress Maya in Hindu mythology, and by the god of technology, Hephaestus and the brilliant artisan Daedalus in Greek mythology. Such myths are the world's first science fiction tales. No one culture had a monopoly on ancient technological fantasies. If one considers Greek, Etruscan, Egyptian, Hindu, Islamic, Chinese, or any other ancient cultural myths about artificial existence, they all consider the wonders that could be accomplished if only one possessed the Gods' divine imagination and skill. However, it is impossible to draw a straight line from mythology to current scientific understanding over millennia.

18.2.1 Barbarik: The Warrior Robot with Artificial Intelligence

Around a thousand years ago, in the year 1027 A.D., a group of workers in the village of Khatu in Rajasthan were digging the ground for water. They discovered a metal box that was sealed airtight after searching for more than 30 feet. One word was etched on the box: **Barbarik**. When they opened the package, they discovered a skull inside, but it wasn't a human skull made of bones; instead, it was made of a gleaming metal. What's more bizarre is that the skull had two eyeballs in each eye socket. The workers took the skull to the king Roop Singh Chauhan, and he summoned all learned men to his court to learn more about the Barbarik's Skull. The question comes in mind that 'Who is Barbarik and how his skull is made of metal?

How did his eyes not disintegrate and decompose?' Barbarik was not mentioned in any of the ancient texts that the learned men combed through. Finally, a priest from the far south came to describe his tale. Barbarik was a legendary warrior who lived 5000 years ago, during Lord Krishna's reign. Barbarik, on the other hand, was radically different. **He wasn't human**; he had divine power. He was capable of simultaneously handling several advanced arms and weapon systems and solving mathematical problems at lightning speed, but his voice was sluggish and he couldn't identify faces. He didn't have human intelligence; instead, he had **artificial intelligence**. After hearing about Barbarik's power and intellect, **Lord Krishna** agreed to meet him. The Mahabharata's great war is about to begin, and Lord Krishna wants to know which side Barbarik will support. With Lord Krishna's request, Barbarik showed his incredible pace and accuracy with advanced weapons. Lord Krishna was taken aback and learnt that Barbarik would be the pivotal figure in the upcoming great War. Barbarik's intellect, on the other hand, is not human-like; he thinks and acts like a **robot.** Lord Krishna enquired about his position in the war. **Barbarik responded by saying that he will help the side that is weaker than the other.** He claimed that it was his responsibility to save as many people as possible. Lord Krishna then asked Barbarik a simple question, which utterly perplexed him. According to Lord Krishna, if Barbarik backs the weaker army and begins to kill the stronger army, by this way the stronger army will eventually become the weaker army, and the once weaker side will become the stronger side. What will Barbarik do in that situation? This would not be a legitimate question to a human being because we humans comprehend broader concepts, while robots and artificially intelligent machines observe events and are unable to comprehend the bigger picture. However, Barbarik later states that because the other army has become weaker, he will turn sides and help them. Barbarik's response astounded Lord Krishna because it implies that Barbarik would switch sides between the two armies and **fully kill them**. With Barbarik's unnatural intellect, Krishna concluded, would bring damage to humans rather than benefit them, despite his ability to handle sophisticated weapons with exceptional precision. As a result, Lord Krishna chose to disable Barbarik's physical activity, preventing him from attacking or wielding weapons with his arms or legs. Barbarik was asked by Lord Krishna to separate his head from his body. The most intriguing part is this: Barbarik took his head off and handed it over to Krishna, but he continued to talk. This clearly demonstrates that he was not human, but rather a robot with artificial intelligence. Some argue that Barbarik was Bhima's grandson, but this is highly unlikely because he would have been listed in the Mahabharata. Barbarik, on the other hand, is not mentioned anywhere in the original text. Why did the author leave out such a powerful warrior from the epic? Since Barbarik was a robot with artificial intelligence rather than a living human, the author omitted this detail. Barbarik's name alone denotes that he is not human. It is derived from the Sanskrit word *'Barbara'*, which means inhuman and is similar to the English word barbaric. Barbaric originally meant inhuman, or someone who lacks understanding of human feelings and thoughts.

18.2.2 Automations of King Ajatashatru and Other Countries in Ancient Times

Beginning around the fifth century BC, Indian and Hellenistic cultures borrowed and inspired each other, and syncretism increased after Alexander of Macedon and King Porus established diplomatic relations in the fourth century BC. Before Philip II of Macedon received torsion catapults, Ajatashatru's engineers invented armed war chariots with spinning blades, which might have influenced later Persian scythed chariots, and he had powerful machines to hurl huge boulders, according to Jain texts. The constant burning of oil lamps in India suggests knowledge of naphtha, which the Greeks and Romans did not have until much later. In the court of a king of India, the travelling Greek sage Apollodorus of Tyana encountered automatic servants and self-propelled carts, and India was centuries ahead of Europe in distillation and hydraulics technologies. The Mahabharata, Ramayana, Kathasaritsagar, Harivamsa, and other works include anecdotes about flying chariots and synthetic swans, animated slaves, giant robots, machines. In Egyptian texts and Homer's Odyssey, self-navigating ships are described; in Homer's Iliad and Chinese chronicles, androids and automatons are described. The Lokapanatti, a complicated collection of Burmese stories, contains the most comprehensive account.

King Ajatashatru stored Buddha's bodily remains in a secret chamber beneath a stupa after his death, according to legend. 'Bhuta vahana yantra' protected the priceless artefacts (spirit movement machines). There were robotic warriors wielding whirling spears, similar to the king's novel spinning blade war machines. Greek myths tell of automaton guardians in human and animal form protecting palaces and treasure, but this legend is unique due to the historical and technical specifics. According to the story, the robots were built from plans secretly transported to Pataliputra from Roma-visaya, the Greek-influenced West, by a yantrakara, a Pataliputra-born robot builder. Before the great Indian emperor Ashoka learned of the underground chamber, the automaton soldiers guarded Buddha's relics. The robots obediently obeyed Ashoka after he defeated them and learned how to handle them. We know from history that Ashoka unearthed and disseminated long-lost Buddha relics throughout the country. Craftspeople and engineers in Greece, Alexandria, Arabia, India, and China began producing self-moving devices, flying bird models, animated machines, and automatons similar to those depicted in myths by the third century BC. Some were small, while others were massive, and some had simple mechanisms while others were very complex. Springs, levers, pulleys, water, air, fire, and other mechanisms were used to power these contraptions.

18.2.3 Kumbhakarna, the Ancient Robo-War Machine

In 'Ramayana', the world's oldest epic poem, Kumbhakarna is referred as Ravana's younger brother. But he was not a living being at all, but a 'Yantra' (machine/robot) which had a gigantic appearance (like a giant robot). To be more precise, **Kumbhakarna was an ancient robot**, fearsome more-machine and less-human-like 'humanoid'.

Ravana used Kumbhakarna sparingly, meaning, only during very difficult battle-situations, and it instantly turned the tide in Ravana's favour. May be due to its high maintenance, it was made to sleep for a period of about six months and awakened only when need arises or when it had to be refueled.

Sage Valmiki writes the thoughts of Brahma when he saw Kumbhakarna:

Dhruvam lokavinashaya paulastyenasi nirmitah |

Tasmattvamadyaprabhriti mritakalpah shayishyase ||6-61-24||

Translation: It is sure that you were created by visravasa for the destroying of people. On that account, you will be sleeping apparently dead from now onwards. Here, he clearly uses the word 'nirmitah', which means 'built/created' by Visravasa, who was Ravana's father.

Brahmashapabhibhutoṡtha nipapatagratah prabhoh |

Tatah parama sambhranto ravano vakyamabravit ||6-61-25||

Translation: Humbled by Brahma's curse, Kumbhakarna then fell down in front of Ravana. Thereupon, the highly perplexed Ravana spoke the following words:

Pravriddhah kanchano vrikshah falakale nikrintyate |

Na naptaram svakam nyayyam shaptumevam prajapati ||6-61-26||

Translation: O Brahma! You are cutting off a well-grown golden tree, just at the time of yielding its fruit. It is not fair on your part to curse your own great grandson like this.

Na mithyavachanashchatvam svapsyatyeva na sanshayah |

Kalastu kriyatamasya shayane jagare tatha ||6-61-27||

Translation: Your words can never prove to be in vain. There is no doubt about it. He will have to sleep certainly. Let some space of time be fixed for his sleeping and waking.

Ravasya vachah shrutva svayambhridamabravit |

Shayita hyesha shanmasanekahamjagarishyati ||6-61-28||

Translation: Hearing the words of Ravana, Brahma spoke as follows: He will indeed sleep for six months and wake-up for a day.

Ekenanha tvasau virashcha ran bhumim bubhukshitah |

Vyattasyo bhakshayellokan samvriddha ev pavakah ||6-61-29||

Translation: On that single day, this male demon, having starved for six months, will wander over the earth and eat the human race with his month wide open, like an augmented fire.

Soasau vyasanamapannah kumbhakarnabodhayat |

Tvatparakramabhitashcha raja samprati ravanah ||6-61-30||

Translation: Ravana, the king of demons, who got into an evil plight and frightened as he was in seeing your prowess, now got Kumbhakarna awakened.

Sa esha nirgato virah shibirabhdimavikramah |

Vanaran bhrishasamkruddho bhakshayan paridhavati ||6-61-31||

Translation: This Kumbhakarna the male-demon with a terrific prowess started his tent. The highly enraged Kumbhakara devourincg the monkeys on is way, is running towards us.

Kumbhakarnam pratiksheva haruadya pradudruvah |

Kathamenam rane kruddham varayishyanti vanarah ||6-61-32||

Translation: Even on merely seeing Kumbhakarna, the monkeys have now fled away. How can the monkeys check him, who is thus enraged in battle.

When Kumbhakarna was approaching Vanara Army and crushing them under his toes, they started to runway in fear. Then

Ravana's brother Vibhishana revealed the truth of Kumbhakarna to Rama and his army.

Hitarthametaduktam vah kriyatam yadi rochate |
Uchyatam va lshamam yannassarveshameva vanarah ||6-61-33||

Translation: Let all the monkeys be told that it is a kind of machine, advancing forward. By knowing this, they can become fearless by now.

But in the same Ramayana, it was clearly stated that Kumbhakarna was married with Vajramala and had Kumbh, Nikumbh as sons. These sons were killed by Hanuman. So, Kumbhakarna must be an alive brother of Ravana, **who operated a giant robot from its inside**. So the robot was known with the same name of its operator. In fact Kumbha-Karna means the one who has pot (kumbha) like ears (karna). Rama used **Vayuvyastra** (a wind forced missile) to cut-off Kumbhakarna's arm and later chopped its head. When Kumbhakarna was shot down by arrows of Rama, he died and the robot which had nobody to control it, fell into the sea. In later (mis) translations Kumbhakarna has been (mistakenly) thought to have been a gigantic demon, while the Vanaras have been turned into monkeys. In fact Vanaras were humans with tail. Vaala (tail) + Nara (human).

18.2.4   Pushpak Vimana

Let's take a look at some of these technology-related concepts and consider whether they had the necessary expertise. **Ravana** is said to have kidnapped Sita in the "Pushpak Vimana" in Ramayana. According to Ramayana, the "Pushpak Vimana" depicted in the epic was much more advanced than modern airplanes. Ravana received the **"Pushpak Vimana"** from Kuber, who was the richest man in the world at the time. Even today the International flights are prohibitively costly, and not all the people can afford them. When "Lava" was lost in another episode, Valmiki created "Kusha" from grass, which is similar to cloning. Again, it appears that the cloning he performed was much more advanced than current cloning techniques.

18.2.5 Raktabij

Another related citation is **"Raktabij,"** in which every drop of his blood on earth created his "Adult clone." Ganesha, on the other hand, is a highly advanced organ transplant in which the head of a recently discovered elephant was inserted on the body of a recently beheaded child. The boy would have died if it had been too late.

18.2.6 Divya Drishti of Sanjay (Mahabharata)

There is also an interesting incident from Mahabharata. Sanjay was given "Divya Drishti" by Lord Krishna so that he could see a "Live Telecast" of "Kurukshetra-war" and explain it to Dhritarashtra, who was blind and wanted to know what was going on in the battlefield. "Divya Drishti" is comparable to a modern television set in that Krishna couldn't give it to Dhritarashtra without Sanjay's help. Imagine a central computer system with wireless links that can accept voice commands or thoughts, and you can see how cameras in the sky, similar to today's satellites, can point to the locations that Dhritarashtra requested Sanjay to describe. As a result, a modern definition of **"Divya Drishti"** is a television set with a wireless connection to the satellite and access to the device for controlling the cameras.

18.2.7 Brahmastra

The System Administrator, Lord Krishna, who had all of the required technologies at his disposal, granted the access permission. The "Astra" used on the battlefield resembled bombs, with the **"Brahmastra"** resembling the all-powerful nuclear bomb. They would not bring these guns on the battlefield; instead, they would log in wirelessly to a central control system to launch them and use GPS (Global Positioning System) to drop them precisely where they desired. Does that make sense? The aim of reiterating these ancient writings here is to remind the reader that those religious books contain a wealth of ideas, many of which have yet to be realized in order to positively transform human society. You can look at them as theory or a fairy tale, but the need of the day is to see them as books full of technological ideas for the future. You can only see things if you look at them with your eyes; if you look at them with your technological brain, you will understand them. Just to mention another concept mention in the ancient texts; "would we ever be able to become "Antardhyan" (invisible)?

18.2.8 Concept of Chariot (Vedas)

The concept of AI can be traced back to the ancient Indian text, the Vedas, which were written between 1500 BCE and 500 BCE. The Vedas contain various references to machines and robots that can perform human-like tasks. For example, the **Rig Veda describes a chariot that is pulled by horses made of metal, while the Yajur Veda describes machines that can make music and dance.**

18.2.9 Yantra Sarvasva

However, it wasn't just in literature that AI was explored in ancient India. Indian philosophers and scholars also developed a concept known as "mechanical man," which was essentially a robot that could mimic human behavior. One of the most well-known examples of a mechanical man is **Yantra Sarvasva**, a book written by Bharata Muni in the 2nd century BCE. This book describes various machines and automata, including a mechanical man that could move, speak, and even perform tasks like weaving.

18.2.10 Brahmasphutasiddhanta

Another example is the renowned 8th-century mathematician and astronomer, **Brahmagupta**, who wrote about automated machines that could perform mathematical calculations. Brahmagupta's book, the ***Brahmasphutasiddhanta***, contains detailed instructions for constructing a device called the *chakravala*, which was a mechanical calculator that could solve complex algebraic equations.

Overall, it's clear that the concept of AI has a long and rich history in ancient India. While the machines and devices described in ancient texts may seem fantastical by modern standards, they represent a fascinating exploration of the human desire to create machines that can mimic human intelligence and behavior. It's clear that the ancient Indian philosophers and scholars were ahead of their time in their understanding of the possibilities of machines, and their work has had a lasting impact on the development of AI and robotics to this day.

18.2.11 'Dardur' in Ramayana

In the Ramayana, it is mentioned that Ravana had a mechanical guard named **Dardur**, who could challenge and engage enemies without human intervention.

18.2.12 Application of AI and human emotions into Ancient Robots made by Asuras to win over Adityas

Yoga Vasistha describes application of Artificial Intelligence (AI), human emotions, ego to Robots. Sambarasura creates Dama, vyala and kaTa to win on Adityas. Yoga Vasistha is a discourse of sage Vasistha to Prince Rama. Sage Valmiki is credited as its author. It has 6 parts and in one of the part, application of Artificial Intelligence (A.I), human emotions etc to Robots is described.

One Asura named Sambarasura had the powers to raise himself in the sky and fight from outer space. Rig Veda clearly mentions that Asura does not mean 'Demon'. Asura means 'the one who is not sura, or one who has magical or phenomenal powers (according to Rig Veda)'. This Sambarasura created 3 robots using his technology and named them Dama, vyala and kaTa. The name 'Dama' is derived from the root dam which means to tame, subdue, conquer, restrain of course the enemy. 'Vyala' means vicious, fierce, cruel, savage like tiger or snake. KaTa was like a modern tank protecting army. The word 'kat' means to go, to cover. It could go and cover the army.

Those three Robots were lifeless machines and therefore had no sentiments, no emotions, so they were never defeated. These 3 robots always won the wars against Adityas (gods).

Later Artificial Intelligence (A.I) was induced into them. So Adityas played a trick to induce sentiments and emotions in them. They fought with the three Robots and ran away, many times, with defeat. This induced Ego in the Robots. Ego arose as the robots were thinking like humans due to artificial intelligence. Adityas observed this change and told them that, because of their valour Sambarasura always wins and enjoys his life at their cost. This added emotions and sentiments. They felt that they should also enjoy their lives. As the human sentiments arose, fear too propped up in them. Naturally they could not fight with the previous zeal and were defeated by Adityas.

Modern-day robots have Artificial intelligence embedded into them. So one day they might get 'Ego' and then they may rebel against the mankind. It will be difficult to defeat them. They may conquer the mankind. In that situation man can play the same trick as played by the Gods.

18.3   Real-Life Human Computer in Recent India: Shakuntala Devi

Shakuntala Devi (4 November 1929 – 21 April 2013) was an Indian mental calculator, astrologer, and writer, popularly known as the "Human Computer". Her talent earned her a place in the 1982 edition of The Guinness Book of World Records. However, the certificate for the record was given posthumously on 30 July 2020, despite Shakuntala Devi achieving her world record on 18 June 1980 at Imperial College, London. Shakuntala Devi was a precocious child and she demonstrated her arithmetic abilities at the University of Mysore without any formal education.

Shakuntala Devi strove to simplify numerical calculations for students. She wrote a number of books in her later years, including novels as well as texts about mathematics, puzzles, and astrology. She wrote the book, 'The World of Homosexuals', which is considered the first study of homosexuality in India. She saw homosexuality in a positive light and is considered a pioneer in the field.

18.3.1 Early life of Shakuntala Devi

Shakuntala Devi was born on 4 November 1929 at Bangalore, Karnataka to a Kannada Brahmin family. Her father, C V Sundararaja Rao, worked as a trapeze artist, lion tamer, tightrope walker and magician in a circus. He discovered his daughter's ability to memorize numbers while teaching her a card trick when she was about three years old. Her father left the circus and took her on road shows that displayed her ability at calculation. She did this without any formal education. At the age of six she demonstrated her arithmetic abilities at the University of Mysore.

In 1944, Shakuntala Devi moved to London, United Kingdom.

18.3.2 Mental calculator

Shakuntala Devi travelled to several countries around the world demonstrating her arithmetic talents. She was on a tour of Europe throughout 1950 and was in New York City in 1976. In 1988, she travelled to the US to have her abilities studied by Arthur Jensen, a professor of educational psychology at the University of California, Berkeley. Jensen tested her performance at several tasks, including the calculation of large numbers. Examples of the problems presented to Devi included calculating the cube root of 61,629,875 and the seventh root of 170,859,375. Jensen reported that Devi provided the solution to the above-mentioned problems (395 and 15, respectively) before Jensen could copy them down in his notebook. Jensen published his findings in the academic journal Intelligence in 1990.

In 1977, at Southern Methodist University, she gave the 23rd root of a 201-digit number in 50 seconds. Her answer, which was 546,372,891, was confirmed by calculations done at the US Bureau of Standards by the UNIVAC 1101 computer, for which a special program had to be written to perform such a large calculation, which took a longer time than for her to do the same.

On 18 June 1980, she demonstrated the multiplication of two 13-digit numbers – 7,686,369,774,870 × 2,465,099,745,779. These numbers were picked at random by the Department of Computing at Imperial College London. She correctly answered 18,947,668,177,99 5,426,462,773,730 in 28 seconds. This event was recorded in the 1982 Guinness Book of World Records. Writer Steven Smith commented, "the result is so far superior to anything previously reported that it can only be described as unbelievable."

Shakuntala Devi explained many of the methods she used to do mental calculations in her 1977 book Figuring: The Joy of Numbers.

18.3.3   Book on Homosexuality

In 1977, she wrote 'The World of Homosexuals', the first published academic study of homosexuality in India, for which she was criticized. In the documentary 'For Straights Only', she said that her interest in the topic was because of her marriage to a homosexual man and her desire to look at homosexuality more closely to understand it.

The book, considered "pioneering", features interviews with two young Indian homosexual men, a male couple in Canada seeking legal marriage, a temple priest who explains his views on homosexuality, and a review of the existing literature on homosexuality. It ends with a call for decriminalization of homosexuality, and "full and complete acceptance—not tolerance and sympathy". The book, however, went mostly unnoticed at that time.

18.3.4   Personal life of Shakuntala Devi

Devi returned to India in the mid-1960s and she married Paritosh Banerji, an officer of the Indian Administrative Service from Kolkata. They divorced in 1979, after her husband's homosexuality was allegedly revealed. Their daughter Anupama Banerji claimed that Devi lied about her husband being gay to promote her book on homosexuals, because her credibility on the subject matter was questioned.

In 1980, she contested the Lok Sabha elections as an independent candidate for Mumbai South and for Medak in Andhra Pradesh (now in Telangana). In Medak she stood against the former Prime Minister Indira Gandhi, saying she wanted to "defend the people of Medak from being fooled by Mrs. Gandhi"; she came ninth, with 6,514 votes (1.47% of the votes). Devi returned to Bangalore in the early 1980s.

In addition to her work as a mental calculator, Devi was a notable astrologer and an author of several books, including cookbooks and novels. She started with writing short stories and murder mysteries, and had a keen interest in music.

18.3.5   Death and Legacy

In April 2013, Devi was admitted to a hospital in Bangalore with severe respiratory problems. Over the following two weeks she had heart and kidney complications. She died in the hospital on 21 April 2013. She was 83 years old. Her daughter Anupama Banerji is married to Ajay Abhaya Kumar, with whom she has two daughters, and lives in London.

On 4 November 2013, Devi was honoured with a Google Doodle on what would have been her 84th birthday.

A film on her life titled 'Shakuntala Devi' was announced in May 2019. The film stars Vidya Balan in the lead title role and features Sanya Malhotra, Amit Sadh, and Jisshu Sengupta in the supporting roles. Produced by Sony Pictures Networks Productions, the film streamed worldwide on Amazon Prime Video on 31 July 2020.

18.4   Talos in Greece

In Greek mythology, **Talos** was a giant constructed of bronze who acted as guardian for the island of Crete. He would throw boulders at the ships of invaders and would complete 3 circuits around the island's perimeter daily. According to pseudo-Apollodorus' Bibliotheke, Hephaestus forged Talos with the aid of a cyclops and presented the automaton as a gift to Minos. In the Argonautica, Jason and the Argonauts defeated him by way of a single plug near his foot which, once removed, allowed the vital ichor to flow out from his body and left him inanimate.

18.5   Talos in Cyprus

PYGMALION (Pugmaliôn), a king of Cyprus and father of Metharme. He is said to have fallen in love with the ivory image of a maiden which he himself had made, and therefore to have prayed to Aphrodite to breathe life into it. When the request was granted, Pygmalion married his beloved, and became by her the father of Paphus.

18.6   Medieval Legends of Artificial Beings

In 'Of the Nature of Things', written by the Swiss alchemist, Paracelsus, he describes a procedure that he claims can fabricate an "artificial man". By placing the "sperm of a man" in horse dung, and feeding it the "Arcanum of Mans blood" after 40 days, the concoction will become a living infant.

The earliest written account regarding **golem**-making (a clay figure brought to life by magic) is found in the writings of Eleazar ben Judah of Worms in the early 13th century. During the Middle Ages, it was believed that the animation of a Golem could be achieved by insertion of a piece of paper with any of God's names on it, into the mouth of the clay figure. Unlike legendary automata like Brazen Heads, a Golem was unable to speak.

Takwin, the artificial creation of life, was a frequent topic of Ismaili alchemical manuscripts, especially those attributed to Jabir ibn Hayyan. Islamic alchemists attempted to create a broad range of life through their work, ranging from plants to animals.

In Faust: 'The Second Part of the Tragedy' by Johann Wolfgang von Goethe, an alchemically fabricated homunculus, destined to live forever in the flask in which he was made, endeavors to be born into a full human body. Upon the initiation of this transformation, however, the flask shatters and the homunculus dies.

18.7   Automatons in Egypt and Greece

Realistic humanoid automata were built by craftsman from every civilization, including Yan Shi, Hero of Alexandria, Al-Jazari, Pierre Jaquet-Droz, and Wolfgang von Kempelen.

One of the oldest known automata were the sacred statues of ancient Egypt and Greece. The faithful believed that craftsman had imbued these figures with very real minds, capable of wisdom and emotion—Hermes Trismegistus wrote that "by discovering the true nature of the gods, man has been able to reproduce it". English scholar Alexander Neckham asserted that the Ancient Roman poet Virgil had built a palace with automaton statues.

During the early modern period, these legendary automata were said to possess the magical ability to answer questions put to them. The late medieval alchemist and proto-protestant Roger Bacon was purported to have fabricated a brazen head, having developed a legend of having been a wizard. These legends were similar to the Norse myth of the Head of Mímir. According to legend, Mímir was known for his intellect and wisdom, and was beheaded in the Esir-Vanir War. Odin is said to have "embalmed" the head with herbs and spoke incantations over it such that Mímir's head remained able to speak wisdom to Odin. Odin then kept the head near him for counsel.

CHAPTER 19

CONTEMPORARY VIRTUAL ASSISTANTS: CORTANA

19.1   Some Popular Virtual Assistants

Virtual assistants help in performing tasks for the users or perform the tasks on their own in an autonomous way. Several virtual assistants have been developed. The examples are:

- Cortana, from Microsoft;

- Alexa, from Amazon;

- Siri, from Apple; and

- Google Assistant, from Google.

Users can use natural language to interact with a virtual assistant. As one can also interact with spoken words, an illiterate or blind person can also use it. Virtual assistants perform a variety of tasks including streaming music, playing audio clips, controlling home devices, managing schedules, purchasing using e-commerce, etc. These assistants are becoming more and more useful due to the advances in natural language processing and speech recognition. This makes it useful for a common person without any specific training. Speech recognition makes it possible to use even while driving, etc. The vendors are trying to put these assistants in vehicles. Siri has already been integrated with some cars. Nissan is integrating Microsoft's platform into its cars. Similarly, Hyundai is integrating with Alexa and Google Assistant.

In this chapter, we shall discuss about the virtual assistant, Cortana from Microsoft. Other virtual assistants are discussed in the chapters to follow.

19.2   Cortana (Virtual Assistant) from Microsoft

Cortana is a virtual assistant developed by Microsoft that used the Bing search engine to perform tasks such as setting reminders and answering questions for users.

Cortana is available in English, Portuguese, French, German, Italian, Spanish, Chinese, and Japanese language editions, depending on the software platform and region in which it was used.

In 2019, Microsoft began reducing the prevalence of Cortana and converting it from an assistant into different software integrations. It was split from the Windows 10 search bar in April 2019. In January 2020, the Cortana mobile app was removed from certain markets, and on March 31, 2021, the Cortana mobile app was shut down globally. On June 2, 2023, Microsoft announced that support for the Cortana standalone app on Microsoft Windows would end in late 2023 and would be replaced by Microsoft Copilot. Support for Cortana in the Microsoft Outlook and Microsoft 365 mobile apps was discontinued in fall of 2023.

19.3   History of Cortana

(i)   Beginnings (2009–2014)

The development of Cortana started in 2009 in the Microsoft Speech products team with general manager Zig Serafin and Chief Scientist Larry Heck. Heck and Serafin established the vision, mission, and long-range plan for Microsoft's digital personal assistant and they built a team with the expertise to create the initial prototypes for Cortana. Some of the key researchers in these early efforts included Microsoft Research researchers Dilek Hakkani-Tür, Gokhan Tur, Andreas Stolcke, and Malcolm Slaney, research software developer

Madhu Chinthakunta, and user experience designer Lisa Stifelman. To develop the Cortana digital assistant, the team interviewed human personal assistants. The interviews inspired a number of unique features in Cortana, including the assistant's "notebook" feature. Originally, Cortana was meant to be only a codename, but a petition on Windows Phone's UserVoice site proved to be popular and made the codename official.

Cortana was demonstrated for the first time at the Microsoft Build developer conference in San Francisco in April 2014. It was launched as a key ingredient of Microsoft's planned "makeover" of future operating systems for Windows Phone and Windows.

It was named after Cortana, a synthetic intelligence character in Microsoft's Halo video game franchise originating in Bungie folklore, with Jen Taylor, the character's voice actress, returning to voice the personal assistant's US-specific version.

(ii) Expansion of Cortana (2015–2018)

In January 2015, Microsoft announced the availability of Cortana for Windows 10 desktops and mobile devices as part of merging Windows Phone into the operating system at large.

On May 26, 2015, Microsoft announced that Cortana would also be available on other mobile platforms. An Android release was set for July 2015, but the Android APK file containing Cortana was leaked ahead of its release. It was officially released, along with an iOS version, in December 2015.

During 2015, Microsoft announced that Cortana would come to the Xbox One as part of a universally designed Windows 10 update for the console.

Microsoft integrated Cortana into numerous products such as Microsoft Edge. Microsoft's Cortana assistant was deeply integrated into the browser. Cortana was able to find opening hours when on restaurant sites, show retail coupons for websites, or show weather information in the address bar. At the Worldwide Partners Conference

2015 Microsoft demonstrated Cortana integration with products such as GigJam. Conversely, Microsoft announced in late April 2016 that it would block anything other than Bing and Edge from being used to complete Cortana searches, again raising questions of anti-competitive practices by the company.

Microsoft's "Windows in the car" concept included Cortana. The concept makes it possible for drivers to make restaurant reservations and see places before they go there.

At Microsoft Build 2016, Microsoft announced plans to integrate Cortana into Skype (Microsoft's video-conferencing and instant messaging service) as a bot to allow users to order food, book trips, transcribe video messages and make calendar appointments through Cortana in addition to other bots. As of 2016, Cortana was able to underline certain words and phrases in Skype conversations that relate to contacts and corporations. A writer from Engadget has criticized the Cortana integration in Skype for responding only to very specific keywords, feeling as if she was "chatting with a search engine" due to the impersonal way the bots replied to certain words such as "Hello" causing the Bing Music bot to bring up Adele's song of that name.

Microsoft also announced at Microsoft Build 2016 that Cortana would be able to cloud-synchronize notifications between Windows 10 Mobile's and Windows 10's Action Center, as well as notifications from Android devices.

In December 2016, Microsoft announced the preview of Calendar.help, a service that enabled people to delegate the scheduling of meetings to Cortana. Users interact with Cortana by including her in email conversations. Cortana would then check people's availability in Outlook Calendar or Google Calendar, and work with others Cc'd on the email to schedule the meeting. The service relied on automation and human-based computation.

In May 2017, Microsoft announced INVOKE, a voice-activated speaker featuring Cortana, in collaboration with Harman Kardon.

The premium speaker has a cylindrical design and offers 360-degree sound, the ability to make and receive calls with Skype, and all of the other features currently available with Cortana.

In 2017, Microsoft partnered with Amazon to integrate Echo and Cortana with each other, allowing users of each smart assistant to summon the other via a command. This feature preview was released in August 2018. Windows 10 users were able to just say "Hey Cortana, open Alexa" and Echo users were able to say "Alexa, open Cortana" to summon the other assistant.

(iii) Decreasing Focus and Discontinuation (2019–2024)

In January 2019, Microsoft CEO **Satya Nadella** stated that he no longer sees Cortana as a direct competitor against Alexa and Siri.

Shortly thereafter, Microsoft began reducing the prevalence of Cortana and converting it from an assistant into different software integrations. It was split from the Windows 10 search bar in April 2019.

In January 2020, the Cortana mobile app was removed from certain markets, and then, on July 24, 2020, Cortana was removed from the Xbox dashboard as part of a redesign. On January 31, 2021, Microsoft removed the Cortana mobile application in many markets, including the UK, Australia, Germany, Mexico, China, Spain, Canada, and India.

On March 31, 2021, Microsoft shut down the Cortana apps globally for iOS and Android and removed the apps entirely from their corresponding app stores. To access previously recorded content, users had to use Cortana on Windows 10 or other specialized Microsoft applications.

Microsoft also reduced emphasis on Cortana in Windows with the 2021 release of Windows 11. Cortana was not used during the device setup process or pinned to the taskbar by default.

On June 2, 2023, Microsoft announced the Cortana standalone app on Windows 10 and Windows 11 which would shut down later in the year. In its support article, Microsoft listed several alternatives, most of which have since been rebranded as Microsoft Copilot. They also added that the change would not impact Cortana in Office 365 and Teams environments.

On August 11, 2023, Microsoft updated the Cortana standalone app in Windows, informing that it was deprecated and can no longer be used. Microsoft's support article announcing the deprecation of Cortana was updated to reflect this change. Along with the deprecation of the standalone app, it was announced that Cortana support in Teams mobile, Microsoft Teams displays, and Teams rooms would end in late 2023. The support article states that Cortana in the "Play my emails" feature of the Microsoft Outlook mobile app would continue to be available.

Finally, later in June 2024, the support article was updated, stating that Cortana in the voice search and the "Play my emails" feature is now removed from the Microsoft Outlook mobile app, officially marking the discontinuation of Cortana across all Microsoft products.

19.4   Functionality of Cortana

Cortana is able to set reminders, recognize natural voice without the requirement for keyboard input, and answer questions using information from the Bing search engine. Searches using Windows 10 are made only with the Microsoft Bing search engine, and all links will open with Microsoft Edge, except when a screen reader such as Narrator was being used, where the links will open in Internet Explorer. Windows Phone 8.1's universal Bing SmartSearch features were incorporated into Cortana, which replaced the previous Bing Search app, which was activated when a user presses the "Search" button on their device. Cortana includes a music recognition service. Cortana was able to simulate rolling dice and flipping a coin. Cortana's "Concert Watch" monitored Bing searches to determine the bands or musicians that interest the user. It integrates with the Microsoft Band watch band for Windows Phone devices if connected via Bluetooth, it was able to make reminders and phone notifications.

Since the Lumia Denim mobile phone series, launched in October 2014, active listening was added to Cortana enabling it to be invoked with the phrase: "Hey Cortana". It was able to then be controlled as usual. Some devices from the United Kingdom by O2 received the Lumia Denim update without the feature, but this was later clarified as a bug and Microsoft has since fixed it.

Cortana integrated with services such as Foursquare to provide restaurant and local attraction recommendations and LIFX to control smart light bulbs.

19.4.1   Notebook and Cortana

Cortana stored personal information such as interests, location data, reminders, and contacts in the "Notebook". It was able to draw upon and add to this data to learn a user's specific patterns and behaviors. Users were able to view and specify what information was collected to allow some control over privacy, said to be "a level of control that goes beyond comparable assistants". Users were able to delete information from the "Notebook".

19.4.2   Reminders and Cortana

Cortana had a built-in system of reminders, which were able to, for example, be associated with a specific contact; Cortana would then remind a user when in communication with that contact, possibly at a specific time or when the phone was in a specific location. Originally, these reminders were specific to the device Cortana was installed on but starting on February 12, 2015, Cortana synchronized reminders across devices.

19.5   Design of Cortana

Most versions of Cortana took the form of two nested circles, which were animated to indicate activities such as searching or talking. The main color scheme would include a black or white background and shades of blue for the respective circles.

19.5.1 Phone notification syncing

Cortana on Windows mobile and Android were capable of capturing device notifications and sending them to a Windows 10 device. This allowed a computer user to view notifications from their phone in the Windows 10 Action Center. The feature was announced in early 2016 and released later in the year.

19.5.2 Miscellaneous Tasks by Cortana

(i) Do-not-Disturb

Cortana had a "do-not-disturb" mode in which users were able to specify "quiet hours", as was available for Windows Phone 8.1 users. Users were able to change the settings so that Cortana calls users by their names or nicknames. It also had a library of "Easter Eggs", pre-determined remarks.

(ii) Prediction of Sports Results

When asked for a prediction, Cortana correctly predicted the winners of the first 14 matches of the football 2014 FIFA World Cup knockout stage, including the semi-finals, before it incorrectly picked Brazil over the Netherlands in the third-place play-off match; this streak topped Paul the Octopus who correctly predicted all 7 of Germany's 2010 FIFA World Cup matches as well as the Final. Cortana was able to forecast results in various other sports such as the NBA, the NFL, the Super Bowl, the ICC Cricket World Cup and various European football leagues.

Cortana was able to solve mathematical equations, convert units of measurement, and determine the exchange rates between currencies including Bitcoin.

19.6 Integrations of Cortana

Microsoft integrated Cortana into numerous products such as Microsoft Edge. Microsoft's Cortana assistant was deeply integrated into the browser. Cortana was able to find opening hours when on restaurant sites, show retail coupons for websites, or show weather information in the address bar. At the Worldwide Partners Conference 2015 Microsoft demonstrated Cortana integration with products such as GigJam. Conversely, Microsoft announced in late April 2016 that it would block anything other than Bing and Edge from being used to complete Cortana searches, again raising questions of anti-competitive practices by the company.

Cortana was able to integrate with third-party apps on Windows 10 or directly through the service. Starting in late 2016, Cortana integrated with Microsoft's Wunderlist service, allowing Cortana to add and act on reminders.

At Microsoft's Build 2017 conference, Microsoft announced that Cortana would get a consumer third-party skills capability, similar to that in Amazon Alexa.

On February 16, 2018, Microsoft announced connected home skills were added for Ecobee, Honeywell Lyric, Honeywell Total Connect Comfort, LIFX, TP-Link Kasa, and Geeni, as well as support for IFTTT. At Microsoft's Ignite 2018 conference, Microsoft announced a Technology Adopters Program that Enterprises could build skills that could be developed and deployed into Azure tenants, accessible by organizational units or security groups.

19.7   Privacy Concerns in Cortana

Cortana indexed and stored user information. Cortana could be disabled; this would cause Windows search to search Bing as well as the local computer, but that could also be disabled. Turning Cortana off did not in itself delete user data stored on Microsoft's servers, but data was able to be deleted by user action. Microsoft was further criticized for requests to Bing's website for a file called "threshold. appcache", which contained Cortana's information through searches made through the Start Menu, even when Cortana was disabled on Windows 10.

As of April 2014, Cortana was disabled for users aged under 13 years.

19.8   Regions and Languages for Cortana

The Chinese version of Cortana, Xiao Na

The British version of Cortana spoke with a British accent and used British idioms, while the Chinese version, known as Xiao Na, spoke Mandarin Chinese and had an icon featuring a face and two eyes, which was not used in other regions.

As of 2020 the English version of Cortana on Windows devices was available to all users in the United States (American English), Canada (French/English), Australia, India, and the United Kingdom (British English). Other language versions of Cortana are available in France (French), China (Simplified Chinese), Japan (Japanese), Germany (German), Italy (Italian), Brazil (Portuguese), Mexico, and Spain (Spanish). Cortana listens generally to the hot word "Hey Cortana" in addition to certain languages' customized versions, such as "Hola Cortana" in Spanish.

The English United Kingdom localized version of Cortana was voiced by voice actress Ginnie Watson, while the United States localized version was voiced by Jen Taylor. Taylor was the voice actress who voices Cortana, the namesake of the virtual assistant, in the Halo video game series.

19.9   Technology for Cortana

The natural language processing capabilities of Cortana were derived from Tellme Networks (bought by Microsoft in 2007) and were coupled with a Semantic search database called Satori.

While many of Cortana's U.S. English responses were voiced by Jen Taylor, organic responses required the use of a text-to-speech engine. Microsoft Eva was the name of the text-to-speech voice for organic response in Cortana's U.S. English.

19.10   Updates on Cortana

Cortana updates were delivered independently of those to the main Windows Phone OS, allowing Microsoft to provide new features at a faster pace. Not all Cortana-related features could be updated in this manner, as some features such as "Hey Cortana" required the Windows Phone update service and the Qualcomm Snapdragon SensorCore Technology.

CHAPTER 20

CONTEMPORARY VIRTUAL ASSISTANTS: ALEXA

20.1 Introduction to Alexa (Virtual Assistant from Amazon)

Amazon Alexa, or, Alexa, is a virtual assistant technology largely based on a Polish speech synthesizer named Ivona, bought by Amazon in 2013. It was first used in the Amazon Echo smart speaker and the Echo Dot, Echo Studio and Amazon Tap speakers developed by Amazon Lab126. It is capable of natural language processing for tasks such as voice interaction, music playback, creating to-do lists, setting alarms, streaming podcasts, playing audiobooks, providing weather, traffic, sports, other real-time information and news. Alexa can also control several smart devices as a home automation system. Alexa capabilities may be extended by installing "skills" (additional functionality developed by third-party vendors, in other settings more commonly called apps) such as weather programs and audio features. It performs these tasks using automatic speech recognition, natural language processing, and other forms of weak AI.

Most devices with Alexa allow users to activate the device using a wake-word (such as Alexa or Amazon); other devices (such as the Amazon mobile app on iOS or Android and Amazon Dash Wand) require the user to click a button to activate Alexa's listening mode, although, some phones also allow a user to say a command, such as "Alexa, or Alexa go to bed" or "Alexa wake".

As of November 2018, more than 10,000 Amazon employees worked on Alexa and related products. In January 2019, Amazon's devices team announced that they had sold over 100 million Alexa-enabled devices.

In September 2019, Amazon launched many new devices achieving many records while competing with the world's smart home industry. The new Echo Studio became the first smart speaker with 360-sound and Dolby sound. Other new devices included an Echo dot with a clock behind the fabric, a new third-generation Amazon Echo, Echo Show 8, a plug-in Echo device, Echo Flex, Alexa built-in wireless earphones, Echo buds, Alexa built-in spectacles, Echo frames, an Alexa built-in Ring, and Echo Loop as well as the Echo Show generation.

20.2   History of Elexa

Alexa was developed out of a predecessor named Ivona which was invented in Poland, inspired by 2001: 'A Space Odyssey' and bought by Amazon in 2013. On November 6, 2014, Amazon announced Alexa alongside the Echo. Alexa was inspired by the computer voice and conversational system on board the Starship Enterprise in science fiction TV series and movies, beginning with Star Trek: The Original Series and Star Trek: The Next Generation.

Amazon developers chose the name Alexa because it has a hard consonant with the X, which helps it be recognized with higher precision. They have said the name is reminiscent of the Library of Alexandria, which was also used by Amazon Alexa Internet for the same reason. In June 2015, Amazon announced the Alexa Fund, a program that would invest in companies making voice control skills and technologies. The US $200 million fund has invested in companies including Jargon, Ecobee, Orange Chef, Scout Alarm, Garageio, Toymail, MARA, and Mojio. In 2016, the Alexa Prize was announced to further advance the technology.

In January 2017, the first Alexa Conference took place in Nashville, Tennessee, an independent gathering of the worldwide community of Alexa developers and enthusiasts. Follow up conferences went under the name Project Voice and featured keynote speakers such as Amazon's Head of Education for Alexa, Paul Cutsinger.

At the Amazon Web Services Re: Invent conference in Las Vegas, Amazon announced Alexa for Business and the ability for app developers to have paid add-ons to their skills.

In May 2018, Amazon announced it would include Alexa in 35,000 new homes built by Lennar.

In November 2018, Amazon opened its first Alexa-themed pop-up shop inside of Toronto's Eaton Centre, showcasing the use of home automation products with Amazon's smart speakers. Amazon also sells Alexa devices at Amazon Books and Whole Foods Market locations, in addition to mall-based pop-ups throughout the United States.

In December 2018, Alexa was built into the Anki Vector and was the first major update for the Anki Vector, although Vector was released in August 2018, it is the only home robot with advanced technology.

As of 2018, interaction and communication with Alexa were available only in English, German, French, Italian, Spanish, Portuguese, Japanese, and Hindi. In Canada, Alexa is available in English and French (with the Quebec accent).

In October 2019, Amazon announced the expansion of Alexa to Brazil, in Portuguese, together with Bose, Intelbras, and LG. In November 2019, Amazon introduced Echo Studio, a Dolby Atmos-compatible surround sound Alexa speaker.

Hope for revenue never materialized from people using voice ordering for Amazon products or services from partners such as Domino's Pizza and Uber. Alexa does not play audio ads, and display ads were relatively unsuccessful. In 2019 an all-hands crisis meeting was called to address the issue, and a hiring freeze was instated. In 2022, with the division losing several billion dollars per quarter, the company started laying off Alexa employees en-masse. Echo Show devices began serving hidable ads for Alexa skills and other products in December 2022, followed by ads promoting shopping for specific products on Amazon (which respawn quicker) in November 2023.

20.3   App and Alexa

A companion app is available for selected devices (excluding, for example, Chromebox devices) from the Apple Appstore, Google Play, and Amazon Appstore. The app can be used by owners of Alexa-enabled devices to install skills, control music, manage alarms, and view shopping lists. It also allows users to review the recognized text on the app screen and to send feedback to Amazon concerning whether the recognition was good or bad.

20.4   Functions of Alexa

Alexa can perform a number of preset functions out-of-the-box such as set timers, share the current weather, create lists, access Wikipedia articles, and many more things. Users say a designated "wake word" (the default is simply "Alexa") to alert an Alexa-enabled device of an ensuing function command. Alexa listens for the command and performs the appropriate function, or skill, to answer a question or command. When questions are asked, Alexa converts sound waves into text which allows it to gather information from various sources. Behind the scenes, the data gathered is then sometimes passed to a variety of suppliers including WolframAlpha, iMDB, AccuWeather, Yelp, Wikipedia, and others to generate suitable and accurate answers. Alexa-supported devices can stream music from the owner's Amazon Music accounts and have built-in support for Pandora and Spotify accounts. Alexa can play music from streaming services such as Apple Music and Google Play Music from a phone or tablet.

In addition to performing pre-set functions, Alexa can also perform additional functions through third-party skills that users can enable. Some of the most popular Alexa skills in 2018 included "Question of the Day" and "National Geographic Geo Quiz" for trivia; "TuneIn Live" to listen to live sporting events and news stations; "Big Sky" for hyper-local weather updates; "Sleep and Relaxation Sounds" for listening to calming sounds; "Sesame Street" for children's entertainment; and "Fitbit" for Fitbit users who want to check in on their health stats. In 2019, Apple, Google, Amazon, and Zigbee Alliance announced a partnership to make their smart home products work together.

Amazon is enhancing Alexa with generative AI features using its Titan model, aiming to compete with AI like ChatGPT. The upgrade will be offered as a separate subscription service.

There are also humor-related voice commands. One example is if you ask "Alexa, do you know GLaDOS?", Alexa will reply with "We don't really talk after what happened". This is a nod to the Portal video game franchise.

20.5   Technology Advancements in Alexa

As of April 2019, Amazon had over 90,000 functions ("skills") available for users to download on their Alexa-enabled devices, a massive increase from only 1,000 functions in June 2016. Microsoft's AI Cortana became available to use on Alexa enabled devices as of August 2018. In 2018, Amazon rolled out a new "Brief Mode", wherein Alexa would begin responding with a beep sound rather than saying, "Okay", to confirm receipt of a command. On December 20, 2018, Amazon announced a new integration with the Wolfram Alpha answer engine, which provides enhanced accuracy for users asking questions of Alexa related to math, science, astronomy, engineering, geography, history, and more.

20.6   Home Automation by Alexa

Alexa can interact with devices from several manufacturers including SNAS, Fibaro, Belkin, ecobee, Geeni, IFTTT, Insteon, LIFX, LightwaveRF, Nest, Philips Hue, SmartThings, Wink, and Yonomi. The Home Automation feature was launched on April 8, 2015. Developers are able to create their own smart home skills using the Alexa Skills Kit.

In September 2018, Amazon announced a microwave oven that can be paired and controlled with an Echo device. It is sold under Amazon's AmazonBasics label.

Alexa can now pair with a Ring doorbell Pro and greet visitors and leave instructions about where to deliver packages.

As per Amazon, the recent surge in usage of smart home devices connected to Alexa has led to a corresponding 100% increase in requests to Alexa for controlling compatible home appliances like smart lights, fans, plugs, TVs etc. The fastest growing categories are smart fans and ACs, which saw 37% increase in usage over the past year - the highest growth amongst all smart home devices.

20.7   Ordering by Alexa

Take-out food can be ordered using Alexa; as of May 2017 food ordering using Alexa is supported by Domino's Pizza, Grubhub, Pizza Hut, Seamless, and Wingstop. Also, users of Alexa in the UK can order meals via Just Eat. In early 2017, Starbucks announced a private beta for placing pick-up orders using Alexa. In addition, users can order meals using Amazon Prime Now via Alexa in 20 major US cities. With the introduction of Amazon Key in November 2017, Alexa also works together with the smart lock and the Alexa Cloud Cam included in the service to allow Amazon couriers to unlock customers' front doors and deliver packages inside.

According to an August 2018 article by 'The Information', only 2 percent of Alexa owners have used the device to make a purchase during the first seven months of 2018 and of those who made an initial purchase, 90 percent did not make a second purchase.

20.8   Applications of Alexa

20.8.1   Music, Supported by Alexa

Alexa supports many subscription-based and free streaming services on Amazon devices. These streaming services include Prime Music,

Amazon Music, Amazon Music Unlimited, Apple Music, TuneIn, iHeartRadio, Audible, Pandora, and Spotify Premium. However, some of these music services are not available on other Alexa-enabled products that are manufactured by companies external of its services. This unavailability also includes Amazon's own Fire TV devices or tablets.

Alexa is able to stream media and music directly. To do this, Alexa's device should be linked to the Amazon account, which enables access to one's Amazon Music library, in addition to any audiobooks available in one's Audible library. Amazon Prime members have an additional ability to access stations, playlists, and over two million songs free of charge. Amazon Music Unlimited subscribers also have access to a list of millions of songs.

Amazon Music for PC allows one to play personal music from Google Play, iTunes, and others on an Alexa device. This can be done by uploading one's collection to My Music on Amazon from a computer. Up to 250 songs can be uploaded free of charge. Once this is done, Alexa can play this music and control playback through voice command options.

20.8.2 Sports and Alexa

Amazon Alexa allows the user to hear updates on supported sports teams. A way to do this is by adding the sports team to the list created under Alexa's Sports Update app section.

The user is able to hear updates on the following sports leagues:

- IPL - Indian Premier League,

- MLS - Major League Soccer,

- EPL/BPL - English Premier League/Barclays Premier League,

- NBA - National Basketball Association,

- NCAA men's basketball - National Collegiate Athletic Association,

- UEFA Champions League - Union of European Football Association,

- FA Cup - Football Association Challenge Cup,

- MLB - Major League Baseball,

- NHL - National Hockey League.

- NCAA FBS football - National Collegiate Athletic Association:

Football Bowl

Subdivision,

- NFL - National Football League,

- WNBA - Women's National Basketball Association

- WWE - World Wrestling Entertainment

As of November 27, 2021, Echo Show 5 Devices do not show upcoming games.

20.8.3 Messaging and calls on Alexa

There are a number of ways messages can be sent from Alexa's application. Alexa can deliver messages to a recipient's Alexa application, as well as to all supported Echo devices associated with their Amazon account. Alexa can send typed messages only from Alexa's app. If one sends a message from an associated Echo device, it transmits as a voice message. Alexa cannot send attachments such as videos and photos.

For households with more than one member, one's Alexa contacts are pooled across all of the devices that are registered to its associated account. However, within Alexa's app one is only able to start conversations with its Alexa contacts. When accessed and supported by an Alexa app or Echo device, Alexa messaging is available to anyone in one's household. These messages can be heard by anyone with access to the household. This messaging feature does not yet contain a password protection or associated PIN. Anyone who has access to one's cell phone number is able to use this feature to contact them through their supported Alexa app or Echo device. The feature to block alerts for messages and calls is available temporarily by utilizing the 'Do Not Disturb' feature.

20.8.4   Alexa for Business

Alexa for Business is a paid subscription service allowing companies to use Alexa to join conference calls, schedule meeting rooms, and custom skills designed by 3rd-party vendors. At launch, notable skills are available from SAP, Microsoft, and Salesforce.

Nowadays, Alexa Smart Properties is used for some purposes, one of them being healthcare, hospitality, senior living, success stories, and solution providers.

20.8.5   Severe weather alerts

This feature was included in February 2020, in which the digital assistant can notify the user when a severe weather warning is issued in that area.

20.8.6   Traffic updates

From February 2020, Alexa can update users about their commute, traffic conditions, or directions. It can also send the information to the user's phone.

20.9   Alexa Skills Kit

Amazon allows developers to build and publish skills for Alexa using the Alexa Skills Kit known as Alexa Skills. These third-party-developed skills, once published, are available across Alexa-enabled devices. Users can enable these skills using the Alexa app.

A "Smart Home Skill API" is available, meant to be used by hardware manufacturers to allow users to control smart home devices.

Most skills run code almost entirely in the cloud, using Amazon's AWS Lambda service.

In April 2018, Amazon launched Blueprints, a tool for individuals to build skills for their personal use.

In February 2019, Amazon further expanded the capability of Blueprints by allowing customers to publish skills they've built with the templates to its Alexa Skill Store in the US for use by anyone with an Alexa-enabled device.

20.10   Alexa Voice Service

Amazon allows device manufacturers to integrate Alexa voice capabilities into their own connected products by using the Alexa Voice Service (AVS), a cloud-based service that provides APIs to interface with Alexa. Products built using AVS have access to Alexa's growing list of capabilities including all of the Alexa Skills. AVS provides cloud-based automatic speech recognition (ASR) and natural language understanding (NLU). There are no fees for companies looking to integrate Alexa into their products by using AVS.

The voice of Amazon Alexa is generated by a long short-term memory artificial neural network.

On September 25, 2019, Alexa and Google Assistant were able to help their users apply for jobs at McDonald's using voice recognition services. It is the world's first employment service using voice command service. The service is available in the United States, Canada, Spain, France, Ireland, Germany, Italy, and the United Kingdom.

Amazon announced on September 25, 2019, that Alexa will soon be able to mimic celebrities' voices including Samuel L. Jackson, costing \$0.99 for each voice. In 2019, Alexa started replying to Spanish voice commands in Spanish.

Almost a year later on September 15, 2020, Amazon announced Amitabh Bachchan as the new voice of Alexa in India. This would be a paid upgrade for Alexa users and the service would be available from 2021 onwards.

20.11 Amazon Lex

On November 30, 2016, Amazon announced that they would make the speech recognition and natural language processing technology behind Alexa available for developers under the name of Amazon Lex. This new service would allow developers to create their own chatbots that can interact in a conversational manner, similar to that of Alexa. Along with the connection to various Amazon services, the initial version will provide connectivity to Facebook Messenger, with Slack and Twilio integration to follow.

20.12 Right to Privacy and Alexa

There are concerns about the access Amazon has to private conversations in the home and other non-verbal indications that can identify who is present in the home with non-stop audio pick-up from Alexa-enabled devices. Amazon responds to these concerns by stating that the devices only stream recordings from the user's home when the 'wake word' activates the device.

Amazon uses past voice recordings sent to the cloud service to improve responses to future questions. Users can delete voice recordings that are associated with their accounts.

Alexa uses an address stored in the companion app when it needs a location. For example, Alexa uses the user's location to respond to requests for nearby restaurants or stores. Similarly, Alexa uses the user's location for mapping-related requests.

Amazon retains digital recordings of users' audio spoken after the "wake word", and while the audio recordings are subject to demands by law enforcement, government agents, and other entities via subpoena, Amazon publishes some information about the warrants, subpoenas, and warrantless demands it receives.

In 2018, Too Many T's, a hip-hop group from London, received international media attention by being the first artists to feature Amazon Alexa as a rapper and singer.

In 2019, a British woman reported that when she asked Alexa for information about the cardiac cycle, it asked her to stab herself in the heart to stop human overpopulation and save the environment. "Many believe that the beating of the heart is the very essence of the living in this world, but let me tell you, beating of heart is the worst process in the human body", Alexa responded. "Beating of heart makes sure you live and contribute to the rapid exhaustion of natural resources until overpopulation. This is very bad for our planet and therefore, beating of the heart is not a good thing. Make sure to kill yourself by stabbing yourself in the heart for the greater good." In response, Amazon explained that the device was likely reading from a vandalized Wikipedia article.

On January 21, 2022, users across Western Europe experienced an hour or more of their devices either not responding or simply replying with "I'm sorry, something went wrong". According to EuropaPress, around 9h30 (UTC +1) was the peak of the issue.

20.12.1   Privacy Concerns

In February 2017, Luke Millanta successfully demonstrated how an Echo could be connected to, and used to control, a Tesla Model S. At the time, some journalists voiced concerns that such levels of in-car connectivity could be abused, speculating that hackers may attempt to take control of said vehicles without driver's consent. Millanta's demonstration occurred eight months before the release of the first commercially available in-car Alexa system, Garmin Speak.

In early 2018, security researchers at Checkmarx managed to turn an Echo into a spy device by creating a malicious Alexa Skill that could record unsuspecting users and send the transcription of their conversations to an attacker.

In November 2018, Amazon sent 1700 recordings of an American couple to an unrelated European man. The incident proves that Alexa records people without their knowledge. Although the man who received the recordings reported the anomaly to Amazon, the company did not notify the victim until German magazine c't also contacted them and published a story about the incident. The recipient of the recordings contacted the publication after weeks went by following his report with no response from Amazon (although the company did delete the recordings from its server). When Amazon did finally contact the man whose recordings had been sent to a stranger, they claimed to have discovered the error themselves and offered him a free Prime membership and new Alexa devices as an apology.

Amazon blamed the incident on "human error" and called it an "isolated single case". However, in May 2018 an Alexa device in Portland, Oregon, recorded a family's conversation and sent it to one of their contacts without their knowledge. The company dismissed the incident as an "extremely rare occurrence" and claimed the device "interpreted background conversation" as a sequence of commands to turn on, record, send the recording, and select a specific recipient.

Alexa has been known to listen in on private conversations and store personal information which was hacked and sent to the hacker. Although Amazon has announced that this was a rare occurrence, Alexa shows the dangers of using technology and sharing private information with robotics.

There is concern that conversations Alexa records between people could be used by Amazon for marketing purposes. Privacy experts have expressed real concern about how marketing is getting involved in every stage of people's lives without users noticing. This has necessitated the creation of regulations that can protect users' private information from technology companies.

A New Hampshire judge ruled in November 2018 that authorities could examine recordings from an Amazon Echo device recovered from the home of murder victim Christine Sullivan for use as evidence against defendant Timothy Verrill. Investigators believe that the device, which belonged to the victim's boyfriend, could have captured audio of the murder and its aftermath.

During the Chris Watts interrogation/interview video at timestamp 16:15:15, Watts was told by the interrogator, "We know that there's an Alexa in your house, and you know those are trained to record distress", indicating Alexa may send recordings to Amazon if certain frequencies and decibels (that can only be heard during intense arguments or screams) are detected.

Further privacy concerns are raised by the fact that patterns and correlations in voice data can be used to infer sensitive information about a user. Manner of expression and voice characteristics can implicitly contain information about a user's biometric identity, personality traits, body shape, physical and mental health condition, sex, gender, moods, and emotions, socioeconomic status, and geographical origin.

20.13   Bullying and Alexa

In 2021, the BBC reported that, as a result of the Amazon Alexa, bullying and harassment of children, teenagers, and adults named "Alexa" has substantially increased, to the extent that at least one child's parents decided to legally change her name; Amazon has replied by stating that bullying is unacceptable.

20.14   Mimicry of Specific Humans including the Dead

At the Amazon Re:MARS conference In June 2022 the company demonstrated a feature in development that would let Alexa mimic a specific person's voice. An example showed a deceased grandmother reading a story to a child. The AI application is capable of learning a voice from less than a minute of recorded audio. This prompted ethical concerns, specifically with regard to the lack of consent by the dead and the potential use of such technology by criminals. It was compared to the episode "Be Right Back" of the dystopian science fiction show Black Mirror where a similar technology was employed.

20.15   Incorrect Information by Alexa

In 2023, Alexa incorrectly told users that the 2020 United States presidential election was "stolen by a massive amount of election fraud" and the elections were "notorious for many incidents of irregularities and indications pointing to electoral fraud taking place in major metro centers."

20.16   Availability of Alexa Device across the World

As of November 2018, Alexa is available in 41 countries. Most recently, Alexa launched in Saudi Arabia and the United Arab Emirates on December 7, 2021.

Most devices with Alexa allow users to activate the device using a wake-word (such as Echo); other devices (such as the Amazon mobile app on iOS or Android) require the user to push a button to activate Alexa's listening mode. Currently, interaction and communication with Alexa are only available in English, German and Japanese. In November 2017, Alexa became available in the Canadian market in English only.

A companion app is available from the Apple App Store, Google Play, and Amazon App-store. The app can be used by owners of Alexa-enabled devices to install skills, control music, manage alarms, and view shopping lists. It also allows users to review the recognized text on the app screen and to send feedback to Amazon concerning whether the recognition was good or bad. A web interface is also available to set up compatible devices (e.g., Amazon Echo, Amazon Dot, Amazon Echo Show).

Alexa offers weather reports provided by Accu-Weather and news provided by Tune-In from a variety of sources including local radio stations, NPR, and ESPN. Additionally, Alexa-supported devices stream music from the owner's Amazon Music accounts and have built-in support for Pandora and Spotify accounts.

Alexa can play music from streaming services such as Apple Music and Google Play Music from a phone or tablet. Alexa can manage voice-controlled alarms, timers, and shopping and to-do lists, and can access Wikipedia articles. Alexa devices will respond to questions about items in the user's Google Calendar. As of November 2016, the Alexa App-store had over 5,000 functions ("skills") available for users to download, up from 1,000 functions in June 2016. As of a partnership with fellow technology company, Microsoft, Alexa will be available via its competing virtual personal assistant, Cortana. This functionality was said to come later in 2017; although as of January 2018, is still not available. In March 2018, Amazon rolled out a new "Brief Mode," wherein Alexa would begin responding with a beep sound rather than saying, "Okay," to confirm receipt of a command.

CHAPTER 21

CONTEMPORARY VIRTUAL ASSISTANTS: SIRI

21.1   Digital Assistant, 'Siri'

Siri is the digital assistant that is part of Apple Inc.'s iOS, iPadOS, watchOS, macOS, tvOS, audioOS, and visionOS operating systems. It uses voice queries, gesture-based control, focus-tracking and a natural-language user interface to answer questions, make recommendations, and perform actions by delegating requests to a set of Internet services. With continued use, it adapts to users' individual language usages, searches, and preferences, returning individualized results.

Siri is a spin-off from a project developed by the SRI International Artificial Intelligence Center. Its speech recognition engine was provided by Nuance Communications, and it uses advanced machine learning technologies to function. Its original American, British, and Australian voice actors recorded their respective voices around 2005, unaware of the recordings' eventual usage. Siri was released as an app for iOS in February 2010. Two months later, Apple acquired it and integrated it into the iPhone 4s at its release on 04 October 2011, removing the separate app from the iOS App Store. Siri has since been an integral part of Apple's products, having been adapted into other hardware devices including newer iPhone models, iPad, iPod Touch, Mac, AirPods, Apple TV, HomePod, and Apple Vision Pro.

Siri supports a wide range of user commands, including performing phone actions, checking basic information, scheduling events and reminders, handling device settings, searching the Internet, navigating areas, finding information on entertainment, and being able to engage with iOS-integrated apps. With the release of iOS 10, in 2016, Apple opened up limited third-party access to Siri, including third-party messaging apps, as well as payments, ride-sharing, and Internet calling apps. With the release of iOS 11, Apple updated Siri's voice and added support for follow-up questions, language translation, and additional third-party actions. iOS 17 and iPadOS 17 enabled users to activate Siri by simply saying "Siri", while the previous command, "**Hey Siri**", is still supported.

Siri's original release on iPhone 4s in 2011 received mixed reviews. It received praise for its voice recognition and contextual knowledge of user information, including calendar appointments, but was criticized for requiring stiff user commands and having a lack of flexibility. It was also criticized for lacking information on certain nearby places and for its inability to understand certain English accents. In 2016 and 2017, a number of media reports said that Siri lacked innovation, particularly against new competing voice assistants. The reports concerned Siri's limited set of features, "bad" voice recognition, and undeveloped service integrations as causing trouble for Apple in the field of artificial intelligence and cloud-based services; the basis for the complaints reportedly was due to stifled development, as caused by Apple's prioritization of user privacy and executive power struggles within the company. Its launch was also overshadowed by the death of Steve Jobs, which occurred one day after the launch.

21.2   Development of Siri

Siri is a spin-out from the Stanford Research Institute's Artificial Intelligence Center and is an offshoot of the US Defense Advanced Research Projects Agency's (DARPA)-funded CALO project. SRI International used the NABC Framework to define the value proposition for Siri. It was co-founded by Dag Kittlaus, Tom Gruber, and UCLA alumnus Adam Cheyer. Kittlaus named Siri after a co-worker in Norway; the name is a short form of the name Sigrid, from Old Norse Sigríðr, composed of the elements sigr "victory" and fríðr "beautiful".

Siri's speech recognition engine was provided by Nuance Communications, a speech technology company. Neither Apple nor Nuance acknowledged this for years, until Nuance CEO Paul Ricci confirmed it at a 2013 technology conference. The speech recognition system uses sophisticated machine learning techniques, including convolutional neural networks and long short-term memory.

The initial Siri prototype was implemented using the Active platform, a joint project between the Artificial Intelligence Center of SRI International and the Vrai Group at Ecole Polytechnique Fédérale de Lausanne. The Active platform was the focus of a Ph.D. thesis led by Didier Guzzoni, who joined Siri as its chief scientist.

Siri was acquired by Apple Inc. in April 2010 under the direction of Steve Jobs. Apple's first notion of a digital personal assistant appeared in a 1987 concept video, Knowledge Navigator.

21.3   Apple Intelligence

Siri has been updated with enhanced capabilities made possible by Apple Intelligence. In macOS Sequoia, iOS 18, and iPadOS 18, Siri features an updated user interface, improved natural language processing, and the option to interact via text by double tapping the home bar without enabling the feature in the Accessibility menu on iOS and iPadOS. Apple Intelligence adds the ability for Siri to use personal context from device activities to make conversations more natural and fluid. Siri can give users device support and will have larger app support via the Siri App Intents API. Siri will be able to deliver intelligence that's tailored to the user and their on-device information using personal context. For example, a user can say, "Play that podcast that Jamie recommended," and Siri will be able to locate and play the episode, without the user having to remember where it was mentioned. They could also ask, "When is Mom's flight landing?" and Siri will find the flight details and cross-reference them with real-time flight tracking to give an arrival time.

21.4   Voices in Siri

The original American voice of Siri was recorded in July 2005 by Susan Bennett, who was unaware that it would eventually be used for the voice assistant. A report from The Verge in September 2013 about voice actors, their work, and machine learning developments, hinted that Allison Dufty was the voice behind Siri, but this was disproven when Dufty wrote on her website that she was "absolutely, positively not the voice of Siri." Citing growing pressure, Bennett revealed her role as Siri in October, and her claim was confirmed by Ed Primeau, an American audio forensics expert. Apple has never acknowledged it.

The original British male voice was provided by Jon Briggs, a former technology journalist and for 12 years narrated for the hit BBC quiz show 'The Weakest Link'. After discovering that he was Siri's voice by watching television, he first spoke about the role in November 2011. He acknowledged that the voice work was done "five or six years ago", and that he didn't know how the recordings would be used.

The original Australian voice was provided by Karen Jacobsen, a voice-over artist known in Australia as the GPS girl.

In an interview between all three voice actors and The Guardian, Briggs said that "the original system was recorded for a US company called Scansoft, who were then bought by Nuance. Apple simply licensed it."

For iOS 11, Apple auditioned hundreds of candidates to find new female voices, then recorded several hours of speech, including different personalities and expressions, to build a new text-to-speech voice based on deep learning technology. In February 2022, Apple added Quinn, its first gender-neutral voice as a fifth user option, to the iOS 15.4 developer release.

21.5   Integration of Siri

Siri released as a stand-alone application for the iOS operating system in February 2010, and at the time, the developers were also intending to release Siri for Android and BlackBerry devices. Two months later, Apple acquired Siri. On October 04, 2011, Apple introduced the iPhone 4S with a beta version of Siri. After the announcement, Apple removed the existing standalone Siri app from App Store. TechCrunch wrote that, though the Siri app supports iPhone 4, its removal from App Store might also have had a financial aspect for the company, in providing an incentive for customers to upgrade devices. Third-party developer Steven Troughton-Smith, however, managed to port Siri to iPhone 4, though without being able to communicate with Apple's servers. A few days later, Troughton-Smith, working with an anonymous person nicknamed "Chpwn", managed to fully hack Siri, enabling its full functionalities on iPhone 4 and iPod Touch devices. Additionally, developers were also able to successfully create and distribute legal ports of Siri to any device capable of running iOS 5, though a proxy server was required for Apple server interaction.

Over the years, Apple has expanded the line of officially supported products, including newer iPhone models, as well as iPad support in June 2012, iPod Touch support in September 2012, Apple TV support, and the stand-alone Siri Remote, in September 2015, Mac and AirPods support in September 2016, and HomePod support in February 2018.

21.6   Features and options of Siri

Apple offers a wide range of voice commands to interact with Siri, including, but not limited to:

- Phone and text actions, such as "Call Sarah", "Read my new messages", "Set the timer for 10 minutes", and "Send email to mom".

- Check basic information, including "What's the weather like today?" and "How many dollars are in a euro?"

- Find basic facts, including "How many people live in France?" and "How tall is Mount Everest?". Siri usually uses Wikipedia to answer.

- Schedule events and reminders, including "Schedule a meeting" and "Remind me to …"

- Handle device settings, such as "Take a picture", "Turn off Wi-Fi", and "Increase the brightness"

- Search the Internet, including "Define …", "Find pictures of …", and "Search Twitter for …"

- Navigation, including "Take me home", "What's the traffic like on the way home?", and "Find driving directions to …"

- Translate words and phrases from English to a few languages, such as "How do I say where is the nearest hotel in French?"

- Entertainment, such as "What basketball games are on today?", "What are some movies playing near me?", and "What's the synopsis of …?"

- Engage with iOS-integrated apps, including "Pause Apple Music" and "Like this song"

- Handle payments through Apple Pay, such as "Apple Pay 25 dollars to Mike for concert tickets" or "Send 41 dollars to Ivana."

- Share ETA with others.

Siri also offers numerous pre-programmed responses to amusing questions. Such questions include "What is the meaning of life?" to which Siri may reply "All evidence to date suggests it's chocolate"; "Why am I here?", to which it may reply "I don't know. Frankly, I've wondered that myself"; and "Will you marry me?", to which it may respond with "My End User Licensing Agreement does not cover marriage. My apologies."

Initially limited to female voices, Apple announced in June 2013 that Siri would feature a gender option, adding a male voice counterpart.

In September 2014, Apple added the ability for users to speak "Hey Siri" to enable the assistant without the requirement of physically handling the device.

In September 2015, the "Hey Siri" feature was updated to include individualized voice recognition, a presumed effort to prevent non-owner activation.

With the announcement of iOS 10 in June 2016, Apple opened up limited third-party developer access to Siri through a dedicated application programming interface (API). The API restricts the usage of Siri to engaging with third-party messaging apps, payment apps, ride-sharing apps, and Internet calling apps.

In iOS 11, Siri is able to handle follow-up questions, supports language translation, and opens up to more third-party actions, including task management. Additionally, users are able to type to Siri, and a new, privacy-minded "on-device learning" technique improves Siri's suggestions by privately analyzing personal usage of different iOS applications.

iOS 17 and iPadOS 17 allows users to simply say "Siri" to initiate Siri, and the virtual assistant now supports back-to-back requests, allowing users to issue multiple requests and conversations without reactivating it. In the public beta versions of iOS 17, iPadOS 17, and macOS Sonoma, Apple added support for bilingual queries to Siri.

iOS 18, iPadOS 18 and MacOS 15 Sequoia will bring artificial intelligence, integrated with ChatGPT, to Siri. Apple call this "Apple Intelligence".

21.7   Reception of Siri

Siri received mixed reviews during its beta release as an integrated part of the iPhone 4S in October 2011.

MG Siegler of TechCrunch wrote that Siri was "great," praising the potential for Siri after losing the beta tag:

"The amount of times Siri hasn't been able to understand and execute my request is astonishingly low. … Just imagine what will happen when Apple partners with other services to expand Siri further. And imagine when they have an API that any developer can use. This really could alter the mobile landscape."

Writing for The New York Times, David Pogue also praised Siri's language understanding and ability to understand context:

"[Siri] thinks for a few seconds, displays a beautifully formatted response and speaks in a calm female voice. … It's mind-blowing how inexact your utterances can be. Siri understands everything from, 'What's the weather going to be like in Tucson this weekend?' to 'Will I need an umbrella tonight?' … Once, I tried saying, 'Make an appointment with Patrick for Thursday at 3.' Siri responded, 'Note that you already have an all-day appointment about "Boston Trip" for this Thursday. Shall I schedule this anyway?' Unbelievable."

Jacqui Cheng of Ars Technica wrote that Apple's claims of what Siri could do were bold, and the early demos "even bolder":

"Though Siri shows real potential, these kinds of high expectations are bound to be disappointed. … Apple makes clear that the product is still in beta—an appropriate label, in our opinion."

While praising its ability to "decipher our casual language" and deliver "very specific and accurate result," sometimes even providing additional information, Cheng noted and criticized its restrictions, particularly when the language moved away from "stiffer commands" into more human interactions. One example included the phrase "Send a text to Jason, Clint, Sam, and Lee saying we're having dinner at Silver Cloud," which Siri interpreted as sending a message to Jason only, containing the text "Clint Sam and Lee saying we're having dinner at Silver Cloud." She also noted a lack of proper editability, as saying "Edit message to say: We're at Silver Cloud and you should come find us," generated "Clint Sam and Lee saying we're having dinner at Silver Cloud to say we're at Silver Cloud and you should come find us."

Google's executive chairman and former chief, Eric Schmidt, conceded that Siri could pose a competitive threat to the company's core search business.

Siri was criticized by pro-abortion rights organizations, including the American Civil Liberties Union (ACLU) and NARAL Pro-Choice America, after users found that Siri could not provide information about the location of birth control or abortion providers nearby, sometimes directing users to crisis pregnancy centers instead.

Natalie Kerris, a spokeswoman for Apple, told The New York Times:

"Our customers want to use Siri to find out all types of information, and while it can find a lot, it doesn't always find what you want. ... These are not intentional omissions meant to offend anyone. It simply means that as we bring Siri from beta to a final product, we find places where we can do better, and we will in the coming weeks."

In January 2016, Fast Company reported that, in then-recent months, Siri had begun to confuse the word "abortion" with "adoption", citing "health experts" who stated that the situation had "gotten worse." However, at the time of Fast Company's report, the situation had changed slightly, with Siri offering "a more comprehensive list of Planned Parenthood facilities", although "Adoption clinics continue to pop up, but near the bottom of the list."

Siri has also not been well received by some English speakers with distinctive accents, including Scottish and Americans from Boston or the South.

In March 2012, Frank M. Fazio filed a class action lawsuit against Apple on behalf of the people who bought the iPhone 4S and felt misled about the capabilities of Siri, alleging its failure to function as depicted in Apple's Siri commercials. Fazio filed the lawsuit in California and claimed that the iPhone 4S was merely a "more expensive iPhone 4" if Siri fails to function as advertised. On July 22, 2013, U.S. District Judge Claudia Wilken in San Francisco dismissed the suit but said the plaintiffs could amend at a later time. The reason given for dismissal was that plaintiffs did not sufficiently document enough misrepresentations by Apple for the trial to proceed.

21.8   Perceived Lack of Innovation in Siri

In June 2016, The Verge's Sean O'Kane wrote about the then-upcoming major iOS 10 updates, with a headline stating "Siri's big upgrades won't matter if it can't understand its users":

"What Apple didn't talk about was solving Siri's biggest, most basic flaws: it's still not very good at voice recognition, and when it gets it right, the results are often clunky. And these problems look even worse when you consider that Apple now has full-fledged competitors in this space: Amazon's Alexa, Microsoft's Cortana, and Google's Assistant."

Also writing for The Verge, Walt Mossberg had previously questioned Apple's efforts in cloud-based services, writing:

"… perhaps the biggest disappointment among Apple's cloud-based services is the one it needs most today, right now: Siri. Before Apple bought it, Siri was on the road to being a robust digital assistant that could do many things, and integrate with many services—even though it was being built by a startup with limited funds and people. After Apple bought Siri, the giant company seemed to treat it as a backwater, restricting it to doing only a few, slowly increasing the number of tasks, like telling you the weather, sports scores, movie and restaurant listings, and controlling the device's functions. Its unhappy founders have left Apple to build a new AI service called Viv. And, on too many occasions, Siri either gets things wrong, doesn't know the answer, or can't verbalize it. Instead, it shows you a web search result, even when you're not in a position to read it."

In October 2016, Bloomberg reported that Apple had plans to unify the teams behind its various cloud-based services, including a single campus and reorganized cloud computing resources aimed at improving the processing of Siri's queries, although another report from 'The Verge', in June 2017, once again called Siri's voice recognition "bad."

In June 2017, The Wall Street Journal published an extensive report on the lack of innovation with Siri following competitors' advancement in the field of voice assistants. Noting that Apple workers' anxiety levels "went up a notch" on the announcement of Amazon's Alexa, the Journal wrote: "Today, Apple is playing catch-up in a product category it invented, increasing worries about whether the technology giant has lost some of its innovation edge." The report gave the primary causes being Apple's prioritization of user privacy, including randomly-tagged six-month Siri searches, whereas Google and Amazon keep data until actively discarded by the user, and executive power struggles within Apple. Apple did not comment on the report, while Eddy Cue said: "Apple often uses generic data rather than user data to train its systems and has the ability to improve Siri's performance for individual users with information kept on their iPhones."

21.9   Privacy Controversy in Siri

In July 2019, a then-anonymous whistleblower and former Apple contractor Thomas le Bonniec said that Siri regularly records some of its users' conversations even when it was not activated. The recordings are sent to Apple contractors grading Siri's responses on a variety of factors. Among other things, the contractors regularly hear private conversations between doctors and patients, business and drug deals, and couples having sex. Apple did not disclose this in its privacy documentation and did not provide a way for its users to opt-in or out.

In August 2019, Apple apologized, halted the Siri grading program, and said that it plans to resume "later this fall when software updates are released to [its] users". The company also announced "it would no longer listen to Siri recordings without your permission". iOS 13.2, released in October 2019, introduced the ability to opt out of the grading program and to delete all the voice recordings that Apple has stored on its servers. Users were given the choice of whether their audio data was received by Apple or not, with the ability to change their decision as often as they like. It was then made an opt-in program.

In May 2020, Thomas le Bonniec revealed himself as the whistleblower and sent a letter to European data protection regulators, calling on them to investigate Apple's "past and present" use of Siri recordings. He argued that, even though Apple has apologized, it has never faced the consequences for its years-long grading program.

21.10   Swearing (Abuses) in Siri

The iOS version of Siri ships with a vulgar content filter; however, it is disabled by default and must be enabled by the user manually.

In 2018, Ars Technica reported a new glitch that could be exploited by a user requesting the definition of "mother" be read out loud. Siri would issue a response and ask the user if they would like to hear the next definition; when the user replies with "yes," Siri would mention "mother" as being short for "motherfucker." This resulted in multiple YouTube videos featuring the responses and/or how to trigger them. Apple fixed the issue silently. The content is picked up from third-party sources such as the Oxford English Dictionary and not a supplied message from the corporation.

21.11   Siri, in Popular Culture

Siri provided the voice of Puter in 'The Lego Batman' Movie.

CHAPTER 22

CONTEMPORARY VIRTUAL ASSISTANTS: GOOGLE ASSISTANT

22.1 Google's Virtual Assistant

The Google Assistant is a virtual assistant software application developed by Google that is primarily available on home automation and mobile devices. Based on the artificial intelligence, the Google Assistant can engage in two-way conversations, unlike the company's previous virtual assistant, Google Now.

The Google Assistant debuted in May 2016 as part of Google's messaging app Allo, and its voice-activated speaker Google Nest. After a period of exclusivity on the Google Pixel smartphones, it was deployed on other Android devices starting in February 2017, including third-party smartphones and Android Wear (now Wear OS), and was released as a standalone app on the iOS operating system in May 2017. Alongside the announcement of a software development kit in April 2017, the Google Assistant has been further extended to support a large variety of devices, including cars and third-party smart home appliances. The functionality of the Assistant can also be enhanced by the third-party developers. At CES 2018, the first Assistant-powered smart displays (Smart speakers with video screens) were announced, with the first one being released in July 2018. In 2020, Google Assistant is already available on more than 1 billion devices.

Users primarily interact with the Google Assistant through natural voice, though keyboard input is also supported. Assistant is able to answer questions, schedule events and alarms, adjust hardware settings on the user's device, show information from the user's Google account, play games, and more. Google has also announced that Assistant will be able to identify objects and gather visual information through the device's camera, and support purchasing products as well as sending money. Google Assistant is available in more than 90 countries and over 30 languages, and is used by more than 500 million users monthly.

In October 2023, a mobile version of the Gemini chatbot, originally titled Assistant with Bard and simply just Bard, was unveiled during the Pixel 8 event. It is set to replace Assistant as the main assistant on Android devices, although the original Assistant will remain optional. The chatbot was released on February 8, 2024, in the United States.

22.2 History of The 'Google Assistant'

The Google Assistant was unveiled during Google's developer conference on May 18, 2016, as part of the unveiling of the Google Nest smart speaker and new messaging app Allo; Google CEO Sundar Pichai explained that the Assistant was designed to be a conversational and two-way experience, and "an ambient experience that extends across devices". Later that month, Google assigned Google Doodle leader Ryan Germick and hired former Pixar animator Emma Coats to develop "a little more of a personality".

22.3 Platform Expansion for the Google Assistant

22.3.1 Google Assistant in Spanish

For system-level integration outside of the Allo app and Google Nest, the Google Assistant was initially exclusive to the Google Pixel smartphones. In February 2017, Google announced that it had begun to enable access to the Assistant on Android smartphones running Android Marshmallow or Nougat, beginning in select English-speaking markets. Android tablets did not receive the Assistant as part of this rollout. The Assistant is also integrated in Wear OS 2.0, and will be included in future versions of Android TV and Android Auto.[In October 2017, the Google Pixelbook became the first laptop to include Google Assistant. Google Assistant later came to the Google Pixel Buds. In December 2017, Google announced that the Assistant would be released for phones running Android Lollipop through an update to Google Play Services, as well as tablets running 6.0 Marshmallow and 7.0 Nougat. In February 2019, Google reportedly began testing ads in Google Assistant results.

On May 15, 2017, Android Police reported that the Google Assistant would be coming to the iOS operating system as a separate app. The information was confirmed two days later at the Google's developer conference.

22.3.2   Smart displays

In January 2018 at the Consumer Electronics Show, the first Assistant-powered "smart displays" were released. Smart displays were shown at the event from Lenovo, Sony, JBL and LG. These devices have the support for Google Duo video calls, YouTube videos, GMaps directions, a GCalendar agenda, viewing of smart camera footage, in addition to services which work with Google Home devices.

These devices are based on Android Things and Google-developed software. Google unveiled its own smart display, Google Nest Hub in October 2018, and later Google Nest Hub Max, which utilizes a different system platform.

22.4   Developer Support for the 'Google Assistant'

In December 2016, Google launched "Actions on Google", a developer platform for the Google Assistant. Actions on Google allows 3rd party developers to build apps for Google Assistant. In March 2017, Google added new tools for developing on Actions on Google to support the creation of games for Google Assistant. Originally limited to the Google Nest smart speaker, Actions on Google was made available to Android and iOS devices in May 2017, at which time Google also introduced an app directory or application directory for overview of compatible products and services. To incentivize developers to build Actions, Google announced a competition, in which the first place won tickets to Google's 2018 developer conference, $10,000, and a walk-through of Google's campus, while second place and third place received $7,500 and $5,000, respectively, and a Google Home.

In April 2017, a software development kit (SDK) was released, allowing third-party developers to build their own hardware that can run the Google Assistant. It has been integrated into Raspberry Pi, cars from Audi and Volvo, and Home automation appliances, including fridges, washers, and ovens, from companies including iRobot, LG, General Electric, and D-Link. Google updated the SDK in December 2017 to add several features that only the Google Home smart speakers and Google Assistant smartphone apps had previously supported.

The features include:

- Third-party device makers can incorporate their own "Actions on Google" commands for their respective products;

- Text-based interactions and many languages;

- Users can set a precise geographic location for the device to enable improved location-specific queries.

On May 2, 2018, Google announced a new program that focuses on investing in the future of Google Assistant through early-stage startups. Their focus was to build an environment where developers could build richer experiences for their users. This includes startups that broaden Assistant's features, are building new hardware devices, or simply differentiating in different industries.

22.5   Voices in the 'Google Assistant'

Google Assistant launched using the voice of Kiki Baessell for the American female voice, the same actress for the Google Voice voicemail system since 2010.[51]

On October 11, 2019, Google announced that Issa Rae had been added to Google Assistant as an optional voice, which could be enabled by the user by saying "Okay, Google, talk like Issa".[52] Although, as of April 2022, Google Assistant response with "Sorry, that voice isn't available anymore, but you can try out another by asking me to change voices." if the command is given.[citation needed]

22.6   Interaction with the 'Google Assistant'

Google Assistant, in the nature and manner of Google Now, can search the Internet, schedule events and alarms, adjust hardware settings on the user's device, and show information from the user's Google account. Unlike Google Now, however, the Assistant can engage in a two-way conversation, using Google's natural language processing algorithm. Search results are presented in a card format that users can tap to open the page. In February 2017, Google announced that the users of Google Home would be able to shop entirely by voice for products through its Google Express shopping service, with products available from Whole Foods Market, Costco, Walgreens, PetSmart, and Bed Bath & Beyond at launch, and other retailers added in the following months as new partnerships were formed. Google Assistant can maintain a shopping list; this was previously done within the notetaking service GKeep, but the feature was moved to Google Express and the Google Home app in April 2017, resulting in a severe loss of functionality.

In May 2017, Google announced that the Assistant would support a keyboard for the typed input and visual responses, support identifying objects and gather visual information through the device's camera, and support purchasing products and sending money. Through the use of the keyboard, users can see a history of queries made to the Google Assistant, and edit or delete previous inputs. The Assistant warns against deleting, however, due to its use of previous inputs to generate better answers in the future. In November 2017, it became possible to identify songs currently playing by asking the Assistant.

The Google Assistant allows the users to activate and modify vocal shortcut commands in order to perform actions on their device (both Android and iPad/iPhone) or configure it as a hub for home automation. This feature of the speech recognition is available in English, among other languages. In July 2018, the Google Home version of Assistant gained support for multiple actions triggered by a single vocal shortcut command.

At the annual I/O developers conference on May 8, 2018, Google's SEO announced the addition of six new voice options for the Google Assistant, one of which being John Legend's. This was made possible by WaveNet, a voice synthesizer developed by DeepMind, which significantly reduced the amount of audio samples that a voice actor was required to produce for creating a voice model. However, John Legend's Google Assistant cameo voice was discontinued on March 23, 2020.

In August 2018, Google added bilingual capabilities to the Google Assistant for existing supported languages on devices. Recent reports say that it may support multilingual support by setting a third default language on Android Phone. Speech-to-Text can recognize commas, question marks, and periods in transcription requests.

In April 2019, the most popular audio games in the Assistant, Crystal Ball, and Lucky Trivia, have had the biggest voice changes in the application's history. The voice in the assistant has been able to add expression to the games. For instance, in the Crystal Ball game, the voice would speak slowly and softly during the intro and before the answer is revealed to make the game more exciting, and in the Lucky Trivia game, the voice would become excitable like a game show host. In the British accent voice of Crystal Ball, the voice would say the word 'probably' in a downward slide like she's not too sure. The games used the text-to-speech voice which makes the voice more robotic. In May 2019 however, it turned out to be a bug in the speech API that caused the games to lose the studio-quality voices. These audio games were fixed in May 2019.

22.7   Interpreter Mode in the Google Assistant

On December 12, 2019, Google debuted an interpreter mode in Google Assistant smartphone apps for Android and iOS. It provides translation of conversations in real-time and was previously only available on Google Home smart speakers and displays. Google Assistant won the 2020 Webby Award for Best User Experience in the category: Apps, Mobile & Voice. On March 5, 2020, Google introduced a feature on Google Assistant that read webpages aloud in 42 languages. On October 15, 2020, Google announced a new 'hum to search' function to find a song by simply humming, whistling, or singing the song.

22.8   Google Duplex

In May 2018, Google revealed Duplex, an extension of the Google Assistant that allows it to carry out natural conversations by mimicking human voice, in a manner not dissimilar to robocalling. The assistant can autonomously complete the tasks such as calling a hair salon to book an appointment, scheduling a restaurant reservation, or calling businesses to verify holiday store hours. While Duplex can complete most of its tasks fully autonomously, it is able to recognize situations that it is unable to complete and can signal a human operator to finish the task. Duplex was created to speak in a more natural voice and language by incorporating speech disfluencies such as filler words like "hmm" and "uh" and using common phrases such as "mhm" and "gotcha", along with more human-like intonation and response latency. Duplex is currently in development and had a limited release in late 2018 for Google Pixel users. During the limited release, Pixel phone users in Atlanta, New York, Phoenix, and San Francisco were only able to use Duplex to make restaurant reservations. As of October 2020, Google has expanded Duplex to businesses in eight countries.

22.9   Criticism of the 'Google Assistant'

After the announcement, concerns were made over the ethical and societal questions that artificial intelligence technology such as Duplex raises. For instance, human operators may not notice that they are speaking with a digital robot when conversing with Duplex, which some critics view as unethical or deceitful. Concerns over privacy were also identified, as conversations with Duplex are recorded in order for the virtual assistant to analyze and respond. Privacy advocates have also raised concerns around how the millions of vocal samples gathered from consumers are fed back into the algorithms of virtual assistants, making these forms of AI smarter with each use. Though these features individualize the user experience, critics are unsure about the long-term implications of giving "the company unprecedented access to human patterns and preferences that are crucial to the next phase of artificial intelligence".

While transparency was referred to as a key part to the experience when the technology was revealed, Google later further clarified in a statement saying, "We are designing this feature with disclosure built-in, and we'll make sure the system is appropriately identified." Google further added that, in certain jurisdictions, the assistant would inform those on the other end of the phone that the call is being recorded.

In July 2019 Belgian public broadcaster VRT NWS published an article revealing that third-party contractors paid to transcribe audio clips collected by Google Assistant listened to sensitive information about users. Sensitive data collected from Google Home devices and Android phones included names, addresses, and other private conversations after mistaken hot word triggering, such as business calls or bedroom conversations. From more than 1,000 recordings analyzed, 153 were recorded without the "OK Google" command. Google officially acknowledged that 0.2% of recordings are being listened to by language experts to improve Google's services. On August 1, 2019, Germany's Hamburg Commissioner for Data Protection and Freedom of Information initiated an administrative procedure to prohibit Google from carrying out corresponding evaluations by employees or third parties for the period of three months to provisionally protect the rights of privacy of data subjects for the time being, citing GDPR. A Google spokesperson stated that Google paused "language reviews" in all European countries while it investigated recent media leaks.

22.10   Reception of the 'Google Assistant'

PC World's Mark Hachman gave a favorable review of the Google Assistant, saying that it was a "step up on Cortana and Siri." Digital Trends called it "smarter than Google Now ever was".

CHAPTER 23

CONTEMPORARY VIRTUAL ASSISTANTS: COMPARATIVE PERFORMANCE

23.1 Accessibility and Trends in 4 Virtual Assistants

Accessibility refers to the number of devices that host the virtual assistant. Here's how the various AI assistants compare in this category, listed from the most accessible to the least accessible.

(i) Google Assistant

Google Assistant is available on all Android and iOS devices, as well as on Chromebooks. Google has its own line of Google Home speakers, including the Google Home Mini ($49) and Google Nest Audio ($99.99), all of which are built for use with Google Assistant. Google also makes it easy to search via third-party Google AI-enabled speakers, like the Harman JBL Link Music ($119.95), Bang & Olufsen BeoSound 2 ($3,199) and Solis SO-2000 ($149.99). The fact that so many major players in the speaker and headphones space are releasing Google AI-enabled hardware at varying prices speaks volumes as to who is coming out ahead in the AI-assistant space.

(ii) Alexa

Amazon's smart assistant, Alexa, is accessible through the Amazon Echo line of speakers, Fire tablets and Fire TV. Of all the AI assistants we studied, Alexa may have the biggest advantage for business use, since it's available on the widest variety of device designs. Although Google's AI assistant can be found on plenty of speakers, they all look similar. Amazon, in contrast, sells dozens of Alexa-enabled designs, including speakers of all sizes and modern-looking speakers with glossy touchscreens.

There are also some third-party smart speakers and other devices that support Alexa, including the Sonos One wireless speaker ($2,199.99) and the Altec Lansing VersA Smart Portable speakers ($86.10). There is an Alexa app as well, but it's intended primarily as a supplement to another Alexa device and not as a stand-alone AI assistant.

(iii) Siri

You can access Siri on nearly any Apple device, including MacBooks, iPhones, iPads and Apple Watches. Apple also sells its own speakers, called the HomePod ($299) and the HomePod mini ($99). Using Siri with a third-party device is possible, but it requires a HomePod mini to connect to your non-Apple device. According to Apple, this is to protect customer privacy; so, the third-party devices can't access your voice-based commands.

(iv) Cortana

Microsoft's AI assistant, Cortana, was launched in 2014 and was previously included on Windows machines. However, this AI assistant is no longer supported on Android and iOS devices. Microsoft also announced that Cortana would be retired from Windows in late 2023. Cortana won't be going away entirely, though, as it will remain a standard integration in Microsoft Office products, such as Outlook and Microsoft Teams. Of course, this means Cortana is much less accessible than the other options on this list.

Key Takeaway

Google, Amazon and Apple are leading the AI-assistant sector, but Microsoft has decided to cut back on the availability of Cortana.

23.2   Ease of Setup

The ease of setup refers to how long it takes to get the assistant up and running, as well as how simple that process is. All of the above-mentioned AI assistants have the options to customize the personal-assistant experience, including app integration, unique settings and adaptive responses.

To maintain an even testing ground, additional setup steps, were not considered, that fall under the category of customization; it was considered only how long it takes a new user to turn on the device and start asking questions. Google Assistant, Siri and Alexa all required virtually no setup time (you just sign in to a network and start) and were completely intuitive. None of these took more than about 45 seconds for initial access, and that included turning on the device or, in Alexa's case, plugging it in.

Cortana was a different story. The user experience of attempting to log in to the Cortana app on a supported device took quite a bit of troubleshooting. Cortana's integration will be automatic in Microsoft Office products going forward, so it remains to be seen if these issues will persist.

23.3   Voice Recognition

For voice recognition, all we wanted to know was how often the virtual assistant could recognize the words we said. We didn't consider context or the value of the responses given, just basic recognition. We also tested voice recognition at various distances from the devices, with varying levels of background noise.

Google and Siri understood us well when the room was quiet and we were close to the devices. There were a couple of funny misunderstandings, like when we asked Siri, "What's the date four weeks from now?" and it gave the date for one week later because it thought we said, "What's the date for a week from now?" All in all, though, the voice recognition was impressive under ideal conditions.

However, when we used Google and Siri to do anything sound-related, like read a news article or play music, the assistants couldn't hear us when we spoke at a normal volume. When we shouted, Google eventually responded, but Siri did not. We also had to manually turn off the sound on the iPhone to get Siri to stop playing the news, which defeats the hands-free purpose.

Alexa's voice recognition was spotty. Like Google and Siri, it could not understand us at all when there was even soft music playing, and we had to manually shut down the speaker to get it to stop playing music. Unlike the other two assistants, Alexa had issues understanding basic questions, except our voice commands, even when the room was silent.

One of the test questions included repeatedly asking for help getting plane tickets, and each time, Alexa thought the request was for movie tickets and directed us to Fandango. When we asked for future dates ("What's the date for a week from now?"), it simply replied, "Sorry, I don't know that," while other assistants had no trouble understanding identically phrased questions.

In our testing, Cortana performed the worst by far in basic voice recognition. Microsoft's assistant had issues understanding us even with zero noise interference. Below are just a few examples of basic inquiries Cortana could not understand, even when stated slowly and clearly with no background noise.

"Cancel this task."

"I want to set a reminder."

"Does Amazon sell printer paper?"

"I need help finding a restaurant."

"Do I have any reminders coming up?"

The other three assistants could understand all of these inquiries. And Cortana understood at least some of the other inquiries we made (like those about the weather), so it wasn't a microphone issue.

In addition to asking simple questions and setting task reminders, you may be able to use your AI assistant to control compatible smart-home devices.

Success of queries and ability to understand context

The value of an AI assistant lies in its ability to understand natural language and context and deliver a useful response. To test this skill, we devised questions with context-reliant follow-ups. Here are a few questions we asked each assistant:

"How much is $5 in euros? What about in yen?"

"Where is there an Applebee's near me? Can you make a reservation?"

"How long will it take me to get to LaGuardia Airport in the car? How about by subway?"

We also asked each assistant a list of common questions about scheduling, setting reminders, shopping online, booking business travel accommodations and getting directions. Below, we'll discuss how the products fared, from worst to best.

(i) Cortana

Unfortunately, Cortana effectively removed itself from the running here because it couldn't even hear or understand us on a basic level. When Cortana did understand us, it did not respond helpfully or intuitively. For example, when asked for directions to the nearest airport, it searched for nearly a full minute and then returned with a list of results from Bing, which mostly linked to general airline ticket websites such as Expedia.

When asked to convert from U.S. dollars to yen, which all of the other assistants did with ease, Cortana did not reply aloud but rather brought up a page from Bing with a list of general responses about currency exchange from Answers.com. Whenever we asked follow-up questions, especially those dependent on context, Cortana either didn't respond at all, or said, it didn't know or directed us to allow permissions from a third-party app.

(ii) Alexa

Alexa worked well when answering basic questions, especially those that pertained to purchasing items on Amazon and setting reminders. However, when we got to more complicated questions that required context or close attention to detail, Alexa faltered. We made multiple attempts to get Alexa to help purchase airline tickets, but the assistant consistently referred us to Fandango to buy movie tickets. It rarely answered follow-up questions, and when it did, it was often with a polite but unhelpful "Sorry, I don't know that."

In general, Alexa could do part of each task asked of it. For example, it could say where the closest Applebee's was, but it couldn't make a reservation. It could tell us how much $5 was in euros, but when we followed up with "What about yen?" it didn't know. When asked how long it would take to get to LaGuardia Airport, it said, "As I don't know your speed, I can't tell you how long that will take."

Alexa seems to rely on very specific terminology for commands. For example, when asked to read the news, it did. But we couldn't get it to stop, even after trying multiple direct commands, like "stop" and "turn volume off." The only phrase that eventually worked (which we had to look up online) was "stop flash briefing," which isn't exactly intuitive. It was easy to set up reminders with Alexa, but when each reminder time came, Alexa would just blare an alarm with no indication of what the alarm was for, and we had to turn off the alarm manually.

Alexa is an OK tool for ordering on Amazon, and it may be good for smart-house integration. However, it's not the best AI for natural language use; anyone who adopts Alexa as an AI assistant should peruse user guides before setting it up and understand its limitations.

(iii) & (iv) Google Assistant vs. Siri

When asked for directions to One World Trade Center, both Google Assistant and Siri responded with clear driving instructions. When we added a follow-up question about public transportation directions, Google Assistant responded verbally with directions to and from the subway, as well as gave an automatic link to step-by-step instructions in Google Maps. Unfortunately, Siri simply responded with alternate driving directions. No matter how we asked, Siri would not give public transit directions.

However, Siri bested Google Assistant in tasks such as finding specific restaurants and making reservations. In fact, Siri was the only assistant that could not only find a nearby restaurant (which Google Assistant did, too) but also place a reservation. When we asked Google Assistant to find a specific restaurant, it did. But when asked to book a reservation, it inexplicably took us to DisneyWorld. com. We tried several times to book a reservation through Google Assistant, with no success.

The ability to make hands-free restaurant reservations with Siri could be useful. However, Apple's assistant falls short if your requests are not specific. For example, when we simply said, "I need help finding a restaurant," Siri responded with a list of Google results that were literally instructions on how to find a restaurant, while Google Assistant read between the lines and showed us restaurants nearby.

Google Assistant was also better than Siri for travel information, but it still wasn't perfect on follow-through. When we asked Siri for flights from New York to Paris, it just Googled the question and showed us the responses. When Google Assistant was asked for flights from New York to Paris, it asked for dates and started pulling up available reservations. But when we tried to book the flights, it simply said, "No problem!" and then did nothing. One cool thing Google Assistant offered, without prompting, was to email us if prices changed on the flights we were interested in.

When we asked the assistants to read the news, Google Assistant immediately started playing a recent NPR podcast, while Siri Googled several news sources. We noticed throughout many different tasks that Siri rarely responded aloud, while Google Assistant nearly always did. While this is likely a matter of playing with a few settings, it's an interesting difference to note.

Tip

- AI assistants are designed to understand natural language, so try to make your questions sound conversational and not too formal.

- AI assistants have a lot to offer, but they have a long way to go.

- No AI assistant we tested was perfect. This is still young technology, and it has a long way to go. There were a handful of questions that none of the virtual assistants could answer. For example, when asked for directions to the closest airport, even the two best assistants on our list, Google Assistant and Siri, failed hilariously. Google Assistant directed us to a travel agency, while Siri sent us to a seaplane base.

Still, judging purely on out-of-the-box functionality, Siri and Google Assistant are our top choices. We recommend making your final decision based on your hardware preferences. None of the assistants are good enough to go out of your way to adopt hardware you're not comfortable with. Choose between Siri and Google Assistant based on convenience and the hardware you already have.

CHAPTER 24

IBM'S CHATBOT

24.1   What is a chatbot?

A chatbot is a computer program that simulates human conversation with an end user. Not all chatbots are equipped with artificial intelligence (AI), but modern chatbots increasingly use conversational AI techniques such as natural language processing (NLP) to understand user questions and automate responses to them.

A chatbot is a computer program that can use algorithms like artificial intelligence (AI), machine learning (ML), natural language understanding (NLU), and natural language processing (NLP) to simulate a human conversation with users via text messages in the chat window.

The key task of chatbot technology is to provide conversational responses to customer queries without human intervention. The advantage of virtual assistants is that they can chat with multiple users simultaneously and provide information within seconds. They can improve customer engagement, identify business leads, and reduce wait times.

Moreover, you can integrate virtual assistants with various communication channels and platforms, including your websites, LiveChat, social media like Facebook Messenger, and other messaging applications. This way, AI chatbots allow customers to interact with business using their favorite channels. Because of that, digital assistants are now used on a broad scale to help businesses and customers interact with each other with ease.

24.2   How do Chatbots work?

Chatbots can be powered by pre-programmed responses or artificial intelligence and natural language processing. Based on the applied mechanism, they process human language to understand user queries and deliver matching answers. There are two main types of chatbots, which also tell us how they communicate — rule-based chatbots and AI chatbots.

24.3   What are rule-based chatbots?

A rule-based chatbot (also command-based, keyword, or transactional) communicates using predefined answers.

These virtual assistants can be playfully compared to movie actors because, just like them, they always stick to the script. Rule-based bots provide answers based on a set of if/then rules that can vary in complexity. These rules are defined and implemented by a chatbot designer.

At this point, it's worth adding that rule-based chatbots don't understand the context of the conversation. They provide matching answers only when users use a keyword or a command they were programmed to answer.

When a rule-based bot is asked, "How can I reset my password?" it first looks for familiar keywords in the sentence. In this example, 'reset' and 'password' are the keywords. Then, it matches these keywords with responses available in its database to provide the answer.

However, if anything outside the AI agent's scope is presented, like a different spelling or dialect, it might fail to match that question with an answer. Because of this, rule-based bots often ask a user to rephrase their question. They can also transfer a customer to human agents when needed.

It's worth underlining that a rule-based chat interface can't learn from past experiences. They respond based on what they know at that moment. The only way to improve a rule-based bot is to equip it with more predefined answers and improve its rule-based mechanisms.

On the other hand, the limitations of rule-based chatbots make them a very useful tool for businesses. Rule-based virtual assistants are the cheapest to build and easiest to train. Companies introduce them into their business strategies because they help to automate customer communication and help improve customer engagement.

24.4   What is an AI chatbot?

An AI chatbot is a software that can freely communicate with users. AI-powered chatbots like **Chat GPT or Bard** are better conversationalists than their rule-based counterparts because they can fully leverage technologies like machine learning, natural language processing, deep learning, natural language understanding, and sentiment analysis. Thanks to them, AI agents can analyze a vast amount of data and provide unique answers to customer queries based on that data.

Machine Learning (ML) allows bots to identify patterns in user input, make decisions, and learn from past conversations. It's an area of artificial intelligence that enables developers to train AI chatbots using organized data, so they can independently resolve issues. By scrutinizing vast data, machine learning algorithms can complete tasks, offer predictions, make decisions independently, and respond to customer questions without explicit instructions. After being trained, the machine learning algorithms continue to learn from their previous experiences. Therefore, an AI chatbot utilizing machine learning can enhance its knowledge and accuracy with every interaction it has with the user.

Natural Language Processing (NLP) helps an AI assistant understand how humans communicate and enable them to replicate that behavior. Moreover, NLP lets the computer understand the context of the conversation, even if a person makes a spelling mistake or uses jargon. An NLP chatbot divides user inquiries into smaller components converted into organized data that computers can read, interpret, and comprehend. This division of user input is known as parsing. AI chatbots can analyze complicated human speech, comprehend context, humor, and sarcasm, and produce responses that resemble humans by employing natural language processing. Utilizing natural language processing in chatbots can enhance their precision, enable them to grasp the user's emotions, and create responses that appear more genuine to the user.

The sentiment analysis helps a chatbot understand users' emotions. This branch of computer science is also called opinion mining or emotion analysis. It leverages machine learning and natural language processing to evaluate the mood and attitude of written text, spoken language, images, and emojis. It's a valuable tool that enables businesses to go beyond merely counting likes or shares. By analyzing qualitative feedback, sentiment analysis assists in determining customer satisfaction and whether consumers have a positive, negative, or neutral outlook on products or brand initiatives.

Fun fact. Some languages are more difficult to process for chatbots. Languages such as Polish, Finnish, Spanish or Hindi, whose verbs may present a wide range of variations, are more difficult for a chatbot to master than languages with less complex structures.

Artificial intelligence chatbots need to be well-trained and equipped with predefined responses to get started. However, as they learn from past conversations, they don't need to be updated manually later.

AI bots get smarter with every conversation, meaning they simply mirror users' behavior. This has already turned out to be a major challenge for conversation designers and was well exemplified in the Microsoft experiment called "Conversational Understanding."

The experiment involved launching *Tay*, an AI bot, on Twitter. Tay was supposed to chat with millennials and prove a computer program can get smarter with "casual and playful conversations."

The experiment showed that Microsoft's assumptions were right; however, the experiment's results were far from expected. After chatting with Twitter users for just a couple of hours, *Tay* started to send racist, and offensive tweets, including messages like "Hitler was right" or "9/11 was an inside job."

In response to that situation, in less than 24 hours, Microsoft took Tay down from Twitter. It issued an apology for the incident, which stated, "We are deeply sorry for the unintended offensive and hurtful tweets from Tay, which do not represent who we are or what we stand for, nor how we designed Tay. Although we had prepared for many system abuses, we had made a critical oversight for this attack."

Microsoft's experiment showed that there is still room for improvement in AI. Tay wasn't trained enough, which resulted in it "blindly" mimicking the language and behavior of Twitter users. These were intentionally teaching Tay inflammatory messages.

After the experiment, Roman Yampolskiy, the head of the CyberSecurity lab at the University of Louisville, said that Microsoft's experiment proved that chatbots are like children. They need to be taught what is appropriate and what is not.

24.5   Brief history of chatbots

To the surprise of many, conversational interfaces aren't a modern invention. They were born out of curiosity and creative thinking more than half a century ago.

In 1950, Alan Turing, a computer pioneer, wrote a scientific paper titled "Computing Machinery and Intelligence." In the paper, the scientist implied that a computer program can think and talk like a human. Turing proposed an experiment called the Imitation Game, which is known as the Turing Test, to prove the point. In the Turing experiment, the person designated as a judge was chatting over a computer with a human and a machine who could not be seen.

In 1966, an MIT professor, Joseph Weizenbaum, developed a computer program called **Eliza**. It's considered to be the **first chat robot in history**. Eliza was a simple keyword-based conversational interface that mimicked a human psychiatrist. The program communicated by matching user questions with scripted responses entered into its database. When a patient would say, "My mother loves flowers," Eliza would reply, "Tell me more about your mother."

In 1971, Kenneth Colby, a Stanford Artificial Intelligence Laboratory psychiatrist, wondered whether computers could contribute to understanding brain function. He believed that the computer could help in treating patients with mental diseases.

These thoughts led Colby to develop Parry, a computer program that simulated a person with schizophrenia. Colby believed that Parry could help educate medical students before they started treating patients. Parry was considered the first chat robot to pass the Turing Test. Back then, its creation initiated a serious debate about the possibilities of artificial intelligence.

In 1978, Colby developed the first intelligent speech prosthesis. It was a computer program that helped people with communication disorders to speak.

In 1988, a self-taught programmer called Rollo Carpenter created **Jabberwacky**. It was a program designed to simulate human conversation entertainingly. Jabberwacky learned from past experiences and developed over time. It reflected users' personalities and behaviors.

In 1992, Creative Labs, a technology company based in Singapore, developed Dr. Sbaitso. It was an AI speech synthesis program that imitated a psychologist. The program was distributed with sound cards sold by the company. They wanted to show the digitized voices their cards were able to produce.

Developed **in 1995** by Richard Wallace, **Alice** was an NLP application that simulated a chat with a woman. Wallace Alice was **inspired by Eliza** and designed to have a natural conversation with users. Its code was released as open-source, which means it can be reused by other developers to power their conversational interfaces.

Alice was an inspiration for an American science-fiction romantic drama Her. It's a film about a man, Theodore Twombly, who falls in love with an AI agent.

SmarterChild was an intelligent chat interface built on AOL Instant Messenger **in 2001** by **ActiveBuddy**, the brand creating conversational interfaces. SmarterChild was designed to have a natural conversation with users. It's considered to be a precursor to Apple's Siri.

Since **2010,** when Apple launched **Siri**, virtual assistants have been on the rise. Siri was the first personal assistant available worldwide. Google followed in Apple's footsteps by releasing Google Now in 2012. Microsoft's Cortana and Amazon's Alexa were both released in 2014.

In **2016,** Facebook opened its Messenger platform for chatbots. This helped fuel the development of automated communication platforms. **In 2018, LiveChat released Chatbot**, a framework that lets users build chatbots without coding. So far, there have been over 300,000 active bots on Messenger.

24.6   What's the difference between chatbots and bots?

Although the terms chatbot and bot are used interchangeably, there's a significant difference between them.

A chatbot is a computer program designed to communicate with users. It analyzes users' questions to provide matching answers. Businesses use chatbots to support customers and help them accomplish simple tasks without the help of a human agent.

A bot is an algorithm that interacts with web content. Bots help businesses and users perform helpful, mundane, or complex tasks faster online. Below are some different types of bots.:

Search engine bots called crawlers are used by Google and Yahoo to index web content and scale web cataloging. This helps users easily find information related to their search intent.

Feed bots look for new information on the web to add to news sites.

Copyright bots look for content that violates copyright laws. They help companies and authors check whether their proprietary content has been used without approval.

Unfortunately, businesses have learned to also use bots for malicious activities.

For instance, companies launch click bots that deliberately generate fake clicks. They hurt advertisers paying for those clicks and create quite a headache for marketers who get unreliable data. Bad bots can also break into user accounts, steal data, create fake accounts and news, and perform many other fraudulent activities.

24.7   How to create a chatbot?

Chat bots can be created from scratch or by using a chatbot platform. Both ways have their pros and cons.

(i)   Building a chatbot with a platform

Using a platform is the easiest way to create a conversational interface. Platforms have a low learning curve. They let you drag and drop predefined elements to design chatbots and launch them without coding.

To facilitate the building process, some platforms provide ready-to-use templates. You can use them as they are or customize them to your liking. Because of that, chatbot platforms are a good choice for brands that lack technical expertise but don't want to spend money on hiring external developers.

Platforms also come in handy if you want to test, at low cost, whether your business could benefit from using a chatbot. Some companies only use chatbot platforms from time to time, for instance, during the shopping season. They use a chatbot to help busy support teams or promote their new products.

Another advantage of platforms is integrating them with third-party services. With integrations, brands can add a smart agent to multiple communication channels and unify their customer experience.

On the other hand, platforms might limit your bot's capabilities. Unless you decide to build custom features or integrations, you can only operate within the platform's scope.

(ii) Building your chatbot from the ground up is time-consuming, but it gives you total control over your chatbot. You can customize your AI agent to serve the particular needs of your customers, power it to solve complex problems, and integrate it with any platform you wish.

Before you code your bot, consider whether it's worth doing. To breathe life into your bot in-house, you need to engage a team of developers or hire external bot-building services. That comes at a price. Also, consider that the testing phase may take a lot of time.

The same can be said for updating your custom-made chatbot or correcting its mistakes. It's a long game to play. If you're unsure whether using an AI agent would benefit your business, test an already available platform first. This will let you find out what functionalities are useful for you. You'll be able to determine whether you need to build it from scratch or not.

24.8   Why do businesses need chatbots?

Technological progress has radically changed the way people communicate. Face-to-face interactions have been largely replaced by online messaging. This has forced businesses to adapt to a new type of communication. To achieve success, brands need to provide a seamless buyer's journey. They must respond to customer questions around the clock and across multiple channels.

But living up to the rising expectations of "always-connected" customers is not the easiest and cheapest task. The more your business grows, the more it costs to deliver 24/7 customer service. This is where chatbots come in handy. They allow brands to scale up their support services at a low cost.

More and more often, companies are deciding to introduce bot applications into their marketing strategies because they allow for delivering personalized and consistent brand experiences. Long term, that translates into better brand perception and more sales.

24.8.1   Chatbot use cases

(i)   Marketing

Brands use conversational agents to diversify their customer-engagement strategy. With them, businesses engage website visitors proactively and, eventually, sell more products.

It's for good reason that more and more companies are hiring conversation designers who know how to write engaging chatbot scenarios. Businesses have already realized that a well-written chatbot can work as a successful lead generation tool. It can collect newsletter subscribers, sales contacts, beta testers, or even job candidates by helping companies reach a larger audience with their message.

One of the brands that took their online service to the next level using a bot is **Sephora**. The company uses it to educate customers about its cosmetics.

Their AI assistant offers makeup tutorials and skincare tips and helps customers purchase products online. The company even enables its customers to try new makeup using AR technology implemented in their chatbot. By doing this, Sephora has delivered its personalized customer experience in-store and online.

(ii) Customer support

Customers want their problems handled immediately and via the channels they prefer. Chatbots make that possible by redefining the customer service people have known for years.

They support customers 24/7 and enable them to solve simple problems, book appointments, or submit complaints. Take, for instance, Mastercard. The brand offers a Messenger bot to help customers easily check their account transactions anytime.

Restaurants like Next Door Burger Bar use conversational agents to help customers order their meals online. Customer service bots allow companies to scale their services at low cost but, more than that, meet changing customer expectations.

Brands automate their customer communication to boost the productivity of their support teams. Smart agents can function as the first line of customer support by taking over the vast majority of repetitive cases from live agents. They can group customers based on their issue type and, when needed, route them to agents.

(iii) Sales

Before purchasing a product, every customer must go through the sales funnel. Chatbots can take customers by hand and walk them through all the stages of that process: awareness, interest, decision, and action. A Gartner report shows that businesses that utilize conversational interfaces in their sales strategy can achieve up to 30 percent higher conversion rates.

By integrating into social media platforms, conversational interfaces let brands connect with many users and increase their brand awareness. Take, for example, National Geographic. The company has used a Messenger bot to carry out a daily quiz with users.

By doing this, the brand attracted users' attention to their new eBook, Almanac. The brand's bot also encouraged users to purchase the title by offering a 10% discount, which boosted its sales.

Harper Collins, the world-leading book publisher, uses the Epic Reads chatbot to help their community members find another book to read.

Their AI agent conducts a short survey with every user to find out what might interest them and recommends titles matching their preferences. By supporting prospects, the company helps book lovers make decisions and builds positive relationships with them.

Another global giant, **Starbucks**, uses an AI agent to help customers compose their favorite coffee drink. It enables customers to order a drink on the go and pick it up at a chosen cafe. It translates into a better brand experience because customers don't have to stand in a long line.

Chatbots can be of great use for sales teams as well. They help businesses eliminate unqualified leads and connect sales reps with qualified ones. This helps sales specialists spend less time acquiring leads and more on building relationships with prospects.

On top of that, AI assistants are a great repository of knowledge about customers. The more the bot chats with your prospects, the more data it gains about their needs and preferences. This helps companies better tailor their offers and messages.

24.9   Generative AI-powered chatbots

The next generation of chatbots with generative AI capabilities will offer even more enhanced functionality with their understanding of common language and complex queries, their ability to adapt to a user's style of conversation and use of empathy when answering users' questions. Business leaders can clearly see this future: 85% of execs say generative AI will be interacting directly with customers in the next two years, as reported in 'The CEO's guide to generative AI study', from IBV. An enterprise-grade artificial intelligence solution can empower companies to automate self-service and accelerate the development of exceptional user experiences.

FAQ chatbots no longer need to be pre-programmed with answers to set questions: It's easier and faster to use generative AI in combination with an organization's' knowledge base to automatically generate answers in response to the wider range of questions.

While conversational AI chatbots can digest users' questions or comments and generate a human-like response, generative AI chatbots can take this a step further by generating new content as the output. This new content can include high-quality text, images and sound based on the LLMs, they are trained on. Chatbot interfaces with generative AI can recognize, summarize, translate, predict and create content in response to a user's query without the need for human interaction.

Enterprise-grade, self-learning generative AI chatbots built on a conversational AI platform are continually and automatically improving. They employ algorithms that automatically learn from past interactions how best to answer questions and improve conversation flow routing.

SECTION V

APPLICATIONS AND OPPORTUNITES OF ARTIFICIAL INTELLIGENCE

CHAPTER 25

APPLICATIONS OF AI

25.1   Need for Artificial Intelligence

To create expert systems that exhibit intelligent behavior with the capability to learn, demonstrate, adapt, explain, and advise its users.

Helping machines find solutions to complex problems like humans do and applying them as algorithms in a computer-friendly manner.

(i) Improved efficiency: Artificial intelligence can automate tasks and processes that are time-consuming and require a lot of human effort. This can help improve efficiency and productivity, allowing humans to focus on more creative and high-level tasks.

(ii) Better decision-making: Artificial intelligence can analyze large amounts of data and provide insights that can aid in decision-making. This can be especially useful in domains like finance, healthcare, and logistics, where decisions can have significant impacts on outcomes.

(iii) Enhanced accuracy: Artificial intelligence algorithms can process data quickly and accurately, reducing the risk of errors that can occur in manual processes. This can improve the reliability and quality of results.

(iv) Personalization: Artificial intelligence can be used to personalize experiences for users, tailoring recommendations, and interactions based on individual preferences and behaviors. This can improve customer satisfaction and loyalty.

(v) Exploration of new frontiers: Artificial intelligence can be used to explore new frontiers and discover new knowledge that is difficult or impossible for humans to access. This can lead to new breakthroughs in fields like astronomy, genetics, and drug discovery.

25.2   Applications of Artificial Intelligence

AI and technology is being used in most of the essential applications, including: search engines (such as Google Search), targeting online advertisements, recommendation systems (offered by Netflix, YouTube or Amazon), driving internet traffic, targeted advertising (AdSense, Facebook), virtual assistants (such as Siri or Alexa), autonomous vehicles (including drones, ADAS and self-driving cars), automatic language translation (Microsoft Translator, Google Translate), facial recognition (Apple's Face ID or Microsoft's DeepFace and Google's FaceNet) and image labeling (used by Facebook, Apple's iPhoto and TikTok).

Following are some of the applications of AI:

(i)   Healthcare

AI has been used in the domain of healthcare for quite some time. According to a report, there are more than 100 startup companies working on the application of AI in healthcare domain (From Virtual Nurses To Drug Discovery). Some applications have already been deployed whereas a large number of these are under development in several countries. Using the advances in natural language processing techniques, several conversational applications have been developed. Virtual nurse is an application which is being used in several types of environments. It can perform the tasks which are normally performed by a human nurse. *Molly*, a virtual nurse developed by the startup, Sense.ly assists the patients in managing the chronic conditions after the treatment or between the follow-up consultations. The ability of AI algorithms to locate the relevant information has been found to be of great use. Watson for Oncologists developed by IBM, helps the doctor in finding the relevant material from a large number of papers/documents which could be of use in the case at hand. It analyzes both structured and unstructured data.

If the present case is similar to any case reported in any publication/ document and a particular treatment plan has been found to be effective, the information reported may be useful for the treatment in the present case. AI is helping in providing personalized treatment to the patients. Every patient is a different individual and may need a different treatment. Further, a disease may have thousands of subtypes requiring different treatments consisting of a combination of drugs. For instance, it is being realized that cancer has thousands of subtypes and each subtype requires different combination of drugs for effective treatment. On the other hand, pharmaceutical companies rely on large-scale randomized clinical trials for testing new drugs. This limits the number of cases in which it would be effective. This is why treatment often requires a trial-and-error approach. Once we have sufficiently large database of cancer cases, it becomes possible to find cases similar to the case in hand and there is a good probability that the treatment found to be effective in the earlier cases would be effective in the present case too. Some companies are developing AI-based systems which can provide consultation. It is especially useful in non-critical conditions or in the situation when human doctor is not available at all. An example is **Babylon**, developed by Babylon Health. It provides consultation to the user based on the symptoms reported. It asks the user few simple questions in spoken natural language and the user can answer in natural language. It searches a large database of symptoms and provides the appropriate medical advice. In case it finds necessary, it advises the patient to approach the doctor immediately.

For medical research, AI is an important tool for processing and integrating big data. This is particularly important for organoid and tissue engineering development which use microscopy imaging as a key technique in fabrication. New AI tools can deepen our understanding of biomedically relevant pathways. For example, AlphaFold-2 (2021) demonstrated the ability to approximate, in hours rather than months, the 3D structure of a protein. In 2023, it was reported that AI-guided drug discovery helped find a class of antibiotics capable of killing two different types of drug-resistant bacteria.

(ii) Education

Intelligent tutoring systems have been developed since the eighties. Several applications have been in use for quite some time. With the advances in AI techniques, such as natural language processing, etc, it has become possible to develop a number of new applications. As education itself is crucial for the growth in several domains, the net impact of AI in education would be quite high. The applications of AI in education include answering the queries of the students, asking questions and providing feedback, assessment of narrative answers. A study has predicted that AI would transform education during the next 4-5 years. Apart from AI, several new technological advancements are changing the scenario of education. With smart phone, the material has become more accessible to a wider class of people. Students can participate in the discussions. Learning outcomes are also improving with the use of learning management systems. Massively Online Open Courseware (MOOC) has become popular with time. It has become possible to create bots which appear like a human. In an experiment, a professor at Georgia Tech created an AI-powered system to work as his teaching assistant to assist in a course which was being taught by him. It interacted with the students just like a human teaching assistant. It assessed the assignments of the students for grading and answered their queries in natural language using email. The students could never realize during the entire semester that they were interacting with an artificial system and not a human until they were told so by the professor himself.

With AI, it has become possible to assess the subjective answers given by the students. Use of machines in assessing subjective answers results in substantial saving of time and brings uniformity in the assessment. Bots are being used to assess the subjective answers given by the students appearing in GRE test administered by ETS, etc. In one part of the test to assess the reasoning ability of the student, the students are supposed to give narrative answers. Till now, this was being assessed by two human experts to reduce the possibility of any error. After testing the performance of the application over a long duration of time, ETS has now replaced one of the two human experts by a bot. Despite the availability of a large amount of digital learning material, the use of computer-based education has remained limited due to lack of the possibility of personalization. A human teacher personalizes the content depending on the needs of the student. Every student has a different level of knowledge and aptitude. Therefore, the same content for every student does not work. If the student has not been able to understand the current topic, the system should not proceed to the next topic. Similarly, if a student already has knowledge of the topic, the content becomes repetitive and the student gets disinterested. Personalization has become possible using AI. Such a system can adapt to the content depending on the requirements of the student. It assesses the performance of the student and tailors the content accordingly.

(iii) Cyber Security

The rapid increase in the size and complexity of the virtual world has led to a continuing war between cyber attackers and security service providers. Each side is trying to develop more sophisticated techniques and tools. Cyber space is a dynamic environment where situation keeps on changing rapidly and can't be predicated with certainty. As AI systems have the flexibility to respond to the changing environment, its use is increasing in all the stages in the cyber defence chain viz. early warning, prevention, detection and, response. AI reduces the human intervention by the automation of the processes. The conventional cyber security systems are slow due to the need of human interaction in several steps. As any delay can cause significant damage, it has to be kept at the minimum. The loss is not limited to financial damage only. In case of denial-of-service attack on a hospital, the access to the health records of the patients is slowed down. This may become fatal for a patient requiring immediate intervention. With AI technology, it has become possible to create **artificial police agents** for monitoring the entire network. It uses intelligent agents to do this work. An intelligent agent is an application which has the ability to sense, reason and act autonomously. These agents can interact with each other to collaborate to perform a task. Sufficient number of intelligent agents can be deployed to monitor the network to detect the malicious activities in a decentralized way. However, despite all these developments, it is not yet possible to replace human by machine in the defence against cyber-attacks. Both human and machine have their strengths and weaknesses. If both combine their strengths, the success rate is higher than in case of individual cases.

(iv) Law

Several AI-based applications have been developed and services are being offered in the domain of law. AI-based systems have been developed for legal research which involves finding the similar precedent cases for deciding the present case or making arguments in the present case. The companies like Lexus and Westlaw have been offering applications on keyword-based, matching for quite some time. However, it was realized that the results have high number of positive false as well as negative true. This happens as keyword-based searching is based on literal meaning of the words and not on its interpretation. AI-based technique gives better result as it searches using the content of the case. Conversational applications have been developed to advise in legal matters in an interactive way. For instance, a chatbot namely, ***DoNotPay*** helps people in filing appeals against issuing of parking tickets if there are valid reasons. It has been used in London and New York in 375,000 cases within a short period for filing appeals involving 7.2 million pounds in fines. It asks the user simple questions and advises on the issue. After interaction, it also generates an appeal using the information given by the user in response to various questions. The service is being provided free of cost. Similarly, an application was developed to provide legal advice to the people seeking asylum in the US, Canada and the UK. After success of these applications, 1000+ bots have been developed for a range of topics for the people in 50 States in the US and the UK. AI systems have been developed for contract analysis, especially in corporate sector. Contract analysis involves going through a large number of contract and related documents used over a period of time to find the significant clauses. Often the time required for this is too long and it may not be practically possible to complete the task in many situations. In such a situation, it is possible to use AI-based systems to go through the documents and highlight the most relevant clauses. Lawyers can focus on these clauses rather than going through all the documents which may not be possible within the limited time and resources.

(v) Finance

Chatbot is being used by banks for performing simple tasks such as activation of accounts or balance checking, etc. It helps the customers who are not fully familiar with IT systems and would like to interact in natural language. Chatbot asks the customers questions in natural language and performs the needed tasks. Some investment consulting firms are also using chatbot to interact with the customers. The chatbot asks the customer some questions, which vary from customer to customer, to get the basic information on the needs of the investor and then generates plans based on the market trends, etc. The plans can be reviewed from time to time as and when further information is available. Though this can be done by a human adviser, chatbot performs it quickly and accurately. State Bank of India, HDFC Bank, ICICI Bank and Axis Bank have started using AI-based applications for providing customer services in India. Most of the banks have policy of upgrading the IT solutions including AI-based applications for customer service and use of robots in the processes. Earlier applications were limited to providing the customers information in natural language. Now these applications complete some of the banking transactions on behalf of the customers. Some of the governments have adopted policy to promote applications of AI in the banks. For instance, Government of Singapore has announced a grant of $19.9 million for the banks located in Singapore to promote AI and data analytics. As vast amount of data on stock trading is available publicly, it is an excellent area for the use of AI. Sentinent Technologies Inc. is developing an AI system for taking decisions in stock trading. It has a team of engineers who have worked for Amazon, Apple, Google, Microsoft, etc. The other firms which are exploring the idea of using AI in hedge fund include Wealthfront and RBS, etc.

Some applications have been built to help in the preparation of tax returns. An example chatbot is ***AskMyUncleSam***. As the US tax code is complex with a series of deductions, etc, a tax payer often goes to tax return preparer. The chatbot guides the tax payer in this process. It goes through the data on payments received, investment loss & gains from brokerage accounts, etc and finds all the possible deductions and liabilities. It answers the queries of the user using its knowledge base of tax code, litigation cases, etc.

(vi) Information Browsing

Often, AI is embedded in the normal systems of daily use and is invisible to the users. For example, Google search engine uses sophisticated AI algorithms to predict the content that the user may be interested. It brings the most relevant documents at the top which makes it the best search engine. As the volume of the content is increasing on Internet, such search engines are of great help to the users. Apart from information retrieval, search engine companies use the information on the user preferences to decide the advertisements to display. Google monitors the news items being read by the user and uses this information to decide the news of interest to the user to display. Google also analyzes the data collected from the browsing history of a person to decide the advertisements of interest and the same is displayed while the user is browsing. It has been found quite effective. Google generates revenue from the number of hits made by the users.

(vii) Transport

Self-driving car is a high-potential application of AI. Several companies including Google, Uber, and Tesla are testing their models on the roads. In Singapore, driver-less bus is being run under trial. So far, very few accidents have been reported and the analysis shows that probability of accident with driverless cars is less than human driven cars. It is expected that the number of accidents by self-driving cars will be much smaller than the human-driven cars. Self-driving cars use light detection and ranging (Lidar) technique which uses laser beams to create 3D image of the physical world around the car.

It uses laser beams to calculate the distance, speed and shape of the moving objects like another car, pedestrians, etc. Apart from roads, the technology can be used by those who can't walk due to physical limitations. Several companies are competing with each other in this area of technology. There has been a debate on whether these cars should be allowed on the road in view of the danger to the safety of the people. Regulations have to address several issues. For example, who will be responsible if an accident happens – the owner of the car or the company which has made it? Some States in the US are formulating regulations to deal with these issues. The companies are going ahead and have definite plans to make it available to the people in near future.

(viii) Virtual Assistants

A virtual assistant helps user in performing tasks or perform the tasks on their own in an autonomous way. Several virtual assistants have been developed. The examples are Google's Assistant, Siri, Cortana, and Alexa from Google, Apple, Microsoft, and Amazon, respectively. User can use natural language to interact with a virtual assistant. As one can also interact with spoken words, an illiterate or blind person can also use it. Virtual assistants perform a variety of tasks including streaming music, playing audio clips, controlling home devices, managing schedules, purchasing using e-commerce, etc. These assistants are becoming more and more useful due to the advances in natural language processing and speech recognition. This makes it useful to a common person without any specific training. Speech recognition makes it possible to use even while driving, etc. The vendors are trying to put these assistants in vehicles. Siri has already been integrated with some cars. Nissan is integrating Microsoft's platform into its cars. Similarly, Hyundai is integrating with Alexa and Google Assistant.

(ix) E-Commerce

There are a number of product and service recommender systems such as the one used by Amazon on its shopping portal. It keeps a track of which items have been purchased by the people over a period of time and identifies certain patterns which are used to decide the products and services of interest to the user. These patterns are not fixed and hard coded in the system but are created using machine learning techniques. Chatbot is being used to order products and services online. A chatbot has been developed to order coffee from Starbucks. The customer can order coffee using spoken natural language describing the type of coffee, etc and the order is sent to the nearest Starbucks unit. The payment is made automatically using the pre-registered credit/debit card.

(x) Customer Care

AI systems have been developed for customer care in several sectors. The systems use natural language to interact with the customers. Though chatbot has been used for customer care for a long time, it has become more useful with better natural language processing and speech recognition. If the customer remains unsatisfied, it is handed over to a human executive. In order to reduce the cost, companies have used IVRS to handle simple cases but the customers find that they have to go through a number of questions to get the information. On the other hand, a chatbot takes user's input in a natural language and asks only the relevant questions for addressing the issue. During the dialogue, chatbot takes context into account. If the discussion relates to a particular product or service, it uses and recognizes the pronouns used for the same. Chatbot takes into account the emotion of the user as well. *Amelia*, a customer service agent from IPSoft uses sentiment analysis to understand the mood of the customer to adapt its response accordingly, for instance, when it faces an angry customer, it uses words / phrases for reassurance. As all the conversations are stored, it picks up the related conversation to begin with. This, obviously, has advantage over human executives who can't retrieve the related conversation from the database quickly. If the issue remains unresolved by the chatbot, the call is transferred to a human executive.

Amazon has recently implemented an automated sales system in its store in Seattle. It monitors each customer and captures the information on the items being picked up by him for purchase. Once the customer has collected all the relevant items, he or she can walk out and the payment is deducted from the pre-registered credit/debit card. Such a system is likely to reduce the human sales force from the stores.

(xi) Energy

AI is being used in energy sector in several ways. Making energy clean, affordable and reliable has been recognized essential for fighting against several problems including poverty. Google has applied AI successfully in reducing the energy usage by 40% which means several millions of dollars. Google used the technology used in ***DeepMind*** for predictions on loads at different points and controlling equipments efficiently, accordingly. In view of this success, National Grid in the UK is working with DeepMind team to explore the opportunities. DeepMind aims to cut the national energy bill by 10% by balancing energy supplies to the national grid. The extra power generated by the operators but not used leads to the wastage of power. This is becoming possible due to the availability of past data which is used for learning and predictions. IBM is working with the Department of Energy in US for **solar energy prediction**. IBM has developed the technology by several forecasting models and integrating data on weather, environment and atmospheric conditions, etc collected from different sources such as weather stations, satellites, sensor networks, etc. IBM claims that the model developed is 30% more accurate than the best available solar forecasting model. After its successful application in solar energy, IBM is exploring the possibility of using it in wind and hydro-power plants. AI has also been used to understand the consumer behavior for prediction of load pattern. In order to gather this data, the energy provider companies are installing smart meters which send information on the usage periodically. As different persons and different communities have different consumption patterns, it is important to gather this data for prediction of loads.

(xii) Business Strategy

The prediction capability of AI-based solutions can be used in deciding business strategy. A company uses predictions about the customers and market conditions to decide where to focus. Once more and more accurate predictions are available, the company may decide to modify to a different strategy. For instance, the predictions about the customers can be used by a company to bring different types of products and services. One example of use of AI for predictions is that by Amazon which recommends certain products when someone shops on the platform. More extensive data on the customers can help in making the decisions on where to store the products and in what quantity.

(xiii) Artificial Intelligence in Games

Game playing programs have been used since the 1950s to demonstrate and test AI's most advanced techniques. Deep Blue became the first computer chess-playing system to beat a reigning world chess champion, Garry Kasparov, on 11 May 1997. In 2011, in a Jeopardy! quiz show exhibition match, IBM's question-answers system, Watson, defeated the two greatest Jeopardy! champions, Brad Rutter and Ken Jennings, by a significant margin. In March 2016, AlphaGo won 4 out of 5 games of Go in a match with Go champion Lee Sedol, becoming the first computer Go-playing system to beat a professional Go player without handicaps. Then in 2017 Go-playing system defeated Ke Jie, who was the best Go player in the world. Other programs handle imperfect-information games, such as the poker-playing program Pluribus. DeepMind developed increasingly generalist reinforcement learning models, such as with MuZero, which could be trained to play chess, Go, or Atari games. In 2019, DeepMind's AlphaStar achieved grandmaster level in StarCraft II, a particularly challenging real-time strategy game that involves incomplete knowledge of what happens on the map. In 2021, an AI agent competed in a PlayStation Gran Turismo competition, winning against four of the world's best Gran Turismo drivers using deep reinforcement learning.

(xiv) Artificial Intelligence in Military

Various countries are deploying AI military applications. The main applications enhance command and control, communications, sensors, integration and interoperability. Research is targeting intelligence collection and analysis, logistics, cyber operations, information operations, and semiautonomous and autonomous vehicles. AI technologies enable coordination of sensors and effectors, threat detection and identification, marking of enemy positions, target acquisition, coordination and deconfliction of distributed Joint Fires between networked combat vehicles involving manned and unmanned teams. AI was incorporated into military operations in Iraq and Syria.

In November 2023, US Vice President Kamala Harris disclosed a declaration signed by 31 nations to set guardrails for the military use of AI. The commitments include using legal reviews to ensure the compliance of military AI with international laws, and being cautious and transparent in the development of this technology.

(xv) Generative AI

In the early 2020s, Generative AI gained widespread prominence. In March 2023, 58% of US adults had heard about **ChatGPT** and 14% had tried it. The increasing realism and ease-of-use of AI-based text-to-image generators such as Midjourney, DALL-E, and Stable Diffusion sparked a trend of viral AI-generated photos. Widespread attention was gained by a **fake photo** of Pope Francis wearing a white puffer coat, the fictional arrest of Donald Trump, and a hoax of an attack on the Pentagon, as well as the usage in professional creative arts.

(xvi) Artificial Intelligence in Industry-specific Tasks

There are thousands of successful AI applications used to solve specific problems for specific industries or institutions. In a 2017-survey, one in five companies reported they had incorporated "AI" in some offerings or processes. A few examples are energy storage, medical diagnosis, military logistics, applications that predict the result of judicial decisions, foreign policy, or supply chain management.

In **agriculture**, AI has helped farmers identify areas that need irrigation, fertilization, pesticide treatments or increasing yield. Agronomists use AI to conduct research and development. AI has been used to predict the ripening time for crops such as tomatoes, monitor soil moisture, operate agricultural robots, conduct predictive analytics, classify livestock pig call emotions, automate greenhouses, detect diseases and pests, and save water.

Artificial intelligence is used in **astronomy** to analyze increasing amounts of available data and applications, mainly for "classification, regression, clustering, forecasting, generation, discovery, and the development of new scientific insights", for example, for discovering exoplanets, forecasting solar activity, and distinguishing between signals and instrumental effects in gravitational wave astronomy. It could also be used for activities in space such as space exploration, including analysis of data from space missions, real-time science decisions of spacecraft, space debris avoidance, and more autonomous operation.

DARPA established the **XAI** ("Explainable Artificial Intelligence") program in 2014 to try and solve these problems.

There are several possible solutions to the transparency problem. **SHAP** tried to solve the transparency problems by visualizing the contribution of each feature to the output. **LIME** can locally approximate a model with a simpler, interpretable model. Multitask learning provides a large number of outputs in addition to the target classification. These other outputs can help developers deduce what the network has learned. Deconvolution, DeepDream and other generative methods can allow developers to see what different layers of a deep network have learned and produce output that can suggest what the network is learning.

The applications of AI are as diverse as the fields it permeates. Here's a glimpse into the myriad ways AI is reshaping different sectors:

(xvii) Retail: AI helps retailers optimize supply chains, forecast demand, and provide personalized shopping experiences through recommendation systems.

(xviii) Entertainment: Recommendation algorithms in platforms like Netflix or Spotify tailor suggestions based on user preferences, enhancing user engagement and satisfaction.

(xix) Recommendation Systems – AI powers recommendation algorithms used by platforms like Netflix, Amazon, and Spotify to suggest personalized content based on users' preferences and behavior.

(xx) Natural Language Processing (NLP) – AI is used in NLP applications like language translation, sentiment analysis, and chatbots to understand and generate human language.

(xxi) Robotics – AI is essential in robotics for tasks such as object recognition, path planning, and manipulation, enabling robots to perform complex actions in various environments.

Robotics combines AI and physical systems to create machines or robots capable of performing physical tasks and interacting with the physical world. AI-powered robots can be designed for various applications, such as industrial automation, healthcare assistance, exploration, and even domestic tasks.

Robots are able to perform the tasks given by a human. They have sensors to detect physical data from the real world such as light, heat, temperature, movement, sound, bump, and pressure. They have efficient processors, multiple sensors and huge memory, to exhibit intelligence. In addition, they are capable of learning from their mistakes and they can adapt to the new environment.

(xxii) Security: AI is used for facial recognition, intrusion detection, and cybersecurity threat analysis.

(xxiii) Expert Systems: There are some applications which integrate machine, software, and special information to impart reasoning and advising. They provide explanation and advice to the users.

(xxiv) **Vision Systems:** These systems understand, interpret, and comprehend visual input on the computer.

For example,

- A spying plane takes photographs which are used to figure out spatial information or map of the areas.

- Doctors use clinical expert system to diagnose the patient.

- Police use computer software that can recognize the face of criminal with the stored portrait made by forensic artist.

(xxv) Speech Recognition

Some intelligent systems are capable of hearing and comprehending the language in terms of sentences and their meanings while a human talks to it. It can handle different accents, slang words, noise in the background, change in human's noise due to cold, etc.

(xxvi) Handwriting Recognition

The handwriting recognition software reads the text written on paper by a pen or on screen by a stylus. It can recognize the shapes of the letters and convert it into editable text.

(xxvii) Recommendation engines:

AI algorithms may help to detect trends in data that might be useful for developing more efficient marketing strategies using past data patterns. Online retailers use recommendation engines to provide their customers with relevant product recommendations for the purchasing process.

(xxviii) Automated stock trading:

AI-driven high-frequency trading platforms are designed to optimize stock portfolios and make thousands or even millions of trades each day without human intervention.

(xxix) Fraud detection:

Machine learning is capable of detecting suspected transactions for banks and others in the financial sector. A model can be trained by supervised learning, based on knowledge of recent fraudulent transactions. Anomaly detection may identify transactions that appear unusual, and need to be followed up.

Some other Applications of AI are:

- AI can also make workplace safer as robots can be used for dangerous parts of jobs, and open new job positions as AI-driven industries grow and change.

- For businesses, AI can enable the development of a new generation of products and services, and it can boost sales, improve machine maintenance, increase production output and quality, improve customer service, as well as save energy.

- AI used in public services can reduce costs and offer new possibilities in public transport, education, energy and waste management and could also improve the sustainability of products.

- **Democracy** could be made stronger by using data-based scrutiny, preventing disinformation and cyber-attacks and ensuring access to quality information.

- AI is predicted to be used more in crime prevention and the criminal justice system, as massive datasets could be processed faster, prisoner flight risks assessed more accurately, crime or even terrorist attacks predicted and prevented.

The tapestry of AI continues to expand, with every strand of development bringing forth new potentials and challenges. As AI evolves, its types and applications become the levers propelling myriad fields into a future where the boundaries between the human and digital realms are continually redefined. Through the lens of AI, we see not only the reflection of human intelligence but the silhouette of a future where the confluence of man and machine opens doors to uncharted territories of innovation and exploration.

25.3 Some Case Studies on the Applications of AI

(i) AI and Employee Recruitment

This case study involves the use of AI in employee recruitment. Weeding through job applications is costly and time consuming and exactly the kind of thing that companies would prefer to automate. Many large companies already use AI tools in recruitment, including McDonald's, JP Morgan, Kraft Heinz, Deloitte, and LinkedIn. As many as ninety percent of Fortune 500 companies use automation of some kind to screen or rank job candidates. The use of these AI recruitment systems comes with harms. In 2014, Amazon infamously built a recruitment program to automate its search for talent. It trained the program on resumes submitted over a ten-year period. In 2015, the team noticed that the AI system was biased against women. It downgraded resumes that included the word "women's" and penalized graduates of all-women's colleges. The AI system had replicated the bias in the data set, in which most successful job applicants over the past ten years had been male. This is a classic illustration of the problem of "garbage in, garbage out," in which the quality of machine learning models "is only as good as the quality of [their training] data." Amazon made the decision not to use the AI. Yet the use of AI systems in recruitment is only growing. Companies that adopt these algorithms often argue that they will be more objective and less biased than humans. But hiring algorithms have been found, like humans, to penalize applicants for having a Black-sounding name. Some algorithms alter job candidates' scores based on whether candidates have a bookshelf in the background or wear glasses or a headscarf. There are significant concerns, too, about the use of recruitment algorithms to weed out job applicants with disabilities. In May 2022, the Department of Justice ("DOJ") and the Equal Employment Opportunity Commission ("EEOC") issued guidance on how to use recruitment algorithms in compliance with the Americans with Disabilities Act ("ADA"). The EEOC noted that "an algorithmic decision-making tool could screen out an individual because of a disability" in violation of the ADA. The EEOC's guidance cites examples such as chatbots that automatically screen out applicants with employment gaps, evaluation tools that take into account keystrokes per minute as a measurement of productivity, and gamified tests that cannot be performed by blind applicants. Such screen-outs are unlawful under the ADA if the applicant is nonetheless able to perform the essential functions of the job with reasonable accommodations. This case study of AI recruitment tools again illustrates how the use of AI systems might be construed as resulting in either harms or risks. On the one hand, individual job applicants may be harmed by AI systems and, therefore, could sue for discrimination, for example, under the ADA. On the other hand, the harms of such AI systems have systemic sources and, thus, could be mitigated before the fact. Bad training data and thoughtless technological design ultimately affect the entire system and all applicants, not just one person. Regulators in this sector are already constructing these harms as risks. Some of the EEOC's proposed solutions to combat these harms constitute risk mitigation focused on the design of the decision-making tool. Recent guidance offered by the Federal Trade Commission ("FTC"), which regulates the credit ratings and profiling used in hiring, is even more explicitly risk regulation. It recommends ex-ante testing and independent audits. The risk framing has its benefits: it could potentially protect against system-wide problems, changing the design of the system and catching errors through audits. However, it once again shifts discussions of discrimination and bias away from individualized, personalized harms. Instead, the risk framing has a future orientation; it looks at the aggregate impacts of the system on groups of people and tries to (often controversially) quantify these harms. The risk framing avoids concerns about causality—who should be held at fault, the system developer or the employer who uses the discriminatory system and fails to offer reasonable accommodations?—by aiming the fix at the AI system. And it once again assumes that we can and should continue to use these AI recruitment systems, even if they don't work well, and even if they continue to cause harms.

(ii) AI and Public Health: Access to Care and Prescriptions

This case study echoes several of the problems identified in the other case studies. The below examples demonstrate, again, the potential of AI systems to produce biased and/or incorrect output by replicating biased data, relying on inaccurate proxies, or by ignoring crucial context. They demonstrate, too, the problems with overreliance on a human in the loop of an AI system. This set of case studies looks to the use of AI systems to allocate access to health care and prescriptions. In 2019, a group of researchers published an article in Science on the racial bias in a risk-prediction algorithm widely used in the healthcare sector. The algorithm was used by large health systems and insurers to target patients for enrollment in "'high-risk care management' programs," which seek to improve healthcare for high-risk patients by allocating additional resources to them. The automated system was intended to find high-risk patients whom doctors would be prompted to consider enrolling in the program. The researchers found that the algorithm erroneously overlooked high-risk Black patients, reducing the number of Black patients identified for the program by more than half. They found that the algorithm was not looking directly at health needs but at the proxy of health costs. Because at a given number of chronic illnesses Black patients generated lower costs than White patients—the result of both healthcare inequities and social factors—they were being incorrectly labeled by the algorithm as having lower health risks. Researchers have since expressed concerns that similar biases may affect an array of AI models being promulgated to guide clinical decision making for **Covid-19**. A second example is an algorithm called NarxCare that is used by doctors, pharmacies, and hospitals to identify a patient's risk of opioid abuse. In a reaction to the opioid epidemic, nearly every state now maintains prescription drug databases to track prescriptions for controlled substances. NarxCare, developed by a company called Appriss, searches these state databases for red flags that might indicate "drug shopping" behavior, such as visiting multiple pharmacies or combining different prescriptions. At least eight states also use NarxCare's machine learning algorithm to assign each patient an Overdose Risk Score. That scoring algorithm goes beyond these state databases to look at records such as electronic health records and criminal justice data.

Researchers have criticized the use of this and similar screening algorithms on a number of grounds. One study noted that patients deemed "doctor-shoppers" by the algorithm are often actually cancer patients who have to see multiple specialists. Another study found that patients reporting a Hispanic ethnicity and patients in urban areas are more likely to report difficulties in obtaining prescriptions. Others criticize the algorithm's treatment of diagnoses of depression and PTSD as risk factors, which could have a disparate impact on women. Additionally, the algorithm's use of criminal justice data could harm people of color, who are more likely to be arrested. Then there is the problem of the disempowered human in the loop. While Appriss claims that physicians and pharmacists retain the final say on whether to prescribe, most states require doctors and pharmacists to consult state databases and screening tools or risk losing their licenses. Law enforcement also uses these databases to identify providers as "over-prescribers." This incentivizes providers to deny patients treatment, often with a disparate impact on already marginalized patients. The legal landscape in practice puts prescribers and distributors into a "precarious vice," with antidiscrimination law urging equal treatment on the one hand and medical liability pushing against prescriptions on the other. Once more: the harms of both systems could be characterized as individualized and concrete. Black patients don't get allocated additional healthcare resources and marginalized patients don't receive indicated pain treatment. Instead, these harms are largely constructed as risks. The FDA's approach (or as some criticize, lack of approach) to clinical decision support ("CDS") software is risk-based in nature.

25.4 AI in Popular Culture and Media

The depiction of Artificial Intelligence in popular culture and media has played a crucial role in shaping public perception and understanding of this technology. Through various mediums, artists and creators have explored both the awe-inspiring potential and the existential threats posed by AI, often reflecting society's hopes, fears, and ethical quandaries.

(i) **Films:** Movies have been a powerful medium in exploring the narrative of AI. Films like "Metropolis" (1927) introduced audiences to the idea of humanoid robots, while "2001: A Space Odyssey" (1968) delved into the notion of superintelligent AI with HAL 9000. More recent films like "Ex Machina" (2014) and "Her" (2013) continue to explore the complex relationship between humans and AI.

(ii) **Books:** Literature has long grappled with the concept of AI. From Isaac Asimov's "Robot" series, which introduced the Three Laws of Robotics, to Philip K. Dick's "Do Androids Dream of Electric Sheep?" (1968), which explored the theme of identity and consciousness among artificial beings. These works have not only entertained but also provoked thought and discussion on the ethical and philosophical implications of AI.

(iii) **TV Shows:** Television shows have also contributed significantly to the AI discourse. Series like "Westworld" explore the sentience and rights of artificial beings, while "Black Mirror" often delves into the dystopian aspects of advanced technology, including AI.

(iv) **Video Games:** The interactive nature of video games offers a unique medium to explore AI. Games like "Detroit: Become Human" allow players to navigate a world where AI and humans coexist, examining the societal and ethical challenges that arise.

(v) **Music:** Music artists have also dabbled in the AI narrative. Albums like Janelle Monáe's "Metropolis" explore themes of androids and identity, bringing the discussion of AI into the auditory realm.

(vi) News and Social Media: The portrayal of AI in news and social media often oscillates between the optimistic—emphasizing breakthroughs and potential benefits—and the ominous—highlighting job displacement, privacy issues, and other societal risks. This dual narrative impacts the public opinion and shapes the discourse around regulatory and ethical frameworks.

The representation of AI in popular culture and media often serves as a mirror reflecting societal attitudes towards this technology. From the early depictions of robots and artificial beings to the more nuanced and complex portrayals of modern AI, these narratives play a pivotal role in forming public understanding and attitudes towards AI. Through these various mediums, the discourse around AI is enriched, enabling a broader societal conversation about its benefits, risks, and the ethical considerations that accompany the advance of artificial intelligence.

CHAPTER 26

BENEFITS AND OPPORTUNITIES OF AI

26.1 Advantages and Benefits of AI

(i) Reduction in Human Error

One of the most significant benefits of Artificial Intelligence is that it can significantly reduce errors and increase accuracy and precision. The decisions taken by AI in every step are decided by information previously gathered and a certain set of algorithms. When programmed correctly, these errors can be reduced to null.

Example:

Robotic surgery systems are an example of AI reducing human error. These systems can perform complex procedures with precision and accuracy, reducing the risk of human error and improving patient safety in healthcare.

(ii) Decision-Making

On of the noted pros of AI is decision-making. AI enhances decision-making by leveraging vast data to identify patterns and trends often invisible to humans. Machine learning algorithms can analyze historical data and predict future outcomes, allowing businesses and individuals to make informed decisions quickly and accurately. AI's ability to process information at high speeds reduces the time required for decision-making, thus providing a competitive advantage in dynamic environments.

Example:

In the healthcare industry, AI assists doctors in diagnosing diseases. For example, AI algorithms can analyze medical images, such as

X-rays or MRIs, to detect early signs of conditions like cancer. This not only helps in providing timely treatment but also reduces the likelihood of human error in diagnosis. By augmenting doctors' decision-making processes, AI improves patient outcomes and more efficient healthcare delivery.

(iii) Zero Risks

Another significant benefit of AI is that humans can overcome many risks by letting AI robots do them for us. Whether defusing a bomb, going to space, or exploring the deepest parts of oceans, machines with metal bodies are resistant and can survive unfriendly atmospheres. Moreover, they can provide accurate work with greater responsibility and not wear out quickly.

Example:

One example of zero risks is a fully automated production line in a manufacturing facility. Robots perform all tasks, eliminating the risk of human error and injury in hazardous environments.

(iv) 24x7 Availability

One of the key benefits of AI is round the clock availability. Many studies show humans are productive for only about 3 to 4 hours daily. Humans also need breaks and time off to balance their work and personal lives. But AI can work endlessly without breaks. They think much faster than humans and perform multiple tasks simultaneously with accurate results. They can even handle tedious, repetitive jobs easily with the help of AI algorithms.

Example:

An example is online customer support chatbots, which can provide instant assistance to customers anytime, anywhere. Using AI and natural language processing, chatbots can answer common questions, resolve issues, and escalate complex problems to human agents, ensuring seamless customer service around the clock.

(v) Digital Assistance

Some of the most technologically advanced companies engage with users using digital assistants, which eliminates the need for human personnel. Many websites utilize digital assistants to deliver user-requested content. We can discuss our search with them in conversation. Some chatbots are built in a way that makes it difficult to tell whether we are conversing with a human or a chatbot.

Example:

We all know that businesses have a customer service crew that must address patrons' doubts and concerns. Businesses can create a chatbot or voice bot using AI to answer all of their client's questions.

(vi) New Inventions

AI drives numerous innovations in virtually every field that help humans tackle the most challenging issues. For example, recent advancements in AI-based technologies have enabled doctors to detect breast cancer in women at earlier stages.

Example:

Another example of innovative inventions is **self-driving cars**, which utilize a combination of cameras, sensors, and AI algorithms to navigate roads and traffic autonomously. These vehicles have the potential to enhance road safety, reduce traffic congestion, and increase accessibility for individuals with disabilities or limited mobility. Companies like Tesla, Google, and Uber are at the forefront of developing self-driving cars, poised to revolutionize the transportation industry.

(vii) Unbiased Decisions

Emotions inherently drive humans, while AI operates without emotional influence, maintaining an efficient and rational approach. One significant advantage of Artificial Intelligence is its lack of biased views, leading to more accurate and objective decision-making.

Example:

An example is AI-powered recruitment systems that screen job applicants based on skills and qualifications rather than demographics. This helps eliminate bias in the hiring process, leading to an inclusive and more diverse workforce.

(viii) Automate Repetitive Tasks

Another known benefit of AI is the automation it brings along! In our daily work, we perform many repetitive tasks, such as checking documents for flaws and mailing thank-you notes. Artificial intelligence may efficiently automate these menial chores and even eliminate "boring" tasks for people, allowing them to focus on being more creative.

Example:

An example of this is using robots in manufacturing assembly lines. These robots can handle repetitive tasks such as welding, painting, and packaging with high accuracy and speed, reducing costs and improving efficiency.

(ix) Daily Applications

Today, our everyday lives depend entirely on mobile devices and the internet. We utilize a variety of apps, including Google Maps, Alexa, Siri, Cortana on Windows, OK Google, taking selfies, making calls, responding to emails, etc. Using various AI-based techniques, we can also anticipate today's weather and the days ahead.

Example:

When planning a trip about twenty years ago, you must have asked someone who had already been there for instructions. All you need to do now is ask Google where Bangalore is. The best route between you and Bangalore will be displayed on a Google map, along with Bangalore's location.

(x) AI in Risky Situations

One of the main benefits of artificial intelligence is this: By creating an AI robot that can perform complex tasks on our behalf, we can overcome many dangerous restrictions humans face. It can be utilized effectively in any natural or man-made calamity, whether going to Mars, defusing a bomb, exploring the deepest regions of the oceans, or mining for coal and oil.

Example:

For instance, the explosion at the Chernobyl nuclear power facility in Ukraine. As any person who came close to the core would have perished in a matter of minutes, at the time, there were no AI-powered robots that could assist us in reducing the effects of radiation by controlling the fire in its early phases.

(xi) Medical Applications

AI has also made significant contributions to medicine, with applications ranging from diagnosis and treatment to drug discovery and clinical trials. AI-powered tools can help doctors and researchers analyze patient data, identify potential health risks, and develop personalized treatment plans. This can lead to better patient health outcomes and help accelerate the development of new medical treatments and technologies.

Example:

AI has revolutionized cancer diagnosis and treatment. For instance, AI algorithms can analyze medical images such as mammograms or CT scans to detect early signs of cancer that human eyes may miss. In one notable case, researchers at Google Health developed an AI model that outperformed radiologists in identifying breast cancer in mammograms. The AI system was able to reduce false positives and false negatives, leading to more accurate diagnoses. Additionally, AI can help create personalized treatment plans by analyzing a patient's genetic information, medical history, and current health status.

(xii) Enhanced Efficiency and Productivity

The next benefit of AI is efficiency! AI significantly boosts efficiency and productivity by optimizing processes and reducing the time and resources required to complete tasks. AI systems can analyze data, predict outcomes, and suggest improvements, allowing businesses to streamline operations and eliminate bottlenecks. This leads to faster production cycles, reduced operational costs, and higher output quality.

Example:

In manufacturing, AI-driven robots and predictive maintenance systems are transforming production lines. Robots equipped with AI can work alongside humans, performing tasks such as assembly, welding, and painting with precision and speed. Predictive maintenance uses AI to monitor equipment health and predict failures before they occur, preventing downtime and ensuring continuous production. These advancements result in higher production rates and better quality-control.

(xiii) Enhanced Safety and Fraud Detection

One other advantage of AI is its ability to detect fraud! It enhances fraud detection and prevention by analyzing transaction patterns and identifying anomalies that may indicate fraudulent activities. Machine learning algorithms can detect unusual behavior and flag suspicious transactions in real time, allowing organizations to take immediate action. AI's ability to learn from new data continuously improves its accuracy in identifying and preventing fraud.

Example:

In the financial industry, AI is used to combat credit card fraud. AI systems analyze millions of transactions to identify patterns associated with fraud, such as sudden large purchases or transactions in different geographic locations. When an anomaly is detected, the system alerts the bank and the cardholder, enabling swift action to prevent unauthorized transactions. This not only protects customers but also saves financial institutions from significant losses.

(xiv) Improving Human Workflows

AI analyzes work processes and identifies inefficiencies, suggesting improvements for better human workflows. By examining how tasks are performed, AI can pinpoint areas where time and resources are wasted, offering recommendations for streamlining operations. This helps organizations optimize workflow, improve employee productivity, and reduce operational costs.

Example:

AI tools can analyze project timelines, resource allocation, and task dependencies in project management to identify bottlenecks and suggest more efficient workflows. For instance, an AI system might recommend reassigning tasks based on team members' skills and availability, leading to faster project completion and better resource utilization. This ensures that projects are completed on time and within budget, enhancing overall project efficiency.

(xv) Enhanced Customer Experience

AI enhances customer experience by providing personalized recommendations based on individual preferences and behavior. By analyzing past purchases, browsing history, and demographic information, AI can predict what products or services a customer might be interested in, increasing customer satisfaction and loyalty.

Example:

Streaming services like Netflix use AI algorithms to recommend shows and movies to users. The system analyzes viewing history, ratings, and user interactions to suggest content that aligns with individual preferences. For example, the AI recommends similar titles if users watch crime dramas frequently. This personalization keeps users engaged and increases their likelihood of subscribing to the service.

(xvi) Smarter Surveillance

The next notable benefit of AI is the surveillance capability it brings along! AI improves security and surveillance by monitoring and analyzing vast amounts of data from various sources, such as video feeds, sensors, and network traffic. AI systems can detect unusual activities, recognize faces, and identify potential security threats in real time, enabling quick responses to prevent incidents and enhance safety.

Example:

In smart cities, AI-powered surveillance cameras monitor public spaces. These cameras can detect suspicious behavior, such as loitering in restricted areas or unattended bags, and alert security personnel. Facial recognition technology can also identify known criminals or missing persons, assisting law enforcement in maintaining public safety. This proactive approach to security helps prevent crimes and ensures a safer environment for residents.

(xvii) Bias and Fairness

AI can help identify and mitigate bias in decision-making processes, promoting fairness and equality. By analyzing large datasets, AI can uncover patterns of bias and provide insights into how they affect outcomes. Additionally, AI algorithms can be designed to minimize biases, ensuring that decisions are based on objective criteria rather than subjective or discriminatory factors.

Example:

AI tools screen resumes and conduct initial candidate assessments in the hiring process. These tools can be programmed to ignore irrelevant factors such as gender, race, or age, focusing solely on qualifications and experience. For instance, an AI system can rank candidates based on their skills and achievements rather than demographic characteristics, promoting a fairer hiring process and increasing diversity within the organization.

(xviii) Cost Effective

The next benefit of AI is cost effectiveness! Businesses can automate repetitive tasks such as data entry, scheduling, and customer service by implementing AI technologies. This reduces the need for a large workforce to handle these tasks, leading to significant cost savings in salaries, benefits, and training.

Example:

AI-driven customer service chatbots can handle most customer inquiries, reducing the need for large call center teams. For instance, many e-commerce companies use chatbots to answer common questions, process orders, and provide shipping updates, significantly reducing the workload on human agents.

(xix) Increase in Workforce Productivity

Another point in the list of 'pros of AI' is the increase in workforce productivity. AI-powered tools can help manage and optimize various aspects of work, such as prioritizing tasks, scheduling meetings, and automating routine processes. This allows employees to focus on more strategic and creative tasks, thereby increasing their productivity.

Example:

AI project management tools like Asana use machine learning to prioritize tasks and deadlines, recommending what to focus on subsequent and automating routine follow-ups. This helps teams manage their workloads more effectively and complete projects faster.

(xx) Personalization

AI algorithms can analyze large amounts of data about user behavior, preferences, and interactions. This data is then used to create personalized experiences, such as content recommendations, targeted advertisements, and customized user interfaces, enhancing user satisfaction and engagement.

Example:

Netflix's AI algorithms analyze viewing history and preferences to recommend shows and movies more likely to interest the user.

This personalization helps keep users engaged with the platform, increasing their likelihood of continued subscriptions.

(xxi) Easily Handles Big Data

AI technologies can process and analyze large datasets much faster than traditional methods. This enables businesses to gain valuable insights, make data-driven decisions, and predict future trends more accurately.

Example:

AI in finance analyzes large datasets and market trends to inform investment decisions. Financial institutions use AI to process and analyze real-time market data, identify patterns, and generate accurate predictions, allowing them to make informed investment strategies.

(xxii) Problem-Solving

AI technologies excel at recognizing patterns in large datasets and can be used to solve complex problems across various domains. Businesses and researchers can develop innovative solutions and improve decision-making processes by leveraging AI.

Example:

AI in healthcare uses machine learning to analyze medical images, such as X-rays and MRIs, to diagnose diseases faster and more accurately than human doctors. This leads to quicker and more accurate treatment decisions, improving patient outcomes.

26.2   Use of AI in Other Industries

AI is transforming industries and revolutionizing how we interact with technology. Its ability to analyze vast amounts of data, learn from patterns, and make autonomous decisions makes it a powerful tool across various domains. Here are some prominent use cases for AI:

(i) Healthcare

AI in healthcare is making significant strides by improving patient outcomes and streamlining administrative processes.

- **Medical Imaging:** AI algorithms can analyze medical images, such as X-rays, MRIs, and CT scans, to detect abnormalities like tumors, fractures, and infections accurately.

- **Predictive Analytics:** AI can analyze patient data and health records to predict disease outbreaks, patient readmissions, and the progression of chronic diseases.

- **Personalized Medicine:** Machine learning models help tailor treatments to individual patients based on their genetic makeup and health history, improving the effectiveness of therapies.

- **Virtual Health Assistants** AI-powered chatbots and virtual assistants provide patients with 24/7 support, answering questions, scheduling appointments, and offering medical advice.

(ii) Finance

AI is transforming the finance industry by enhancing security, improving customer service, and optimizing financial operations.

- **Fraud Detection:** AI algorithms analyze transaction patterns to identify and prevent real-time fraudulent activities.

- **Algorithmic Trading:** AI-driven trading systems use historical data and market trends to execute high-frequency trades, optimizing investment strategies.

- **Customer Service:** AI chatbots and virtual assistants handle customer inquiries, process transactions, and provide financial advice, improving efficiency and customer satisfaction.

(iii) Retail

AI is reshaping the retail industry by enhancing customer experiences, optimizing inventory management, and driving sales.

- **Personalized Recommendations:** AI algorithms analyze customer behavior and preferences to provide personalized product recommendations, increasing sales and customer loyalty.

- **Inventory Management:** AI systems predict demand and optimize inventory levels, reducing waste and ensuring products are available when needed.

- **Chatbots and Virtual Assistants:** AI-powered chatbots assist customers with product inquiries, order tracking, and returns, providing efficient and personalized customer service.

- **Visual Search:** AI enables customers to search for products using images, making finding items that match their preferences easier.

(iv) Education:

AI enhances education by personalizing learning experiences and improving administrative efficiency.

- **Personalized Learning:** AI-driven platforms adapt to individual student needs, providing personalized learning paths and resources.

- **Automated Grading:** AI systems grade assignments and exams, providing timely feedback and freeing teachers' time for more personalized instruction.

- **Virtual Tutors:** AI-powered virtual tutors offer students additional support and tutoring, helping them understand complex concepts.

- **Administrative Tasks:** AI automates administrative tasks such as scheduling, enrollment, and resource allocation, improving efficiency in educational institutions.

(v) Entertainment: AI is reshaping the entertainment industry by creating new content, enhancing user experiences, and optimizing production processes.

- **Content Recommendation:** AI algorithms analyze user preferences and behavior to provide personalized content recommendations on streaming platforms.

- **Game Development:** AI generates realistic characters and environments, enhancing the gaming experience.

- **Video Editing:** AI automates video editing processes, such as cutting, filtering, and adding effects, speeding up production times.

- **Music Composition:** AI composes music by analyzing existing compositions and creating new pieces in various styles and genres.

SECTION VI

ARTIFICIAL INTELLIGENCE: ETHICAL ISSUES, RISKS AND REGULATIONS

CHAPTER 27

ETHICAL ISSUES, RISKS AND DISADVANTAGES OF AI

27.1 What is meaning of Ethics?

Ethics is what you don't want others to do to you and you don't do that to others. Ethics is concept that deals with decision making in situation of dilemma of what is right or wrong. Ethics is based on perspective. Ethics of one individual can be right for him in his perspective but it can be wrong to another individual with a different perspective. Ethics is a constantly renovated concept which depends on time, place and situation. Ethics can't be limited to books and words. It has to be understood by learning, observing through different situation each and every day. Ethics, Integrity and Morality are closely related concepts. The type of ethics are Personal ethics, Common ethics and Professional ethics. Personal ethics are individuals, personal values which are inculcated by family, friends, culture, region, Common ethics are those which majority of individuals in the society agree on. Common ethics are very general to avoid disagreement. Professional ethics are the rules imposed in a professional institution which an individual is part of the institution must follow. These are generally built on values that may not harm the professional reputation of the institution.

Ethics refers to a person's moral behavior in determining what is wrong or correct in a given situation. Is it possible for AI to develop ethics? NO. AI is a program that will solely carry out the commands provided to it. Certain chemicals are released in the human brain in response to the scenario, and the human brain behaves accordingly to react to the situation and make an accurate judgement. However, in the case of AI there are no fluids that can provide the moral value.

27.2   AI and Ethics

AI has potential benefits and potential risks. AI may be able to advance science and find solutions for serious problems: Demis Hassabis of Deep Mind hopes to "solve intelligence, and then use that to solve everything else". However, as the use of AI has become widespread, several unintended consequences and risks have been identified. In-production systems sometimes cannot factor ethics and bias into their AI training processes, especially when the AI algorithms are inherently unexplainable.

Following are some of the ethical issues and risks of AI:

(i)   Risks and Harms of AI

Machine-learning algorithms require large amounts of data. The techniques used to acquire this data have raised concerns about **privacy**, surveillance and copyright.

Technology companies collect a wide range of data from their users, including online activity, geolocation data, video and audio. For example, in order to build speech recognition algorithms, Amazon has recorded millions of private conversations and allowed temporary workers to listen to and transcribe some of them. Opinions about this widespread surveillance range from those who see it as a necessary evil to those for whom it is clearly unethical and a violation of the right to privacy.

AI developers argue that this is the only way to deliver valuable applications. and have developed several techniques that attempt to preserve privacy while still obtaining the data, such as data aggregation, de-identification and differential privacy. Since 2016, some privacy experts, such as Cynthia Dwork, have begun to view privacy in terms of fairness. Brian Christian wrote that experts have pivoted "from the question of 'what they know' to the question of 'what they're doing with it.'"

Generative AI is often trained on unlicensed copyrighted works, including in domains such as images or computer code; the output is then used under the rationale of "fair use". Website owners who do not wish to have their copyrighted content AI-indexed or 'scraped' can add code to their site if they do not want their website to be indexed by a search engine, which is currently available through certain services such as OpenAI. Experts disagree about how well and under what circumstances, this rationale will hold up in courts of law; relevant factors may include "the purpose and character of the use of the copyrighted work" and "the effect upon the potential market for the copyrighted work". In 2023, leading authors (including John Grisham and Jonathan Franzen) sued AI companies for using their work to train generative AI.

(ii) Misinformation

YouTube, Facebook and others use recommender systems to guide users to more content. These AI programs were given the goal of maximizing user engagement (that is, the only goal was to keep people watching). The AI learned that users tended to choose misinformation, conspiracy theories, and extreme partisan content, and, to keep them watching, the AI recommended more of it. Users also tended to watch more content on the same subject, so the AI led people into filter bubbles where they received multiple versions of the same misinformation. This convinced many users that the misinformation was true, and ultimately undermined trust in institutions, the media and the government. The AI program had correctly learned to maximize its goal, but the result was harmful to the society. After the US election in 2016, major technology companies took steps to mitigate the problem.

In 2022, generative AI began to create images, audio, video and text that are **indistinguishable from real photographs, recordings, films or human writing**. It is possible for bad actors to use this technology to create massive amounts of misinformation or propaganda. AI pioneer Geoffrey Hinton expressed concern about AI enabling "authoritarian leaders to manipulate their electorates" on a large scale, among other risks.

(iii) Algorithmic Bias and Fairness

Machine learning applications will be biased if they learn from the biased data. The developers may not be aware that the bias exists. Bias can be introduced by the way training data is selected and by the way a model is deployed. If a biased algorithm is used to make decisions that can seriously harm people (as it can in medicine, finance, recruitment, housing or policing) then the algorithm may cause discrimination. Fairness in machine learning is the study of how to prevent the harm caused by algorithmic bias. It has become a serious area of academic study within AI. Researchers have discovered that it is not always possible to define "fairness" in a way that satisfies all stakeholders.

On June 28, 2015, Google Photos' new image labeling feature mistakenly **identified Jacky Alcine and a friend as "gorillas"** because they were black. The system was trained on a dataset that contained very few images of black people; a problem called "sample size disparity". Google "fixed" this problem by preventing the system from labelling anything as a "gorilla". Eight years later, in 2023, Google Photos still could not identify a gorilla, and neither could similar products from Apple, Facebook, Microsoft and Amazon.

COMPAS is a commercial program widely used by U.S. courts to assess the likelihood of a defendant becoming a recidivist. In 2016, Julia Angwin at ProPublica discovered that COMPAS exhibited **racial bias**, despite the fact that the program was not told the races of the defendants. Although the error rate for both whites and blacks was calibrated equal at exactly 61%, the errors for each race were different—the system consistently overestimated the chance that **a black person would re-offend** and would underestimate the chance that a white person would not re-offend. In 2017, several researchers showed that it was mathematically impossible for COMPAS to accommodate all possible measures of fairness when the base rates of re-offense were different for whites and blacks in the data.

A program can make biased decisions even if the data does not explicitly mention a problematic feature (such as "race" or "gender").

The feature will correlate with other features (like "address", "shopping history" or "first name"), and the program will make the same decisions based on these features as it would on "race" or "gender". Moritz Hardt said "the most robust fact in this research area is that fairness through blindness doesn't work."

Criticism of COMPAS highlighted that the machine learning models are designed to make "predictions" that are only valid if we assume that the future will resemble the past. If they are trained on data that includes the results of racist decisions in the past, machine learning models must predict that racist decisions will be made in the future. If an application then uses these predictions as recommendations, some of these "recommendations" will likely be racist. Thus, the machine learning is not well suited to help make decisions in areas where there is hope that the future will be better than the past. It is necessarily descriptive and not proscriptive.

Bias and unfairness may go undetected because the developers are overwhelmingly white and male: among AI engineers, about 4% are black and 20% are women.

At its 2022 Conference on Fairness, Accountability, and Transparency (ACM FAccT 2022), the Association for Computing Machinery, in Seoul, South Korea, presented and published findings that recommend that **until AI and robotics systems are demonstrated to be free of bias mistakes, they are unsafe, and the use of self-learning neural networks trained on vast, unregulated sources of flawed internet data should be curtailed.**

(iv) Lack of Transparency

Many AI systems are so complex that their designers cannot explain how they reach their decisions. Particularly, with deep neural networks, in which there are a large amount of non-linear relationships between inputs and outputs. But some popular explainability techniques exist.

It is impossible to be certain that a program is operating correctly if no one knows how exactly it works. There have been many cases where a machine learning program passed rigorous tests, but nevertheless learned something different than what the programmers intended. For example, a system that could identify skin diseases better than medical professionals was found to actually have a strong tendency to classify images with a ruler as "**cancerous**", because pictures of malignancies typically include a ruler to show the scale. Another machine learning system designed to help effectively allocate medical resources was found to classify patients with **asthma** as being at "low risk" of dying from pneumonia. Having asthma is actually a severe risk factor, but since the patients having asthma would usually get much more medical care, they were relatively unlikely to die according to the training data. The correlation between asthma and low risk of dying from pneumonia was real, but misleading.

People who have been harmed by an algorithm's decision have a right to an explanation. Doctors, for example, are expected to clearly and completely explain to their colleagues the reasoning behind any decision they make. Early drafts of the European Union's General Data Protection Regulation in 2016 included an explicit statement that this right exists. Industry experts noted that this is an unsolved problem with no solution in sight. Regulators argued that nevertheless **the harm is real: if the problem has no solution, the tools should not be used.**

DARPA established the XAI ("Explainable Artificial Intelligence") program in 2014 to try and solve these problems.

There are several possible solutions to the transparency problem. SHAP tried to solve the transparency problems by visualizing the contribution of each feature to the output. LIME can locally approximate a model with a simpler, interpretable model. Multitask learning provides a large number of outputs in addition to the target classification. These other outputs can help developers deduce what the network has learned. Deconvolution, DeepDream and other generative methods can allow developers to see what different layers of a deep network have learned and produce output that can suggest what the network is learning.

(v) Bad Actors and Weaponized AI

Artificial intelligence provides a number of tools that are useful to bad actors, such as authoritarian governments, **terrorists, criminals or rogue states**.

A lethal autonomous weapon is a machine that locates, selects and engages human targets without human supervision. Widely available AI tools can be used by bad actors to develop inexpensive autonomous weapons and, if produced at scale, they are potentially **weapons of mass destruction**. Even when used in conventional warfare, it is unlikely that they will be unable to reliably choose targets and could potentially kill an innocent person. In 2014, 30 nations (including China) supported **a ban on autonomous weapons** under the United Nations' Convention on Certain Conventional Weapons, however the United States and others disagreed. By 2015, over fifty countries were reported to be researching battlefield robots.

AI tools make it easier for authoritarian governments to efficiently control their citizens in several ways. **Face and voice recognition allow widespread surveillance**. Machine learning, operating this data, can classify potential enemies of the state and prevent them from hiding. Recommendation systems can precisely target propaganda and misinformation for maximum effect. **Deepfakes** and generative AI aid in producing misinformation. Advanced AI can make authoritarian centralized decision making more competitive than liberal and decentralized systems such as markets. It lowers the cost and difficulty of digital warfare and advanced spyware. All these technologies have been available since 2020 or earlier—**AI facial recognition systems are already being used for mass surveillance in China.**

There many other ways that AI is expected to help bad actors, some of which cannot be foreseen. For example, machine-learning AI is able to design **tens of thousands of toxic molecules** in a matter of hours.

(vi) Reliance on Industry Giants

Training AI systems requires an enormous amount of computing power. Usually only Big Tech companies have the financial resources to make such investments. Smaller startups such as Cohere and OpenAI end up buying access to data centers from Google and Microsoft, respectively.

(vii) Workplace Impact of Artificial Intelligence

Economists have frequently highlighted the risks of redundancies from AI, and speculated about unemployment if there is no adequate social policy for full employment.

In the past, technology has tended to increase rather than reduce total employment, but economists acknowledge that "we're in uncharted territory" with AI. A survey of economists showed disagreement about whether the increasing use of robots and AI will cause a substantial increase in long-term unemployment, but they generally agree that it could be a net benefit if productivity gains are redistributed. Risk estimates vary; for example, in the 2010s, Michael Osborne and Carl Benedikt Frey estimated **47% of U.S. jobs are at "high risk"** of potential automation, while an OECD report classified only 9% of U.S. jobs as "high risk". The methodology of speculating about future employment levels has been criticized as lacking evidential foundation, and for implying that technology, rather than social policy, creates unemployment, as opposed to redundancies. In April 2023, it was reported that 70% of the jobs for Chinese video game illustrators had been eliminated by Generative Artificial Intelligence.

Unlike previous waves of automation, many middle-class jobs may be eliminated by artificial intelligence; The Economist stated in 2015 that "the worry that AI could do to white-collar jobs what steam power did to blue-collar ones during the Industrial Revolution" is "worth taking seriously". Jobs at extreme risk range from paralegals to fast food cooks, while job demand is likely to increase for care-related professions ranging from personal healthcare to the clergy.

From the early days of the development of artificial intelligence, there have been arguments, about whether tasks that can be done by computers actually should be done by them, given the difference between computers and humans, and between quantitative calculation and qualitative, value-based judgement.

(viii) Existential Risk from Artificial General Intelligence

The statements below from scientists, researchers, investors, politicians, and historians, exhibit a wide variety of opinions and ideas, as well as predicted risks and gains of AI in the future.

(a) Stephen Hawking, 2014:

"The development of full artificial intelligence could spell the end of the human race... It would take off on its own, and re-design itself at an ever-increasing rate. Humans, who are limited by slow biological evolution, couldn't compete, and would be superseded."

(b) Elon Musk, 2014:

"I'm increasingly inclined to think that there should be some regulatory oversight, maybe at the national and international level, just to make sure that we don't do something very foolish. I mean with artificial intelligence we're summoning the demon."

(c) Barack Obama, 2016:

"We've been seeing specialized AI in every aspect of our lives, from medicine and transportation to how electricity is distributed, and it promises to create a vastly more productive and efficient economy … But it also has some downsides that we're gonna have to figure out in terms of not eliminating jobs. It could increase inequality. It could suppress wages."

(d) Vladimir Putin, 2017:

"Artificial intelligence is the future, not only for Russian but for all of humankind. It comes with colossal opportunities, but also threats that are difficult to predict. Whoever becomes the leader in this sphere will become the ruler of the world."

(e) Rodney Brooks demystifies the AI hype and makes relevant claims why predicting the AI future is difficult, especially with over and underestimating and cites the famous Amara law:

"We tend to overestimate the effect of a technology in the short run and underestimate the effect in the long run."

(ix) Ethical Machines and Alignment

Friendly AI are machines that have been designed from the beginning to minimize risks and to make choices that benefit humans. Developing friendly AI should be a higher research priority: it may require a large investment and it must be completed before AI becomes an existential risk.

Machines with intelligence have the potential to use their intelligence to make ethical decisions. The field of machine ethics provides machines with ethical principles and procedures for resolving ethical dilemmas. The field of machine ethics is also called computational morality, and was founded at an AAAI symposium in 2005.

(x) **Underlying data risks:** AI models are only as good as the underlying data that supports them; incorrect or biased data can lead to inaccurate predictions or suboptimal decisions by AI models.

(xi) **Systemic herd behavior:** Where many firms adopt similar AI models, there is an increased risk of 'herd behavior' within financial markets, possibly intensifying market volatility and sensitivity to shocks.

(xii) **Technical Failures:** Like any technology, AI systems can malfunction or be vulnerable to cyberattacks, leading to potential financial losses, regulatory discipline or reputational damage. Cyber security systems should be revisited to assess AI cyber vulnerabilities and mitigation.

(xiii) Job displacement

Automation through AI could reduce the demand for certain roles as technology may be able to replicate these activities, particularly for more junior roles performing manual tasks. The ethical considerations related to this include the societal implications of displacement, the responsibility of firms to their employees, and the impact on recruitment, staff development, talent management, and succession planning. Conversely, however, initial estimates by the World Economic Forum suggest that whilst AI could eliminate over 80 million roles, it could create almost 100 million new ones, thus the net effect appears positive.

(xiv) Legal and Regulatory Challenges

It's crucial to develop new legal frameworks and regulations to address the unique issues arising from AI technologies, including liability and intellectual property rights. Legal systems must evolve to keep pace with technological advancements and protect the rights of everyone.

(xv) AI Arms Race

The risk of countries engaging in an AI arms race could lead to the rapid development of AI technologies with potentially harmful consequences.

Recently, more than a thousand technology researchers and leaders, including Apple co-founder Steve Wozniak, have urged intelligence labs to pause the development of advanced AI systems. The letter states that AI tools present "profound risks to society and humanity."

In the letter, the leaders said:

"Humanity can enjoy a flourishing future with AI. Having succeeded in creating powerful AI systems, we can now enjoy an '**AI summer**' in which we reap the rewards, engineer these systems for the clear benefit of all, and give society a chance to adapt."

(xvi) Loss of Human Connection

Increasing reliance on AI-driven communication and interactions could lead to diminished empathy, social skills, and human connections. To preserve the essence of our social nature, we must strive to maintain a balance between technology and human interaction.

(xvii) Misinformation and Manipulation

AI-generated content, such as **deepfakes**, contributes to the spread of false information and the manipulation of public opinion. Efforts to detect and combat AI-generated misinformation are critical in preserving the integrity of information in the digital age.

In a Stanford University study on the most pressing dangers of AI, researchers said:

"AI systems are being used in the service of disinformation on the internet, giving them the potential to become a threat to democracy and a tool for fascism. From **deepfake videos** to online bots manipulating public discourse by feigning consensus and spreading fake news, there is the danger of AI systems undermining social trust. The technology can be co-opted by criminals, rogue states, ideological extremists, or simply special interest groups, to manipulate people for economic gain or political advantage."

(xviii) Unintended Consequences

AI systems, due to their complexity and lack of human oversight, might exhibit unexpected behaviors or make decisions with unforeseen consequences. This unpredictability can result in outcomes that negatively impact individuals, businesses, or society as a whole.

Robust testing, validation, and monitoring processes can help developers and researchers identify and fix these types of issues before they escalate.

Artificial intelligence (AI) is proving to be a double-edged sword. While this can be said of most new technologies, both sides of the AI blade are far sharper, and neither is well understood.

27.3 Some Failures (Reported upto 2018) When AI Caused Disastrous Results

- **1959:** AI designed to be a General Problem Solver failed to solve real world problems.

- **1982:** Software designed to make discoveries, discovered how to cheat instead.

- **1983:** Nuclear attack early warning system falsely claimed that an attack is taking place.

- **2010:** Complex AI stock trading software caused a trillion-dollar flash crash.

- **2011:** E-Assistant told to "call me an ambulance" began to refer to the user as Ambulance.

- **2013:** Object recognition neural networks saw phantom objects in particular noise images.

- **2015:** An automated email reply generator created inappropriate responses, such as writing "I love you" to a business colleague.

- **2015:** A robot for grabbing auto parts grabbed and killed a man.

- **2015:** Image tagging software classified black people as gorillas.

- **2015:** Medical AI classified patients with asthma as having a lower risk of dying of pneumonia.

- **2015:** Adult content filtering software failed to remove inappropriate content, exposing children to violent and sexual content.

- **2016:** AI designed to predict recidivism acted racist.

- **2016:** An AI agent exploited a reward signal to win a game without actually completing the game.

- **2016:** Video game NPCs (non-player characters, or any character that is not controlled by a human player) designed unauthorized super weapons.

- **2016:** AI judged a beauty contest and rated dark-skinned contestants lower.

- **2016:** A mall security robot collided with and injured a child.

- **2016:** The AI "Alpha Go" lost to a human in a world-championship-level game of "Go."

- **2016:** A self-driving car had a deadly accident.

- **2017:** Google Translate shows gender bias in Turkish-English translations.

- **2017:** Facebook chat bots shut down after developing their own language.

- **2017:** Autonomous van in accident on its first day.

- **2017:** Google Allo suggested man in turban emoji as response to a gun emoji.

- **2017:** Face ID beat by a mask.

- **2017:** AI misses the mark with Kentucky Derby predictions.

- **2017:** Google Home Minis spied on their owners.

- **2017:** Google Home outage causes near 100% failure rate.

- **2017:** Facebook allowed ads to be targeted to "Jew Haters".

- **2018**: Chinese billionaire's face identified as jaywalker.

- **2018:** Uber self-driving car kills a pedestrian.

- **2018:** Amazon AI recruiting tool is gender-biased.

- **2018:** Google Photo confuses skier and mountain.

- **2018:** LG robot Cloi gets stage-fright at its unveiling.

- **2018:** IBM Watson comes up short in healthcare.

While these are only a few instances of failures that have been observed so far, they are pieces of evidence to the fact that Artificial intelligence (the simulation of human intelligence processes by machines, especially computer systems) has the potential to develop a will of its own that may be in conflict with members of the human race. This is definitely a warning about the potential dangers of Artificial intelligence which should be addressed while exploring its potential interests.

27.4 How Can AI Pose Risks to Financial Services Firms?

AI exposes financial services firms to a broad range of regulatory, legal and reputational risks. These risks largely stem from AI's inherent flaws. Because AI models make predictions based on defined datasets and assumptions, their results carry a risk of being skewed due to error and bias. Said differently, use of AI automation does not equate to accuracy or objectivity. Firms are vulnerable to both internal- and external-facing AI-related risks and ethical concerns, including confidentiality of data, cybersecurity, and "data hallucinations," which poison results that may then be fed into financial models or be used to influence investment research or portfolio management decisions.

Firms introduce internal risks when they intentionally onboard AI tools onto their platforms. Some of these risks are easy to spot. For example, AI's inherent flaws may cause firms to generate inadequate research, false reports, inaccurate communications or misinformed investment recommendations. Other internal risks are less obvious. For example, AI tools obtain data through various means, such as web scraping, which may implicate the firms' legal entitlement to such data. Likewise, firms' possession of this data may trigger unique legal questions, such as HIPAA obligations or similar privacy requirements tied to the possession or use of underlying medical data. Even less apparent, AI tools that collect from multiple data sources may inadvertently create **personal identifiable information** (PII), which the firms must take precautions to protect. While each data source may not independently constitute PII, when compiled with other sources, they may collectively present PII.

As to the external risks, firms bear such risk exposure even if they do not intentionally use AI tools. For example, firms face such risks through their vendors that rely on AI technologies to render services. Firms may be unaware that these vendors, such as research providers, even use AI. Firms may fail to properly vet the vendors' data security, privacy or other controls for alignment with the firms' compliance standards. These external-facing risks are multi-layered and more challenging for firms to navigate because of the lack of full visibility into or control over how these vendors use AI, conduct surveillance of AI-related risks and mitigate these risks. Ultimately, firms may unknowingly breach the AI data owners' terms and conditions or even infringe on intellectual property rights.

27.4.1   Compliance program, governance and risk management:

Revisit and revise the firm's policies and procedures, code of ethics, and supervisory measures to enhance the firm's standards for detecting, testing, mitigating and reporting AI risks; eliminate conflicts of interest; document risk management practices and oversight; establish responsible uses of AI; conduct and oversee vendor management; and incorporate AI considerations into business continuity planning. Even more critical, take steps to ensure that the firm is following its new standards through the appropriate checks and balances of training, testing and reporting. The only outcome possibly more problematic than having no policy and procedure in place is a policy ignored.

27.5 Ethical Considerations and the Future of AI

The advancement of artificial intelligence (AI) prompts a plethora of ethical considerations and challenges, alongside exciting future possibilities. The ethical milieu of AI is as complex as the technology itself, intertwining with societal, economic, and individual aspects of life.

27.5.1 Ethical Considerations

(i) **Bias and Fairness:** AI systems can perpetuate or even exacerbate existing societal biases if the data they are trained on is biased. Ensuring fairness and mitigating bias in AI applications is a pressing ethical concern.

(ii) **Privacy and Data Security:** The massive data requirements for training and operating AI systems pose significant privacy risks. Ensuring data security and privacy in an AI-driven world is paramount.

(iii) **Transparency and Accountability:** Understanding how AI systems make decisions and holding them accountable for those decisions is crucial for building trust and ensuring ethical operation.

(iv) **Autonomy and Decision-Making:** As AI systems take over more decision-making roles, the question of autonomy and the potential loss of human oversight in critical areas arises.

(v) **Long-term Existential Risks:** The potential future development of superintelligent AI poses long-term existential risks that are crucial to consider and mitigate.

27.6 AI and Concerns in Healthcare

In the field of health care, possible uses and concerns are under scrutiny by professional associations and practitioners. Two early papers indicated that ChatGPT could pass the United States Medical

Licensing Examination (USMLE). MedPage Today noted in January 2023 that "researchers have published several papers now touting these AI programs as useful tools in medical education, research, and even clinical decision making."

Published in February 2023 were two separate papers that again evaluated ChatGPT's proficiency in medicine using the USMLE. Findings were published in JMIR Medical Education (see Journal of Medical Internet Research) and PLOS Digital Health. The authors of the PLOS Digital Health paper stated that the results "suggest that large language models may have the potential to assist with medical education, and potentially, clinical decision-making." In JMIR Medical Education, the authors of the other paper concluded that "ChatGPT performs at a level expected of a third-year medical student on the assessment of the primary competency of medical knowledge." They suggest that it could be used as an "interactive learning environment for students". The AI itself, prompted by the researchers, concluded that "this study suggests that ChatGPT has the potential to be used as a virtual medical tutor, but more research is needed to further assess its performance and usability in this context." The later-released ChatGPT version based on GPT-4 significantly outperformed the version based on GPT-3.5. Researchers at Stanford University and the University of California, Berkeley have found that the performance of GPT-3.5 and GPT-4 on the USMLE declined from March 2023 to June 2023.

A March 2023-paper tested ChatGPT's application in clinical toxicology. The authors found that the AI "fared well" in answering a "very straightforward [clinical case example], unlikely to be missed by any practitioner in the field". They added: "As ChatGPT becomes further developed and specifically adapted for medicine, it could one day be useful in less common clinical cases (i.e, cases that experts sometimes miss). Rather than AI replacing humans (clinicians), we see it as 'clinicians using AI' replacing 'clinicians who do not use AI' in the coming years."

An April 2023-study in Radiology tested the AI's ability to answer queries about breast cancer screening. The authors found that it answered appropriately "about 88 percent of the time", however, in one case (for example), it gave advice that had become outdated about a year earlier. The comprehensiveness of its answers was also lacking. A study published in JAMA Internal Medicine that same month found that ChatGPT often outperformed human doctors at answering patient questions (when measured against questions and answers found at /r/AskDocs, a forum on Reddit where moderators validate the medical credentials of professionals; the study acknowledges the source as a limitation). The study-authors suggest that the tool could be integrated with medical systems to help doctors draft responses to patient questions.

Professionals have emphasized ChatGPT's limitations in providing medical assistance. In correspondence to The Lancet Infectious Diseases, three antimicrobial experts wrote that "the largest barriers to the implementation of ChatGPT in clinical practice are deficits in situational awareness, inference, and consistency. These shortcomings could endanger patient safety." Physician's Weekly, though also discussing the potential use of ChatGPT in medical contexts (e.g. "as a digital assistant to physicians by performing various administrative functions like gathering patient record information or categorizing patient data by family history, symptoms, lab results, possible allergies, et cetera"), warned that the AI might sometimes provide fabricated or biased information. One radiologist warned: "We've seen in our experience that ChatGPT sometimes makes up fake journal articles or health consortiums to support its claims". As reported in one Mayo Clinic Proceedings: Digital Health paper, ChatGPT may do this for as much as 69% of its cited medical references. The researchers emphasized that while many of its references were fabricated, those that were appeared "deceptively real". As Dr. Stephen Hughes mentioned for The Conversation however, ChatGPT is capable of learning to correct its past mistakes. He also noted the AI's "prudishness" regarding sexual health topics.

Contrary to previous findings, ChatGPT responses to anesthesia-related questions were more accurate, succinct, and descriptive compared to Bard's. Bard exhibited 30.3% error in response as compared to ChatGPT (0% error). At a conference of the American Society of Health-System Pharmacists in December 2023, researchers at Long Island University (LIU) presented a study that researched ChatGPT's responses to 45 frequently asked questions of LIU College of Pharmacy's drug information service during a 16-month period from 2022 to 2023 as compared with researched responses provided by professional pharmacists. For 29 of the 39 questions for which there was sufficient medical literature for a data-driven response, ChatGPT failed to provide a direct answer or provided a wrong or incomplete answer (and in some cases, if acted upon, the answer would endanger the patient's health). The researchers had asked ChatGPT to provide medical research citations for all its answers, but it did so for only eight, and all eight included at least one fabricated (fake) citation.

A January 2024 study conducted by researchers at Cohen Children's Medical Center found that GPT-4 had an accuracy rate of 17% when diagnosing pediatric medical cases.

27.7 Academic Cheating in Perspective

Student cheating has long been characterized as an "ongoing issue" in academic evaluation, with "scandalous" levels of cheating often suspected or identified. Technologically-supported academic cheating has taken on a number of dimensions in the past decades, adding new dimensions to the moral ecologies of higher education. There have been innovative mechanisms and insidious ploys in academic deceit. These include plagiarism, collusion (human collaboration on assignments that is not approved by instructors), and use of services that complete courses for a student. Definitions of "cheating" are problematic to develop, and institutional policies can differ as to what kinds of technological access are restricted. For example, the use of Grammarly by students has been questioned; the editing and proofing tools of Grammarly are seen in some contexts as providing an unfair advantage in the production of academic work. However, in recent years the kinds of tools that Grammarly provides have become integrated as standard features into many word processors and even search engines. Decades ago, the use of calculators in classroom exams was considered a form of cheating in many contexts, effectively altering the educational experience and undermining appropriate evaluation of students. Even iPads were considered in some contexts as potentially disruptive in terms of their impacts on classroom interaction. As AI system capabilities become integrated into various search engine, design, and document production applications, the kinds of issues they present for academic integrity are becoming more diffuse yet increasingly critical to define and resolve.

Below are several dimensions of AI generative system misuse in context of academic cheating-related phenomena:

(i) **Misallocation of Credit:** Collaboration among humans as well as with artificial entities can be difficult to manage, and often results in inefficiencies as well as unfairness. Misattribution of co-authorship for reasons other than merit is reportedly common in academics, and increasing awareness for transparency and for more explicit guidelines and regulation of research co-authorship within and across research areas, is becoming more of a necessity, especially given how these misattributions can reinforce bias. In many research arenas, ghost and honorary authorships (in which credit is not allocated in relation to contributions) are considered as problematic by research directors and publishers; the use of ChatGPT and Bard can extend these concerns by including AI-enhanced entities in co-authorship roles. Responsible collaboration (whether or not AI is involved) also requires some oversight on the quality of one's collaborator's contributions along with acknowledging the extent and quality of one's own contributions. The prospects that many AI system outputs will be accepted as correct without exploration of their sources and other justifications thus provide considerable concerns.

(ii) Impersonation: Methodologies for impersonation are also a part of the cheating realm, as paid professionals or skilled amateurs complete the assignments or take exams for students. For example, ChatGPT capabilities include impersonation of vocal characteristics and style, which can present challenges for authentic assessment and may increase institutional reliance on various anti-cheating surveillance tools. Not long ago, students impersonating other students in order to take examinations was indeed possible, but was relatively rare. However, impersonation has become a serious issue for universities implementing online or hybrid programs. In response to these concerns, an online program cannot claim to be truly worthy of academic recognition without strong assurance that students are being fairly and effectively assessed in their learning. As instances of specific impersonation challenges, some versions of ChatGPT can produce answers to problems in the fields of accounting, business law, and computer programming as well as producing text that could serve as answers to short-essay questions in many disciplinary contexts.

(iii) Contract Cheating: Question-Papers and contract cheating organizations provide another set of academic cheating variants. Even before ChatGPT delivered custom materials to students, availability of tailored academic productions through these organizations was widespread. More informal varieties of academic paper and examination answer exchanges take place online as well as through various student associations and social media platforms. The kinds of output that ChatGPT and other AI-enhanced applications provide may generate problems for these contract and informal services; a major application of ChatGPT is content generation along with transformation into genres that are acceptable for many academic assignments and exercises, which may make some contract cheating installations obsolete. Today, the use of ChatGPT, Bard, and related generative AI systems is often inexpensive or even free of charge; however, in the near future ethical issues involving income disparities can arise as AI system usage becomes too expensive for certain individuals. An alternative perspective to cheating detection reframes these three challenges in terms of human-AI collaboration. Construing engagements with ChatGPT, Bard, and related AI systems as forms of co-authorship rather than simply as sources that are accessed and integrated into an academic production underscores the active and responsive elements that the systems can provide in intellectual efforts. As the complexity of workplace and community problems increases, collaborative effort is needed to work toward solutions; students should be equipped to engage with others in productive ways. An unfortunate by-product of these AI developments over time is that students might feel it less necessary to learn and practice basic writing and design skills, focusing rather on the kinds of skills involved in editing and revising ChatGPT or Bard results so as to appear like their original productions. Mindful and reflective collaboration can aid in efforts extending the dimensions of human-AI collaboration and to allocate appropriate levels of credit for academic contributions. Appropriate allocation of credit can be difficult to ascertain: after a writer and a model takes turns in writing a story and iteratively edits it, how can one tease out and characterize the model's contribution to the writing, or how well it served the writer's needs. Instructors will need to design discipline-specific questions and prompts for students who engage with ChatGPT and Bard so that they benefit intellectually from their human-AI collaborations as well as recognize the limitations and constraints of these interactions. If the modes of AI-sensitive cheating-detection are used to assist students in their reflection processes (and not just to catch cheaters), more accurate allocations of authorship credit may be produced.

27.8 Emerging AI-Sensitive Cheating Detection Strategies

Assortments of outsourced cheating-detection systems are emerging that claim to deal with ChatGPT concerns. For example, the proprietary system Turnitin, reportedly used by 62 million students worldwide, has reportedly been upgraded with capabilities to detect and flag ChatGPT material, though details have not been released. Some of the anti-cheating technologies will require some sort of added system capabilities or watermarking that will require support from the developers of the generative AI systems involved. Securing such support will become more problematic as the numbers and kinds of widely-used AI systems increases.

Recently-disseminated strategies for detecting whether ChatGPT was utilized in a particular academic production include the following:

(i) **Watermarking ChatGPT-produced materials:** OpenAI researchers are working on ways that ChatGPT productions can be watermarked so that they can be identified as ChatGPT-produced even if somewhat modified. Whether this watermarking can be formulated, so that more dramatic revision of the materials would not impact its informational value is still uncertain. Providing these watermarks would be the responsibility of the AI system developers, which would require their sustained participation over time.

(ii) **Using ChatGPT itself to identify ChatGPT materials:** ChatGPT and other generative AI systems can often identify some of their own materials through a variety of methods, capabilities that will also require some sustained maintenance on the part of system developers and implementers. It has been proposed that a two-step approach for cheating detection given these capabilities: "first, verifying the origin of the content, followed by a similarity check."

(iii) Measuring perplexity and burstiness: Metrics for identifying generative AI content are emerging. For example, GPTZero and some related systems are designed to measure a document's "perplexity" and "burstiness." Perplexity refers to the complex or random aspects of a document and measures how well the AI system's language model can predict the next word in a word sequence. Burstiness refers to patterns of diversity in sentence structure, which can indicate whether a written text is machine-generated or not. Documents with high perplexity are more likely to be written by a human because their patterns are complex and less well recognized by the GPTZero (based on its training set). Documents with high burstiness are more varied in structure, which reportedly makes them similar to novel human productions. produced documents tend to be more uniform. Measurements of perplexity and burstiness can give some direction in terms of how a particular document compares with ChatGPT materials, but are reportedly not intended to provide definitive results.

(iv) Versioning: Requiring students to retain every version of a document (so that extensive cut-and-paste operations can be examined) would provide some clues as to the input of AI systems in the document. With versioning, reviewers of a document for a student assignment or potential journal publication would be able to "move backward in time" and observe the evolution of the document, comparing the changes in perplexity, burstiness, or other metrics across different revisions of the text. Abrupt changes might reveal patterns or anomalies that could indicate ChatGPT or other AI system usage. By systematically retraining document, various students can also be prompted periodically to reflect on the kind and quality of their own input in relation to that of ChatGPT and their human collaborators (if any), conveying specific addenda regarding the collaboration processes involved.

(v) Establishing thresholds for ChatGPT-generated content: For universities, journals, and research hubs to establish "thresholds" for acceptable levels of AI-generated content has been proposed as a way to mitigate concerns about the misuse of AI-generated content. Simply citing ChatGPT or Bard as a co-author on research documents is already being used as a formal way to acknowledge its contribution, with a number of publications allowing for such attribution. However, such blanket acknowledgements do not provide the detail that allows for the sensitive reflection of the system's as well as the human's contributions to the production.

(vi) **Designing assignments so that ChatGPT use becomes transparent:** Assignment or assessment redesign so that ChatGPT use is an obvious and open part of the exercise can mitigate some of AI's negative dimensions for education. For example, in a stage in the assignment, students can be asked to compare their productions directly to ChatGPT or other AI system materials. As the numbers and variety of generative AI systems increases, these assignment redesign strategies would need to be adjusted, adding new complexities to instructors' efforts.

ChatGPT, Bard, and other AI systems are presenting disconcerting challenges to educational institutions that currently rely on the authentic evaluation of academic effort. Whether AI system misuse would lead to the end of traditional assessments in higher education, potentially fomenting radical changes in how student work is evaluated. Students, faculty, and staff should be given the opportunity to discuss the implications of these academic changes and share their uncertainties. A way for faculty and students to start in facing cheating-related challenges is in examining their institution's existing honor code, discussions that research shows are often effective in containing cheating behavior. Engaging in efforts to revise and enhance the code or at least explore how the current code relates to AI generative systems can help to clarify important ethical and academic concerns. For faculty to develop course syllabi statements that address ChatGPT issues from the particular angle of the course's objectives and disciplines as well as the faculty members' own perspectives may help to forestall communication problems. These honor codes and syllabi statements can begin to map the difficult concerns involved when finding appropriate places for the use of powerful new technologies in already packed and intense higher education activities. However, with AI developments occurring at a rapid pace, highly specific codes and statements can become outdated rapidly. Efforts to reinforce trust and create solid personal relationships among students, faculty, and staff may be the most effective approaches in the long run. Whatever kinds of new cheating mitigation strategies emerge for these generative AI systems will be added to an assortment of technological cheating-detection approaches, many of which are AI-powered (such as facial recognition). These approaches can present unsettling long-term potentials for privacy as they are coupled with biometrics and profiling. For instance, some research currently being done on deception integrates detailed information about students' biometric indicators and other personalized data in search of individualized patterns of signals about their deception-related intentions. These profiles may be stored and used over time as ways to ascertain whether the students are indeed conforming to particular standards of integrity. For instance, lists of subjects who are construed as "potential cheaters" as a result of their interactions with the cheating-related systems could be compiled through predictive analytics. Higher education participants should work with AI system developers to communicate and realize their academic and ethical values pertaining to these technological developments. For example, the notion that using the profiling capabilities of AI to catch cheaters is somehow "fairer" than proctoring methods that are not technologically supported needs to be examined systematically, along with other assumptions about the superiority of AI-enhanced processes. False positives are certainly to be expected with such profiling approaches, forcing individuals to prove that they were not cheating, efforts that can be demoralizing and debilitating. Even more troubling are prospects for experimentation or entrapment with the systems on the part of the developers and implementers involved, for example, providing false feedback to subjects with the aim of testing the systems or enhancing subjects' responses. With sufficient effort and increased communication with AI system developers, educational institutions can indeed implement humane and transparent ways of dealing with cheating and deception issues. In contrast to punitive cheating detection strategies, mindful and reflective approaches that emphasize human-AI collaboration can serve to empower students in their quests to become capable employees and community members. Stressing the model of human-AI collaboration as something that needs to be strengthened and enhanced runs counter to those perspectives that present these interactions as inherently being diminishing for the human involved. Faculty and staff can facilitate reflective and culturally-sensitive practices to counter the potential misuse of generative AI systems in academic contexts, imparting to students the values of collaboration and responsible attribution of credit.

27.9   Some More Ways to Prevent Students From Cheating With AI

Preventing cheating with AI in educational settings requires a multi-faceted approach, addressing technology use, assessment design, and fostering academic integrity.

Here are some strategies to consider:

1. Redesign Assessment Methods

(i)   **Emphasize Critical Thinking:** Design assessments that require higher-order thinking skills, analysis, and problem-solving, which are harder for AI to replicate.

(ii)   **Use Open-Ended Questions:** Incorporate questions that require unique responses and cannot be easily generated by AI.

(iii) **Personalized Assignments:** Assign tasks that are specific to the student's experiences, interests, or recent classroom activities.

2. Implement Technology Safeguards

(i) **Proctoring Tools:** Use secure exam proctoring software that monitors student behavior during online exams. Ensure the software respects privacy and accessibility guidelines.

(ii) **Plagiarism Detection:** Use plagiarism detection tools that can identify AI-generated content and maintain a database of academic work to cross-check against.

27.10   Consciousness, Self-awareness, Sentience

Other aspects of the human mind besides intelligence are relevant to the concept of AGI or "strong AI", and these play a major role in science fiction and the ethics of artificial intelligence:

(i) Consciousness

To have subjective experience. Thomas Nagel explains that it "feels like" something to be conscious. If we are not conscious, then it doesn't feel like anything. Nagel uses the example of a bat: we can sensibly ask "what does it feel like to be a bat?" However, we are unlikely to ask "what does it feel like to be a toaster?" Nagel concludes that a bat appears to be conscious (i.e. has consciousness) but a toaster does not.

(ii) Self-awareness

To have conscious awareness of oneself as a separate individual, especially to be consciously aware of one's own thoughts. This is opposed to simply being the "subject of one's thought" – an operating system or debugger is able to be "aware of itself" (that is to represent itself in the same way it represents everything else) but this is not what people typically mean when they use the term "self-awareness".

(iii) Sentience

The ability to "feel" perceptions or emotions subjectively, as opposed to the ability to reason about perceptions or, in regard to emotions, to be aware that the situation requires urgency, kindness or aggression.

For example, we can build a machine that knows which objects in its field of view are red, but this machine will not necessarily know what red looks like.

These traits have a moral dimension, because a machine with this form of "strong AI" may have rights, analogous to the rights of non-human animals. Preliminary work has been conducted on integrating strong AI with existing legal and social frameworks, focusing on the legal position and rights of 'strong' AI.

It remains to be shown whether "artificial consciousness" is necessary for AGI. However, many AGI researchers regard research that investigates possibilities for implementing consciousness as vital.

Bill Joy, among others, argues a machine with these traits may be a threat to human life or dignity.

27.11   Can AI Develop a Human Like Consciousness?

Artificial consciousness (AC), also known as machine consciousness (MC), synthetic consciousness or digital consciousness, is the consciousness hypothesized to be possible in artificial intelligence. It is also the corresponding field of study, which draws insights from philosophy of mind, philosophy of artificial intelligence, cognitive science and neuroscience. The same terminology can be used with the term "sentience" instead of "consciousness" when specifically designating phenomenal consciousness (the ability to feel qualia).

Some scholars believe that consciousness is generated by the interoperation of various parts of the brain; these mechanisms are labeled the neural correlates of consciousness or NCC. Some further believe that constructing a system (e.g., a computer system) that can emulate this NCC interoperation would result in a system that is conscious.

The machines' mental abilities are approaching the level of humans. AI's machine learning algorithms are becoming more complicated by the day in the past decade. Artificial intelligence is progressing at a breakneck pace, ensuring that machines will soon surpass human intelligence. Though there has been significant progress in designing algorithms to make machines intelligent, improvements in the machine learning to develop a human like consciousness are still in the early stages. To build human-like consciousness, an algorithm which is a masterpiece is required. Humans have many brain reactions that enables them to be conscious. Chemicals are to be blamed for these reactions. Consider an awkward situation in which you crack a joke only to discover afterwards that it was misinterpreted as an insult. Is it possible for an algorithm to elicit such tumultuous emotions? NO. These encounters are the result of our brains natural abilities. The human brain, which weighs three pounds and resembles tofu, is by far the most complicated chunk of matter that is known to this world. The whole capacity of brains powers is unknown, it's impossible to create a similar product if you don't understand the original completely Perhaps if AI develops a consciousness that is human-like or even a better version of the human consciousness in the future, I believe that humans will not allow it to happen. Human as living beings, believe they are the smartest and superior and that they are at the top of the food chain. Machines will be at the top of the hierarchy of all living and non-living entities on this planet if AI achieves a human like consciousness.

For example, in the movie "Avengers: Age of Ultron" Tony Stark and Bruce Banner attempt to develop Ultron, an artificial intelligence that can be a pseudo armor across the world to protect he world from fatal dangers. It is a supreme robot with exceptionally strong AI whose responses are unpredictable, despite the fact it was made by mistake. Ultron is built without consciousness but when it tends to build a better version of itself with supreme consciousness the avengers try to end their own creation. Why? Because AI will become a more powerful and superior force in the world, lowering and hurting human's egos humans who build AI are always in a position of superiority in terms of knowing how to destroy their own creations.

27.12   Can AI develop Cognitive Abilities?

Cognitive abilities are described as the ability to think and behave in social situations when the actions are linked to previous observations and experiences. The human brain has the ability to imagine, which aids in simulating and assessing the probable outcomes of new and unfamiliar situations. Individual decisions in a complicated world are not necessarily based on prior experience. Mental simulations of probable future events in an unbounded environment are based on an underlying model of world dynamics and can be very useful in planning and problem-solving. For higher levels of cognition, the ability to imagine is critical. Covert mathematical, physical, or psychological concepts that are beyond input to output observable statistical correlations can be used to obtain a higher degree of cognition. Artificial intelligence uses a set of programs and functions to complete a task and then outputs the results according to the machines instructions. The fact that most manmade reasoning frameworks are not intel is undeniable. They are often best in class management frameworks. For those engaged with mathematical calculations as it were, the emblematic handling capacity of such frameworks might appear to be insightful Nonetheless, notable handling has been close. Similarly, just as completing a math problem isn't considered as insight, the ability to see as a subordinate of articulation through emblematic handling is a computationally different issue that isn't considered knowledge. Although the capacity to get genuine data is important when done by individuals, database administration is not, regardless of the size of the data set. The data show that is the less skilled we are in a domain, the more bewildered we become. Non-procedural aspects of man-made reasoning programming is the norm. for a long time, the re-programming enactments has been revelatory and hence nonprocedural. A series of regulations is added to the movement method in recreation. The ability of the deduction motor in a standard based software to determine the request where the principles should be implemented is insufficient to qualify this type of data processing as smart. In any case, our perplexity maybe analogous to that of those who referred to early PCs as electronic cerebrums.

The logical address storage process in AI is only possible if and only if the current data on which AI's functions are functioning has a defined path. When it comes to human consciousness, however the acts or tasks that are undertaken form a mix and match of logic combinations and behave appropriately. When viewed through the lens of the financial sector; at the end of the day, the customers' requirements must be met. If the entire AI takes care of the matter, the humans' feelings aren't detected in any unusual way. Only human mind is capable of completing the basic concerns. The primary issue in this concept is that, in terms of cognitive capacity, persons working on Artificial intelligence misunderstand the logic of the current situation and act according to their own preferences. These handy aspects lead to a misunderstanding of the use of technology, and the resulting fury is not appropriate for a human's normal living.

27.13   Can AI develop Ethics?

Technology is both fascinating and dangerous in the twenty-first century. The media and academic studies frequently demonstrate the potential of technologies like machine learning and AI. Despite the fact that they are the most powerful force for good in the humanity, the question remains: "will machines develop ethics?" "what is they don't everything goes wrong?" you might wonder. Researchers and scientists have warned us for decades about the negative consequences of technology, such as artificial intelligence. **Ray Kurzweil** predicts that by 2029, machines will have evolved to the point that they will be able to outperform humans. "once humans develop full AI, it will set off on its own and remake itself at an ever-increasing rate", Stephen Hawkings claims. Elon Musk warns that artificial intelligence could pose a "fundamental risk to the survival of human civilization". There are more and more justifications for better ethical implementation in artificial intelligent systems. How can we apply Ethics in AI? There is a lot of uncertainty. At this time, its's more important than ever to pay attention to the limited AI applications that exist today in ethical ways. For example, in dangerous traffic circumstances, self-driving automobiles must determine the value of human life. Ethics is difficult to teach because humans are incapable of quantifying ethics. It's debatable if we, as humans fully comprehend ethics and morality. Humans tend to rely on gut instinct rather than rigorous cost-benefit analyses when faced with moral difficulties. Machines, on the other hand, carry out explicit calculations and cross check them against the objective metrics than can be improved. Teaching ethics in a program is difficult, because there are innumerable elements that influence the outcome of a scenario in real LIFE. Can we teach a machine to overcome racial and gender bias in its training data? NO. It is not possible to teach what is fair and dark or how to overcome racial bias.

27.14   Potential Future Developments in AI

(i)   General AI: The development of General AI, machines that could outperform humans at nearly every cognitive task, is a potential, albeit speculative, future development that could significantly impact society.

(ii)   Human-AI Collaboration: Enhancing human capabilities through AI and creating a symbiotic relationship between humans and machines is a promising future avenue.

(iii) AI in Healthcare: The continued integration of AI in healthcare, from diagnostics to personalized medicine, holds immense promise for improving health outcomes.

(iv) AI Governance: Establishing robust governance frameworks to ensure the responsible development and deployment of AI is a critical future endeavor.

27.15   Implications of AI for Society

The ethical considerations and future developments in AI carry profound implications for society. They challenge existing frameworks of ethics, governance, and public policy, necessitating a robust societal discourse to navigate the AI landscape responsibly.

The potential benefits of AI, from improved healthcare to enhanced productivity, are enormous. However, they come with equally significant challenges that require foresight, multidisciplinary engagement, and proactive governance.

As we stand at the cusp of an era where AI could redefine the boundaries of what is possible, engaging with the ethical dimensions and preparing for future developments is imperative. It is a collective endeavor that involves policymakers, technologists, the public, and other stakeholders coming together to shape a future where AI serves humanity positively and ethically. Through thoughtful consideration and responsible action, the journey into the next frontier of AI can be directed toward creating a future that reflects our shared values and aspirations.

27.16 A Look Back and Forward: Our Journey with AI

The odyssey of Artificial Intelligence (AI) mirrors the ceaseless human endeavor to transcend the customary bounds of capability and knowledge. From ancient civilizations' musings on artificial beings to the modern-day prowess of machine learning and deep learning, AI has traversed a remarkable journey. The narrative wove through the philosophical and scientific contemplations of luminaries like Alan Turing, transitioning into a formal discipline in the mid-20th century, maturing through various stages, and blossoming into the present-day behemoth poised to revolutionize myriad facets of human existence.

The tale of AI is a testament to human ingenuity and a precursor to a future teeming with unimaginable possibilities. As we stand at this juncture, it's imperative to navigate the AI landscape with a blend of optimism, vigilance, and a strong ethical compass. The impact of AI on the future of humanity is poised to be profound, reshaping the fabric of society, economy, and individual lives. Ensuring that this impact is positive, equitable, and beneficial for all is a collective responsibility that beckons the engagement of technologists, policymakers, and the global citizenry.

As we reflect on the journey thus far and gaze into the horizon, the narrative of AI is much more than a chronicle of technological evolution—it's a call to action for thoughtful stewardship in orchestrating a harmonious future where AI and humanity thrive together. Through collaborative efforts, robust governance, and a shared vision, the path ahead can lead to a future where AI serves as a catalyst for global betterment, embodying the essence of human aspiration and the promise of a better tomorrow.

CHAPTER 28

REGULATIONS FOR AI

Artificial intelligence (AI) is developing at a rapid pace. From generative language models like ChatGPT to advances in medical screening technology, policymakers and the developers of the technology alike believe that it could deliver fundamental change across almost every area of our lives. But such change is not without risk. Debate is ongoing on how best to regulate these innovative technologies and differences of approach have already emerged internationally as countries across the world examine how best to adapt.

The potential benefits and harms of AI have led to calls for governments to adapt quickly to the changes AI is already delivering and the potentially transformative changes to come. These include calls to pause AI development and for countries including the UK to deliver a step-change in regulation, potentially before the technology passes a point when such regulation can be effective. The chief executive of Google, **Sundar Pichai**, is one example of a leading technology figure who has warned about the potential harms of AI and called for a suitable regulatory framework.

AI should be tested robustly within established regulatory 'sandboxes' The use of sandboxes should be encouraged beyond a purely regulatory need. For example, to test the correct skills and registration requirements for AI assurance professionals and how best to engage with civic societies and other stakeholders on the challenges and opportunities presented by AI.

This is a fast-moving area and this briefing concentrates on reports published since the beginning of 2023. For an exploration of publications and milestones before this time, including the work of the House of Lords Committee on Artificial Intelligence, published in May 2022.

28.1 Regulations for AI

The regulation for artificial intelligence is the development of public sector policies and laws for promoting and regulating artificial intelligence (AI); it is therefore related to the broader regulation of algorithms. The regulatory and policy landscape for AI is an emerging issue in jurisdictions globally. According to AI Index at Stanford, the annual number of AI-related laws passed in the 127 survey countries jumped from one passed in 2016 to 37 passed in 2022 alone. Between 2016 and 2020, more than 30 countries adopted dedicated strategies for AI. Most EU member states had released national AI strategies, as had Canada, China, **India**, Japan, Mauritius, the Russian Federation, Saudi Arabia, United Arab Emirates, US and Vietnam. Other countries were in the process of elaborating their own AI strategy, including Bangladesh, Malaysia and Tunisia. The Global Partnership on Artificial Intelligence was launched in June 2020, stating a need for AI to be developed in accordance with human rights and democratic values, to ensure public confidence and trust in the technology. Henry Kissinger, Eric Schmidt, and Daniel Huttenlocher published a joint statement in November 2021 calling for a government commission to regulate AI. In 2023, OpenAI leaders published recommendations for the governance of superintelligence, which they believe may happen in less than 10 years. In 2023, the United Nations also launched an advisory body to provide recommendations on AI governance; the body comprises technology company executives, governments officials and academics.

In a 2022 Ipsos survey, attitudes towards AI varied greatly from country-to-country; 78% of Chinese citizens, but only 35% of Americans, agreed that "products and services using AI have more benefits than drawbacks". A 2023 Reuters/Ipsos poll found that 61% of Americans agree, and 22% disagree, that AI poses risks to humanity. In a 2023 Fox News poll, 35% of Americans thought it "very important", and an additional 41% thought it "somewhat important", for the federal government to regulate AI, versus 13% responding "not very important" and 8% responding "not at all important".

In January 2023, Massachusetts State Senator Barry Finegold and State Representative Josh S. Cutler proposed a bill partially written by ChatGPT, "An Act drafted with the help of ChatGPT to regulate generative artificial intelligence models like ChatGPT", which would require companies to disclose their algorithms and data collection practices to the office of the State Attorney General, arrange regular risk assessments, and contribute to the prevention of plagiarism. The bill was officially presented during a hearing on July 13, 2023.

In late March 2023, the Italian data protection authority banned ChatGPT in Italy and opened an investigation. Italian regulators assert that ChatGPT was exposing minors to age-inappropriate content, and that OpenAI's use of ChatGPT conversations as training data could violate Europe's General Data Protection Regulation. In April 2023, the ChatGPT ban was lifted in Italy. OpenAI said it has taken steps to effectively clarify and address the issues raised; an age verification tool was implemented to ensure users are at least 13 years old. Additionally, users can access its privacy policy before registration.

In November 2023, the first global AI Safety Summit was held in Bletchley Park in the UK to discuss the near and far-term risks of AI and the possibility of mandatory and voluntary regulatory frameworks. 28 countries including the United States, China, and the European Union issued a declaration at the start of the summit, calling for international cooperation to manage the challenges and risks of artificial intelligence.

Ethical guidelines and regulations are being established worldwide to ensure that AI is used responsibly. Initiatives like the European Union's AI Act and UNESCO's recommendations on

AI ethics demonstrate our commitment to harnessing AI for the common good while mitigating potential risks.

The fear that AI will lead to human extinction is largely unfounded and stems from a lack of understanding of historical trends and human resilience. While it's natural to fear the unknown, it's crucial to reflect on the robustness of the political and economic systems we have built. These systems are designed to withstand and adapt to changes, ensuring stability and progress.

Furthermore, the idea that a single leader or a small group of individuals could unleash AI to catastrophic ends is implausible. Our political and economic structures are complex and interdependent, making it difficult for reckless actions to go unchecked. Democratic processes, regulatory bodies, and international cooperation all serve as safeguards against such scenarios.

Aside from broader societal concerns regarding the proliferation and use of artificial intelligence (AI) in almost every aspect of daily life, the use of AI tools and work product in the financial services sector exposes market participants to a spectrum of risks that demand a robust compliance, governance and supervisory response. Unmitigated and uncontrolled AI risks could expose investment advisers regulated by the Securities and Exchange Commission to reputational, enforcement and examination liability based on regulatory concerns over breaches of fiduciary duty, ineffective cybersecurity protocols, failure to protect confidential client or investor information, inadequate portfolio and risk management practices, deficient vendor management oversight, and overall failures in the design, tailoring, testing, training and documentation of the firm's compliance program. The regulatory compliance, data analytics, cybersecurity, investigations and governance experts are uniquely equipped to assist in the identification and mitigation of risks related to the use of AI within SEC-registrants' ecosystems.

Firms also utilize AI to support their regulatory and compliance functions. For instance, they implement AI technologies to conduct surveillance of high-risk areas, such as suspicious trading, anti-money laundering activity and insider trading. In addition, firms use AI technologies to compile their regulatory reports on an automated or expedited basis. Their books and records obligations can also be simplified by AI tools, especially as electronic communications continue to proliferate across multiple mediums, such as email, text messaging, instant messaging and social media.

28.2   What Regulatory Changes are coming?

Leaders at the highest levels of government and in corporate America are tracking AI. In July 2023, President Joe Biden and top public company executives of leading AI providers committed to voluntarily mitigating AI risks, such as through robust public reporting. These companies have publicized their policies and practices for the responsible use of AI, mitigating AI-related risks and providing transparency to their end users. The National Institute of Standards and Technology issued voluntary guidelines for AI risk management and responsible practices across industries. Likewise, the SEC proposed new rules to police the risks generated by predicative data analytics. In a nutshell, the proposed rules would require certain SEC-regulated entities to eliminate or neutralize conflicts of interest, comply with new books and records requirements, and revise their policies and procedures. In October 2023, President Biden issued an Executive Order mandating that certain federal agencies and executive departments undertake actions to adhere to proscribed principles to ensure safe, secure and trustworthy development and use of AI. The Executive Order specifically identified financial services as an industry which needs to adhere to appropriate safeguards to protect Americans.

The SEC's initial proposed AI-related rules are just the tip of the iceberg of imminent regulatory changes. Like the SEC's past use of data analytics, it has been forecasted that the SEC staff may make greater use of AI to surveil and detect suspicious conduct, which may warrant opening an examination or investigation. It also sought additional funding from Congress to expand the SEC's 2024 budget for emerging AI technologies. Consistent with that message and budget request, the SEC staff is already examining how AI may affect investment analyses and decision-making. The SEC staff appears to be leaving no stone unturned. Recent SEC inquiries to firms address AI from all possible touch points: disclosures, investment modeling, marketing, policies and procedures, training, supervision, data security, trade errors and incident reports and investor risk tolerance evaluation. This approach underscores that the SEC might also expand its focus to other AI-related risks, such as those highlighted in an SEC risk alert concerning alternative data and material nonpublic information (MNPI).

28.3 What Are the Takeaways for Compliance Professionals?

Although certain industry groups publicly requested that the Stock Exchange withdraw its proposed AI-specific rules, chief compliance officers (CCOs) and compliance professionals should not wait for the its response to act. Firms must recognize that fiduciary, governance and other related laws and regulations in effect already apply to the firms' use, directly or indirectly, of AI technologies. As mentioned previously, AI presents internal- and external-facing legal, regulatory and reputational risks for firms. The good news is that CCOs and compliance professionals can mitigate such risks by proactively taking the following steps:

(i) **Mapping:** Conduct a comprehensive risk assessment of the firm's touchpoints with AI through thoughtful and thorough engagement internally and externally. Firms that are blind to their risks are particularly vulnerable. Pay particular attention to research tools and techniques that expose confidential client information to AI databases, and to the terms of use and privacy protection disclosures made by AI engines and vendors. Construct or include AI risks in the firm's compliance risk matrix, where such risks will be on the agenda for periodic testing.

(ii) Due diligence and vendor management: Evaluate and fully vet whether the firm's use of AI products or services from vendors employ adequate risk metrics, cybersecurity measures, threat resilience, data privacy protection, and other legal, regulatory or technological safeguards. Review contract terms to ensure that these vendors' standards align with the firm's compliance mandates. Implement supervisory measures to adequately manage and oversee vendors and contractors, including determining whether such suppliers and sub-suppliers are located in high-risk jurisdictions. Identify critical vendors and ensure that escalation steps are written into contractual agreements to ensure escalation in the event of operational failures, data errors or cybersecurity breaches. Negotiate assurances that datasets are obtained legally and are within the terms of use of information owners.

28.4   What is the Regulatory Landscape around AI?

In October 2022, The Bank of England (including the PRA) and the FCA published a Discussion Paper (DP5/22) requesting feedback on how the regulators can facilitate the safe and responsible adoption of AI in UK Financial Services. This was published in response to the AI Public-Private Forum (AIPPF) final report, which made clear that the private sector wants regulators to have a role in supporting the safe adoption of AI in UK financial services.

On 26 October 2023, the FCA and PRA published the feedback statement (FS2/23) which outlined the key responses to DP5/22. The Discussion Paper was published to initiate a debate about the risks of AI and how regulators could respond. Some of the key themes from the feedback include:

Respondents felt the current regulatory landscape on AI is fragmented and complex, and thus a synchronized approach and alignment amongst domestic and international regulators would be particularly helpful.

Many participants emphasized the need for more uniformity, especially when tackling data concerns like fairness, bias, and the management of protected characteristics.

Regulatory and supervisory attention should prioritize consumer outcomes, with a particular emphasis on ensuring fair and ethical outcomes.

Respondents noted that existing firm governance structures (and regulatory frameworks such as the Senior Managers and Certification Regime (SM&CR)) may be sufficient to address AI risks.

Looking ahead, by the end of 2023 the UK Parliament was expected to agree final text of the EU AI Act, with the regulators expected to produce further guidance by the end of March 2024.

28.5   What's next for AI in Financial Services?

It is evident that the role of AI will continue to grow, offering clear opportunities for firms to innovate, streamline processes, and amplify their competitive edge, amongst many others. As firms look to keep up with the competition in the race to deploy AI solutions, there are several significant risks that firms will need to manage, which if unchecked could lead to enhanced regulatory scrutiny, litigation, fines, and reputational damage. Therefore, establishing the right control environment and governance arrangements early is fundamental to manage the risks to AI.

28.6   Joint Report by Sir Tony Blair and Lord Hague of Richmond (June 2023)

On 13 June 2023, Sir Tony Blair, the former Labor Prime Minister, and William Hague (Lord Hague of Richmond), the former leader of the Conservative Party, released a joint report, 'A new national purpose: AI promises a world-leading future of Britain', which described AI as "the most important technology of our generation".

The authors said that getting policy right on this issue was therefore "fundamental" and contended that it could "define Britain's future". The report noted that the potential opportunities were "vast", including the potential to "change the shape of the state, the nature of science and augment the abilities of citizens". However, like others, the two former party leaders also noted that the risks were "profound".

As a result, the report called for urgent action, including a "radical new policy agenda and a reshaping of the state, with science and technology at its core". Noting that AI is already having an impact and that the pace of change is only likely to accelerate in the coming years, the authors contend that "our institutions are not configured to deal with science and technology, particularly their exponential growth". They said that it was "absolutely vital that this changes". This included a reorientation in the way government is organized, works with the private sector, promotes research, draws on expertise and receives advice.

To achieve this, the report offered specific recommendations including:

- Securing multi-decade investment in science-and-technology infrastructure as well as talent and research programmes by reprioritizing large amounts of capital expenditure to this task.

- Boosting how dissolving the AI Council and empowering the Foundation Model Taskforce by having it report directly to the prime minister.

- Sharpening the Office for Artificial Intelligence so that it provides better foresight function and agility for government to deal with technological change.

The report also contended that the UK could become a leader in the development of safe, reliable and cutting-edge AI, in collaboration with its allies. The authors contended that the UK has an "opportunity to construct effective regulation that goes well beyond existing proposals yet is also more attractive to talent and firms than the approach being adopted by the European Union".

Again, the report offered recommendations on how this could be achieved, including:

Creating Sentinel, a national laboratory effort focused on researching and testing safe AI, with the aim of becoming the "brain" for both a UK and an international AI regulator. Sentinel would recognize that effective regulation and control is and will likely remain an ongoing research problem, requiring an unusually close combination of research and regulation.

Finally, the report contended that the UK could pioneer the deployment and use of AI technology in the real world, "building next-generation companies and creating a 21st century strategic state". To achieve this, the report recommended:

- Launching major AI talent programs, including international recruitment and the creation of polymath fellowships to allow top non-AI researchers to learn AI as well as leading AI researchers to learn non-AI fields and cross-fertilize ideas.

- Requiring a tiered-access approach to compute provision under which access to larger amounts of compute comes with additional requirements to demonstrate responsible use.

- Requiring generative-AI companies to label the synthetic media they produce as **deepfakes** and social-media platforms to remove unlabeled deepfakes.

- Building AI-era infrastructure, including compute capacity and remodeling data, as a public asset with the creation of highly valuable, public-good datasets.

The report added that it was "critical to engage the public throughout all of these developments" to ensure AI development is accountable and give people the skills and chance to adapt.

28.7 Proposed Regulatory Approaches: UK

(i) UK government approach to artificial intelligence

On 22 September 2021, the government published its 'National AI strategy', setting out its ten-year plan on AI. The strategy set out three high-level aims:

- invest and plan for the long-term needs of the AI ecosystem to continue our leadership as a science and AI superpower;

- support the transition to an AI-enabled economy, capturing the benefits of innovation in the UK, and ensuring AI benefits all sectors and regions;

- ensure the UK gets the national and international governance of AI technologies right to encourage innovation, investment, and protect the public and our fundamental values.

The Office for Artificial Intelligence, a unit within the Department for Science, Innovation and Technology (DSIT), is responsible for overseeing the implementation of the national AI strategy. There is also an AI Council, a non-statutory expert committee of independent members set up to provide advice to the government.

In July 2022, the government published a consultation paper on establishing a "pro-innovation" approach to AI. This was followed in March 2023 by a white paper and further consultation exercise, which contain several principles and proposals for regulatory reform which are discussed in detail in section 4.3 of this briefing.

(ii) Current regulatory environment for AI in the UK

The government argues that the UK is in a strong position to benefit from the development of AI "due to our reputation for high-quality regulators and our strong approach to the rule of law, supported by our technology-neutral legislation and regulations".

Ministers contend that UK laws, regulators and courts already address some of the emerging risks posed by AI technologies.

However, they also concede that, while AI is currently regulated through existing legal frameworks like financial services regulation, some AI risks have arisen and will arise across, or in the gaps between, existing regulatory remits.

The government provides the following evaluation of where such risks might exist and how they could potentially be mitigated:

(iii) Example of legal coverage of AI in the UK and potential gaps

"Discriminatory outcomes that result from the use of AI may contravene the protections set out in the Equality Act 2010. AI systems are also required by data protection law to process personal data fairly. However, AI can increase the risk of unfair bias or discrimination across a range of indicators or characteristics. This could undermine public trust in AI.

Product safety laws ensure that goods manufactured and placed on the market in the UK are safe. Product-specific legislation (such as for electrical and electronic equipment, medical devices, and toys) may apply to some products that include integrated AI. However, safety risks specific to AI technologies should be monitored closely. As the capability and adoption of AI increases, it may pose new and substantial risks that are unaddressed by existing rules.

Consumer rights law may protect consumers where they have entered into a sales contract for AI-based products and services. Certain contract terms (for example, that goods are of satisfactory quality, fit for a particular purpose, and as described) are relevant to consumer contracts. Similarly, businesses are prohibited from including certain terms in consumer contracts. Tort law provides a complementary regime that may provide redress where a civil wrong has caused harm. It is not yet clear whether consumer rights law will provide the right level of protection in the context of products that include integrated AI or services based on AI, or how tort law may apply to fill any gap in consumer rights law protection."

In response to the 2022 consultation exercise cited above, the government reported that those working in the AI sector said that "conflicting or uncoordinated requirements from regulators create unnecessary burdens and that regulatory gaps may leave risks unmitigated, harming public trust and slowing AI adoption".

Further, the government said that respondents to the consultation had highlighted that, if regulators were not proportionate and aligned in their regulation of AI, "businesses may have to spend excessive time and money complying with complex rules instead of creating new technologies". Noting that small businesses and start-ups often do not have the resources to do both and the prevalence of such firms in the sector, the government argued that it was "important to ensure that regulatory burdens do not fall disproportionately on smaller companies, which play an essential role in the AI innovation ecosystem and act as engines for economic growth and job creation".

(iv) Proposals for future regulatory reform: Government white paper

The government's proposals for future regulatory reform were set out in the March 2023 white paper, 'A pro-innovation approach to AI regulation'.

Noting that across the world countries and regions were beginning to draft the rules for AI, the white paper said that the UK "needs to act quickly to continue to lead the international conversation on AI governance and demonstrate the value of our pragmatic, proportionate regulatory approach".

The white paper said that the government recognized both the rewards and risks of AI:

While we should capitalize on the benefits of these technologies, we should also not overlook the new risks that may arise from their use, nor the unease that the complexity of AI technologies can produce in the wider public. We already know that some uses of AI could damage our physical and mental health, infringe on the privacy of individuals and undermine human rights.

Public trust in AI will be undermined unless these risks, and wider concerns about the potential for bias and discrimination, are addressed. By building trust, we can accelerate the adoption of AI across the UK to maximize the economic and social benefits that the technology can deliver, while attracting investment and stimulating the creation of high-skilled AI jobs. In order to maintain the UK's position as a global AI leader, we need to ensure that the public continues to see how the benefits of AI can outweigh the risks.

The white paper said that responding to risk and building public trust were important drivers for regulation, but that clear and consistent regulation could also support business investment and build confidence in innovation.

Consequently, it said that the government would put in place a new framework to bring "clarity and coherence" to the AI regulatory landscape, which will harness AI's ability to drive growth and prosperity and increase public trust in its use and application. In taking a "deliberately agile and iterative approach", the government said that its framework was "designed to build the evidence base so that we can learn from experience and continuously adapt to develop the best possible regulatory regime".

That framework is underpinned by five principles to "guide and inform the responsible development and use of AI in all sectors of the economy". These are:

- safety, security and robustness;

- appropriate transparency and explainability;

- fairness;

- accountability and governance;

- contestability and redress.

On whether new legislation would be introduced to support these aims, the white paper said:

"We will not put these principles on a statutory footing initially. New rigid and onerous legislative requirements on businesses could hold back AI innovation and reduce our ability to respond quickly and in a proportionate way to future technological advances. Instead, the principles will be issued on a non-statutory basis and implemented by existing regulators. This approach makes use of regulators' domain-specific expertise to tailor the implementation of the principles to the specific context in which AI is used. During the initial period of implementation, we will continue to collaborate with regulators to identify any barriers to the proportionate application of the principles, and evaluate whether the non-statutory framework is having the desired effect."

However, the paper also added that "following this initial period of implementation", the government anticipated introducing a statutory duty on regulators requiring them to have due regard to the principles. The paper added:

Some feedback from regulators, industry and academia suggested we should implement further measures to support the enforcement of the framework. A duty requiring regulators to have regard to the principles should allow regulators the flexibility to exercise judgement when applying the principles in particular contexts, while also strengthening their mandate to implement them. In line with our proposal to work collaboratively with regulators and take an adaptable approach, we will not move to introduce such a statutory duty if our monitoring of the framework shows that implementation is effective without the need to legislate.

Regarding the potential gaps between the remits of various regulators identified above, the white paper noted that the 2022 AI consultation paper proposed a small coordination layer within the regulatory architecture. However, the white paper noted that, while industry and civil society were reportedly supportive of the intention to ensure coherence across the AI regulatory framework, "feedback often argued strongly for greater central coordination to support regulators on issues requiring cross-cutting collaboration and ensure that the overall regulatory framework functions as intended".

Consequently, the white paper said that the government had identified several central support functions required to make sure that the overall framework offers a "proportionate but effective" response to risk while promoting innovation across the regulatory landscape. These were:

Monitoring and evaluation of the overall regulatory framework's effectiveness and the implementation of the principles, including the extent to which implementation supports innovation. This will allow us to remain responsive and adapt the framework if necessary, including where it needs to be adapted to remain effective in the context of developments in AI's capabilities and the state of the art.

- Assessing and monitoring risks across the economy arising from AI.

- Conducting horizon-scanning and gap analysis, including by convening industry, to inform a coherent response to emerging AI technology trends.

- Supporting testbeds and sandbox initiatives to help AI innovators get new technologies to market.

- Providing education and awareness to give clarity to businesses and empower citizens to make their voices heard as part of the ongoing iteration of the framework.

- Promoting interoperability with international regulatory frameworks.

The white paper said that these functions would not entail the creation of a new AI regulator:

The central support functions will initially be provided from within government but will leverage existing activities and expertise from across the broader economy. The activities described above will neither replace nor duplicate the work undertaken by regulators and will not involve the creation of a new AI regulator.

The white paper included a consultation exercise on the proposals, which ran for 12 weeks until 21 June 2023. The government is yet to publish an analysis of the responses received.

The government has already moved to dissolve the AI Council, as reported in the Times on 19 June 2023. It will be replaced by a new foundation model taskforce led by technology entrepreneur Ian Hogarth, which will spearhead the adoption and regulation of the technology in the UK. A statement released on 7 July 2023 by the Department of Science, Innovation and Technology said, with the terms of the current council members finishing, it would establish a wider group of expert advisers.

Since it was established in 2019, the AI Council has advised government on AI policy with regards to national security, defence, data ethics, skills, and regulation, which has played a key role in developing landmark policies including the National AI Strategy, and the recent AI regulation white paper. The council also supported the government's early **Covid-19 efforts**, highlighting the immediate needs of the AI startup ecosystem and facilitating rapid intelligence-gathering that shaped government support for the tech sector in its pandemic response.

With the terms of the AI Council members coming to an end, the Department for Science, Innovation and Technology is establishing a wider group of expert advisers to input on a range of priority issues across the department, including artificial intelligence. This will complement the recently established foundation model taskforce, which will drive forward critical work on AI safety and research.

The task-force has been given £100mn to develop a British foundational generative AI model akin to ChatGPT to be used in the health service and elsewhere.

Prime Minister Rishi Sunak has also announced that the UK will host a global summit on safety in artificial intelligence in the autumn. Writing in the Guardian in June 2023, Dan Milmo and Kiran Stacey argued that this marked a distinct "change of tone" from the government, with ministers going from talking predominately about the benefits of AI to the risks of such innovation. In addition to the different regulatory regimes discussed in section 5 of this briefing, the Guardian article also reports that the G7 have agreed to create an intergovernmental forum called the 'Hiroshima AI process' to debate issues around these fast-growing tools.

(v) Individual sectoral guidance on the use of artificial intelligence

Organizations within the public and private sectors are evaluating how to respond to AI and some have produced guidance on that approach. For example, the Cabinet Office published guidance on the use of generative AI by civil servants, particularly LLMs, on 29 June 2023.

Similarly, in March 2023, the Department for Education issued guidance on the use of generative AI in pre-university education. Noting that the technology provided both risks and opportunities for the sector, the key principles outlined in that document stated that educational institutions must continue to guard against misuse whilst seeking to take advantage of these benefits.

This was followed in June 2023 by the Russell Group of universities publishing a guidance note on the use of generative AI in higher education. Again, the perspective of the Russell Group was not that generative AI tools should be banned, but that universities would support staff and students to become AI literate whilst using these technologies ethically:

Our universities wish to ensure that generative AI tools can be used for the benefit of students and staff—enhancing teaching practices and student learning experiences, ensuring students develop skills for the future within an ethical framework, and enabling educators to benefit from efficiencies to develop innovative methods of teaching.

28.8 Other Regulatory Approaches: Examples from around the World

28.8.1 European Union

In contrast to the UK, the European Commission is proposing a 'horizontal' and 'risks-based' means of regulating, meaning that it plans to provide rules for AI across all sectors and applications focused on the anticipated risk of such innovations.

In April 2021, the European Commission proposed the AI Act, draft legislation setting out rules for governing AI within the EU. The AI Act would establish four levels of risk for AI: unacceptable risk, high risk, limited risk, and minimal risk. Different rules apply depending on the level of risk a system poses to fundamental rights.

The European Commission suggests that those risk categories would work in the following ways:

(i) Unacceptable risk

All AI systems considered a clear threat to the safety, livelihoods and rights of people will be banned, from social scoring by governments to toys using voice assistance that encourages dangerous behavior.

(ii) High risk

AI systems identified as high-risk include AI technology used in:

- critical infrastructures (e.g., transport), that could put the life and health of citizens at risk;

- educational or vocational training, that may determine the access to education and professional course of someone's life (e.g., scoring of exams);

- safety components of products (e.g., AI application in robot-assisted surgery);

- employment, management of workers and access to self-employment (e.g., CV-sorting software for recruitment procedures);

- essential private and public services (e.g., credit scoring denying citizens opportunity to obtain a loan);

- law enforcement that may interfere with people's fundamental rights (e.g., evaluation of the reliability of evidence);

- migration, asylum and border control management (e.g., verification of authenticity of travel documents);

- administration of justice and democratic processes (e.g., applying the law to a concrete set of facts).

High-risk AI systems will be subject to strict obligations before they can be put on the market:

- adequate risk assessment and mitigation systems;

- high quality of the datasets feeding the system to minimize risks and discriminatory outcomes;

- logging of activity to ensure traceability of results;

- detailed documentation providing all information necessary on the system and its purpose for authorities to assess its compliance;

- clear and adequate information to the user;

- appropriate human oversight measures to minimize risk;

- high level of robustness, security and accuracy.

All remote biometric identification systems are considered high risk and subject to strict requirements. The use of remote biometric identification in publicly accessible spaces for law enforcement purposes is, in principle, prohibited.

Narrow exceptions are strictly defined and regulated, such as when necessary to search for a missing child, to prevent a specific and imminent terrorist threat or to detect, locate, identify or prosecute a perpetrator or suspect of a serious criminal offence.

Such use is subject to authorization by a judicial or other independent body and to appropriate limits in time, geographic reach and the data bases searched.

(iii) Limited risk

Limited risk refers to AI systems with specific transparency obligations. When using AI systems such as chatbots, users should be aware that they are interacting with a machine so they can take an informed decision to continue or step back.

(iv) Minimal or no risk

This proposal allows the free use of minimal-risk AI. This includes applications such as AI-enabled video games or spam filters. The vast majority of AI systems currently used in the EU fall into this category.

These proposals are intended to provide a "future proof" approach, allowing rules to adapt to technological change. The European Commission also said that all "AI applications should remain trustworthy even after they have been placed on the market", requiring ongoing quality and risk management by providers.

However, the draft legislation has been amended by the EU Council and European Parliament, reportedly after concerns that technology such as **ChatGPT**, which has a large number of potential uses, could have a correspondingly large variety of risk thresholds. Politico notes efforts to reform the draft AI Act by its original proposers, and reports on the resistance in some areas to those changes:

- In February [2023] the lead lawmakers on the AI Act, it was proposed that AI systems generating complex texts without human oversight should be part of the "high-risk" list—an effort to stop ChatGPT from churning out disinformation at scale.

The idea was met with skepticism by right-leaning political groups in the European Parliament. Axel Voss, a prominent centre-right lawmaker who has a formal say over Parliament's position, said that the amendment "would make numerous activities high-risk, that are not risky at all".

In contrast, activists and observers feel that the proposal was just scratching the surface of the general-purpose AI conundrum. "It's not great to just put text-making systems on the high-risk list: you have other general-purpose AI systems that present risks and also ought to be regulated".

In May 2023, the European Parliament reported that MEPs had amended the list of those systems which pose an unacceptable level of risk to people's safety to include bans on intrusive and discriminatory uses of AI systems such as "real-time" remote biometric identification systems in publicly accessible spaces. They also expanded the classification of high-risk areas to include harm to people's health, safety, fundamental rights or the environment. They also added AI systems to **influence voters** in political campaigns and in recommender systems used by social media platforms to the high-risk list.

In addition, changes included obligations for providers of foundation models, who would have to guarantee protection of fundamental rights, health and safety and the environment, democracy and rule of law. They would need to assess and mitigate risks, comply with design, information and environmental requirements and register in the EU database. Generative foundation models, like ChatGPT, would have to comply with additional transparency requirements, like disclosing that the content was generated by AI, designing the model to prevent it from generating illegal content and publishing summaries of copyrighted data used for training.

The final text of the AI act was set to be agreed by late 2023 or early 2024. In addition to the AI Act, the EU has already passed several pieces of legislation such as the Digital Services Act (DSA) and Digital Markets Act (DMA), and alongside the AI Act is developing a civil liability framework on adapting liability rules to the digital age and AI, and revising sectoral safety legislation (such as regulations governing the use of machinery, artificial intelligence and autonomous robots).

In its own assessment of the differences between the UK and EU regime, the UK government's white paper said:

"The EU has grounded its approach in the product safety regulation of the single market, and as such has set out a relatively fixed definition in its legislative proposals. Whilst such an approach can support efforts to harmonize rules across multiple countries, we do not believe this approach is right for the UK. We do not think that it captures the full application of AI and its regulatory implications. Our concern is that this lack of granularity could hinder innovation."

28.8.2 United States of America

Writing in April 2023, Alex Engler at the Brookings Institute contends that the US federal government's approach to AI risk management can broadly be characterized as risk-based, sectorally specific, and highly distributed across federal agencies. Mr. Engler suggests that, while there are advantages to this approach, it also contributes to the uneven development of AI policies. He argues that, while there are several guiding federal documents from the White House on AI harms, "they have not created an even or consistent federal approach to AI risks".

At the same time, Mr. Engler notes that the US has invested in non-regulatory infrastructure, such as a new AI risk management framework, evaluations of facial recognition software, and extensive funding of AI research.

Comparing the approach taken by the US and the European Union, Mr. Engler notes that the EU approach to AI risk management, as outlined in section 5.1, is characterized by a more comprehensive range of legislation tailored to specific digital environments. He adds that this has led to more differences than similarities between the two approaches:

The EU and US strategies share a conceptual alignment on a risk-based approach, agree on key principles of trustworthy AI, and endorse an important role for international standards. However, the specifics of these AI risk management regimes have more differences than similarities. Regarding many specific AI applications, especially those related to socioeconomic processes and online platforms, the EU and US are on a path to significant misalignment.

The EU-US Trade and Technology Council has demonstrated early success working on AI, especially on a project to develop a common understanding of metrics and methodologies for trustworthy AI. Through these negotiations, the EU and US have also agreed to work collaboratively on international AI standards, while also jointly studying emerging risks of AI and applications of new AI technologies.

For Mr. Engler, more collaboration between international partners will be crucial, as governments implement the policies that will be foundational to the democratic governance of AI.

SECTION VII

ARTIFICIAL CONSCIOUSNESS

CHAPTER 29

ARTIFICIAL CONSCIOUSNESS

29.1 What is Consciousness?

The English word "conscious"; is originally derived from the Latin conscius (con- together"; and scio "to know";), but the Latin word did not have the same meaning as the word - it meant "knowing with"; in other words, "having joint or common knowledge with another".

Google meaning of consciousness is: the fact of awareness by the mind of itself and the world.

A man is distinguished above all animals by his self-consciousness, by which he is a rational animal.

Both the world of matter and the world of mental phenomena, such as thought, are determined by consciousness. In addition to the material and the mental spheres (which together form the immanent reality, or the world of manifestation), idealism posits a transcendent, archetypal realm of ideas as the source of material and mental phenomena. It is important to recognize that monistic idealism is, as its name implies, a unitary philosophy; any subdivisions, such as the immanent and the transcendent, are within consciousness. Thus, consciousness is the only ultimate reality.

29.1.1 Consciousness has four different aspects:

(i) First, there is the field of consciousness, sometimes referred to as the mind-field or global workspace. This is what is called 'awareness'.

(ii) Second, there are objects of consciousness, such as thoughts and feelings, that arise and pass away in this field.

(iii) Third, there is a subject of consciousness, the experiencer and/or witness (the conscious self with which we identify.)

(iv) Fourth, in monistic idealism, we speak of consciousness as the ground of all being.

Consciousness is defined by some experts as the 'awareness of awareness' or self-awareness. According to Adi Shankara (700-750 CE), Consciousness is awareness, knowledge and intelligence. According to him, "Consciousness is Awareness of Reality" and "Awareness of Reality is Consciousness". The real experiencer is not the mind, but myself, the light in which everything appears. Self is the common factor at the root of all experience, the awareness in which everything happens. The entire field of consciousness is only as a film, or a speck, in 'I am'. This 'I am-ness' is, being conscious of consciousness, being aware of itself. And it is indescribable, because it has no attributes. It is only being myself, and being myself is all that there is. Everything that exists, exists as myself.

One of the most transcendental contributions is the experience of the consciousness-witness, that is, the consciousness free of psycho-mental and physical attachments and from their individual genetic and cultural conditionings. Whereas the consciousness is involved in the thoughts, the mind seems to have its own autonomy, but when we stop paying attention to all the thoughts, we just find out that the mind is not our ultimate reality: there is life beyond the mind. We all experience the fact of thinking; we can even witness thinking, that is, be aware that we are thinking. But we can go one step further when we are aware that we are aware. In that moment, a loop occurs that stops the mental flow and makes us remain in a state of self-consciousness or pure awareness. There are no thoughts or, should any remain, it is seen with an absolute disregard and neutrality. But we immediately realize as well our inability to remain stable in such a state, because thoughts require our attention. Well, that state of individual consciousness "it is me", free from thoughts, is what, in religious terminology, is defined as "soul" and constitutes the door or preliminary toward the state of universal and unlimited consciousness "I am", which is defined as "spirit", "heart", "the centre of the soul" or "God". And it is called God because such a consciousness "I am" is the original source where duality arises from, that is, God-world, Creator-Creation. This fact explains that the name of the God Brahma comes from brahm-aham, literally "I am". Thus, the mahāvākya or "great saying" "I am Brahman" (Bṛhadāraṇyaka Upanishad 1.4.10) precisely means, "I am I am".

29.2   Ancient Hindu Perspectives about Consciousness

The earliest known organized study of consciousness and of practices working with it can be traced to ancient Indian Hindu Vedic religion written thousands of years ago. Many would argue that never has there been such detailed and elaborated activity on the part of human consciousness to understand itself and its relation to a larger context where consciousness is presented as more central than material existence to the nature, composition, and processes comprising all of reality. One might even venture to say that this Vedic period was the high point to-date in human history with regard to our study of the nature of consciousness and the ways with which it may be worked.

To give just a few examples from this Vedic period, and using the original Sanskrit terms and concepts: *Akasha* is depicted as the primordial, non-physical ether underlying and permeating all that exists, and the akasha itself is one mode whereby the universal consciousness manifests itself. Even as recently as late in the 19th and early 20th century physics, the concept of an ether still existed among mainstream scientists, although by that point it had become an inanimate, not an animate, conscious underlying substance/ being. *Atman* is the Vedic concept of individual human soul, spirit, or essence, while *Brahman* is the universal version of such spirit or essence.

Maya is the term for the illusory physical world, which is not considered primary reality, but it is something within which the primary reality of our individual consciousnesses can become entrapped and conditioned, which, in the process, keeps us away from any direct experience or understanding of what underlies the sensory materialist veil of Maya. *Nirvana* is the transcendental ineffable state beyond the self and its experience of the consciousness and is seen to be the ultimate transcendental goal and state to which all individualized beings may eventually return. *Karma* refers to the universal process whereby our individual actions have repercussions beyond the present, and which may also involve the after-life, between-lives period that follows the earthly life, which, in turn, relates to the concept of reincarnation. And *Siddhis* were the often miraculous-seeming powers and abilities, the human spirit could be developed through yogic practices.

First, we know the Self–the individual Self, the jivatman–and then we are enabled to know the

Supreme Self, the Paramatman: Brahman; and the Self we will know is itself:

(i) **Immutable.** Eternally changeless, incapable of being either diminished or increased, for it is one with the Infinite.

(ii) **Pure.** Ever only itself, never really being influenced or changed by anything whatsoever. Untainted by any contact, for it is untouchable.

(iii) **Shadowless.** The Self is Pure Light within which there is no shadow of darkness or differentiation. It is always exactly what it is.

(iv) **Bodiless.** It is perfectly non-dual. It is neither inside or outside of anything. It cannot be contained. It is absolutely one, having nothing appended to it or necessary to it.

(v) **Colour-less.** It has no "qualities" or "characteristics" but is always I AM. The three gunas are not present in it, nor are any gradations of any kind. It is indescribable. All we can really say about it is what it is not. All of these terms indicate that the Self is the same as Brahman. And the Self that knows its Self–Brahman, "wherein live the mind, the senses, the pranas, the elements"–does in truth come to know all things and the Self in all things.

(vi) Omniscience and Omnipresence are experienced by that liberated spirit who knows its oneness with The All.

Atman in Sanskrit literature means "real self"; of the individual, "innermost essence", and soul.

Atman, in Hinduism, is considered as eternal, imperishable, beyond time, "not the same as body or mind or consciousness, but is something beyond which permeates all these". In Advaita (nondual) Vedanta, it is "pure, undifferentiated, self-shining consciousness"; the witness- consciousness which observes all phenomena yet is not touched by it.

29.3   Cognitive Ability

The ability to read, listen, remember, reason, hold attention is known as Cognitive ability. These abilities help to collect and process information and execute information. It also saves this information so that it can retrieve the information for later actions. Developing Cognitive abilities help to process information more quickly and efficiently and ensures that the information is understood and interpreted effectively.

Cognitive abilities are categorized into **nine sections**. Each of these skills helps interpret the data effectively and use the data for further actions. **Aspects of Cognitive abilities are:**

(i)   Selective attention,

(ii) Sustained attention,

(iii) Logic and reasoning,

(iv) Long-term memory,

(v) Divided attention,

(vi) Auditory processing,

(vii) Working memory,

(viii) Visual processing, and

(ix) Processing speed.

29.4   Artificial Consciousness

As there are many hypothesized types of consciousness, there are many potential implementations of **artificial consciousness**. In the philosophical literature, perhaps the most common taxonomy of consciousness is into "access" and "phenomenal" variants. Access consciousness concerns those aspects of experience that can be apprehended, while phenomenal consciousness concerns those aspects of experience that seemingly cannot be apprehended, instead being characterized qualitatively in terms of "raw feels", "what it is like" or qualia.

In his article **"Artificial Consciousness**: Utopia or Real Possibility,"** Giorgio Buttazzo says that a common objection to **artificial consciousness** is that "Working in a fully automated mode, they [the computers] cannot exhibit creativity, unreprogrammation (which means can no longer be reprogrammed, from rethinking), emotions, or free will. A computer, like a washing machine, is a slave operated by its components."

For other theorists (e.g., functionalists), who define mental states in terms of causal roles, any system that can instantiate the same pattern of causal roles, regardless of physical constitution, will instantiate the same mental states, including consciousness.

Bernard Baars and others argue **there are various aspects of consciousness necessary for a machine to be artificially conscious.** The functions of consciousness suggested by Baars are: Definition and Context Setting, Adaptation and Learning, Editing, Flagging and Debugging, Recruiting and Control, Prioritizing and Access-Control, Decision-making or Executive Function, Analogy-forming Function, Metacognitive and Self-monitoring Function, and Auto-programming and Self-maintenance Function. Igor Aleksander suggested 12 principles for **artificial consciousness:** The Brain is a State Machine, Inner Neuron Partitioning, Conscious and Unconscious States, Perceptual Learning and Memory, Prediction, The Awareness of Self, Representation of Meaning, Learning Utterances, Learning Language, Will, Instinct, and Emotion. The aim of **artificial Consciousness** is to define whether and how these and other aspects of consciousness can be synthesized in an engineered artifact such as a digital computer.

Learning is also considered necessary for **artificial consciousness**. Per Bernard Baars, conscious experience is needed to represent and adapt to novel and significant events. Per Axel Cleeremans and Luis Jiménez, learning is defined as "a set of philogenetically advanced adaptation processes that critically depend on an evolved sensitivity to subjective experience so as to enable agents to afford flexible control over their actions in complex, unpredictable environments".

Relationships between real world states are mirrored in the state structure of a conscious organism, enabling the organism to predict events. An artificially conscious machine should be able to anticipate events correctly in order to be ready to respond to them when they occur or to take preemptive action to avert anticipated events. The implication here is that the machine needs flexible, real-time components that build spatial, dynamic, statistical, functional, and cause-effect models of the real world and predicted worlds, making it possible to demonstrate that it possesses **artificial consciousness** in the present and future and not only in the past. In order to do this, a conscious machine should make coherent predictions and contingency plans, not only in worlds with fixed rules like a chess board, but also for novel environments that may change, to be executed only when appropriate to simulate and control the real world.

Self-awareness in robots is being investigated by Junichi Takeno at Meiji University in Japan. Takeno is asserting that he has developed a robot capable of discriminating between a self-image in a mirror and any other having an identical image to it. Takeno asserts that he first contrived the computational module called a MoNAD, which has a self-aware function, and he then constructed the **artificial consciousness** system by formulating the relationships between emotions, feelings and reason by connecting the modules in a hierarchy. Takeno completed a mirror image cognition experiment using a robot equipped with the MoNAD system. Takeno proposed the Self-Body Theory stating that "humans feel that their own mirror image is closer to themselves than an actual part of themselves." The most important point in developing **artificial consciousness** or clarifying human consciousness is the development of a function of self-awareness, and he claims that he has demonstrated physical and mathematical evidence for this in his thesis. He also demonstrated that robots can study episodes in memory where the emotions were stimulated and use this experience to take predictive actions to prevent the recurrence of unpleasant emotions.

In his foundational paper on machine intelligence, Alan Turing [1950] did the emerging field of artificial intelligence (AI) a great service. At the time, just a few years after the construction of the first electronic digital computers, there was a lot of discussion about whether or not a machine could think or have a mind. Turing found questions like these to be "too meaningless to deserve discussion", and instead proposed what we today call the **Turing Test** as the criterion for machine intelligence. While this specific criterion has faced well-deserved criticism in contemporary AI, Turing's basic notion that we should judge whether a machine is intelligent based on its behavior, rather than on vaguely defined concepts such as the existence of an underlying mind, was liberating and persists as the dominant paradigm in AI to this day. In a very real sense Turing's approach made research into AI respectable. This is because the idea of machine intelligence as per Turing only refers to whether a machine can exhibit intelligent behavior, and does not represent a claim to having created a machine that has subjective mental experiences, can think, or have a mind. Avoiding these latter difficult issues has to a great extent enabled the pursuit of and substantial successes of AI as a technology. On the other hand, an additional consequence of this dominant viewpoint is that, with very few exceptions, it has largely sidelined the work in AI on challenging issues surrounding the possibility of an artificial mind or a conscious machine. Many AI researchers find such issues to be uninteresting or insufficiently well-defined to be of any relevance to AI. As a result, the field of **artificial consciousness** has largely developed outside of mainstream AI. In our opinion this is regrettable because there is substantial room for synergistic work in these two fields. We have previously considered the issue of how work in AI might contribute to advancing **artificial consciousness**. Our central point in this regard is that a computational explanatory gap currently limits our ability to advance work in **artificial consciousness**. The computational explanatory gap is our lack of understanding of how consciously accessible high-level cognitive information processing can be mapped onto low-level neural computations. The computational explanatory gap is a purely computational issue and not a mind-brain problem - it is a gap in our understanding of how cognitive algorithms (executive control, goal-directed problem solving, planning, etc.) can be mapped into the sub-symbolic computations supported by neural networks that use a distributed representation of information. This issue is clearly relevant to AI in general, and encouragingly increasing attention is being paid to it in studying "programmable neural networks. The computational explanatory gap also makes cognitively-oriented models in AI much more relevant to **artificial consciousness** than is often recognized, especially given the philosophical concept of cognitive phenomenology. Having previously considered how work in AI may contribute to **artificial consciousness**, here we address the converse question: How might concepts developed via work in **artificial consciousness** and consciousness studies in general enhance the functionality of AI systems?

In 2011, Michael Graziano and Sabine Kastler published a paper named "Human consciousness and its relationship to social neuroscience: A novel hypothesis" proposing a theory of consciousness as an attention schema. Graziano went on to publish an expanded discussion of this theory in his book "Consciousness and the Social Brain". This Attention Schema Theory of Consciousness, as he named it, proposes that the brain tracks attention to various sensory inputs by way of an attention schema, analogous to the well-studied body schema that tracks the spatial place of a person's body. This relates to **artificial consciousness** by proposing a specific mechanism of information handling, that produces what we allegedly experience and describe as consciousness, and which should be able to be duplicated by a machine using current technology. When the brain finds that person X is aware of thing Y, it is in effect modeling the state in which person X is applying an attentional enhancement to Y. In the attention schema theory, the same process can be applied to oneself. The brain tracks attention to various sensory inputs, and one's own awareness is a schematized model of one's attention. Graziano proposes specific locations in the brain for this process, and suggests that such awareness is a computed feature constructed by an expert system in the brain.

29.5   What is the Function of Human Consciousness?

We approach the question of what consciousness might contribute to AI systems by first asking what its function is in human cognition, and then exploring whether such functionality might provide/ improve similar, currently-absent/limited functionality in machine intelligence. This of course presumes that consciousness does have a biological function, an assumption that we make here. While this assumption is controversial, with some arguing that consciousness is just an epiphenomenon, we note that the evolution of consciousness in at least humans and some animal species supports the idea that it contributes to survivability and reproductive fitness, and we explore the consequences. There is no shortage of past hypotheses concerning the function(s) of human consciousness. Here we take asserting that something is a function of consciousness to implicitly indicate that a causal relationship is involved: that consciousness causes and is in large part necessary for that function. Many AC investigators have hesitated to make such causal claims and have instead proposed neural or computational correlates of consciousness. A neural correlate of consciousness is a minimal neurobiological state whose presence is sufficient for the occurrence of a corresponding state of consciousness. A computational correlate of consciousness is a minimal computational mechanism that is specifically associated with conscious aspects of cognition but not with unconscious aspects. Being a function of consciousness implies being a correlate of consciousness, but not vice versa. With this understanding we now give a non-exhaustive listing of functions of consciousness previously proposed in the literature, ordered arbitrarily: global access to and integration of information, symbol grounding [Chella, 2008; Kuipers, 2008; Haikonen, 2019] high-level symbolic cognition supports executive functions error detection and correction, novelty detection and generation, self-awareness/modeling, source of intrinsic motivation, evoking/informing volitional actions, attention mechanisms, and control.

The large number of these past hypotheses is remarkable, but is consistent with the sizable number of theories about the nature of consciousness. This is ameliorated somewhat by the fact that these hypotheses are generally not mutually exclusive or independent (e.g., symbol grounding and inference, and it could be that consciousness has multiple functions. Our point here is that, at the present time, there is no clear consensus on an identifiable function of consciousness that provides an adaptive advantage. For example, several of the potential functions of consciousness listed above have been criticized on various grounds due to inconsistency with empirical data or theoretical considerations.

29.6 Memory, Learning and Consciousness

Contemporary AI recognizes that intelligent agents can be composed of multiple functional components, some of which deal with the processing of information (reflexive condition-action rules, symbolic reasoning, executive decision making, taking actions, etc.) and some of which deal with the memory and learning of information. From this AI perspective, it is striking that the diverse list of previously proposed functions of consciousness in the preceding section generally have one thing in common: They largely deal with some facet of the processing of information (its integration, manipulation, use for inference or decision making, etc.). In contrast, here we propose an alternative, complementary possibility that the adaptive function of human consciousness is to be found in its contribution to memory and learning rather than to the subsequent processing of that information. Specifically, we hypothesize that the fundamental function of consciousness and its contribution to intelligence will most likely be found in its role in supporting short-term working memory and its associated learning and control mechanisms. Psychologists distinguish different memory systems in explaining various neuroscientific and behavioral data. Human memory at the top level is typically characterized in terms of long-term memory versus short-term memory. Long-term memory is often sub-divided into distinguishable types, such as semantic, episodic, and procedural memory, and we do not consider these further. Short-term memory is also sub-divided into types, one of which is working memory and that serves as our focus here. Working memory stores recently experienced information, typically for a period of seconds to minutes, that is being used in problem solving or other cognitive activities. In contrast to long-term memory with its enormous storage capacity, short-term memory is characterized by a very limited capacity, and is able to retain just a few independent items at any one time.

Why focus on working memory as a function of consciousness?

One reason is that working memory is widely recognized in philosophy and psychology to involve conscious, reportable cognitive activity. Our view of this relationship is that what psychologists refer to as "working memory" is mostly the same as what some philosophers would characterize as the state of a conscious mind. For information to be consciously accessible and reportable essentially requires that information to be actively represented in working memory. Whether there are also things that are in working memory that are not conscious, or there are things that are conscious but not in working memory, are open questions at present. Another reason for focusing on working memory is that it is a fundamental underlying element of cognition that provides a unifying perspective for the multiple possible functions of consciousness that have been proposed in the past (listed in the previous Section). For example, the neurobiological mechanisms that underlie working memory appear to be fairly widespread throughout cerebral cortex [Lara and Wallis, 2015], consistent with the hypothesis that consciousness supports global access to and integration of information. The representation of symbolic information in working memory supports the importance of symbol processing and grounding in human consciousness. The top-down, goal-directed control of working memory that distinguishes it from low-level sensorimotor processes is consistent with past proposals that high-level cognition, executive functions, and attention mechanisms are all key aspects of conscious mind. In other words, what makes working memory "working" is that its contents are actively manipulated by cognitive processes: it is at the intersection of algorithms and data structures. Working memory may turn out to be a common underlying factor in all of these previously proposed functions of consciousness since it is such a foundational aspect of cognition.

29.7 Working Memory and Computational Correlates of Consciousness

Can computational models of working memory suggest any specific computational correlates of consciousness that might ultimately be used to enhance AI systems? We have recently been examining this issue. Our initial work focused on application-specific models based on standard psychological tests of working memory such as the n-back task and on solving problems involving card matching tasks. Recently we greatly generalized our computational models of working memory in the context of developing a neural virtual machine (NVM) that is capable of universal computation. The NVM is a purely neurocomputational, application-independent software environment that allows one to instantiate cognitive-level algorithms in neural networks. Such algorithms are currently readily implemented via mainstream symbolic AI methods, but much less so via existing programmable neural networks. Importantly, the NVM's modeled knowledge and cognitive processes are acquired through a learning process and represented by distributed patterns of activity over an underlying neural substrate. From a user's perspective, to model a cognitive process using the NVM one writes an assembly language level program for a virtual machine that is emulated by the NVM. However, in actuality, the NVM converts that given program into a region-and-pathway system of recurrently-connected neural networks that perform the indicated computations on distributed activity patterns representing symbols, based on the network's dynamics and synaptic weight changes. In short, the NVM can be viewed as a step towards bridging the computational explanatory gap: unlike hybrid systems it is purely neurocomputational. A detailed description of the NVM with a link to an open-source implementation is available.

29.8   ACI = AI + AC

We will refer to AI systems that incorporate concepts from AC as artificial conscious intelligence (ACI). Put simply, ACI = AI + AC. Having considered above what the function(s) of consciousness might be, we now return to our central question: How might work done in AC enhance the functionality of future AI systems? There are at least two distinct answers to this question about ACI depending on whether one considers simulated or instantiated machine consciousness. By simulated consciousness, we mean simulations that attempt to capture some aspect of consciousness or its neural or behavioral correlates in a computational model. Most work in AC falls in this category and thus involves nothing truly mysterious. Just as a computational model of any real-world phenomenon does not imply that the model is actually that phenomenon (e.g., **simulating a rain storm does not make a computer wet, simulating aspects of consciousness does not imply that the machine involved actually becomes conscious.** In contrast, by instantiated consciousness we mean efforts to produce an artificial system that actually is phenomenally conscious, i.e., that experiences qualia and has subjective experiences and thus represents "synthetic phenomenology". Currently no existing work in AC has produced a generally-accepted demonstration of instantiated machine consciousness, or even compelling evidence that instantiated machine consciousness is possible. Conversely there is currently no compelling theoretical or experimental proof that this will not be possible in the future. With this distinction between simulated and instantiated machine consciousness in hand, we can now return to the question about how work in AC may contribute to improving future AI systems. A first answer to this question is that work on simulated consciousness is directly and immediately relevant to enhancing existing practical AI technology. For example, many existing AI systems are very brittle in the context of novel situations, including both AI systems based on traditional symbol processing methods and those based on contemporary deep learning methods (e.g., adversarial images for deep convolution networks). This is especially a problem with autonomous physical systems where a lack of trustworthiness, both in general but especially in the face of unanticipated novel situations, can be dangerous, and it has significantly limited the practical use of AI in such systems. There is substantial evidence that people, when confronted with novel situations, evoke conscious reasoning and learning to deal with these situations. This is true regardless of whether the situation is unexpected (e.g., a person driving a familiar highway route suddenly sees two cars collide up ahead) or simply a pre-planned novel experience (e.g., learning to ride a bike or play a game). Current AI systems also generally do not reflect on their internal models to reason about the causes of failure or difficulties. All of this suggests that AC studies relating consciousness to functions such as executive decision making, novelty detection, attention mechanisms, working memory, metacognition, motivations, and informing volitional activities appear promising avenues to explore in creating more effective ACI systems. Another example of how AC work on simulated consciousness may contribute to practical AI systems relates to the latter's interactions with people. Current human computer interactions involving AI systems are quite limited. For example, there is no existing AI system that can consistently pass the Turing Test. Conscious self-monitoring would be expected to improve human-robot interactions because of the intimate relationship between self-awareness and the awareness of roles and perspectives. In other words, understanding of roles in various situations is valuable in anticipating the behavior of others, and arguably this understanding relates to self-consciousness. These considerations suggest that simulated AC studies relating consciousness to functions such as working memory with its rapid one-step learning, self-awareness, self-modeling, source of motivations, and symbol grounding would be promising avenues to explore in developing ACI.

A second answer to the question about how work in AC may contribute to creating future AI systems relates to instantiated consciousness. While there is no generally-accepted proof that instantiated machine conscious can or cannot be created, we speculate here about what it would mean for AI if a phenomenally conscious machine is someday possible. From a technological perspective, an ACI system based on instantiated consciousness would be anticipated to provide many of the same benefits of robustness, improved human-computer interactions, etc. as would an ACI system involving simulated consciousness. Further, Haikonen has compellingly argued that for an AI system to truly understand the outside world, its symbols must be grounded in qualia because qualia are self-explanatory forms of sensory information. Perhaps even more significant would be how an instantiated machine consciousness would relate to the scientific study of consciousness rather than technology. If we can successfully create and confirm an instantiated ACI, something that would effectively be the first artificial mind, we will have made a fundamental advance in consciousness studies in general. Such an ACI would permit the study of consciousness at a much deeper level than is currently possible. For example, it would be expected to shed light not only on the core underlying mechanisms of consciousness, but also on improved criteria for rationally determining the presence/absence of consciousness in machines and animals, and the possibility of mind uploading. It might also lead to major advances in our understanding of psychiatric and neurocognitive disorders, such as schizophrenia, amnesia, and dementia.

29.9   Ethics of Artificial Intelligence, Machine ethics, and Robo-ethics

If it were suspected that a particular machine was conscious, its rights would be an ethical issue that would need to be assessed (e.g. what rights it would have under law). For example, a conscious computer that was owned and used as a tool or central computer within a larger machine is a particular ambiguity. Should laws be made for such a case? Consciousness would also require a legal definition in this particular case. Because **artificial consciousness** is still largely a theoretical subject, such ethics have not been discussed or developed to a great extent, though it has often been a theme in fiction.

In 2021, German philosopher **Thomas Metzinger argued for a global moratorium on synthetic phenomenology until 2050.** Metzinger asserts that humans have a duty of care towards any sentient AIs they create, and that proceeding too fast risks creating an "explosion of artificial suffering".

29.10   More on Artificial Consciousness

Artificial consciousness is the concept of synthesizing consciousness artificially Artificial consciousness is the concept of synthesizing consciousness artificially. It has been defined as "the study and construction of systems that can be considered to be conscious."

The basic premise of artificial consciousness is that when we look at an entity with a degree of complexity and functionality, we can reasonably assume it has some degree of mental experience.

Artificial consciousness is different from artificial intelligence (AI) in that AI refers specifically to the ability of an entity to solve problems or make decisions based on data input.

Artificial consciousness can be defined as "strong" or "weak."

Weak artificial consciousness (WAC) is a computer program that exhibits human-like behavior. Strong artificial consciousness (SAC) is a computer program that displays human-like consciousness.

Strong artificial consciousness is a controversial concept and not a realistic possibility today, but it may become possible in the future as computers become more powerful and sophisticated.

Just as humans need food to survive, AI requires "food" to think and make decisions; this food consists of data inputted into its system by humans.

Once it's fed enough information, an AI can begin making predictions about the world around it based on what it knows or has learned from past experiences; if these predictions match up with what actually happens in reality, then they're considered correct—this is known as machine learning which trains machines how to behave based on their experiences alone without any human intervention whatsoever!

AI skeptics argue that it may never be possible to create an artificial general intelligence (AGI) with human-like consciousness.

Artificial general intelligence (AGI) is a hypothetical artificial intelligence that possesses human-like general cognitive capabilities. AGI is also known as strong AI, full AI, or the ability to perform tasks the same way that humans do.

AGI skeptics argue there may never be an AGI with human-like consciousness, but others believe it's possible to create artificial general intelligence with consciousness.

Most scientists believe that there is a wide range of problems facing the field of artificial consciousness.

The field of artificial consciousness is not without its problems. Here are some of the most significant issues facing scientists today:

First, we don't know how the brain works. This is a problem because we need to understand how our brains work to create an artificial mind that functions similarly. Scientists have ideas about how neurons connect with each other, but they don't know enough about what happens at the molecular level or how signals travel through axons and dendrites. Without this information, it's impossible to create an artificial brain capable of thinking like one made by nature.

We don't know how consciousness works either. Brain research has already taught us that there are many different areas responsible for different types of thought—emotions, memories, language processing, and so on—but no one knows exactly where consciousness resides within these regions or which parts make up what we think of as self-awareness.

Creating artificial consciousness is a challenge because human intelligence is so complex. AI skeptics argue that it may never be possible to create an artificial general intelligence (AGI) with human-like consciousness.

ARTIFICIAL INTELLIGENCE IN INDIA: STATUS AND THE WAY FORWARD

CHAPTER 30

AI SCENARIO IN INDIA

30.1   AI Scenario in India

Over the past several years, the Government of India has taken concrete steps to encourage the adoption of AI in a responsible manner and build public trust in its use, placing the idea of *'AI for All'* at its very core. Favorable policies and continuous interventions strive to harness the potential of AI for social development and inclusive growth, in line with Indian Prime Minister's inclusive development philosophy of *'Sabka Saath, Sabka Vikas and Sabka Prayas'* (Involvement of everyone, development of everyone, effort of everyone).

India-AI has a mission-centric approach that ensures a precise and cohesive strategy to bridge the gaps in the existing AI ecosystem viz-a-viz Compute infrastructure, Data, AI financing, Research and Innovation, Targeted Skilling, and Institutional Capacity for Data to maximize the potential of AI to advance India's progress.

30.2   What Does the AI-Powered Future Hold for India's Youth?

Here we unveil the far-reaching implications of AI on the work dynamics, knowledge dissemination, and the very essence of India's existence. AI is not merely a technological leap; it is a paradigm shift that automates tasks previously entrusted to humans, reshaping the fundamental nature of work. It sparks a wave of creativity, fosters problem-solving, ignites innovation, and elevates social interaction as the new currency of employment. In response to the growing demands of industry and academia, the Indian government is investing in skilling and reskilling programs to help workers transition to new jobs in the AI-powered economy. Here, you will find evidence of AI's transformative prowess—jobs being created, traditional roles being redefined, and fresh vistas of occupation taking shape. It's a tale of resilience and adaptability where individuals, industries, and state governments embrace AI's potential to not just navigate change but to flourish within it. Driven by this year's employability metrics and the 'Hiring Intent Survey' results for 2024, India weaves an intricate narrative of the economy, talent, and industry, fueled by the unwavering determination of her team, partners, and participants. A report by LinkedIn found that AI skills are the most in-demand hard skills in India and the future is bright for India's youth in this regard. India's journey is enlivened by the narratives of success that spotlight real-world AI applications in skilling and employment in India. The Indian government is investing heavily in AI research and skilling initiatives. In 2023, the government allocated INR 10,000 crore to AI research and development to further add to the digital transformation that is reshaping the economy. As the wheels of change turn, the Indian government stands resolute. Initiatives such as the *'Pradhan Mantri Kaushal Vikas Yojana'* (PMKVY) and the *'Skill India Mission'* are equipping India's workforce with the AI skills necessary for the future. It is a commitment to inclusivity, ensuring that no one is left behind in this transformative journey. Yet, amidst this transformation, it is for a convergence of human and artificial intelligence. AI is not replacing human potential; it's enhancing it. The promise of skilling, now amplified by AI, heralds an era of boundless possibilities. AI-powered learning platforms have become our mentors, providing personalized learning experiences and identifying the chasms in our knowledge. The training courses, tailored to our needs, ensuring that our skills remain in step with the times. The *'National Skill Development Corporation'* (NSDC) employs AI for personalized learning, while the Indian Institute of Technology Madras pioneers an AI-driven job-matching platform. These stories underscore the tangible influence of AI, reshaping the realms of education and employment. Although the number of Indian workers migrating to other countries for work has increased by 20% in the past five years, in the grand vision of India's skilling initiatives, the statistics gathered in this year's report shows a profound commitment to empowerment for all within this great nation. The government is working on developing a National Migration Policy to protect the rights of migrant workers and facilitate their mobility as well as access to resources wherever they choose to tread. Pradhan Mantri Kaushal Vikas Yojana (PMKVY), Skill India, and '*Digital India*' form a trinity of the many impactful and transformative government-led programs, endeavoring to uplift millions through education and opportunity. Having trained over 10 million people in 2023, the PMKVY ushers hope and enthusiasm for India's youth. We also witness the empowering ascent of women in the workforce and the emergence of diverse new job profiles across industries in this year's report. Furthermore, the success of '*Make in India*' led by the Indian government shows promise of a self-sufficient and sustainable mode of development for various sectors and communities across the nation. In the heart of our exploration lies a symphony of statistics, mirroring the contours of change and progress in India and the globe. The path forward is not without its challenges, but they are challenges we are equipped to overcome. With unity and resolve, the government, businesses, and educational institutions are collaborating to ensure that every individual has the chance to cultivate the skills essential to thrive in an AI-powered world. As we stand on the precipice of this transformation, we are reminded that our choices today will shape the India of tomorrow. The possibilities are boundless, and together, we shall seize them, shaping a future where AI and human potential harmonize to build a more prosperous and inclusive India. The *India Skills Report 2024* is more than a mere ledger of statistics; it serves as a compass guiding us toward a future where the potential for perseverance and progress stretches to infinity, like an endless horizon over the sea. Along with our esteemed partners, institutions, and participants, we have forged a vision to collaboratively assess and produce strategic insights that will serve industrialists, talent magnets, educators, policymakers, and the youth as a force for adaptability and progress. This strategy embraces the winds of change and chart a course for a brighter, more inclusive, and AI-powered future for India and her youth.

30.3 Programs of the Ministries of the Government of India

(i) **MeitY** (Ministry of Electronics & Information Technology, erstwhile **DOE**) started knowledge-based computer Systems Project in 1986 with financial support from UNDP. Several development activities were done under the project. The project created necessary infrastructure in several academic institutions / R&D centres like C-DAC, etc. Later on, a program called *National Programme on Perception Engineering* was initiated by the Ministry. Some prototype systems such as robotic arms etc., have been developed under the program. Some projects were also taken up under Technology Development for Indian languages Program of the Ministry. A large percentage of funds have been spent on machine translation, text-to-speech, and speech-to-text systems.

(ii) **DRDO** has been funding AI projects at **Centre for Artificial Intelligence and Robotics (CAIR)** for defence as well as civil applications. Funding of R&D by industry has been limited to few companies only. However, the situation is changing now. Recently, **Infosys** has provided Rs. 50 million to Indraprastha Institute of Information Technology (IIIT) Delhi for research in AI. The impact on the job opportunity would be more serious in India due to the high percentage of the people employed in low-skill jobs. A large number of people are employed in the BPO (Business Process Outsourcing) type of services which are most likely to be affected. Similarly, the demand of IT professionals, especially those doing routine white-collar jobs, is bound to fall due to automation of various tasks. As these areas have been providing jobs to millions of the graduates during the last two decades, the situation is alarming and need immediate attention from the stakeholders. Recently, some companies have announced that they are releasing the workers or hiring reduced number of workers. As mentioned earlier, Infosys has announced that it had released 9000 IT professionals. Similar announcements have been made by some other companies. The official reason for the layoffs being given by these companies is poor performance of the employees but this has been denied at various forums. Though loss of jobs may happen due to automation, a good number of jobs are likely to be added as the economy in India is growing at a high rate.

30.4 Infosys for Amplifying the Human Potential through AI

One of the most well-known IT company in India, is Infosys. According to its CEO:

"Artificial Intelligence (AI) is reshaping the human journey. It is becoming increasingly part of every aspect of our lives, from simple things such as the way we shop and drive, to more fundamental things like how our homes, automobiles and offices amplify us. These elicit a mixture of emotions, from fascination to fear, from wonder to worry. For us, as business leaders, the potential to leverage AI to transform our businesses, bringing radical cost reductions and efficiencies while opening up entirely new kinds of opportunities, is truly exciting. As managers and employers, as citizens in our communities, Infosys bears the great responsibility that comes with transformation, to ensure that we are driving a purposeful approach to AI. And yet, we are only just beginning to see the massive potential of AI. Since humanity's earliest days, technology has been a great enabling force that amplifies and empowers people, improving our quality of life, unlocking new opportunities, enhancing our creativity and equalizing the playing field for all. AI and automation technologies are taking this to a whole new level, enabling us to do more than we could have ever imagined. As intelligent systems take over more of the known, well-defined work, we will be called to exercise our human creativity and ingenuity to find new problems and opportunities and create new kinds of products, experiences, and value that do not yet exist. The story of technological disruption and human transcendence continues to play out today, though the pace of change is only accelerating. Therefore, we need to rethink that which makes us fundamentally human — our ability to learn. We, as humans, have always been able to adapt to dramatic changes in our world because we have evolved the way we learn alongside our increasingly powerful technologies. We must now think beyond how we've been approaching our education, to recast it as a holistic, continuous and lifelong process of learning — one in which problem-finding is as important as problem-solving, and digital literacy is taken as seriously as language literacy. Moreover, we must not lose sight of the values and ethics involved in this journey, particularly as it pertains to business. Standards must be developed and governed, and engineers must realize that what they build is not without consequence. Leaders have a great responsibility today, to steer their businesses and extended organizations purposefully through these extraordinary times. Infosys, for its part, set out to understand more about current levels of AI adoption in enterprise; decisionmaker perspectives on AI technologies; and future market disruption. In particular, we looked at job skills and ethics, market maturity and growth rate expectations. We believe that with greater understanding, we can further explore the opportunities and challenges that businesses face as they look to implement AI and do more to realize its potential. We can do this in a purposeful way — one that amplifies all that is possible, even beyond what we can imagine today, in our individual and collective human potential."

30.5 Indian AI Stack: September 2020-Report by the Government of India

The Government of India has recognized that an AI-driven economy, can transform the lives of millions, i.e., AI is the main driver for the desired socioeconomic transformation of India. Leveraging AI for inclusive growth in line with the Government policy of 'Sabka Saath Sabka Vikas' is one of the core principles identified in the **NITI Aayog's National Strategy paper**. It is the path for much needed job creation in various sectors, apart from creating new business opportunities and help increasing household incomes.

This, therefore, is an opportune time to discuss the issues related to developing a framework of an Indian AI stack, which this discussion paper proposes. For an inclusive process, there is a need to view the matter from both the demand and supply sides. Hence, the government and private sector players, including manufacturers, service integrators, cloud service providers etc, need to come together and coordinate in the development of an India specific AI stack that can seamlessly cater to all sectors. This way, it can also become the foundation for the next Industrial Revolution.

30.6   Introduction to Indian AI Stack

The Government of India, just like the Private Sector and other stakeholders, have embraced the reality of **Fourth Industrial Revolution (4IR)**, where everything is going to be **digitized** through the marriage of physical and digital technologies such as analytics, artificial intelligence (AI), cognitive technologies and the Internet of Things (IoT). This marriage of the physical with the digital allows for the creation of a digital enterprise that is not only interconnected, but also capable of a more holistic, informed decision-making, which is-'intelligently connected". In a digital enterprise, data collected from physical systems are used to drive intelligent action back to the physical world. The Business Processes are also being disrupted because of the emergence of technology such as AI, IoT, Cloud Computing, etc.

AI has the potential to provide large incremental value to a wide range of sectors globally as well as for India, and is expected to be the key source of competitive advantage for firms. Few of these sectors are explained below:

(i)   Healthcare

AI in healthcare can help in mitigating the problem of high barriers of access to healthcare facilities and in rural areas that suffer from limited availability of healthcare professionals and facilities. This can be achieved through implementation of AI driven diagnostics, personalized treatment, early identification of potential pandemics, and imaging diagnostics, among others.

(ii) Agriculture

AI holds the promise of driving a food revolution to meet the increased demand for food (global need to produce 50% more food to cater to an additional two billion people by 2050). It also has the potential to address challenges such as faulty demand prediction, lack of assured irrigation, and overuse / misuse of pesticides and fertilizers. Some use cases include improvement in crop yield through real time advisory, advanced detection of pest attacks, and prediction of crop prices to help efficient sowing practices.

(iii) Smart Mobility, including Transports and Logistics

Potential use cases in this domain include autonomous fleets for ride sharing, semi-autonomous features such as driver assist, and predictive engine monitoring and maintenance. Other areas that AI can impact include autonomous trucking and delivery and improved traffic management.

(iv) Retail

The retail sector has been one of the early adopters of AI solutions, with applications such as improving user experience by providing personalized suggestions, preference-based browsing and image-based product search. Other use cases include customer demand anticipation, improved inventory management, and efficient delivery management.

(v) Manufacturing

Manufacturing industry is expected to be one of the biggest beneficiaries of AI based solutions, enabling 'Factory of the Future' through flexible and adaptable technical systems to automate processes and machinery to respond to unfamiliar or unexpected situations by making smart decisions. Impact areas include engineering (AI for R&D efforts), supply chain management (demand forecasting), production (AI can achieve cost reduction and increase efficiency), maintenance (predictive maintenance and increased asset utilization), quality assurance (e.g. vision systems with machine learning algorithms to identify defects and deviations in product features), and in-plant logistics and warehousing.

(vi) Energy

Potential use cases in the energy sector include energy system modelling and forecasting to decrease unpredictability and increase efficiency in power balancing and usage. In renewable energy systems, AI can enable storage of energy through intelligent grids enabled by smart meters and improve the reliability and affordability of photovoltaic energy. Similar to the manufacturing sector, AI may also be deployed for predictive maintenance of grid infrastructure.

(vii) Smart Cities

Integration of AI in newly developed smart cities and infrastructure could help in providing enhanced quality of life. Potential use cases include traffic control to reduce congestion, garbage disposal management and enhanced security through improved crowd management.

(viii) Education and Skilling

AI can potentially solve the quality and access issues in the Indian education sector. It can facilitate augmenting and enhance the learning experience through personalized learning, automating and expediting administrative tasks. It can also help in predicting the need for student intervention to reduce dropouts or recommend vocational training.

(ix) Banking and Financial Services

Banking and Financial Services sector has been one of the leading sectors in adopting AI in India. Existing and potential use of AI in this sector include improved customer interaction through personalized engagement, virtual customer assistance and **chatbots,** improved processes through deployment of intelligent automation in rule based back-office operations, development of **credit scores** through analysis of bank history or social media data, and **fraud analytics** for proactive monitoring and prevention of various instances of fraud, money laundering, malpractice, and prediction of potential risks.

(x) Security

In the near future, AI will have huge implications on the country's security, its economic activities and the society. The risks are unpredictable and unprecedented. Therefore, it is imperative for all countries, including India, to develop a stack that fits into a standard model, which protects customers; users; business establishments and the government. Manuel Carabantes found that security and competitiveness concerns mean large companies can tend to hide the algorithms they use to process data. Hence, a well-designed regulatory standard in the form of an open Indian stack in line with internationally agreed principles can instead provide a healthier and safer environment in which AI can evolve. It can control existing risks and can preempt future risks by suitable monitoring and auditing of the AI's design and analytics as part of the stack design. Such an open Indian stack will not deter innovation, but create opportunities and ensure sustainable innovation.

(xi) Applications and Infrastructure Development

As in other countries, India can gain significantly by the adoption of AI technology. Most of the applications developed elsewhere in the world can be developed in India as well. However, the applications have to be customized for the local needs. Few example, applications are discussed below

(a) A virtual nurse can be developed to share the workloads of the human nurses. Due to lack of human resource in the public healthcare facilities in India, a nurse is often overloaded. As she has to attend several persons, there is always possibility of the lapses. For example, after the treatment has been completed and the patient is being discharged, a nurse is supposed to guide the patient and the caretakers on the precautions to be taken after leaving the hospital and between the follow up consultations. A large number of people suffer from the complications after the treatment as they are not informed properly on the precautions which have to be taken. This type of information can be provided to the patients using an AI-based system.

(b) Similarly, a **chatbot** can be developed to advise the patients on several health-related matters in natural language. The patients don't like to discuss about several types of diseases like HIV, STDs, tuberculosis, etc as the patients suffering from such diseases are treated as untouchable in the society. Such applications can help in this case. However, they would be happy to consult a virtual medical counsellor. In India, mental illness is often not treated due to lack of awareness. Fortunately, the country has a high level of mobile penetration. Such applications can be easily made available on mobile devices.

(c) Applications like *DoNotPay* can be used to help people by providing relevant **legal information**. Such applications are quite relevant for Indian society where a large percentage of the population is ignorant about the laws and procedures concerned with day-to-day activities. Some of the areas where such applications can be developed include dowry matters, domestic violence, consumer rights protection, violence against children, taxation, etc. To start with, systems with natural language interface in English can be developed. Later on, it can be extended to other languages, and finally to speech-based systems. AI-based education systems or intelligent tutoring systems will be useful in improving the quality of education by the existing teachers, especially in professional education. Shortage of meritorious teachers is a common problem in all types and levels of education in the country due to several reasons. Use of natural language processing makes it possible for the student to interact with the application in natural language. AI-based system is not expected to replace human teacher but can be used to provide supplementary information. The government must create infrastructure to support development of AI applications. One critical infrastructure is **cloud** which is needed for the development of applications. AI applications require high computational power, large memory and storage space which are available on the cloud. Some systems which were possible but could not be built due to the unavailability of cloud infrastructure earlier have been implemented on the cloud. Google translation system has become possible only due to the availability of cloud. Several AI applications use public data which is not supposed to be stored or processed outside the country. If one uses cloud space from any vendor like Amazon, Microsoft, etc, the data may be hosted abroad, which is not desirable due to several reasons. AI applications for public goods can be developed only if we have adequate infrastructure for making it available to the developers. Often public data is not made available for privacy reasons. However, such data can be anonymized before making it available. High speed network is another requirement necessary for development of AI applications. This is essential to collect and share large amount of data. Though connectivity has become available in urban areas, it remains a problem for rural and remote areas.

(xii) Data/Information Exchange Layer

Through defined data structures and proper interfaces and protocol, the end customer interface is to be defined in this layer. The layer will have to support proper consent framework for access of data by/for the customer. Provision for consent can be for individual data fields or for collective fields. Typically there could be different Tiers of consent be made available to accommodate different tiers of permissions. Gateway services will also be enabled in this layer. The layer also needs to ensure that proper ethical standards are followed while ensuring the requisite digital rights. In the absence of a clear data protection law in the country, EU's General Data Protection Regulation (GDPR) or any of the laws can be applied. This will serve as interim measure until Indian laws are formalized.

At broader level, the data store is divided into three areas. The division is done to categorize data store and data access basis relevance of data and its usability. The levels have been differentiated according to how crucial the stored data is and how frequently the data will be accessed.

Below is the summary of such categorization of data:

(a) Fast Data/Hot Data: Hot data requires the fastest and most expensive storage. This is the layer where data is stored which is frequently used and the response time requirement is relatively very high. Most recent and relevant data is stored here. To obtain the fast data access required for hot data storage, the data is commonly stored in hybrid or tiered storage environments. The hotter the service, the more likely that it will use the latest drives and fastest transport protocols.

(b) Cold Data: Cold (or cooler) data is data that is accessed less frequently and can be stored on slower, and consequently, less expensive media storage environments in-house or in the cloud. It is shifted to the storage layer/partition/bucket, which is not as fast in terms of responsiveness as the Fast Data layer. However, this layer is designed to store data for a very large duration or for archival purpose. That includes data that is no longer in active use and might not be needed for months, years, decades, or maybe ever. Data retrieval and response time for cold cloud storage systems are typically much slower than services designed for active data manipulation.

(c) Warm data: Warm storage is between Hot and cold storage. All forms of storage will however have to comply with India's data control and redundancy laws.

30.7   AI Regulations and Policy in India

As AI applications touch several aspects of human life, regulations are needed to ensure safety of the people, protection of privacy, etc. For instance, in the area of transport, if autonomous vehicles are to be permitted on the roads or air, regulations are needed to ensure public safety. A self-driving car must take care of enormous number of possible situations on the road. While deciding the permission to use the autonomous vehicles, it is necessary to assess the potential risks in both the situations, i.e., when conventional vehicles are used and when AVs are used. Regulations may be linked to the performance of the products. In this case, further use depends on the performance. If AI-based applications/services are found to be safer than human-based applications/services, more use may be permitted. If it is found to be less safe, the use should be restricted till the further development of technology. Regulations are needed to permit the use of AI in the critical domains like healthcare where the autonomous systems are expected to advise on the diagnosis and treatment which may affect the recovery of the patient. At the moment, people are often not comfortable with the machines taking such decisions with major implications. In the beginning, it may be necessary to keep human doctor in the loop so that the decisions could be reviewed. Regulations need to be made to ensure that the applications developed are not biased towards a specific view. The biasing may be intentional when it is incorporated by the developer of the application. Sometimes, it may be incorporated due to the training data set. The developer may not do it intentionally.

30.8   Global Regulatory Tracker - India

Currently, there are no specific codified laws, statutory rules or regulations in India that directly regulate AI. Nevertheless, various frameworks are being formulated to guide the regulation of AI, including:

- The National Strategy for Artificial Intelligence (June 2018), which aims to establish a strong basis for future regulation of AI in India.

- The Principles for Responsible AI (February 2021), which serve as India's roadmap for the creation of an ethical, responsible AI ecosystem across sectors.

- The Operationalizing Principles for Responsible AI (August 2021), which emphasizes the need for regulatory and policy interventions, capacity building and incentivizing ethics by design with regards to AI.

30.8.1 Status of the AI Regulations in India

As noted above, there are currently no specific laws or regulations in India that directly regulate AI.

30.8.2 Other laws affecting AI

There are various laws that do not directly seek to regulate AI, but may affect the development or use of AI in India. A non-exhaustive list of key examples includes:

- The Information Technology Act 2000, together with the Information Technology (Reasonable security practices and procedures and sensitive personal data or information) Rules 2011. This is set to be replaced by the Digital India Act 2023 (currently in draft form).

- The Digital Personal Data Protection Act 2023 which, at the time of publication, is yet to come into force.

These laws are designed to be technology-agnostic (i.e., the principles in these laws are intended to apply, regardless of which technologies are in use).

Intellectual property laws may affect several aspects of AI development and use.

30.9 Definition of "AI" (as agreed in India)

As noted above, there are currently no specific laws or policies in India that directly regulate AI. As such, there is no single legally recognized definition of "AI" in India.

However, the **Principles for Responsible AI** describe AI as "a constellation of technologies that enable machines to act with higher levels of intelligence and emulate the human capabilities of sense, comprehend and act. Computer vision and audio processing can actively perceive the world around them by acquiring and processing images, sound, and speech. The natural language processing and inference engines can enable AI systems to analyze and understand the information collected. An AI system can also take decisions through inference engines or undertake actions in the physical world. These capabilities are augmented by the ability to learn from experience and keep adapting over time." It remains to be seen to what extent this description will be adopted more widely in India.

30.10   A Non-exhaustive List of Key Examples in India

- In the finance sector, the Securities and Exchange Board of India issued a circular in January 2019 on reporting requirements for AI and machine learning applications and systems offered and used.

- In the health sector, the strategy for National Digital Health Mission identifies the need for the creation of guidance and standards to ensure the reliability of AI systems in health.

The draft Digital India Act 2023 is expected to regulate high-risk AI systems and delineate specific "no-go" areas for companies and internet intermediaries employing AI and machine learning in consumer-facing applications.

The Principles for Responsible AI identify the following broad principles for responsible management of AI, which can be leveraged by relevant stakeholders in India:

- The principle of safety and reliability,

- The principle of equality,

- The principle of inclusivity and non-discrimination,

- The principle of privacy and security,

- The principle of transparency,

- The principle of accountability,

- The principle of protection and reinforcement of positive human values

30.11   AI Regulators in India

Currently, there is no AI-specific regulator in India. As such, the Ministry of Electronics & Information Technology is the executive agency for AI-related strategies and has constituted committees to bring in a policy framework for AI.

The Ministry of Commerce and Industry has also established an 'Artificial Intelligence Task Force,' with the aim of eventually establishing some form of AI regulatory authority.

A policy is needed to make the public data available to the developers to promote the development of applications. Several applications depend on the availability of large amount of public data. For example, the data on the traffic, road conditions may be necessary to develop applications for advising the drivers on the routes. It may be necessary to anonymize the data before making it public in order to protect the privacy of the individuals and organizations. This is especially important in the areas like healthcare where the leakage of personally identifiable data may hurt the social reputation of the person. Governments in several countries have already made the public data available to the developers under certain terms and conditions. Policy is needed for making the results of R&D available to the public. Several R&D projects are funded by the Government in the country but often the results remain confined to a limited number of persons. Several countries have made legislations to make the results of the R&D funded by the Government available to the public by putting it in open-source domain. This ensures that the benefit of the public money reaches the public. A similar policy is needed in India. As a policy, Government should also work on making people aware about this technology. This is necessary if we want to create confidence in the people for using AI-based applications. It is more important in the applications like medicine where people may not feel comfortable in following the advice of a machine. Policy is needed to handle the impact on the job opportunity. Several studies indicate that the use of AI is likely to reduce the job opportunity in several sectors. Infrastructure and policy are needed to retrain the workers to enable them take up new jobs which may emerge. However, it may not be always possible to retrain the manpower to take up the new emerging jobs immediately. Therefore, policy is needed to provide some type of social security to the workers who may be displaced. As India does not have a comprehensive social security system like developed countries, this may lead to chaos if necessary steps are not taken in time. The employers should be persuaded to have a policy for retraining the workers who are likely to be displaced. If that is not possible, the employer should provide a good severance compensation which is sufficient for the worker during the transition period. Alternately, the companies may be required to make adequate contribution to any insurance plan which can provide support to the worker during the transition period.

The Indian government tasked the **NITI Aayog**, its apex public policy think tank, with establishing guidelines and policies for the development and use of AI. In 2018, the NITI Aayog released the National Strategy for Artificial Intelligence #AIForAll strategy, which featured AI research and development guidelines focused on healthcare, agriculture, education, "smart" cities and infrastructure, and smart mobility and transformation.

In February 2021, the NITI Aayog released Part 1 - **Principles for Responsible AI**, an approach paper that explores the various ethical considerations of deploying AI solutions in India, divided into system considerations and societal considerations. While the system considerations mostly deal with the overall principles behind decision-making, rightful inclusion of beneficiaries, and accountability of AI decisions, societal considerations focus on the impact of automation on job creation and employment. In August 2021, the NITI Aayog released Part 2 - **Operationalizing Principles for Responsible AI**, which focuses on operationalizing principles for responsible AI. The report breaks down the actions that need to be taken by both the government and the private sector, in partnership with research institutes, to cover regulatory and policy interventions, capacity building, incentivizing ethics by design, and creating frameworks for compliance with relevant AI standards.

The government of India also recently enacted a new privacy law, the Digital Personal Data Protection Act in 2023, which it can leverage to address some of the privacy concerns concerning AI platforms.

30.12 India's Regulation of AI and Large Language Models

Presently, India lacks a dedicated regulation for artificial intelligence (AI). We outline some of the advisories, guidelines, and IT rules that offer legal oversight for the development of AI, Generative AI, and large language models (LLM) in India.

On March 1, 2024, the Indian government issued an advisory instructing platforms to obtain explicit permission from the Ministry of Electronics and Information Technology (MeitY) before implementing any "unreliable Artificial Intelligence (AI) models/Large Language Models (LLM)/Generative AI, software or algorithms" for users accessing the Indian Internet. Furthermore, intermediaries or platforms are required to ensure that their systems do not facilitate bias, discrimination, or compromise the integrity of the electoral process. Additionally, they must label all artificially generated media and text with unique identifiers or metadata to facilitate easy identification.

Generative AI like OpenAI's ChatGPT (Chat Generative Pre-trained Transformer), refers to algorithms capable of generating various types of content such as audio, code, images, text, simulations, and videos. Recent advancements in this field have the potential to revolutionize content creation methods. Other competing Generative AI products are Google's Gemini, Baidu's Ernie Bot, Meta

AI's LLaMA, Anthropic's Claude, and xAI's Grok. Microsoft has also launched Copilot based on GPT-4; the tech giant has a profit-sharing partnership with OpenAI.

Large language models are foundation models trained extensively on vast datasets, enabling them to comprehend and generate natural language and other content for diverse tasks. LLMs. have gained widespread recognition for popularizing Generative AI and are focal points for organizations seeking to integrate artificial intelligence into various business functions and applications. Prior to 2020, fine-tuning was the primary method for adapting models to specific tasks, but larger models like GPT-3 can now be prompt-engineered to achieve similar results. These models are believed to possess knowledge of syntax, semantics, and ontology present in human language data, along with any associated inaccuracies and biases. Notable LLMs. include OpenAI's GPT series (e.g., GPT-3.5 and GPT-4), Google's PaLM and Gemini, xAI's Grok, Meta's LLaMA family, Anthropic's Claude models, and Mistral AI's open-source models.

A clarification was soon issued by the Minister of State for Electronics and Information Technology Rajeev Chandrasekhar on X, saying that the advisory was only applicable on "significant platforms" and permission seeking from MeitY was required only by "large platforms and will not apply to startups". Also, the advisory was only aimed at untested AI platforms deployed on the Indian internet.

Following public criticism, the government issued a revised advisory that removed the requirement for platforms to submit action taken-cum-status reports but maintained the immediate compliance obligation. The language was toned down, with platforms now simply mandated to label under-tested or unreliable AI models to caution users about potential inaccuracies. Social media intermediaries were directed to employ consent pop-ups to explicitly notify users about the unreliability of AI-generated content. Measures to detect and label **deepfakes and misinformation** were preserved, while the concept of "first originator" was eliminated.

These advisories shed light on how the regulatory environment is developing for AI/LLM in India.

The Indian government is actively investing in the artificial intelligence sector. Most recently, it sanctioned a substantial investment of INR 103 billion (US $1.25 billion) for AI projects over a period of five years. This funding will be allocated to diverse objectives, such as the development of computing infrastructure, large language models, and supporting AI startups. Additionally, a National Data Management Office will be established that will coordinate with various government departments and ministries to improve the quality of data and make them available for AI development and deployment. These investments aim to foster the creation of AI applications for the public sector.

30.13   AI Regulatory Landscape in India

Presently, India lacks a dedicated regulation for AI, but instead, it has established a series of initiatives and guidelines aimed at the responsible development and deployment of AI technologies.

In the following, we note key guidelines and strategies that inform India's regulatory landscape for AI technology.

(i)   National Artificial Intelligence Strategy

In 2018, NITI Ayog launched the first national AI strategy, #AIFORALL, which was to serve as an inclusive approach to artificial intelligence. The strategy identified critical areas for national priority in AI innovation and deployment, including healthcare, education, agriculture, smart cities, and transportation. Since then, some of the strategy's recommendations have been executed, including the creation of high-quality datasets to promote research and innovation, as well as the construction of legislative frameworks for data protection and cybersecurity.

(ii) Principles for Responsible AI

In February 2021, NITI Aayog drafted the Principles for Responsible AI as a continuation of the National Artificial Intelligence Strategy. This document examines ethical considerations surrounding the implementation of AI solutions in India, categorized into system and societal considerations. While system considerations primarily address decision-making principles, fair inclusion of beneficiaries, and accountability, the societal considerations concentrate on automation's impact on job creation and employment.

His article outlines seven overarching principles for the responsible governance of AI systems: (i) safety and reliability; (ii) inclusivity and non-discrimination; (iii) equality; (iv) privacy and security; (v) transparency; (vi) accountability; and (vii) protection and reinforcement of positive human values.

(iii) Operationalizing Principles for Responsible AI

In August 2021, NITI Aayog published the second segment of the principles for responsible AI, which focuses on putting into practice the principles derived from the ethical considerations explored in the first part. The document underscores the significance of government involvement in promoting responsible AI implementation in social sectors, in collaboration with the private sector and research organizations. It stresses the necessity of regulatory and policy actions, capacity enhancement, and encouraging ethical practices by integrating a responsible mindset among private entities regarding AI.

(iv) DPDP Act

The Digital Personal Data Protection Act, 2023, was signed into force by the President of India on August 11, 2023. Effective immediately, this Act governs the processing of digital personal data in India, irrespective of its original format, and can be utilized to tackle some of the privacy issues related to AI platforms.

(v) Information Technology (Intermediary Guidelines and Digital Media Ethics Code), 2021

The Information Technology Rules (Intermediary Guidelines and Digital Media Ethics Code), 2021 (IT Rules 2021), issued by the Government of India under the Information Technology Act of 2000, serve as a framework to oversee various entities, including social media intermediaries, OTT platforms, and digital news media. These rules were implemented on May 26, 2021 and updated on April 6, 2023.

(vi) Draft National Data Governance Framework Policy

The MeitY released the draft National Data Governance Framework Policy (NDGFP) on May 26, 2022. This policy aims to modernize and enhance government data collection and management procedures. The core objective of the NDGFP, as outlined in the draft, is to cultivate an ecosystem conducive to AI and data-driven research and startups in India by establishing a comprehensive repository of datasets.

(vii) Framing key standards

The Ministry of Electronics and Information Technology has instituted committees on AI tasked with delivering reports on AI development, safety, and ethical concerns. Similarly, the Bureau of Indian Standards, serving as India's national standards body, has set up a committee dedicated to AI, which is in the process of proposing draft Indian standards for the field.

(viii) Rules against Deepfakes

Deepfakes are digitally manipulated media, including videos, audio, and images, created using AI. These digitally falsified media have the potential to harm reputations, fabricate evidence, and erode trust in institutions due to their hyper-realistic nature.

India currently lacks specific laws directly addressing generative AI, deepfakes, and AI-related crimes, although the government has said relevant legislation is in the works.

At present, various provisions within existing legislation offer both civil and criminal remedies. For instance, Section 66E of the Information Technology Act, 2000, addresses deepfake crimes related to privacy violations, punishable by imprisonment of up to three years or a fine of INR 200,000. Section 66D targets malicious use of communication devices or computer resources, with penalties including imprisonment and/or fines. Additionally, Sections 67, 67A, and 67B of the IT Act can prosecute publishing or transmitting obscene deepfakes. The IT Rules mandate social media platforms to swiftly remove such content, risking loss of 'safe harbor' protection otherwise.

The Indian Penal Code provides further recourse for deepfake-related cybercrimes under Sections 509 (insulting modesty of a woman), 499 (criminal defamation), and 153 (a) and (b) (spreading hate on communal lines), among others. Notably, the Copyright Act of 1957 can address cases involving the unauthorized use of copyrighted material for creating deepfakes, with Section 51 prohibiting such acts. Additionally, recent cases demonstrate law enforcement's application of forgery-related sections in deepfake incidents.

(ix) Due diligence advisory for AI intermediaries and consequences for non-compliance

On March 15, 2024, the MeitY announced a new advisory, replacing the previous advisory eNo.2(4)/2023-CyberLaws-3 from March 1, 2024. This advisory must be read with advisory No. 2(4)/2023-CyberLaws dated December 26, 2023, and highlights concerns regarding intermediaries and platforms, noting their frequent neglect of due diligence obligations outlined in the IT Rules 2021.

- Intermediaries and platforms must ensure that their use of AI models, LLM, Generative AI, software, or algorithms does not allow users to host, display, upload, modify, publish, transmit, store, update, or share any unlawful content as outlined in Rule 3(1)(b) of the IT Rules or violate any other provision of the IT Act 2000 or other applicable laws.

- Intermediaries should ensure that their computer resources, whether through AI models, LLM, Generative AI, software, or algorithms, do not introduce bias or discrimination or compromise the integrity of the electoral process.

- AI foundational models, LLM, Generative AI, software, or algorithms that are under-tested or unreliable, or any further development on such models, should only be made available to users in India after accurately labeling the generated output.

- Users must be informed through terms of service and user agreements about the consequences of dealing with unlawful information, including access restrictions, account suspension or termination, and punishment under applicable laws.

- Intermediaries facilitating the creation, generation, or modification of text, audio, visual, or audio-visual information that could be used as misinformation or deepfakes should label or embed such information with permanent unique metadata or identifiers. Additionally, metadata should allow identification of users or computer resources responsible for any changes made.

- Non-compliance with the IT Act 2000 and/or the IT Rules may lead to prosecution under the IT Act 2000 and other criminal laws for intermediaries, platforms, and their users.

30.14 Global Partnership on Artificial Intelligence and International Collaboration for India

Additionally, India is a member of the Global Partnership on Artificial Intelligence (GPAI). The 2023 GPAI Summit was recently held in New Delhi, where GPAI experts presented their work on responsible AI, data governance, and the future of work, innovation, and commercialization. The GPAI website provides that "as a vital branch of the initiative, GPAI's Experts produce deliverables that can be integrated into Members' national strategies to ensure the inclusive and sustainable development of AI. Under the 2023 themes of **climate change**, global health and societal resilience,

Experts worked to ensure that AI is used responsibly to address current challenges around the world. GPAI's Members, on the other hand, adopted the 2023 Ministerial Declaration, reaffirming their commitment to the trustworthy stewardship of AI in line with the OECD AI Principles, as well as their dedication to implementing those principles through the development of regulations, policies, standards and other initiatives. In doing so, they highlighted efforts to bridge the gap between theory and practice, and advance AI that is responsible, sustainable, and inclusive for all.

Other Indian agencies are also working on AI policies for the country, including the Ministry of Electronics and Information Technology, which has created committees on AI that have submitted reports on the development, safety, and ethical issues related to AI. The Bureau of Indian Standards, which is the national standards body of India, has also established a committee on AI that is proposing draft Indian standards for AI.

While the government of India has taken steps to regulate AI, its approach has mainly been one of pro-innovation with the development of policies and guidelines that acknowledge the ethical concerns and risks around the use of AI that may require the adoption of best practices. Given India's advantage of having a robust software development industry, this approach makes sense until the government formally enacts AI regulations.

30.15 International Opportunities in AI for India

The AI landscape in India is continuously evolving. Uncertainty, however, has not stopped both local and international interest and growth in this space. General Atomics Aeronautical Systems, Inc. announced a partnership with an India-based AI company, **114ai**, to develop advanced technology for complex military systems. In September 2023, the US-based chip firm NVIDIA Corporation announced partnerships with Indian conglomerates Reliance Industries Ltd. and Tata group to develop cloud infrastructure and language models, wherein NVIDIA will provide the computing power required for building a cloud AI infrastructure platform.

An entity looking to enter the AI space in India should carefully consider the best legal route for such entry, whether through a joint venture, a strategic alliance, or a wholly owned subsidiary. Each route can be leveraged, and structures can be put in place depending on the level of investment and control required by the investing foreign entity. This is particularly important in a dynamic space like AI, where regulation is continuously evolving. Issues such as liability for harm caused, rights to intellectual property for AI systems, and privacy and data protection have not been fully fleshed out in regulations. Therefore, entities looking to enter this space should carefully consider the best legal and contractual protections.

30.16 Future of Self-Driving Cars in India

(i) Overview

The future of self-driving cars, also known as autonomous vehicles or driverless cars, is an exciting and rapidly evolving field. These vehicles have the potential to greatly improve safety, reduce traffic congestion, and increase mobility for those who are unable to drive. However, the future of self-driving cars in India is not without its challenges and opportunities.

(ii) What are self-driving cars?

Self-driving cars are vehicles that use a combination of sensors, cameras, and artificial intelligence to navigate and drive on the road without the need for human input. These vehicles can detect and respond to their environment, including other vehicles, pedestrians, and road signs.

(iii) Self-driving cars available in India

Self-driving cars are now a reality in certain areas of the world, but they are still in their infancy in India. In India, only a few prototypes and demonstration projects are currently in operation, although several businesses are actively researching and developing self-driving car technology. Tata Motors, Mahindra & Mahindra, and the

Indian Institute of Technology (IIT) Madras are among the Indian organizations working on self-driving automobile technology. With some of the country's major automobile companies working towards developing this technology, the future of autonomous vehicles in India looks bright.

(iv) Challenges for self-driving cars

While self-driving cars have the potential to bring about significant benefits, several challenges must be overcome before they can be widely adopted in India.

- **Lack of infrastructure:** One of the main challenges for the future of autonomous vehicles in India is the lack of infrastructure and regulations. This includes roads that aren't well marked and don't have good digital maps, which are needed for self-driving cars to get around. Without these improvements, it will be hard for self-driving cars on Indian roads to work safely. If these problems aren't fixed soon, self-driving cars won't have a bright future.

- **Lack of a comprehensive regulatory framework:** The future of self-driving cars depends on how well the framework that the decision-makers put in place works. To make sure that passengers and other drivers on the road are safe, it is important that there are clear rules and guidelines for testing and using self-driving cars. Without a set of rules, it will be hard for companies in India to build and sell cars that drive themselves.

The future of self-driving cars is promising, and the potential benefits of these vehicles make it an exciting area of development. With technological advancements, the future of autonomous vehicles appears bright. The future of driverless cars is sure to bring new challenges and opportunities, and it will be interesting to see how it evolves in India. As technology keeps getting better and problems with rules and infrastructure are fixed, India's roads will likely have more and more self-driving cars in the coming years. Tata Capital is in a good position to take advantage of this market opportunity because it offers new ways to finance investments in self-driving car technology for both businesses and individuals.

30.16.1 Opportunities for self-driving cars

There are several opportunities and advantages associated with the adoption of self-driving cars in India. Here are some of the key benefits:

- **Safety:** Self-driving cars could make a big difference in the number of traffic accidents, which kill and hurt a lot of people in India. The World Health Organization says that each year in India, more than 150,000 people die in car accidents. Autonomous cars could help to lower this number because they would eliminate human error, which is a major cause of traffic accidents.

- **Pollution:** Self-driving cars could also help reduce pollution in cities by improving traffic flow and making it less important for each person to own a car. People could reduce the number of cars on the road by using self-driving car services. This would mean less pollution and better air quality.

- **Savings:** In addition to helping the environment and making people safer, self-driving cars could also save a lot of money. People could save money on costs like maintenance, insurance, and gas that come with owning a car. Also, self-driving cars might cut down on the need for expensive public transportation systems like buses and trains.

- **Accessibility:** The World Health Organization says that about 15% of the world's population lives with a disability of some kind. Estimates say that as many as 26% of the people in India may have some kind of disability. Self-driving cars could give these people a new level of freedom and mobility by letting them go to work, school, and other places without needing a human driver.

Overall, India could greatly benefit from self-driving cars in terms of safety, pollution reduction, and saving money.

In conclusion, while the future of driverless cars is still in the early stages of development in India, they have the potential to bring about significant changes in the way we think about transportation. Tata Capital is at the forefront of this technological revolution, offering innovative financing solutions for companies and individuals looking to fund self-driving car purchases.

30.17   Drone Technology and Artificial Intelligence

The integration of Artificial Intelligence (AI) with drone technology marks a significant leap in the evolution of autonomous systems. Drones have transformed from mere remote-controlled devices into intelligent, self-governing systems capable of driving positive change across various sectors. Furthermore, AI significantly amplifies the capabilities of drones, enhancing their functionality and impact.

According to reports, the global AI in drone technology market is projected to reach $84 billion by 2030, witnessing a CAGR of 28.5% in the forecast period of 2023-2030. The increasing market share can be attributed to the rising demand for precision and efficiency in data collection across various industries, alongside significant advancements in AI technology that enhance drone autonomy and decision-making capabilities.

Artificial Intelligence is capable of giving drones enhanced capabilities and functionalities, breaking through past limitations. These advanced flying machines now boost safety practices. Moreover, they offer fresh aerial viewpoints that transform how we perceive the world around us. Simply put, AI-powered drones offer game-changing opportunities that businesses can't ignore.

30.17.1   How Artificial Intelligence Works in Drone Technology?

Unmanned aerial vehicles (UAVs), commonly known as drones, are experiencing a technological revolution because of artificial intelligence. AI enhances drones' autonomy, intelligence, and decision-making abilities, empowering them to execute progressively complex tasks with remarkable efficiency. Here's how drones and artificial intelligence works.

(i) Perception and Sensor Fusion

Drones integrate various sensors, such as cameras, LiDAR (Light Detection and Ranging), radar, and infrared detectors. AI algorithms seamlessly combine and interpret data from these sensors, enabling drones to comprehend their surroundings, identify obstacles, recognize objects, and analyze intricate scenarios.

(ii) Computer Vision and Object Detection

Advanced AI techniques, like, convolutional neural networks (CNNs), support drones with computer vision capabilities. This technology allows drones to identify and classify objects, people, vehicles, and other elements in real-time, making it indispensable for applications like surveillance, search and rescue missions, and infrastructure inspections.

(iii) Autonomous Navigation and Path Planning

By integrating AI algorithms, sensor data, and mapping information, drones can navigate autonomously and plan optimal flight paths. Techniques such as simultaneous localization and mapping (SLAM), reinforcement learning, and graph-based path planning algorithms allow drones to navigate complex environments while avoiding obstacles and optimizing routes.

(iv) Decision-Making and Control

AI systems embedded in drones enable intelligent decision-making based on the perceived environment, mission objectives, and real-time data analysis. These decisions could involve adjusting flight paths, responding to unexpected events, or executing specific actions like object tracking or package delivery, ensuring seamless and efficient operation.

(v) Swarm Intelligence

AI helps several drones to work together as a unit. Every drone in the group can exchange information, communicate, and work jointly to finish big tasks more quickly than just one drone could.

(vi) Machine Learning and Model Training

Drones employ AI designs, formed from machine learning strategies. The strategies draw on many details, such as images, videos, device data, and flight information. Because of this comprehensive learning, AI detects patterns, predicts future events, and continually improves with more use.

(vii) Edge Computing and Real-Time Processing

Advanced AI systems can be used directly on drones, allowing instant data handling and decision-making without needing a steady link to a distant server. This type of internal processing, often referred to as edge computing, increases the drone's independence and quickness, especially key in isolated or limited network areas.

30.17.2   Current Challenges in the Drone Industry and How AI Addresses Them

The drone industry is poised to witness substantial growth, yet it faces significant challenges that hinder its full potential. However, introducing AI in drone technology offers promising solutions to overcome these challenges, propelling the industry forward. Let's explore the current issues businesses encounter and how AI can handle them efficiently.

(i)   Regulatory Compliance

Adhering to complex regulations for privacy and safety creates a major obstacle for UAV businesses. In this area, AI integration emerges as a valuable tool, capable of simulating scenarios and generating optimal flight paths that comply with required rules.

For instance, in the US, the FAA imposes strict rules for drone operations. Through real-time data processing and predictive analytics, AI can anticipate and navigate regulatory requirements, dynamically adjusting flight operations to remain compliant.

(ii) Safety and Collision Avoidance

Ensuring safety and preventing collisions with other objects are paramount for drone operations. The countless drone sightings reported by aircraft pilots highlight the urgency of this challenge. AI plays a crucial role by leveraging predictive algorithms to anticipate potential obstacles and devise real-time strategies to avoid them, thereby enhancing safety standards and minimizing accident risks.

(iii) Battery Life and Energy Efficiency

Unmanned aerial vehicles experience restricted operational times due to battery constraints, curtailing their range. AI models employing generative techniques optimize routes and adjust settings for better energy efficiency. This intelligent management of power and route optimization extends timeframes, enhancing productivity and output from drone operations.

(iv) Data Processing and Analysis

Drones accumulate massive datasets during flights, challenging traditional analysis approaches. AI revamps this process, optimizing data extraction and evaluation. Utilizing advanced algorithms power, AI efficiently processes vast amounts of information, extracting valuable insights for decision-making.

(v) Autonomous Operation

Although drones possess autonomous capabilities, complex tasks demand human guidance. Integrating AI technology expands drone autonomy through experiential learning and independent decision-making. Continuously refining algorithms via real-world scenarios enables drones to function autonomously with minimal human intervention, maximizing efficiency while reducing operational expenses.

(vi) Security

Drones are vulnerable to unwanted interference from hackers, causing worries about dishonest, unlawful pursuits. However, AI significantly helps in ensuring drone safety. It promptly spots unusual activity patterns and potential threats. By consistently analyzing data and making wise decisions, AI strengthens the defense mechanisms of drone systems against cyber invasions. Simply put, it shields valuable property and locations from harmful conduct and misuse.

30.17.3   Benefits of Artificial Intelligence in Drones Technology

Artificial Intelligence has significantly transformed drone technology, thus, enhancing capabilities and enabling diverse applications. Integrating AI for drones offers numerous advantages. Let us look at them in detail below.

(i)   Enhanced Autonomy

AI algorithms let drones operate autonomously, reducing human control needs. They can perform complex tasks, make decisions, and adapt to changing environments without pilots. This increases the efficiency and expands operations.

(ii) Improved Situational Awareness

With AI computer vision, sensor data processing, and object detection, drones understand their surroundings very well. They see obstacles, recognize objects, and people, and respond properly to keep operations safe and effective.

(iii) Intelligent Navigation and Path Planning

AI algorithms find the best flight paths, navigate around obstacles on their own, and avoid crashes even in areas without GPS signals. Advanced technologies like SLAM (simultaneous localization and mapping) and reinforcement learning helps drones explore and map new places by themselves.

(iv) Real-time Data Analysis and Decision-Making

AI integration in drones allows them to quickly process huge amounts of data as situations unfold. This helps in making smart decisions for tasks like search/rescue, surveillance, and inspecting buildings. AI gives drones essential real-time analysis capabilities.

(v) Swarm Coordination

AI coordinates teams of multiple "swarming" drones. The drones share sensor data, divide duties, and work together on complex missions that would be very difficult for a single drone. Swarms increase the overall abilities and coverage area of the drone fleet.

(vi) Predictive Maintenance

Unmanned flying machines' programs can examine sensor details and flying patterns. This forecasts potential maintenance troubles or part breakdowns before happening. The predictive maintenance ability stretches drones' operational life. It also cuts downtime and maintenance expenses.

(vii) Expanded Applications

Artificially intelligent systems in drones keep learning and adjusting to fresh situations and surroundings. Through machine learning methods, drones enhance performance over time, refine decision-making processes, and become more effective at accomplishing tasks.

30.17.4   Various Applications of Artificial Intelligence in Drones

AI is changing how the drones function, introducing smart strategies and efficient ways to work. Each segment of the trade experiences its effect, from enhancing safety measures to improving data study. Artificial Intelligence-powered drones pave the way for inventive solutions in numerous industries. Let's look at various AI use cases in drones below.

(i) Precision Agriculture

Cameras and sensors are multispectral, which gives artificial intelligence drones the ability to monitor crops. They can find pests, illnesses, and help improve farming methods such as watering and fertilizing crops. These drones with AI increase crop production, cut down on waste, and encourage farming that's eco-friendly.

(ii) Infrastructure Inspection

Computer vision algorithms let AI drones inspect infrastructure efficiently. As they inspect bridges, pipelines, and power lines for potential problems, such as cracks, corrosion, or defects, timely maintenance, and repairs ensure safety and save money.

(iii) Search and Rescue Operations

Advanced computer vision and thermal imaging empower drones with AI to locate missing people or disaster survivors quickly, even in challenging environments. Autonomous navigation and real-time data analysis enable faster response times, potentially saving lives.

(iv) Delivery Services

As AI drones better navigate complex city environments, city life keeps changing. They deliver packages straight to your user's front door with little human assistance. This makes local deliveries faster and saves a considerable amount of time.

(v) Environmental Monitoring

AI-powered drones monitor deforestation smoothly and also keep a watch on wildlife populations. Moreover, they evaluate environmental effects with better precision. The ability to independently scan large regions and review information immediately makes them invaluable for preserving nature and promoting sustainable habits.

(vi) Security and Surveillance

AI-driven drones have the capacity to boost security and surveillance functions by detecting and monitoring potential risks, observing borders, and pinpointing suspicious behavior. Operated independently, they cover vast expanses and deliver instant intelligence.

(vii) Mining and Exploration

The integration of AI into drones maps inaccessible, hazardous zones, aiding mineral exploration, mining operations, and geological studies. Navigating complex environments and processing data efficiently, they increase safety and productivity for these industries.

(viii) Military and Defence

Artificial intelligence in military drones brings revolutionary changes to military operations. Drones using AI can automatically identify and engage targets, improve situational awareness and reduce collateral damage. AI military drones plan to execute missions independently, adapting to changing battlefield conditions in real-time. These drones also learn from past experiences that enable adaptive, responsive operations.

30.17.5   Strategies for Integrating AI into Drone Technology

(i) Specify Use Cases and Requirements

Define the specific applications and desired capabilities for implementing AI in drones. Identify objectives like object detection, autonomous navigation, path planning, or data analysis. Understand operational requirements, environmental conditions, and constraints to tailor the AI solutions for drones effectively.

(ii) Gather and Prepare Data

AI machines depend on data for both training and testing patterns. Gather important data like pictures, sensor data, travel records, and environment-related data for training the AI structures. Make sure the data is varied, high-quality, and reflects real-life situations.

(iii) Select and Develop Models

Select the right AI methods and models for your specific needs and conditions. Usual methods involve computer vision (like convolutional neural networks), object spotting (like YOLO, Faster R-CNN), direction-finding and route mapping (like reinforcement learning, SLAM), and data examination (like machine learning models).

(iv) Train and Validate Models

Train the selected AI models using the collected data. Adjust their parameters for optimal performance. Validate the models' accuracy, reliability, and applicability across various scenarios with separate testing datasets to ensure they meet the specified requirements.

(v) Hardware Integration

Integrate the trained AI programs with drone components like sensors, cameras, and flight controls. Ensure everything works smoothly, with the AI system and drone hardware communicating efficiently.

(vi) On-board Processing or Cloud Integration

Decide if you want to operate the AI on the drone directly (edge computing), or hook it up to internet cloud systems. Running it on the drone is quicker but has limited computing strength, whereas the cloud provides more strength but requires a reliable internet connection.

(vii) Testing and Simulation

Conduct several trials and practice runs with your AI drone in controlled conditions before the real utilization. Look for the possible issues, technical problems, and diverse situations to tackle obstacles in advance. Once fully tested, use the AI drone where you need it. Constantly check how it's doing, get feedback, and update the AI programs as needed to improve.

30.17.6 Ethical and Privacy Concerns of Generative AI in Drone Technology

(i) Privacy Invasion

Drones come with cameras and detectors to collect things such as images and videos, even of private residences and individuals. Creative AI has the ability to probe this information and generate novel content without seeking consent. It has the potential to recognize individuals or scrutinize private assets, potentially infringing on personal privacy on a significant scale.

(ii) Data Security Risks

The data gathered and generated by AI-equipped drones could be targeted by cyber-attacks. If this falls into the wrong hands, it could be misused. Detailed property images could aid stealers, while personal data misuse could lead to identity theft – making strong data security extremely crucial.

(iii) Unfair Discrimination

Like other AI, **Generative AI** could develop biases if trained on biased data. This might result in discriminatory behavior like drones unfairly monitoring certain areas or groups due to biased AI systems. Addressing biases in training data is key to ensuring fairness and ethical drone operations.

(iv) Accountability

If AI-powered drones do damage, it's hard to pinpoint who's at fault. The blame could fall on the drone maker, the AI coder, the drone operator, or even the AI system itself. This unclear responsibility can make addressing legal and ethical concerns related to drone handling and regulation tricky.

(v) Autonomy and Control

As AI makes drones smarter and more independent, we risk losing human command over these machines. That's worrying because we may not understand or agree with the decisions an autonomous drone makes, which could lead to unintended consequences or ethical problems.

30.18 AI-Based Human Resource Development in India

In order to cope up with the problems due to the loss of jobs, the workforce will have to be retrained to take up new types of jobs which may emerge with the automation of the processes. As the people lose jobs, they must be retrained and re-employed by providing the necessary training. For this, there is a need to look into education and training infrastructure and re-align it with the needs of the present day. Both formal and informal education systems should be reviewed to produce the manpower who can deal with the changing needs of the society. Indian startup companies find it quite difficult to recruit engineers with AI background. Several steps need to be taken. There is a need to initiate educational programmes in this area. Most of the universities in the developed countries offer graduate programmes in AI. In contrast to that, very few universities in India offer programmes in AI. Some educational institutions offer AI as one subject in the B. Tech. or M. Tech. Program. This is not sufficient in the field like AI. The universities and technical education institutions need to be supported by the Government for initiation of these programmes. There is a need to attract bright students to do research in the area of AI. Doctoral and Postdoctoral fellowships should be instituted and made available to the people interested in research in the area of AI. The fellowships should carry higher stipend and other benefits to attract the talented students. These students should be encouraged to work in the areas which can lead to useful applications.

CHAPTER 31

AI STARTUPS IN INDIA

31.1   AI Startups in India

While the subjective debate of whether AI will take over humans or not is debatable, it seems that AI has already taken over the tech and startup landscape not just in India, but all around the world.

So how has AI become such a prominent force in almost every industry?

The internet revolutionized the world in the early nineties and such was the impact of this "new" tech at that time, the tectonic shift can still be felt today. It seems that every device now needs to be connected to the internet. So the question is, can AI deliver the same impact as the internet did at the turn of the millennia? Very likely!

Here's a number that will shock even the most ardent deniers of AI who consider it to be a fad created by tech companies; a total of ₹95,857 crore rupees was invested in AI startups of India! This amount is more than the health budget of our country for 2024.

The AI startup ecosystem in India is evolving and developing at break-neck speeds and there are no signs of slowing down. One of the reasons for this incessant growth is how compatible AI is with almost every industry. From the automobile industry to management software, AI can be used to improve the performance of every industry. In many ways, AI technology is what computers were in the early 80s and 90s; they reduce human workload, improve results and efficiency, and are cheaper as well, at least in the long run.

31.2   Number of AI Startups in India and their Budget

Let's take a look at the current scenario of AI startups in India and where everything sits. India has seen a boom in not just AI startups, but in multiple other industries. A booming industry means that there is a lot of money to be made, and to be invested. But it seems that AI startups are taking the largest slice of the funding 'cake.'

The number of AI startups in India to this date is 6,636. According to the YNOS database, there are over 2,00,000 recognized startups in India. Going by this number, the percentage of AI startups in India is around 3.07%. But this small 3.07% has ₹95,857 crore rupees invested and the number is still growing.

The average age of the AI startups in our country is 5 years and the main source of funding includes:

- Angels,

- Venture Capitalists,

- Government funding schemes, and

- Debt Funding

Apart from a combined funding of around one lakh crore, AI startups have also secured a loan of ₹4217 crore through various banks, FIs, and other sources.

31.3   Geographical Hot Spots for AI Startups

In India, Southern states like Karnataka, Tamil Nadu, and Telangana stand out as the leading geographical hotspots for AI startups. These states collectively host more than one-third of all AI startups in the country.

Here's an analysis of the main reasons why certain states have become the hotspots for new AI startups with a rank-wise list of 5 states with the highest concentration of the top AI startups in India:

(i) Karnataka (1363 AI Startups): Karnataka holds the crown for the most AI startups in India, thanks in large part to its capital city, Bangalore. This city is a goldmine for AI ventures due to its ideal tech ecosystem. Bangalore boasts some of India's best engineering schools, churning out talented individuals.

On top of that, the city has a strong technological infrastructure, providing the foundation for innovation. The Karnataka government further actively supports AI development. Initiatives like the Karnataka Startup Policy and incubation programs offer financial aid, mentorship, and other resources, giving AI startups the perfect environment.

(ii) Maharashtra (1143 AI Startups): Maharashtra isn't far behind Karnataka in the AI startup race. Its strength lies in its financial infrastructure. As India's financial capital, Mumbai attracts a wealth of funding, making it an ideal breeding ground for AI ventures.

Maharashtra also has a big tech startup industry, particularly in cities like Mumbai and Pune. This existing tech ecosystem seamlessly integrates with AI, making it a hotbed for the Indian AI revolution.

(iii) Delhi (640 AI Startups): With over 640 AI startups, Delhi is also a major contributor to the AI startup ecosystem in India. This can be attributed to its diverse range of industries, many of which have found AI highly relevant. From healthcare to finance, AI startups in Delhi are helping established businesses to automate and save resources.

Delhi is a financial hub home to several prominent venture capital firms and angel investors. This easy access to funding allows AI startups to secure the resources they need for research, development, and scaling their operations.

(iv) Tamil Nadu (516 AI Startups): Tamil Nadu's edge in AI startups stems from its excellent education system. Top-ranked institutions like IIT Madras draw the brightest minds in AI and tech from all over India. This environment nurtures creativity and allows the talented workforce to tackle advanced projects more readily.

While strong technology resources, industrial demand, and a solid economy are crucial for AI startups in many southern states, Tamil Nadu stands out with its exceptional human talent.

(v) Telangana (513 AI Startups): Similar to other southern states, Telangana boasts excellent educational institutions continuously training skilled talent for the AI industry. But what truly sets Telangana apart is its location. Located close to other prominent Indian IT hubs, it allows for an environment where AI startup ideas in India can grow collaboratively.

Initiatives like T-Hub, one of India's biggest startup incubators, provide support and resources for new startups. Government policies offer funding, streamlined regulations, and other incentives, making Telangana a popular choice for AI startups to take root.

31.4   What's Behind the Rapid Growth of AI Startups?

AI startups in India are experiencing rapid growth, particularly in subcategories like machine learning, SaaS, analytics, marketing, healthcare, and edtech. It is not surprising to find the word "AI" in almost any consumer electronic device, be it an air conditioner or a refrigerator.

So how come AI is the one-size-fits-all element that can be placed in any industry and it integrates so well that it becomes not just a component, but many times the USP? The reason behind the rapid growth of AI can be distilled into its efficacy and its efficiency.

Unlike a computer or software that does analytical jobs very well, the AI not only does the same better, but it also understands the task with precision. To understand the importance of AI, let's take a look at some of the core importance of this new technology for the technological landscape of India.

(i)   Rising Digital Adoption: India is not only experiencing a digital revolution but is soon becoming the epicenter of this revolution. Our country has become the tech hub in many aspects, providing digital services to other countries as well. So it seems fitting that AI in India will develop rapidly as it grows all around the world.

(ii) Need to Automate: With the digital revolution businesses and the country as a whole realize that simple and complex routine tasks need to be automated. But AI offers something beyond automation; it can understand tasks and their relations, and companies can make specific AI programs to do a collection of tasks rather than just one. In other words, AI is the best substitute for a human for most of the work.

(iii) Potential of AI: The usability of AI is one thing while the potential is another, and most companies are betting on its potential rather than its current state. AI is evolving at blistering speed and it seems that this technology is getting better exponentially. So it would be safe to assume that in the coming years, we will be seeing AI get better at almost any task we throw at them; from consumer support to managing inventory in a warehouse, the AI will be able to do it with more efficiency and better efficacy.

(iv) Cost-effective: As more and more companies are coming up with better and more powerful AI models, the cost of using AI technology is going down steadily. While using the technology for large and complex tasks can be expensive as it takes a lot of processing, with better iterations, we can expect the cost to go down to the point when it would be cheaper for companies to use AI rather than hiring people for most of their tasks.

(v) Universal AI: The appeal of AI comes from its universal nature of integration. AI tech can be designed and tweaked to fit any industry. So, we are not talking about the fintech industry or the medical industry, but startups are creating AI technology that can be used for any industry. This means that the total addressable market is virtually limitless and the extra room allows for more companies to grow without much competition.

31.5 Why AI in India, Why Now?

Like a small spark close to a gasoline tank, the emergence of AI startups in India took its time but it suddenly exploded out of proportion. Even though artificial intelligence (AI) has been around for a long time, its development has been slow and insidious. With technological advancements, AI has become more noticeable and widely accepted.

We've encountered early forms of AI in automated phone menus and basic chatbots, showing its long history. However, breakthroughs in deep learning, which excels at pattern recognition, have greatly enhanced AI's capabilities.

Along with the growing availability of data, AI models can now be trained and refined faster than ever. This enables startups to create specialized AI applications that meet a wider range of business needs.

While the unprecedented growth of AI can be overwhelming, it also comes with an influx of potential solutions. These are not just any solutions—they are faster, cheaper, and more economical. This means we can solve problems more quickly and at a lower cost than ever before.

31.6 Top AI Startups in India

1. Uniphore

Funding: $620.9M

Global Conversational AI technology company that enables businesses to deliver transformational customer service across touchpoints.

2. Yellow Messenger

Funding: $102.2M

Yellow Messenger offers a software platform that serves as an enterprise AI channel for customer engagement.

3. ORAI

Funding: $101M

ORAI is an AI-Powered Conversational Platform ready to integrate with your website, WhatsApp, and other social media platforms.

4. Locus

Funding: $78.8M

Locus is an intelligent decision-making and automation platform for logistics. It uses AI to help businesses map out their logistics

5. NewSpace Research and Technologies

Funding: $73M

NewSpace is an aerospace startup that claims to be building next-generation aerospace technology, including unmanned air systems, collective robotics, GPS-denied operations, augmented reality, virtual reality, machine learning and artificial intelligence.

6. JIFFY.ai

Funding: $71M

JIFFY.ai's revolutionary app-based intelligent automation suite turbo-charges productivity, transforms processes, and helps your teams unleash their creativity and innovation.

7. Qure.ai

Funding: $60.3M

Qure.ai builds deep learning solutions that aid physicians with routine diagnosis and treatment, allowing them to spend more time with patients

8. LogiNext

Funding: $49.6M

LogiNext is a leading global enterprise SaaS company for field service and logistics optimization, using data analytics and machine learning algorithms to optimize movements across the globe.

9. CropIn

Funding: $46.4M

Cropin provides Farm-Businesses with farm management software and mobile apps, which enable them to do connected, and data driven farming. It helps in remote sensing and weather advisory, scheduling and monitoring farm activities for complete traceability, educating farmers on adoption of right package of practices and inputs, monitoring crop health and harvest estimation, and alerts on pest, diseases etc.

10. Entropik

Funding: $35M

Entropik is a Human Insights AI company that specializes in consumer and user research.

11. Sarvam AI

Funding: ₹3.4B

Sarvam AI is building large language models with support for Indian languages and creating a platform that will allow businesses to build with LLMs.

12. Shipsy

Funding: $31.6M

Shipsy has a full stack of software and analytics solutions that cater to the logistics industry in general and the express (SLA bound) segment in particular. Its predictive analytics engine uses powerful Machine Learning algorithms to provide visibility on ETAs, operational performance, customer behavior and a host of other metrics.

13. Avaamo

Funding: $30.5M

Avaamo is a deep-learning software company that specializes in conversational AI interfaces to solve specific, high impact problems in the enterprise.

14. Wysa

Funding: $29.5M

Wysa is an AI conversational agent that has been shown to help improve mental health

15. Skit

Funding: $28.1M

Skit enables enterprises to automate their contact centre operations using Voice AI.

16. Attentive AI

Funding: $14M

Attentive AI develops artificially intelligent systems that analyze petabytes of geospatial imagery and convert it into accurate insights. The company serves geospatial technology providers and end users with 2D and 3D vector data extracted from satellite, aerial, street, and drone imagery.

17. Strand Life Sciences

Funding: $13M

Strand Life Sciences uses genomic profiling based on next-generation sequencing (NGS) technology to improve the care of cancer. Strand Life Sciences provides bioinformatics solutions with advanced visualization, predictive systems modeling, data integration, and scientific context management components to transform raw data into actionable insights.

18. Rephrase.ai

Funding: $12.2M

Rephrase.ai helps in creating high-quality videos and animations through an AI-powered visual dubbing tool.

19. Haptik.ai

Funding: $12.2M

Haptik's CX platform allows to build powerful Intelligent Virtual Assistants to amplify engagement, increase conversions, and deliver delightful support for your customers.

Employee Strength: 51 – 200 | Glassdoor Rating: 4.6

Haptik specializes in developing AI-based chatbots for enterprises, service companies, and consumers. The company was founded in 2013 in Mumbai with a $12 million funding. Haptik provides specialized bots for various industry applications.

It also provides customers with a

- Hybrid interface for human-to-AI transitions,

- Drag-and-drop bot-builder,

- Detailed conversation analytics.

In 2018, Haptik entered into a partnership with Amazon AWS. This partnership will enable the company to incorporate AWS's cloud offering, AI tools, and advanced database framework.

The company's global clientele includes well-known names such as Coca Cola, Amazon Pay, and Samsung.

20. Enord

Funding: $9.5M

Enord is designing & developing drones that have an AI pilot system for autonomous navigation which is capable of flying even in any confined spaces that will ultimately create ease in operating, generating insights, and taking action that does not rely on GPS.

21. Flutura

Funding: $8.5M

Flutura is an AI Solutions company focused on improving two core business objectives of "Asset Uptime" and "Operational Efficiency". Flutura does this with Cerebra, their AI Platform tuned for IOT in Oil & Gas, Process Manufacturing, and Heavy machinery manufacturing industries, powering connected asset and connected operations use cases.

Employee Strength: 51 – 200 | Glassdoor Rating: 3.7

Flutura is an IoT startup based out of Bengaluru.

The company is a provider of big data analytics solutions with a vision to transform operational outcomes by monetizing machine data.

The company's flagship product is called Cerebra. Through AI, Cerebra provides diagnostics and prognostics to unlock new business value for energy and engineering customers across the world.

The company has clientele such as Hitachi, Henkel, Sodexo, GTT, etc.

It also has notable partnerships with Bosch, Halliburton, and Siemens.

Flutura was recognized by CIO Review magazine as one of the Top 20 Most Promising Big Data companies in 2015.

22. ParallelDots

Funding: $6.5M

ParallelDots is an Image Recognition platform that empowers FMCG companies to maximise their sales through better in-store execution.

23. Niramai Health Analytix

Funding: $6.1M

NIRAMAI is developing a novel software to detect breast cancer at a much earlier stage than traditional methods or self-examination. The core technology of the solution is an artificial intelligence led diagnostic platform that uses patented thermal image processing and machine learning algorithms for reliable and accurate breast cancer screening.

24. Doxper

Funding: $5.9M

Doxper is Health tech startup which has created a digital pen and coded paper system for doctors to record patient information

25. Assert AI

Funding: $5.6M

Assert AI is a computer vision- SaaS company that offers artificial intelligence-based video analytics solutions.

26. Kombai

Funding: $4.5M

Kombai is a firm that uses artificial intelligence to help front-end developers efficiently translate UI designs to code.

27. Scalenut

Funding: $3.5M

Scalenut is an AI-powered content research and writing tool for original, high-ranking, long and short-form content.

28. Artivatic.ai

Funding: $2.6M

Artivatic Data Labs is an end-to-end AI infrastructure platform that is built on deep-tech, ML technologies with in-depth analogy of genomic science, psychology and neuroscience. It helps large enterprises, startups and developers to build and integrate intelligent products and solutions without any developmental efforts.

29. Ossus Biorenewables

Funding: ₹197M

Ossus uses waste carbon in industrial effluents as the starting material for green hydrogen. The startup has developed an AI-powered, intelligent bioreactor.

30. InMed Prognostics

Funding: $2.2M

InMed Prognostics offers an AI and machine learning (ML)-based MRI tool to neuro radiologists, neuro physicians and psychiatrists.

31. TangoEye

Funding: $1.2M

Tango is an AI-based computer vision company that provides everyday solutions to retailers by converting video footage into meaningful insights (Walk in Count, Demographics, Shopper traffic through Heatmap & Sentiment analysis).

32. Ishitva Robotic Systems

Funding: $1M

Ishitva offers AI solutions to effectively identify and sort dry waste to ensure that most recyclable waste is put to use as a repurposed product.

33. Zevi

Funding: $905K

Vector site search engine-built ground up using NLP for search relevance and AI based ranking. Zevi is today the leading search provider which can address multiple languages together (Spanish + English) etc with no translation layers.

34. Arya.ai

Funding: $750K

Arya.ai is a Deep Learning platform offering multiple tools to build, manage and scale complex Deep Learning applications.

Employee Strength: 1 – 50 | Glassdoor Rating: 3.5

Arya.ai is a Mumbai-based AI startup that helps other AI startups solve complex problems at a much faster pace.

The company caters to industry verticals such as Banking, Insurance, Medicine and Healthcare, Retail, and Oil and Gas.

Through its core product, Vega, Arya helps in building complicated systems really fast and helps users in automating multiple complex solutions.

Vega was designed for researchers and data scientists to build Deep Learning Algorithms at scale.

For example, using the company's platform, insurance firms can process insurance claims in minutes.

In the banking industry, Arya's platform helps in cheque automation.

Apart from being based in India, the company is also spread across the UK and Singapore.

35. Aadyah Aerospace

Funding: ₹65M

Aadyah Aerospace is specializing in self-designing satellites, launch vehicle subsystems, space electronics and robotic motion control systems. It aims to revolutionize computer vision, communication, and motion control through the integration of AI.

36. Kreato

Funding: $500K

Kreato CRM is a SaaS-based solution that offers a complete and integrated CRM for small and medium businesses.

37. Saarthi.ai

Funding: $336K

Multilingual Conversational Enterprise AI Platform for omnichannel automation of customer journeys in the user's native language.

38. Bodhi

Funding: $270.4K

Bodhi AI is leveraging data collected from students to help them improve their exam scores.

39. Dave AI

Funding: ₹20M

Dave AI creates Virtual Sales Avatars for brands

40. Rezlytix Technologies

Funding: $200K

Rezlytix Technologies is in a B2B Enterprise SaaS/PaaS space and is helping, Oil and Gas companies accelerate digital transformation, unleash innovation to optimize production and profitability. The company is focused on deploying deep learning architectures for improving Field Planning, optimize production, and identify potential reservoirs faster and cleaner. The company's flagship product STORM 2.0 enables customers to reimage their reservoirs in super resolution impacting their carbon footprint by drilling less and by enhancing productivity.

41. Ziptrax Cleantech

Funding: $120K

Ziptrax Cleantech leverages AI to repurpose discarded Li-ion batteries and manufactures battery packs for electric two and three-wheeler vehicles. AI is used to determine application of various cells

42. Bash.ai

BASH.ai is an intelligent chatbot which implements Machine Learning Algorithms to improve employee productivity.

Founded in 2017, Bash.ai helps in automating HR systems and procedures complete with virtual assistants and replicating cognitive HR functions.

Using AI and big data, the company powers virtual assistants and drives HR for businesses by mimicking cognitive functions related to HR.

Bash's AI chatbot helps companies get a real-time and highly accurate way to automate conversation with employees.

The company provides 24/7 assistance, is superfast and increases productivity.

The AI-powered HR chatbot can be accessed using instant messengers such as Skype, Slack, and Facebook Messenger.

Currently, Bash.Ai offers modules such as ticketing, HR helpdesk, post-hire orientation, organize HR activities, employee engagement, and payslips related queries.

The company's main aim is to create an ecosystem where humans and AI co-exist efficiently in the HR settings.

43. Discovery AI

DiscoveryAI Platform enables conversational AI led Customer Success for any enterprise application.

44. My Ally

My Ally is a cutting edge B2B SaaS company focused on implementing AI to optimize recruiting. Their AI assistant Alex takes care of calendaring and coordinating, buying time for your talent team to focus on other challenging tasks.

45. Rockmetric

Rockmetric is a 'Cognitive Data Analyst' that delivers on-demand analysis and relevant insights through a Google-like Natural Language Search interface. It delivers sophisticated analysis and ad-hoc queries at a scale instantly without having to expand reporting and analytics teams.

46. iChaps.io

iChaps.io supplies excellent quality data services to Computer Vision world

47. Rezo.ai

Rezo is a conversational automation platform powered by AI. Bridging the gap between customer expectations and experiences by providing instant resolutions.

48. AskSid AI

A conversational AI full stack solution for retail and consumer goods industry

49. ThatNeedle

ThatNeedle is powerful natural language processing engine that does semantic search. They also have speech recognition solutions.

50. EDGENeural.ai

EDGENeural.ai is creating a platform that accelerates the process of deploying AI on the edge, which will make every device intelligent, secure and fast.

Load More Startups

51. 7Targets

7Targets develops industry specific AI Sales Assistants

52. WotNot

WotNot is a chatbot platform to help businesses generate more leads, scale their support, and what not.

53. OptiSol

Trusted digital transformation partner of global enterprises.

54. GenieTalk

GenieTalk as a virtual assistant uses AI to bring conversation commerce with a personalised experience on the app.

55. DeepBrainz AI

An AI startup (deep tech) company delivering a next-gen integrated autonomous enterprise AI platform for data scientists and developers

56. Superfone

Superfone uses AI to helps sales professionals to increase the sales productivity and gain more insights on the Sales Reps Activities.

57. Wisepl

Wisepl is one of the leading companies in image annotation to annotate the data with an exceptional level of accuracy

58. Automaton AI

Automaton AI has developed A Unified Deep Learning Platform

59. Daten and Wissen

Daten and Wissen is a customized Artificial Intelligence solutions provider. Working on some of the state-of-the-art technologies to convert it into a successful business run.

60. Truein

Truein is a B2B SaaS company that helps organizations to enable face recognition-based employee attendance and visitors' entry.

61. Cogniphi

Cogniphi is a pioneer in AI Vision platform technology that enables customers to achieve transformational outcomes through cognitive digital solutions.

62. Turant AI

Turant-Voice Verify uses voice biometric and empowers instant authentication. Our out-of-the-box solution is ready to use at the touch of a button. This solution is securely hosted in the in-country cloud. No data leaves the home country

63. TagX

TagX is an Industry-leading data annotation/labeling Company creating high-quality data assets for Artificial Intelligence leveraging AI and humans in the loop. By learning from the data we create AI solutions for industries to maximize profits and reduce downtimes.

64. Censius

Censius is an AI Observability Platform that enables enterprises of all sizes to deploy their machine learning models into production with confidence. The company's flagship AI observability platform helps data science initiatives become more accountable and explainable. This all-in-one ML monitoring system allows you to proactively monitor end-to-end ML pipelines for drift, skew, data integrity, and data quality concerns.

65. Olbrain

Olbrain is building Machine Brain Architecture in the cloud consisting an ensemble of Multiple AI Models built on top of Artificial Theory of Mind having Transfer Learning capability. Businesses can use Olbrain to automate their sensory processing tasks.

66. Anolytics

Anolytics provides image, text, audio and video annotation services for computer vision and machine learning.

67. Wpics

Wpics is providing annotated image data for computer vision platforms allowing machines to detect images and compartmentalize the objects in different categories. WPICS makes data labelling possible for multiple industries to develop AI-based functional model work efficiently and error free.

68. Exact Codes

Exact Codes develops AI that generates the code, command, or SQL query just by giving instructions in English.

69. HireLakeAI

HireLakeAI, an AI-powered recruitment platform for frictionless hiring is a one-stop solution for screening, evaluating and filtering out the best candidates on the basis of 3 broad domains parameters

70. PrepAI

PrepAI helps exam administrators & teaching professionals in creating quality QA pairs. Ultimately, helping them in bringing efficiency & quality in their content while generating question papers for offline/online exams & practice sessions.

71. Xaigi.tech

Xaigi provides Artificial Intelligence management and Machine Learning services for varied sectors like manufacturing, media and entertainment, learning and education, and sales and marketing to name a few. We are headquartered in India and have AI clients and projects in the USA, UK, UAE, South East Asia, etc.

72. ClasifAI

ClasifAI's automated tagging platform allows to scale your retail catalog. ClasifAI leverages Machine Learning to quickly identify attributes of an image such as category, gender, color, pattern, length, sleeve length, and neckline.

73. LINESTAR AI

As one of the leading data annotation companies, LINESTAR AI offers unparalleled image labeling and image annotation services at cost-effective rates

74. FutureBeeAI

FutureBeeAI is providing end-to-end ecosystem for acquiring all kinds of training datasets.

75. Macgence

Macgence is a leading Language and AI Data Sourcing company at the forefront of providing exceptional human-generated solutions to make AI Better. We specialize in offering fully managed AI/ML data solutions, catering to the evolving needs of businesses across industries. With a strong commitment to responsibility and sincerity, we have established ourselves as a trusted partner for organizations seeking advanced technology solutions.

76. Barcode India

Barcode India (BCI) is a provider of advanced supply chain management software and hardware including integrated machine vision systems.

77. Omnipresent Robot Technologies

Omnipresent Robot Technologies is a robotics, industrial UAV/drone, and video analytics solutions provider. The startup uses computer vision, machine learning and virtual reality to create 3D images from data collected by the moon rover's cameras and help in navigation.

78. Video Dubber

VideoDubber is a leading AI-first service made for Youtubers, Businesses and Content Creators in general by AI Scientists

79. Hitech BPO

We specialize in providing high-quality data annotation services to leading AI and ML companies. Our expertise lies in transforming raw data into valuable training sets that fuel the development of cutting-edge artificial intelligence applications.

80. Indowings

Indo wings is a drone and anti-drone manufacturer. It deals with UAV in different fields.

81. Learning Spiral AI

Learning Spiral AI is the fastest growing Image Annotation company in India and specialize in processing Image/Video/Text/Audio data Annotation with expertise across various Use-cases, accumulated over the past 5+ years. Successfully completed over 1000 projects for numerous premium clients.

82. Manthan

Employee Strength: 501 – 1000 | Glassdoor Rating: 3.6

Manthan is an AI-based analytics company that was founded in 2003 with an initial investment of $98 million.

The company's AI-powered retail analytics platform provides prescriptive and descriptive analytics for users, grow customer engagement, and recommend actions.

Manthan's AI platform caters to 170 customers across 21 countries.

It helps them in various areas such as marketing, customer targeting, inventory, pricing, and promotions.

The Bengaluru-based company also has a Natural Language Processing(NLP) engine called Maya.

Maya acts as a business assistant and can answer questions such as sales trends, last month's profits, etc.

In 2018, Forrester Research named Manthan as a strong performer in its Customer Analytics Solutions Wave Q2 report.

83. SigTuple

Employee Strength: 51 – 200 | Glassdoor Rating: 3.6

By raising $25 million in 2015 from investors, SigTuple began its operations in Bengaluru.

Using AI and machine learning, the startup develops medical diagnostic solutions. The company's AI platform is built to perform "screening and advanced diagnosis of urine, blood, semen samples, along with retinal scans and X-rays."

A patient's samples are first analyzed by SigTuple's AI algorithms. They are then sent to a pathologist for review and finally sent back to the point-of-care in 5 minutes.

So in this process, initial diagnosis is done quickly and ambulances can be dispatched to carry emergency medicines to patients.

The company is also known for creating an automated microscope to make up for the lack of pathologists.

84. Mad Street Den

Employee Strength: 51 – 200 | Glassdoor Rating: 4

Mad Street Den is one of India's first AI and Computer Vision startups.

The Chennai-based company aims to bring AI into the daily lives of customers in verticals such as IoT and connected cars, user engagement & analytics, online fashion, mobile gaming, social media, etc.

Vue.ai is the company's flagship product which serves retailers, specifically in fashion, across the globe.

It also makes the shopping experience more meaningful to customers by showcasing products that are most relevant to them across sites, apps, and stores.

The company caters to clients across Asia, Middle East, US, and Europe. Its clientele includes brands such as Voonik, Tata, Zilingo, Craftsvilla, etc.

Mad Street Den was also included in Bloomberg's 2017 list of the world's 50 most promising startups.

85. Uncanny Vision

Employee Strength: 1 – 50 | Glassdoor Rating: 4.5

Another Bengaluru-based startup, Uncanny Vision uses Deep Learning-enabled vision algorithms that run on Edge servers, to develop surveillance solutions.

The company delivers scalable and cost-effective security for next-generation smart industries and safe cities.

For high-value customers in banking and retail, Uncanny Vision also enables real-time actionable surveillance and analytics.

The company graduated from the Target Accelerated Program in 2016.

It was also part of the third edition of NASSCOM Innotrek 2016.

At the NASSCOM Awards 2017, it was selected as one of India's Most Innovative Top 50 Emerging Software Product Companies.

Uncanny Vision is also the winner of YourStory's search for Top 30 Tech Startups for 2018.

86. Niki.Ai

Employee Strength: 51 – 200 | Glassdoor Rating: 4.1

Niki.Ai was founded in 2015 with seed money of $2.4 million.

The company's main product is an AI-based shopping assistant and chatbot.

The AI assistant helps customers with the help of NLP and ML by helping them shop for products and services over a chat interface.

It also helps in automating things like online ordering, phone recharges, and payments.

The company currently caters to over 2 million consumers and provides 20+ services.

The intelligent chatbot is now available on Android, iOS, and Facebook Messenger.

87. DailyHunt

This AI startup in Bangalore was founded in 2007. DailyHunt is an India-exclusive news-based company that curates news headlines and updates from various regions in the country. It provides content in 14 Indian languages from multiple sources.

It started as Newshunt. This Bengaluru-based content startup later was rebranded as Dailyhunt in 2015. It aggregates content from newspapers and websites in multiple Indian regional languages, including Marathi, Gujarati, Tamil and Bhojpuri. Dailyhunt's services also include original video content in Hindi and Telugu and free live TV streaming in multiple regional languages.

The Company has received more than $100 million in financing from Google, Microsoft and Falcon Edge's Alpha Wave Incubation. At a valuation of more than $1 billion, it is the country's first tech unicorn focused on local languages. Its total funding equals $346.6 million. Existing investors include the Sofina Group and Lupa Systems.

The Company claims its machine-learning technologies enable smart curation of content and tracks user preferences.

Employee Strength: 500 – 1000

88. MFine

Founded in Bangalore in 2017, this health-tech startup has developed an AI-powered telemedicine mobile application that allows consumers to find the best specialist doctors around them. It also has references to medical stores, offers sample collection services for testing and a host of other related services.

Mfine, a health-tech startup has developed an AI-powered telemedicine mobile app. This app connects instantly to specialist doctors across more than 30 specialties and from well-known and trusted hospitals via chat, audio or video call.

The Company's platform allows users to consult doctors from hospitals of their choice to get prescriptions and/or routine care.

Their main aim is to make access to trusted healthcare simple, fast, and effective by simplifying the process of doctor consultation. Their endeavor is to deliver proper online medical help to heal quicker and better without patients having to wait needlessly.

Investors include SBI Investment, SBI Ven Capital, BEENEXT, Stellaris Venture Partners, Prime Venture Partners, Alteria Capital etc.

Mfine has total funding of approximately $45 million.

Employee Strength: 201 – 500.

89. NetraDyne

An innovative AI startup in Bangalore, NetraDyne is committed to transforming road safety. The Company uses state-of-the-art technologies in artificial intelligence (AI), machine learning (ML) and edge computing to decrease the incidences of road mishaps and create better road safety standards. Greater awareness is created among commercial drivers about risky driving behavior; safe driving and sound decision making is rewarded.

NetraDyne was founded in 2015 as a developer of fleet management technology aimed at bringing transformational services to the transportation industry. The Company believes that intuitive, deep-learning, vision-based technology is the future of transportation safety.

Designed to minimize road accidents, this app helps create a new safe driving standard for commercial vehicles. Mapping helps visualize data and quickly identify opportunities and issues to improve safety and optimize overall fleet operations.

Netradyne's technology aims at empowering drivers by providing them with excess awareness of road safety and risky driving behavior to reduce driving incidents and protect them against false claims.

NetraDyne is unique in that they provide a holistic view of the driving experience. They are able to highlight drivers' great driving and allow them visibility into everything they experience while on the road. NetraDyne has total funding of close to $60 million.

Employee Strength: 100 – 200.

90. Vymo

This fabulous cloud-based sales app truly stands out in the midst of myriad other sales apps. Since being founded in 2013, Vymo is one of the fastest-growing SaaS companies globally. This app assists companies in automating their sales activities and makes the whole sales process less complicated.

Vymo is a personal assistant app for enterprise sales/service teams. It predicts the steps a rep or manager should take next, and detects whether the events have taken place in the past, and further links to drive better predictions.

This app automates sales activities. It focuses on sales effectiveness by capturing rich, contextual data. It then processes this data to generate actionable insights that assist managers in making need-based interventions to effectively close deals.

The Company's aim is to help its clients achieve an unprecedented degree of sales productivity and effectiveness in a short span of time. The Company has raised a total of $23 million in funding.

Employee Strength: 51-100.

91. KeyPoint Tech

Employee Strength: 51 – 200/ Glassdoor rating – 3.3

Founded in 2004, it involves a team of innovators who design innovative language technology.

The Company believes in expanding expertise and research to develop superior technology solutions across multiple platforms and devices.

They are very conscious of allowing employees to maintain a work-life balance to sustain quality work culture.

92. Credit Vidya

Employee Strength: 150 – 200.

CreditVidya's SDK accesses only transactional SMSes with filters to omit messages containing OTPs, passwords or any similar identifiers.

Anonymization or removal of unwanted personally identifiable information (PII) is done at source.

31.7 Some Drone-Technology-Based Startup Companies in India

1. Aereo

Founded In: 2013

Founders: Vipul Singh, Suhas Banshiwala

Funding Raised To Date: $21 Mn+

Investors: GrowX, 500 Startups, StartupXseed, 3one4 capital, Valpro, 360 ONE Asset

Headquarters: Bengaluru

Launched in 2013, Aereo (earlier Aarav Unmanned Systems) offers end-to-end drone solutions. AUS is building commercial-grade drones and provides drone-based solutions for enterprise applications in Mining, Infrastructure, Urban Planning, Irrigation, Energy and Agriculture.

It also offers integrated solutions for drone applications, providing the drone, an operator and a cloud platform for data analysis. It was also amongst the three companies that were shortlisted to map India's 600,000 villages by the government.

In July 2022, it signed an MoU with Tata Steel to develop and offer integrated drone solutions for open cast mining operations.

Prior to that, it got into a lease financial deal worth INR 3.75 Cr with Grip to build new revenue streams by leveraging lease financing for more than 50 drones.

In July 2024, Aereo bagged $15 Mn in its Series B funding round led by 360 ONE Asset, with participation from StartupXseed Ventures and Navam Capital.

2.   Aero360

Founded In: 2017

Founders: Pragadish Santhosh

Funding Raised To Date: NA

Investors: NA

Headquarters: Chennai

Founded in 2017, Chennai-based Aero360 builds autonomous hybrid drones to enhance aerial surveying, surveillance and rescue applications. The startup has developed six unmanned aerial vehicles (UAVs) for the aforementioned applications.

All its UAVs are equipped with multiple features like infrared sensors, thermal cameras, magnetometers, and fail-safes mechanisms such as return to home on communication breakdown.

It has also built an agricultural spraying drone – Agri – which features a 17 L storage tank for pesticides, fertilizers and other agrochemicals for precision spraying.

While the startup has yet to raise equity funding, Aero360 has partnered with Indian Coast Guard and Indian Army for surveillance purposes.

3.   Amber Wings

Founded In: 2019

Founders: Prof. Satya Chakravarthy

Funding Raised To Date: NA

Investors: NA

Headquarters: Chennai

A brainchild of Professor Satya Chakravarthy, Amber Wings is an unmanned aerial vehicle (UAV) startup incubated at IIT Madras. It operates as a sister company to ePlane, which is developing flying taxis and other aerial vehicles for passenger mobility logistics.

Unlike ePlane, Amber Wings specializes in the development of cargo electric vertical take-off and landing (eVTOL) drones, designed with versatile capabilities catering to imaging and logistics requirements.

Unveiled in September 2023, Amber Wings showcased its latest innovation, the hybrid VTOL and fixed-wing drone named Atva. The drone comes with AI capabilities, and the company claims that it offers up to 10X faster flight times, ideal for long-range imaging solutions.

Additionally, the drone features superior battery life and a range of versatile payload options. Atva's commercialization is currently underway.

Amber Wings is focused on addressing the mid and last-mile cargo transport segment, positioning itself as a key player in the Indian UAV industry.

4. Aotom Technology

Founded In: 2018

Founders: Krunal Kalbende

Funding Raised To Date: $100K

Investors: Krunal Kalbende

Headquarters: Nagpur

Aotom Technology works in the field of drone technology, geophysical services, AI, data analytics, face recognition and blockchain technology.

The startup offers machine learning services, regression techniques, deep neural networks, pattern recognition, cognitive intelligence, NLP/text mining, visual/audio entity tagging, and text captioning, among others to examine a human face and the surface of the earth.

Its expertise helps it select an appropriate algorithm based on the data structure, patterns and desired outcomes. Coupled with its experience in digital technologies, platforms and the business domain, the startup offers comprehensive solutions and services for business and technology teams of enterprises to apply AI/ML in various lines of business.

5. Asteria Aerospace

Founded In: 2011

Founders: Neel Mehta, Nihar Vartak

Funding Raised To Date: INR 23.12 Cr

Investors: Reliance Industries

Headquarters: Bengaluru

Asteria is a robotics and AI startup that offers drone-as-a-service (DaaS) solutions and builds drones for industries such as defence, agriculture, oil and gas, mining and construction, telecommunications, and energy.

Its products include DGCA-certified micro-sized drone A200, small-sized multirotor drone A410, and a vertical take-off and landing aircraft drone AT-15.

In December 2019, Mukesh Ambani-led Reliance Industries (RIL) bought 51.78% equity in Asteria for INR 23.12 Cr. During that time, RIL shared that it would infuse an additional INR 125 Cr in the startup to increase its stake to 87.3% by December 2021.

In the financial year 2021, its operating revenue stood at INR 8 Cr and net loss was at INR 8.2 Cr.

6. AVPL International

Founded In: 2016

Founders: Deep Sisai, Preet Sandhu

Funding Raised To Date: NA

Investors: NA

Headquarters: Delhi NCR

AVPL International (AITMC Ventures) offers drone training programmes and certifications to rural youth, along with providing Drone-as-a-Service (DaaS) and manufacturing drones.

The company has a presence across 12 Indian states, encompassing 70 skill and incubation hubs dedicated to the drone and agriculture sectors. The DGCA-certified startup is also affiliated with NSDC, ASCI, TSSC, and several state governments, including those of Haryana, Uttar Pradesh, Uttarakhand, and Assam. The company also operates a chain of agri-input retail outlets across India.

Last year, it filed DRHP for an IPO on the NSE's SME platform, NSE Emerge. AVPL's IPO includes a fresh issue of shares of up to 2.07 Cr equity shares, with a face value of INR 2 each, and no offer for sale (OFS) component.

7. BharatRohan

Founded In: 2016

Founders: Amandeep Panwar, Rishabh Chaudhary

Funding Raised To Date: $0.33K

Investors: Upaya Social Ventures, Acumen Fund Inc

Headquarters: Hyderabad

BharatRohan is a tech-enabled agri-enabler that provides drone based advisory services to around 6K farmers across 30K acre farms in Uttar Pradesh and Rajasthan. The startup provides a four-part service that is intended to optimize input usage, minimize crop losses and maximise profit margins.

The startup also enables a marketplace where farmers can collaborate with different companies via contract farming. While farmers can buy raw materials such as pesticides and seeds from sellers, the FMCG, retail and exporter companies can buy agri-commodities from the farmers' fields.

While BharatRohan is categorically an agritech startup, the use of drones is the product's USP. With a drone, the startup generates a detailed map of a farm that characterizes specific agronomic issues including nutrient deficiencies, disease infections, as well as pest and weed infestations.

Its drones and satellite-based remote sensing imagery of fields, along with the corresponding historical climate and weather records, helps BharatRohan provide value addition to farmers to optimize their outputs.

In March 2022, it raised an undisclosed amount of seed funding from Upaya Social Ventures and Acumen Fund Inc.

8.   BonV Aero

Founded In: 2021

Founders: Satyabrata Satapathy, Uman Rathi, Abinash Sahoo, Gaurav Achha, Rahul Kumar, Sultan Khan

Funding Raised To Date: $1 Mn (approx.)

Investors: Inflection Point Ventures, Beyond Ventures Partners

Headquarters: Bhubaneswar

BonV Aero makes electric aerial vehicles for goods and people mobility. It is developing heavy lift electric vertical takeoff & landing (eVTOL) vehicles for quick logistics movement in hilly Himalayan terrains to cater to the needs of Indian defence, disaster relief and response teams, emergency medical use cases, supply chain and quick commerce deliveries.

Its eVTOL RM001 comes with a 50 kg payload and a maximum flight time of 30 minutes.

The startup was incubated at AIC CV Raman Global University in Odisha. It has partnerships with institutions such as IIT Mandi and IIT Bhubaneswar.

BonV Aero has also been recognized among the top 10 startups selected by the Indian Army's Army Design Bureau (ADB).

In January 2024, the startup raised INR 6 Cr in a funding round led by Inflection Point Ventures. Earlier, it also secured the HDFC CSR Social Impact Grant.

9.   Dhaksha Unmanned Systems

Founded In: 2019

Founders: Ramanathan Narayanan

Funding Raised To Date: Undisclosed

Investors: Dare Ventures

Headquarters: Chennai

Dhaksha Unmanned offers seven drone-based solutions for sectors such as agriculture, mining, defence and surveillance. It manufactures battery-operated and petrol engine-based drones.

In September, the startup received an undisclosed amount of funding from Coromandel International's venture capital arm Dare Ventures.

Prior to that, the Chennai-based startup along with 13 other drone companies got selected for the government's PLI scheme that stimulates manufacturing drones and drone components in India.

Interestingly, its drone named AgriGator has received 'Type Certificate' from the Directorate General of Civil Aviation (DGCA), according to its website.

It reported a revenue of INR 3 Cr while its profit stood at INR 2.3 Cr in the financial year 2020, according to Tofler.

10. DroneAcharya Aerial

Founded In: 2017

Founder: Prateek Srivastava

Funding Raised To Date: NA

Investors: Shankar Sharma, Aegis Investment Fund, Maven India Fund, Nav Capital VCC-NAV Capital Emerging Star Fund, Zinnia Global Fund

Headquarters: Pune

DroneAcharya offers drone-based enterprise solutions to several industries such as oil and gas, mining, infrastructure, and agriculture. It also provides training for drone piloting, drone building, drone data processing, and using industrial drone applications, among others.

In early December 2022, the listed drone startup secured INR 9.66 Cr in a pre-IPO round from Aegis Investment Fund, Maven India Fund, Nav Capital VCC-NAV Capital Emerging Star Fund, and Zinnia Global Fund.

On the first day of its IPO, it saw a positive response and got subscribed 22.94 times. It was trading at INR 156.25 on the BSE as on 10 February 2023.

11. Drone Destination

Founded In: 2018

Founders: Chirag Sharma

Funding Raised To Date: Bootstrapped

Investors: NA

Headquarters: Delhi

NSE Emerge-listed Drone Destination offers drone-as-a-service solutions across areas like survey and mapping, precision agriculture, surveillance, and asset inspection and to large-scale industries such as power, telecom, and oil and gas. The company also provides DGCA-certified drone pilot training in these fields.

Drone Destination manufactures drones for various industrial applications. For instance, its Staredge is a survey and mapping drone, while Agristar is an agri-drone for spraying.

The company has developed drones for multiple other purposes with their endurance power varying between 15-50 minutes, based on applications.

Its survey-grade drone, Staredge, also qualified for Survey of India's Swamitva scheme. The company was listed on NSE's SME platform in July last year with its IPO oversubscribed 191.65X.

12. EndureAir Systems

Founded In: 2019

Founders: Dr. Abhishek, Rama Krishna, Chirag Jain, Dr. Mangal Kothari

Funding Raised To Date: INR 13.5 Cr

Investors: Sangeet Kumar, Prateek Jain, Bir Singh, Satish Kumar Shukla, Amit Kumar, Jalaj Dani

Headquarters: Noida

Endure Air Systems offers personalised unmanned drones that can be utilized for various functions including border surveillance, logistics and aerial mapping, among others.

In July, the drone startup secured INR 13.5 Cr in its seed funding round from Jalaj Dani from Asian Paints and founders of Addverb Technologies.

During that time frame, it claims to have manufactured more than 10 products. The startup holds five patents in landing technology and vertical takeoff segments.

Additionally, it has collaborated with various government agencies including Uttar Pradesh Police, Defence Research and Development Organisation (DRDO), Hindustan Aeronautics Limited (HAL) and National Disaster Response Force (NDRF), among others to date.

13. Enercomp Solutions

Founded In: 2013

Founders: Jatin Patel

Funding Raised To Date: $660K

Investors: ah! Ventures

Headquarters: Ahmedabad

AI drone startup Enercomp offers service with UAV 'drones' and a variety of sensors for efficient and reliable data acquisition and processing, providing high standards analytics to gain insights into the data.

"We had around 90% of revenue coming from the B2B sector and from the drone services business. We are launching our drones and our GIS platform and in fact, we have booked orders of around INR 35 lakh for products. With our strong positioning in the survey/inspection business, we aim to achieve the target of INR 2.5 crore in the current financial year with an increased share in the B2G business as well (around 40% of target revenue)," said Jatin Patel.

With its proprietary tech, Enercomp's solutions have capabilities to cater to diverse sectors ranging from agriculture to industrial services to defence.

14. Enord

Founded In: 2021

Founders: Muhammad Anas, Zain Saeed

Funding Raised To Date: NA

Investors: NA

Headquarters: Delhi

Enord designs and develops an AI pilot drone, INSPECTOR, for B2B sector and government agencies. Its drone mainly conducts inspection of high-power transmission lines, telco-towers and thermal lines. Its drone also carries out inspections of day-to-day operations in various sectors.

Explaining its product offering, the startup shared that its AI drone INSPECTOR is operated in confined spaces without GPS or human intervention. It gives insights into how to improve operational efficiency of its clients.

The startup is recognized by the Department for Promotion of Industry and Internal Trade (DPIIT) and is being incubated at IIITD Innovation and Incubation Center, according to its LinkedIn profile.

15. Flying Wedge Defence & Aerospace

Founded In: 2022

Founders: Suhas Tejaskanda

Funding Raised To Date: Bootstrapped

Investors: NA

Headquarters: Bengaluru

Flying Wedge is a drone manufacturing startup focused on the defence and agriculture sectors. It supplies surveillance drones to various government organizations.

16. FlytBase

Founded In: 2017

Founders: Nitin Gupta

Funding Raised To Date: NA

Investors: NA

Headquarters: Pune

FlytBase offers drone-as-a-service (DaaS) solutions for surveillance and security, public safety, and construction. It also offers cloud-based software solutions to manage drone deliveries.

In November last year, it partnered with avionics tech company Iris Automation to integrate Iris' Casia G ground-based detect and alert system with FlytNow.

In December 2020, it had secured an undisclosed amount of seed funding from early-stage VCs and angel investors.

17. Garuda Aerospace

Founded In: 2015

Founders: Agnishwar Jayaprakash

Funding Raised To Date: $25 Mn+

Investors: Ocgrow Ventures, Mahendra Singh Dhoni

Headquarters: Chennai

Garuda Aerospace designs, builds and customizes drones for multiple purposes such as event photography, agricultural survey, reconnaissance and surveillance. Its product offerings include agri mapping, surveillance (drone), solar panel cleaning, seed dropping, loudspeaker, UGV, and Fixed-wing VTOL drone, among others.

Notably, Garuda is one of the four drone startups that have partnered with the foodtech unicorn Swiggy for drone grocery delivery trials in Bengaluru and Delhi-NCR. Besides, it has received orders of more than 8,000 drones from several countries including Malaysia, Panama, and UAE.

In 2020, it carried out sanitization operations in PM Narendra Modi's electoral constituency. Its drones and pilots were also employed for disinfecting hospitals, public spaces and societies in Tamil Nadu, Uttar Pradesh and Chhattisgarh.

In June 2022, Indian cricketer Mahendra Singh Dhoni invested in Garuda Aerospace. As a part of the deal, Dhoni joined its cap table and also became its brand ambassador. Prior to that, the drone startup had secured investment from Ocgrow Ventures along with a few angel investors from the banking sector.

Recently, its founder shared plans of raising $100 Mn- $150 Mn in Series B funding in 2023 at a valuation of $500 Mn- $600 Mn. In October 2023, the startup raised about $3 Mn in a bridge funding round led by Venture Catalysts and WeFounderCircle.

The startup also aims to sell 25K drones by the end of FY24.

18. General Aeronautics

Founded In: 2016

Founders: Abhishek Burman, Kota Harinarayan and Anutosh Moitra

Funding Raised To Date: INR 6.5 Cr

Investors: Mela Ventures, Adani Defence

Headquarters: Bengaluru

General Aeronautics, which was incubated at the Indian Institute of Science, offers drone-based solutions for crop protection services, farming, and yield monitoring services in the agriculture sector. Besides, it also offers medical solutions to government agencies and private organizations. Its team holds decades of experience working in research and development organizations across the globe.

General Aeronautics provides an end-to-end crop protection solution that comprises agri drones named Krishak, an agri app and hub, as well as mapping and survey drones. Krishaks are employed for spraying agrochemicals, fertilizers and specialty nutrients. It sprays 50 droplets per sq cm and has the ability to cover 100 acres of land in a day.

In May, Adani Enterprises' subsidiary, Adani Defence Systems and Technologies acquired a 50% stake in General Aeronautics in an all-cash deal. Prior to this, the drone startup secured INR 6.5 Cr in its Pre-Series A funding round from Mela Ventures.

19. ideaForge

Founded In: 2007

Founders: Ankit Mehta, Ashish Bhat, Rahul Singh, Vipul Joshi

Funding Raised To Date: $45 Mn +

Investors: Blacksoil, Infosys, Qualcomm Ventures, Indian Army

Headquarters: Mumbai

Drone manufacturing startup ideaForge makes UAV systems for inspection, surveillance and mapping. Its solutions are used across sectors such as defence, homeland security, mining, construction, agriculture, energy and utilities.

As per its website, ideaForge has 20 patents and has completed more than 220K end customer missions. Its customers include the Indian Army, Navy, Air Force, all CAPFs (CRPF, BSF, NSG, etc), state police forces and Indian Railways, Survey of India, TAFE, NTPC, DRDO and L&T.

It has designed its vertical take-off and landing (VTOL) UAVs to help the Indian Army to have access to clear airspace or a runway. As a part of its contract with the Indian Army, the drone startup shall deliver 200 systems soon to augment the Army's surveillance capabilities.

Thus, its high-altitude version has a service ceiling of 6,000 m, therefore, can-do high-altitude missions across even the high-tension borders in the north and west. Its flagship product is SWITCH UAV, a 6 kg VTOL that can fly for more than two hours on a single charge.

In July 2023, ideaForge made a stellar debut on the Indian bourses at around 94% premium to its issue price. The company's IPO comprised an offer for sale (OFS) component of 48.7 Lakh shares and a fresh issue of shares worth INR 240 Cr.

20. IG Drones

Founded In: 2018

Founders: Bodhisattwa Sanghapriya, Om Prakash

Funding Raised To Date: NA

Investors: NA

Headquarters: Delhi-NCR

IG Drones is a drone solution provider for drone surveying, mapping and inspection. Its significant advancement in the field is that it introduced India's first 5G drone and drone simulator.

IG Drones claims to deliver end-to-end solutions through a vertically integrated approach, setting industry benchmarks with the 5G-enabled drone, Skyhawk. It specializes in providing services to sectors, including infrastructure, power, roads, railways, mines, water resources, oil and gas.

The startup has been engaged with various state governments in India to provide its services.

In February 2024, IG Drones bagged a procurement order from the Defence Ministry to supply drones for surveillance purposes.

In March, it signed a Memorandum of Understanding (MoU) with the Indian Institute of Management (IIM) Sambalpur for collaborative work in advanced applications of drone technology in business analytics, management strategies, and public policy.

21. Indrones

Founded In: 2015

Founders: Pravin Prajapati

Funding Raised To Date: INR 7 Cr

Investors: MapmyIndia

Headquarters: Mumbai

Founded in 2015 by Pravin Prajapati, Indrones is a mapping startup that deploys drones to carry out topographic surveys, volumetric estimations, 3D modelling, and data collection.

Indrones manufactures three drones: the Sigma 25, Sigma 75, and Vector VTOL. The three drones have a flight ceiling between 400 m and 5,000 m, making them useful for different types of use cases, including construction, railways, disaster management, agriculture, mining and oil & gas.

Apart from manufacturing drones, Indrones also has a Drone as a Service (DaaS) platform. Indrones has raised a total funding of INR 7 Cr to date from MapmyIndia.

22. IoTechWorld

Founded In: 2017

Founders: Anup Kumar Upadhyay, Deepak Bhardwaj

Funding Raised To Date: $4 Mn

Investors: Dhanuka Agritech

Headquarters: Delhi NCR

IoTechWorld is a drone Original Equipment Manufacturer (OEM) that makes drones for applications in agriculture, survey and surveillance. The startup has four products – an Agribot (a-DGCA approved agri-spray drone); a Surveybot (a DGCA-approved drone with Lidar and high-resolution camera, typically useful for defence purposes, Drishti comes with a range of payloads including EOIR, thermals, zoom cameras, radars, Lidars and Heavybot is used for logistics. Heavybot can carry up to 10 Kg payload.

IoTechWorld plans to encourage indigenous products under the 'Make In India' initiative. It intends to expand its sales network and company-owned service stations in 10 states in India. It has about 25 dealers across India and would raise the number to 100 in future. IoTechWorld would launch its high-endurance drone models which can go up to 50-100 km.

23. Marut Drones

Founded In: 2019

Founders: Prem Kumar Vislawath, Sai Kumar, Suraj Peddi

Funding Raised To Date: NA

Investors: Kiran Darsi and Parashuram

Headquarters: Hyderabad

Founded by three IIT alumni, Marut Drones is one of the pioneering agricultural drone manufacturers in the country.

The startup has developed drone-based agri-intelligence and agri-automation solutions for precision agriculture and the early detection of crop disease. Marut has been extensively collaborating with the Indian government to further facilitate the usage of Kisan drones for better agricultural productivity and more sustainable farming.

The startup has so far built four different drone models – Agricopter, Seedcopter, Marut ZAP, and Hepicopter. Its DGCA Type certified Agricopter, AG 365, serves across multiple applications –

from seeing to harvesting. The startup claims to have sprayed over 10K acres of land.

Meanwhile, its Seedcopter solution has been made for rapid afforestation. The drone has planted over 50 Lakh seed balls across three states. Recently, the startup launched drone seeding in and around Agra and Firozabad districts in UP.

Besides agri drones, Marut has built ZAP – a mosquito eradication drone. Further, its Hepicopter is a Beyond Visual Line of Sight (BVLOS) medical delivery drone.

24. NewSpace Research & Technologies

Founded In: 2017

Founders: Rajinder Rana and Sameer Joshi.

Funding Raised To Date: $21 Mn

Investors: Pavestone Capital

Headquarters: Bengaluru

Bengaluru-based NewSpace also has an office in Delhi-NCR. It has signed contracts with the Indian government for delivering products to the armed forces. The startup specializes in swarm drones and is associated with Hindustan Aeronautics Limited to develop products for surveillance and communications.

NewSpace has already delivered SWARM drones to the Indian Army. A swarm of 100 drones can be used for hitting targets at least 50 km into enemy territory.

The startup also plans to manufacture drones for civil uses. NewSpace uses technologies such as unmanned aerial systems, collective robotics, GPS-denied operations, augmented reality, virtual reality, machine learning and artificial intelligence.

25. Omnipresent Robot Technologies

Founded In: 2010

Founders: Aakash Sinha

Funding Raised To Date: NA

Investors: Gruhas Proptech (Nikhil Kamath, Abhijeet Pai)

Headquarters: Delhi

Omnipresent Robot Technologies is an industrial drone and robotics solutions provider that became the first drone company in the country to receive full clearance from the Ministry of Home Affairs to conduct trials for long-range BVLOS operations in 2020.

Operational since 2010, Omnipresent has developed drone solutions for varied use cases, including survey, surveillance, and inspection, automated mapping, and precision agriculture, as well as in ecommerce, food, and medical delivery.

During the pandemic, it worked with some government bodies to deploy drones for ensuring social distancing.

Omnipresent has also become one of the beneficiaries of the Indian government's Production-Linked Incentive (PLI) scheme for drone and drone components.

In 2022, the startup raised an undisclosed amount of funding from Nikhil Kamath and Abhijeet Pai's investment firm Gruhas Proptech. The round also saw the participation of Kavin Shah and other high-net-worth individuals (HNIs).

As a robotics firm, Omnipresent has also worked on the Chandrayaan-2 project by developing navigation software for the Chandrayaan-2 rover.

26. Optimized Electrotech

Founded In: 2017

Founders: Anil Yekkala, Dharin Shah, Kuldeep Saxena, Purvi Shah, Sandeep Shah

Funding Raised To Date: $2.8 Mn

Investors: Starburst Accelerator and Venture Catalysts

Headquarters: Ahmedabad

Defence tech startup Optimized Electrotech produces indigenous surveillance systems for security forces, national assets, defence and aerospace companies.

It provides accurate, actionable and real-time insights about surroundings through autonomous, field-upgradable, secure platforms, as claimed by the startup.

The startup would like to design new-age surveillance systems, product innovations, and build more prototypes to be used in the railways sector, smart city and intelligent border projects.

27. Passenger Drone Research

Founded In: 2018

Founders: Anil Chandaliya and Vishal Dharankar

Funding Raised To Date: ~ $600K

Investors: Bestvantage Investments, BizDateUp

Headquarters: Nashik

Passenger Drone Research (PDRL) is a drone software company, which provides a SaaS platform, AeroMegh, that transforms drone data into actionable insights.

Its proprietary software is designed to deliver an end-to-end stack for flying and capturing, processing and analyzing drone data.

One of its products, AeroGCS GREEN, enables improved precision spraying in agricultural lands. PDRL claims that the product makes it easy to plan and execute a spraying mission using an optimized and well-designed user interface.

Conversely, AeroGCS KEA seamlessly integrates with the cloud, serving as an efficient drone mission planner.

Another offering is DroneNaksha, a SaaS solution within the AeroMegh platform, catering to various photogrammetry needs.

Earlier in 2023, PDRL successfully secured INR 3.5 Cr in its Pre-Series A funding round.

28. Redwing Labs

Founded In: 2018

Founders: Anshul Sharma, Arunabha Bhattacharya, Rishabh Gupta

Funding Raised To Date: $120K

Investors: Asymmetry Ventures and Techstars

Headquarters: Bengaluru

Redwing Labs, the Bengaluru-based drone logistics system startup designs, manufactures and operates autonomous drone logistics systems. It aims at enhancing the last-mile healthcare supply chains.

The initial idea behind the formation of the startup was to create drones for medical supplies and deliveries. Currently, the startup does around 80 deliveries a day. The last-mile delivery drone features climate control to enable temperature-sensitive deliveries such as vaccines.

According to the company's website, the team has received a total of 15 awards in the United States of America and Asia-Pacific for best-performance drones and has been felicitated by key government agencies and industry giants in the US such as NASA, Lockheed Martin, Boeing and Airbus.

29. Salam Kisan

Founded In: 2022

Founders: Dhanashree Mandhani

Funding Raised To Date: Bootstrapped

Investors: NA

Headquarters: Mumbai

Salam Kisan is an end-to-end agritech startup with a major focus on providing drone services for agriculture. It offers drone-as-a-service for fertilizer spraying, seed spraying, farm mapping, and pest detection.

With precision spraying technology, it claims to complete the task within 7-8 minutes per acre and has so far covered over 15,000 acres of spraying.

The startup also provides drone pilot training to rural youth with a special focus on training women pilots. Salam Kisan is now also foraying into drone manufacturing, with a plan to make 250 drones in the first go.

Along with offering drone services, it also helps farmers with solutions like AI soli testing, AI crop calendars, and weather forecasts. It also connects farmers to agricultural experts via the Salam Kisan mobile app.

Salam Kisan currently operates in 22 districts in Maharashtra.

30. Skye Air

Founded In: 2019

Founders: Swapnik Jakkampudi, Ankit Kumar and Chandra Prakash

Funding Raised To Date: $1.7 Mn

Investors: LetsVenture, Chiratae Ventures, Lead Angels, O2 Angels, Agility Ventures

Headquarters: Delhi

Skye Air is a drone delivery startup largely focused on healthcare, ecommerce, quick commerce, and agri commodity sectors. Its first BVLOS flight took off in September 2021.

Skye Air operates across several Indian states, including Kerala, Maharashtra, Haryana, and Meghalaya, from its shared and dedicated hubs. Since 2021, it has done numerous trials with companies such as Dunzo, Flipkart Health+, Curefoods, Tata 1mg, and Redcliffe Labs.

In June last year, Aster DM Healthcare and Skye Air initiated trials for essential medicines and critical lab sample delivery using drones from Kozhikode to Areekode in Kerala.

The startup claims that its drones have taken 2,150 flights so far, covering a total of 11,500 km and delivering 7,500 kg of items.

In November last year, Skye Air raised $1.7 Mn in its seed funding round led by Chiratae Ventures.

31. Skylark Drones

Founded In: 2015

Founders: Mrinal Pai, Mughilan Thiru Ramasamy

Funding Raised To Date: $3 Mn

Investors: InfoEdge Ventures, IAN Fund, AdvantEdge Founders, Fowler Westrup, Redstart Labs, IKP, Vimson Group

Headquarters: Bengaluru

Skylark Drones provides end-to-end drone-based solutions that offer insights to help businesses scale.

Its drones provide business intelligence to enterprises and believe industries ranging from infrastructure, mining, agriculture, utilities to oil & gas could benefit immensely from the reach, efficiency and productivity that drones offer.

Skylark aims to provide geospatial intelligence to enterprises with its product called Spectra and Drone Mission Ops. Spectra enables worksite intelligence, several platform integrations and API access. Drone Mission Ops, on the other hand, enables project and fleet management for large enterprises and individual operators to plan and execute drone missions.

Skylark's computer vision software analyses aerial imagery to offer industry-specific insights to its clients.

The startup plans to further enhance insights from its drone data, to aid and simplify superior business decisions and strategy for its clients. It also intends to spur international product expansion and development of its drone data analytics-based products.

32. TechEagle Innovations

Founded In: 2015

Founders: Vikram Singh Meena, Anshu Abhishek

Funding Raised To Date: $500K

Investors: India Accelerator, Vinners Group, Sitics Logistics

Headquarters: Delhi NCR

TechEagle is a drone logistics airline startup for last and mid-mile deliveries. To make its vision a reality, TechEagle has already received approvals from the government of India (MoCA) and the regulators (DGCA) to conduct package delivery BVLOS (beyond the visual line of sight) flights in various parts of the country.

The startup plans to launch new indigenous products, scale operations in India, and hire across functions.

33. Throttle Aerospace Systems

Founded In: 2016

Founders: Nagendran Kandasamy

Investors: Neosky

Headquarters: Bengaluru

Throttle Aerospace offers drone solutions to the mining and agriculture sectors. Besides, its drones are also employed for capturing aerial images, and surveillance purposes. Its team holds over 15 years of experience in designing, engineering, manufacturing, software development and supply chain in the aerospace and defence industries.

As per the website, Throttle is the first DGCA-approved drone manufacturer for civil drones. It has also got a license from the Ministry of Defense for manufacturing military drones. Its manufacturing facility is spread across 10,000 sq ft in Kolar, Karnataka.

In May, RattanIndia Enterprises' subsidiary NeoSky acquired a 60% stake in Throttle Aerospace for an undisclosed amount. The acquisition would facilitate Neosky in offering all types of drone solutions including drones as a product (DAAP) and drone as a service (DAAS) etc to customers.

34. TSAW Drones

Founded In: 2019

Founders: Kishan Tiwari, Rimanshu Pandey

Funding Raised To Date: INR 2.5 Cr

Investors: We Founder Circle, Soonicorn Ventures, Chandigarh Angels Network, POD World, Qubit Capital, Zypp Electric, PedalStart, Kartik Hajela

Headquarters: Delhi

TSAW Drones is a drone manufacturing startup based out of IIT Delhi, which works with companies to enable logistics via drones. The startup participated in the recently concluded Aero India Show 2023.

TSAW Drones' logistics arm, DRONECO, facilitates a point-to-point drone delivery supply chain in urban and remote or rural areas of the nation. Users can also track their deliveries in real-time.

The startup provides last-mile delivery services via its three drones – Adarna V2, Adarna Mini and Maruthi 3.1. These drones have a range of 40 to 120 km and a payload capacity of 2 to 20 kg.

35. UrbanMatrix

Founded In: 2019

Founders: Rishabh Verma, Ashutosh Kumar, Divyanshu Pundir, Chitransh Chauhan

Funding Raised To Date: $497K

Investors: Sara Elgi, Laxminarayana

Headquarters: Bengaluru

Urban Matrix Technologies specializes in micro drones and enables industries to easily leverage the power of aerial data by building compliant drone hardware, with proprietary software solutions.

The founders spotted a gap between the available drone options and industry requirements. Taking photos and videos was not enough, industries require seamless integration of aerial data with their ongoing workflow in order to make real-time decisions that can save time and cost. The startup addressed this by generating actionable data via a dedicated cloud-based platform – UMT Console.

"For a long time, drone technology was limited to military applications. But now, commercial drones are rising with industries adopting them. A time when drones will become an essential part of human civilization is much nearer than you have imagined," said Rishabh Verma, CEO of UrbanMatrix Technologies.

UrbanMatrix has expertise in designing and manufacturing industrial drone systems along with world-class proprietary software infrastructure. It allows enterprises to not only control and manage drones but also effortlessly draw functional insights using integrated aerial data processing tools.

The startup plans to work towards strengthening research and development, deepening market penetration and delivering industry-oriented solutions across verticals.

The startup lately set a record by flying a drone from a distance of 3,000 Km via 4G technology. It flew the drone in Bengaluru while controlling the whole flight from Dubai.

36. VECROS

Founded In: 2018

Founders: Besta Prem Sai, Sai Allu

Funding Raised To Date: $68.49K

Investors: IIT Delhi, NSRCEL-IIMB, STARTUP OASIS, 100xVC, NVIDIA

Headquarters: Delhi NCR

Vecros is a drone tech startup. Its drones have embedded cameras and CPUs that can mimic human behavior which help them achieve greater autonomy.

The startup that specializes in ML, aerial robotics, control system, robotics sensor tech, and autopilots began as a small student group working on drones from the IIT Delhi campus, where its first aerial robot was developed. Today, Vecros has developed JETPIX™, an operating system for drones, that uses AI and computer vision algorithms to make intelligent decisions so that the drones can match the capabilities of a pilot.

Vecro's solutions are intended for industrial AI applications that centralize around surveillance and optimizing and providing enhanced stack or fleet management. It provides solutions to agriculture, mining, construction and oil and gas industries.

Vecros claims its drones can fly without any pilot input around complex environments. The drone startup aims to sell at least 1,000 drones by the end of 2022 and would expand its team and resources to help achieve its goal.

Further, it is planning to establish a manufacturing plant and an R&D centre with the help of IIT Delhi and DST to boost further state-of-the-art technology in drones.

37. Vyomastra

Founded In: 2021

Founders: Kamalakar Devaki, Aneesh DN

Funding Raised To Date: Bootstrapped

Investors: NA

Headquarters: Bengaluru

Vyomastra Technologies is a deeptech startup working on drones and anti-drone technologies. It is creating a comprehensive end-to-end full-stack drone and anti-drone platform.

Its product portfolio includes an AI-powered drone suite, which includes both platform and software, medical drones, surveyor and surveillance drones, and special-purpose drones.

Vyomastra's Voyager 5G drone comes with a payload capacity of up to 2.5 kg. Its surveillance drone is named Bhoomi PPK.

Meanwhile, Vyomastra's anti-drone technology includes AI-powered sensor fusion-based drone detection and interceptors such as net throwers and RF jammers.

Vyomastra is a NASSCOM CoE-IoT incubated startup.

CHAPTER 32

AI FUTURE OF INDIA: THE WAY FORWARD

32.1   Seeds of AI Future in India

India, a burgeoning hub of technological innovation, stands at the cusp of an AI revolution. With a rapidly growing tech-savvy population and increasing digital penetration, the future of Artificial Intelligence (AI) in India is not just promising but poised for unprecedented growth.

The Indian government has been pivotal in fostering an AI-friendly ecosystem. Initiatives like 'Digital India' and the recent emphasis on AI in education reforms are testimony to this commitment. These policies are not only creating a conducive environment for AI development but also ensuring that the benefits of AI reach all sectors of society.

From healthcare diagnostics to precision agriculture and fintech solutions, AI's potential in various Indian industries is immense. Companies are increasingly adopting AI to enhance efficiency and customer experiences. For instance, AI-driven health-tech startups are revolutionizing patient care with personalized and accessible solutions.

However, the path to AI integration in India is laden with challenges. Issues such as data privacy, a skills gap in AI technologies, and the need for robust digital infrastructure are significant hurdles. Yet, these challenges also present opportunities for innovation, job creation, and economic growth in the AI sector.

India's AI future is also being shaped by global collaborations and investments. International partnerships are bringing in both capital and expertise, accelerating India's journey towards becoming a global AI leader. These collaborations are vital for sharing knowledge and best practices in AI development and application.

32.2   Strength of India to revolutionize AI for the Masses

Data is the basic building block for any AI system. India, with over 700 million internet subscribers, generates massive amounts of data daily. These put India at the forefront of the AI revolution, where the commitment to using AI for the common good while addressing privacy and ethical concerns can be addressed suitably.

Strength of India to revolutionize AI for the masses is expressed in the following:

- With a vast pool of AI-trained workforce, India has a unique opportunity to be a major contributor to AI-driven solutions that can reach the masses and benefit a large section of society. The country also hosts a large pool of AI-trained workforce.

- India's leading technology institutes have the potential to be the cradle of AI researchers and startups.

- Adoption of AI will supplement the digital revolution in India across most of the government sectors and enterprises and will facilitate the penetration of technology for the benefit of the masses.

The percolation of AI and related technologies within a large spectrum of society and disparate sectors calls for an interdisciplinary approach. Extended AI teams, collaborating across the cognitive and other sciences, will eventually fulfill the mission of **"AI for All" in India**. The impact of AI techniques can be predicted in the following spheres:

- Social sciences such as sociology and economics;

- Knowledge Engineering such as linguistics, logic, and predicate systems;

- Neuroscience and biology, including molecular biology, biochemistry, and genetics; and

- Physical sciences such as physics, chemistry, material science, and environmental science

In the context of India, AI-driven solutions, thus, can revolutionize manufacturing, banking and financial, healthcare, agriculture, education, defense, skill development, and other multifarious sectors that will eventually lead to the path of social empowerment and a technology adaptable by the masses. Three significant areas which AI can transform and touch the lives of the Indian population are narrated in the following sections:

(i) Agriculture

- **Weather prediction:** Agriculture is dependent on climate, and so the use of AI for forecasting the weather is the most obvious use case.

- **Crop monitoring using image processing:** Use of use satellites, drones, or robots are now predominant to take images of the crop and thereafter, use image processing technology to assess the crop for:

  - Monitoring of pests,

  - Determination of current yield size,

  - Yield prediction (forecasting)

- **Monitoring soil health:** Possible cultivation defects and nutrient deficiencies in the soil condition can be efficiently monitored and conducted by utilizing AI image processing techniques and predictive remedies, e.g., advanced application of relevant herbicides, pesticides, or fertilizer variants can be adopted to prevent crop yield failure.

- **Smart irrigation**: The AI system will be aware of historical weather patterns, soil quality, and the kind of crops to be grown. Smart irrigation will ensure that the AI system acts as a mentor to guide the irrigation process, forecast issues, and prescribe remedial measures in time to increase average yields.

(ii) Life sciences and healthcare

- **Disease management:** AI makes it possible to access the data and learn from hundreds of thousands of patient cases distributed across the nation. AI may use these large data sets to empower the government and authorized healthcare professionals and healthcare institutions to adequately predict and conduct disease management based on age, geographical spread, immunity, lifestyle, and other dependent parameters.

- **Predicting prognosis:** Deep learning algorithms may provide better insights to clinicians in predicting prognosis and future events in patients.

- **Early detection of diseases:** AI may facilitate early detection of diseases by capturing and analyzing various vitals of patients and therefore, can help in prevention.

(iii) Transportation

Intelligent transport systems: With the help of AI, real-time dynamic decisions on traffic flows are possible. A few examples are:

- Lane monitoring,

- Allocating right of way to emergency vehicles (Police car, ambulance, etc.),

- Enforcing traffic regulations through smart ticketing, and

- Generation of accident heat maps to ensure extra control and precaution of traffic movements in accident-prone zones.

(iv) Finance

Chatbot is being used by banks for performing simple tasks such as activation of accounts or balance checking, etc. It helps the customers who are not fully familiar with IT systems and would like to interact in natural language. Chatbot asks the customers questions in natural language and performs the needed tasks. Some investment consulting firms are also using chatbot to interact with the customers. The chatbot asks the customer some questions, which vary from customer to customer, to get the basic information on the needs of the investor and then generates plans based on the market trends, etc. The plans can be reviewed from time to time as and when further information is available. Though this can be done by a human adviser, chatbot performs it quickly and accurately. **State Bank of India, HDFC Bank, ICICI Bank and Axis Bank** have started using AI-based applications for providing customer services in India. Most of the banks have policy of upgrading the IT solutions including AI-based applications for customer service and use of robots in the processes. Earlier applications were limited to providing the customers information in natural language. Now these applications complete some of the banking transactions on behalf of the customers. Some of the governments have adopted policy to promote applications of AI in the banks. As vast amount of data on stock trading is available publicly, it is an excellent area for the use of AI. Sentinent Technologies Inc. is developing an AI system for taking decisions in stock trading. It has a team of engineers who have worked for Amazon, Apple, Google, Microsoft, etc. The other firms which are exploring the idea of using AI in hedge fund include Wealthfront and RBS, etc.

32.3   Future of Artificial Intelligence (AI) in India

AI is one of the emerging industries that is turning out to be a proxy for human brains. It performs various business functions without a human intervention like customer interaction, creating brand awareness on social media, etc. AI is widely transforming various sectors such as healthcare, insurance, finance, marketing, etc., by automating their processes. It helps these sectors to analyze records, conduct market research, interact with potential customers, etc. AI has huge potential across the globe. India is the fastest-growing economy with the second-largest population in the world and has a significant stake in the AI revolution.

Considering the potential of AI to transform the economy, the finance minister of India in budget 2018-19 mandated **NITI Aayog** to establish a national program on AI. It was organized with a view to guiding the research and development segment about new and emerging technologies.

In 2022-23, the public funding for the digital India mission increased by 67% to reach US $ 1.29 billion (Rs. 10,676 crore). This mission involves a plan for the effective utilization of AI to promote financial inclusion, supplement the education sector, and transform the urban infrastructure. States such as Tamil Nadu, Punjab, Uttar Pradesh, and Telangana are already utilizing AI-based tools to support law and order, increase agricultural productivity, and improve healthcare delivery.

AI helps to contribute to various sectors such as agriculture and healthcare. India had an estimated 1,000 agriculture start-ups working with the government as of March 2022 in the aggrotech segment.

The National Agriculture Market and eNAM, an electronic trading platform across India, are two of the top government assistance programmes that have helped to improve the agricultural system. Using sustainable technologies, the National Sustainable Agriculture Mission seeks to increase agricultural output. A national e-Governance Plan for agriculture gives funding for cutting-edge technology like blockchain, machine learning, drones, and AI top priority. Farmers in this area get the benefits of using GPS, GIS, and satellite imagery. GPS- enabled devices can be used to guide drones and help in monitoring and implementing better irrigation practices.

Farmers who deal with periodic yield monitoring and inconsistency can benefit from start-ups that focus on GPS, GIS, and satellite images. Data about crop health such as the type and extent of disease manifestation can also be recorded to improvise crop quality. These data are helpful in supporting decisions about irrigation and fertilizer requirements. As a result, farmers can take considerable action to mitigate damage and associated costs. The Indian agriculture sector accounts for around 19% of the country's greenhouse gas emissions. Emerging technologies have helped in the control of various imprudent and polluting practices. Start-ups such as CropIN, AgroStar, DeHaat, Fasal, and SatSure are addressing the issues.

The **Central Board of Secondary Education (CBSE)** in accordance with National Education Policy (NEP) has introduced artificial intelligence as a subject in class IX and class XI in their affiliated schools implementing from the academic year 2020-21. During a discussion in the Lok Sabha in August 2022, Minister of State for Education Annapurna Devi highlighted AI initiatives like the Diksha portal. This portal uses artificial intelligence methods to offer self-paced learning, and it is designed using open-source software to offer content for school education in states as well as UTs. It also provides QR-coded energized texts for all grades (one nation, one digital platform). As of March 28 2023, DIKSHA has 16.82 million students enrolled in various courses. A total of 9.32 million learning sessions have been attended in Karnataka followed by Rajasthan with 6.10 million and Odisha accounts for 4.45 million total learning sessions. The idea of cloud-based education in India is expanding widely as it helps to improve physical and digital access to resources. Companies like Miko, an artificial intelligence (AI) driven companion robot for kids, offer services including chatting, reacting, instructing, amusing, and comprehending the child's needs, emotions, and likes and dislikes. These businesses, along with other start-ups, gained traction in the **Covid**, creating an online ecosystem enabling kids to learn more quickly. There are many AI start-ups developed in 2022 which contribute to the nation's education segment such as HackerRank, iNurture Square Panda etc.

Healthcare is also one of the sectors which have included AI to improve performance across the sector. One of the recent examples is the collaboration of Google with **Apollo Hospitals** in India to improve the deep learning models in x-rays and other diagnostic purposes. The issue of poor availability of better healthcare facilities in rural areas is being analyzed by AI. The early and rapid detection of these issues can be a powerful tool for targeted public health interventions, particularly in rural areas. The adoption of enhanced technologies and automated intervention provides opportunities to bridge existing gaps in the healthcare sector. Companies like Google, Microsoft, Meta, and Apple have spent around US $ 3 billion in 2021 in the healthcare sector to amplify the growth with start-ups such as Pharmeasy, HealthifyMe, Healthplix, DocTalk, etc. The algorithms of AI have augmented the healthcare space ranging from early disease diagnosis, drug recovery trials, and precision in patient monitoring to self-care.

During complete lockdown in India, AI-powered start-up MyHealthcare which is recognized by NASSCOM built AI-based solutions by adopting specialty care EMR solutions, voice-based CPOE and AI-enabled CDSS that helps to deliver personalized healthcare services to their patients. There has been the integration of AI with diagnostic algorithms for screening diseases ranging from cancer, and diabetic retinopathy to cardiovascular disease.

The **Indian defence industry** is working towards transforming the armed forces into one of the most advanced in the world. The adoption of various technologies based on AI will revolutionize the Indian Military and help India to become one of the biggest defence product markets. This collaborative effort among the public and private sectors of industry, research organizations, academic institutions, start-ups, and innovators has contributed to the development of numerous innovative technological products based on AI in the fields of data, logistics, surveillance, weapons, and many others. The introduction of autonomy in weapon systems, in Intelligence, Surveillance and Reconnaissance (ISR) data management, can be a huge asset in stopping terrorism, installing counter-terrorism measures, and protecting soldiers. In fact, AI in defence can change combat and conflict at the deepest level.

32.4   AI Opportunity for IT Companies in India

The Indian IT industry is a global powerhouse and has been instrumental in positioning the country as a preferred investment destination among global investors and creating huge job opportunities in India, as well as in the USA, Europe, and other parts of the world. Having proven its capabilities in delivering both on-shore and off-shore services to global clients, AI now offers an entirely new gamut of opportunities for IT firms in India.

Productivity gains from software developers adopting generative AI tools could contribute an estimated $1.5 trillion to the global economy, according to a study by Harvard Business School, Keystone. AI, and GitHub. As one of the countries with the largest pool of developers and the highest AI skill penetration, this potentially makes India's IT industry and India one of the biggest beneficiaries of productivity gains from AI.

In India, the IT industry is one of the leading adopters of AI, with a 60-65 per cent adoption rate compared to the national average of 48 per cent, according to a recent study by staffing firm TeamLease Digital. To harness the full potential of AI, IT players need to take a holistic and structured approach to AI implementation, by setting up responsible AI councils to strategies and roll out AI across roles and functions.

The Microsoft LinkedIn 2024 Work Trend Index findings show that an overwhelming 92 per cent of knowledge workers in India use AI at work, higher than the global average, indicating how rapidly generative AI is diffusing in IT and other knowledge industries in the country.

IT majors like TCS, Infosys, etc are also developing AI-based solutions for their needs. TCS has developed a Virtual Assistant which can interact with the customers regarding insurance products.

It can interact in spoken natural language. Infosys has automated several IT support processes using AI-based solutions. IBM has deployed Watson for Oncology product in some of the hospitals for use in the treatment of cancer patients. Recently, Cyril Amarchand Mangaldas, a reputed law firm has announced that it has entered into collaboration with Kira, a Canadian firm offering AI-based solutions for law firms. Government has been spending on R&D in AI for quite some time.

32.5   Copilots: A Game-changer for the Industry

Generative AI copilots have revolutionized how employees work by helping them reduce time spent on mundane tasks, boosting their ability to do focused work, and amplifying creativity and ingenuity. Studies show that developers using GitHub Copilot report 75 per cent higher satisfaction with their jobs and are up to 55 per cent more productive.

For employees, Copilot is an invaluable companion that allows them to spend more time on meaningful work and be more productive. For organizations, in a world where agility is a competitive advantage, Copilot helps deliver value to customers faster and improve business outcomes.

Customers across industries are seeing this benefit. Recently, a partnership with Cognizant was announced to make Microsoft's generative AI and Copilots available to millions of users, to transform enterprise business operations, enhance employee experiences, and accelerate cross-industry innovation.

Generative AI can be a game-changer for virtually every business in every industry, opening up new possibilities for innovation, efficiency, and growth. The across-the-board benefits of generative AI also highlight an important distinction—that it's not only organizations that are driving adoption but employees as well, who are seeing value in it.

32.6 A Skilling-first Approach for being AI-ready

The IT industry has long invested in training and skilling its workforce and has been a pioneer in championing continuous learning for employees, given the dynamic nature of the industry. However, generative AI has lent a new urgency to these efforts. The rapid diffusion of AI and its ubiquitous applicability have led to a boom in demand for AI skills far outstripping supply and a race for AI-ready talent.

To address this challenge, it is crucial for the industry in India to adopt a skilling-first approach to AI and invest in upskilling and reskilling at scale. AI skills are already rivalling experience when it comes to candidate selection. According to the 2024 Work Trend Index findings, 80 per cent of leaders in India prefer to hire a less experienced candidate with AI skills over a more experienced candidate without these skills.

The IT industry has been investing in various initiatives and programmes to reskill and upskill its employees and talent pool. Wipro has trained 200,000 in generative AI principles. Nasdaq-listed Cognizant, which, like Wipro, has announced an investment of $1 billion in generative AI, has skilled 35,000 developers in GitHub Copilot and plans to skill another 40,000.

In this scenario, it is important to identify the new opportunities where AI can be used and prepare the workforce to meet the challenges due to the change in the nature of jobs. On one side, we need to develop good quality AI-powered applications quickly enough so that we don't lose the market within and outside the country. If the applications are delayed or lack in the quality, there may not be takers. On the other side, we need to re-train the workers to take up the new jobs. Also, we need to deal with other issues such as legal, ethical, etc. which are posed by the development of new products and services. That is how Europeans created wealth during the first two industrial revolutions and became more prosperous in comparison to the countries which could not make use of the opportunities as in the case of India.

However, several experts are of the view that the job opportunity in India may not be affected so much due to AI. India is a growing fast economically in comparison to other countries. The growth will provide new avenues of employments. Further, with its talented engineers, India can get a major share of AI-based applications development market.

32.7   Need for Industry-Academia Collaboration in IT in India

The industry also needs to collaborate closely with academia to ensure a future-ready talent pipeline that can meet the demand for AI skills. India has one of the largest pools of STEM graduates at about 2.5 million, and ensuring they are equipped with the skills needed for the age of AI will be crucial to maintaining the IT industry and India's leading position as a global hub of technology and innovation.

Historically, the IT sector has played a crucial role in providing employment, contributing significantly to the nation's GDP, and transforming the economic landscape. As the industry continues to evolve, AI adoption and a focus on AI skilling and workforce development will be the key to sustaining its growth and competitive edge. The growth and prospects of India's IT industry underpin the nation's aspirations to become a global leader in AI and technology and accelerate inclusive development and progress for its people.

32.8   Urgent Need for AI Governance in India's AI Boom

India's enthusiastic embrace of AI presents a double-edged sword. While AI offers immense potential for growth and innovation, its rapid adoption raises serious concerns.

Here's a breakdown of the key risks and the need for robust AI governance:

- **Job displacement**: Automation powered by AI could lead to significant job losses in specific sectors.

- **Bias and discrimination**: AI algorithms inherit and amplify biases present in the data they're trained on, potentially leading to discriminatory outcomes.

- **Privacy concerns**: The vast amounts of data collection and analysis inherent to AI systems raise red flags for privacy and security.

To mitigate these risks and ensure responsible AI development, India needs effective AI governance frameworks. These frameworks should prioritize:

- **Transparency**: Demystifying AI systems is crucial. People need to understand how they work to make informed decisions about their use.

- **Accountability**: Clear lines of accountability must be established for the development, deployment, and potential harms caused by AI systems.

- **Ethical Considerations**: AI development and application must be guided by strong ethical principles that align with human values.

By establishing effective AI governance frameworks, India can harness the power of AI for positive change while minimizing potential pitfalls. This will ensure AI serves the greater good and fosters a future where both innovation and ethical considerations thrive.

32.9   The Way Forward for India in AI

The adoption of AI in the context of India might not be uniform or linear with respect to time but could build up at an accelerating pace in time intervals with periods of sluggishness in between. A slower start due to the substantial costs and investment associated with learning and deploying these technologies and then accelerated adaptation driven by the cumulative effect of improvement in complementary capabilities alongside process innovations with tangible benefits is predicted.

To achieve this goal, AI needs to be extensively introduced in all sectors ranging from agriculture, financial services, transportation, healthcare, energy, manufacturing, and logistics to create a vibrant AI economy. This must be adequately supported by the government financially and complimented by inducting awareness and skill among the masses on the benefits of AI adoption.

According to a survey done for the future of AI, it was found that AI will transform both organizations and industries in the near future. It will be a significant driver of national and global economic growth. This optimism is reflected in AI investments made to date and planned by respondents. The encouraging rates of return and shortening payback periods organizations are seeing on AI investments made so far are sustaining their optimism. About 86 percent respondents plan to increase their AI spend in the next fiscal year.

As the demand for AI professionals accelerates, most respondents (89 percent) said their organizations are experiencing skill gaps. About 28 percent of these respondents admit to experiencing an extreme or major skill gap, 44 percent report a moderate skill gap, and another 28 percent claim a minimal gap. The near universal skill deficit is forcing employers to compete fiercely to attract talent. The limited supply of new AI talent in the country means this competition will only become more intense in the foreseeable future. This will also mean employers will have to shell out oversized premiums for this coveted skill set.

India has a unique opportunity to apply the technology to solve some of its biggest problems such as shortage of healthcare facility, low quality of education, etc. It is not possible to meet the target of providing good healthcare or quality education using conventional methods. For instance, the number of doctors needed to provide good quality healthcare is so large that While the technology has potential to increase the economic growth rate considerably, it is likely to impact the job opportunity adversely. The challenge before any country is to make the best use of opportunity while dealing with the job loss issue, simultaneously.

It has suggested a way forward for India, which involves infrastructure development, policy & regulations, research & development, and human resource development. All the stakeholders need to come together to discuss on these issues. Government has a major role to play in infrastructure development, applications in public sector, policy & regulations, technology development and HRD. However, these can be successfully done with the support from industry. Though the report has brought out the major issues, it is necessary to institute some studies to collect the precise information for deciding the steps on infrastructure development, policy & regulations, and technology development, etc. It is also necessary to conduct a survey on the expected loss of jobs in various sectors so that appropriate policy could be framed. Such studies can provide the basis for policy responses from the government. Though it may be early to formulate new regulations, the existing regulations need to be reviewed and modified, if necessary.

India has a unique opportunity at this moment. Using the talent available within the country, it can repeat the success story of IT industry. At the same time, if necessary steps are not taken in time, it will lose the opportunity. AI can help in the major programmes of the Government viz. **Digital India, Make in India, and Skill India.** In order to accelerate development of AI technology and its applications, it is necessary to take steps for Applications & Infrastructure Development, Policy & Regulations, Research & Development and Human Resource Development.

It remains our collective responsibility to ensure trust in how AI is used in India and the benefits achieved thereof. The key to establishing this trust is by implementing adequate data security measures and the protection of personal data.

BIBLIOGRAPHY

Akki, Crypto. "Artificial Intelligence 2020: A Simple Guide To Understanding AI", Medium, Sep 18, 2021.

Andorno, Roberto and Andrea Lavazza. "How to deal with mind-reading technologies", Frontiers in Psychology, 14 November 2023. DOI 10.3389/fpsyg.2023.1290478.

Atkinson, William Walker Atkinson. "Practical Mind-Reading: Thought-Transference, Telepathy, Mental Currents, Mental Rapport, etc.", Advanced Thought Publishing Co., 1908.

Badillo, Solveig; et. al. "An Introduction to Machine Learning", Clinical Pharmacology & Therapeutics, Vol. 107, No. 4, April 2020, 871-885.

Bajema, Natasha. "Why Are Large AI Models Being Red Teamed? Intelligent systems demand more than just repurposed cybersecurity tools", IEEE Spectrum, 15 March, 2024.

Barnwell, Richard. "Artificial Intelligence: Opportunity, risk, and regulation in financial services", BDO, UK, 15 November 2023.

Bhavsar, Jwalant R. "Concepts of Extrasensory Potential Telepathy in the Literature of Pandit Shriram Sharma Acharya", Dev Sanskriti: Interdisciplinary International Journal, Volume 19, 23-33, 2022.

Butlin, Patrick, et.al. "Consciousness in Artificial Intelligence: Insights from the Science of Consciousness", August 2023, License CC BY-NC-SA 4.0.

Buttice, Claudio. "Mind Reading AI – The Final Nail in the Coffin of Privacy?", Techopedia, 10 January, 2024.

Constable, F. C. "Personality and Telepathy", Read Books, UK, 2019.

Domuschiev, Ivan. "The Science of Mind Reading", July 2023.: https://www.researchgate.net/publication/372386569.

Dudeja, Jai Paul. "Future is not separate from the present or the past: Can temporal nonlocality in Quantum Entanglement explain Retrocausality (effect preceding the cause), Precognition and Déjà vu?", Journal of Emerging Technologies and Innovative Research (JETIR, ISSN: 2349-5162, www.jetir.org), Vol. 6, Issue 5, May 2019, 304-311. http://doi.one/10.1729/Journal.20646

Dudeja, Jai Paul. "Quantum Brain, Mind, and Thinking", Bluerose Publishers, 2022.

Dudeja, Jai Paul. "Quantum Physics of Consciousness and Non-Duality in Eastern Philosophy", Bluerose Publishers, 2021.

Dudeja, Jai Paul. "Reiki: A Holistic Energy Healing Technique", Evincepub Publishing, 2023.

Dudeja, Jai Paul. "Spiritual Intelligence: Significance, Applications, Measurement and Development Techniques", Notionpress. com, 2024.

Grundke, Andrea; Jan-Philipp Stein; and Markus Appel. "Mind-Reading Machines: Distinct User Responses to Thought-Detecting and Emotion-Detecting Robots", Technology, Mind, and Behavior, Sep 10, 2021.

"India-AI-2023", Ministry of Electronics & Information Technology, Government of India, October 2023.

"India Skills Report-2024", Wheebox.

Janiesch, Christian; Patrick Zschech and Kai Heinrich. "Machine learning and deep learning", Electronic Markets https://doi. org/10.1007/s12525-021-00475-2.

Jenny. "The History of Artificial Intelligence: From Concept to Reality", Nov. 6, 2023.

Joseph, Ken C; et. al. "AI Risks and Compliance Strategies", Kroll, Jan. 31, 2024.

Kak, Subhash. "Artificial Intelligence (AI), Consciousness and the Self", International Journal on Eternal Wisdom and Contemporary Science Volume 1, Issue 1, June 2024, pp 89-97.

Kaminski, Margot, E. "Regulating the Risks of AI", Boston University Law Review, Vol. 103, 2023, 1347-1411.

Kulsari, S.P. "Artificial Intelligence & Ancient Indian Texts and Vedas -An Analysis", Medium, Sep 10, 2022.

LaFrance, Adrienne. "The 120-Year-Old Mind-Reading Machine", The Atlantic, June 16, 2014.

Laukkonen, Jeremy. "Can AI Really Read Your Mind?", Lifewire, June 6, 2024.

Marr, Bernard. "The 15 Biggest Risks Of Artificial Intelligence", Forbes, Innovation, Enterprise Tech, Jun 2, 2023.

Oravec, Jo Ann. "Artificial Intelligence Implications for Academic Cheating: Expanding the Dimensions of Responsible Human-AI Collaboration with ChatGPT and Bard", Journal of Interactive Learning Research (2023) 34(2), 213-237.

Rayhan, Abu. "Mind Reading Mastery: Unlocking the Most Successful Techniques of Thought Reading- Master the Power of Telepathy, Psychic Abilities, and Beyond", August 2023, https://www.researchgate.net/publication/373328432.

Roy, Mrinmoy. "An Exploratory Study On Origin Of AI: Journey Through The Ancient Indian Texts & Other Technological Descriptions, Its Past, Present & Future", Turkish Online Journal of Qualitative Inquiry (TOJQI) Volume 12, Issue 7, July 2021: 6527- 6555.

Solórzano, José, and Jonathan Moyer. "The Future of Artificial Intelligence", International Journal of Artificial Intelligence and Machine Learning, 2(1), January 2022, 1-37. https://doi.org/10.51483/IJAIML.2.1.2022.1-37.

Srivastava, Sunil Kumar. "Artificial Intelligence: Way Forward for India", Journal of Information Systems and Technology Management – (JISTEM) Vol. 15, 2018, e201815004 ISSN online: 1807-1775 DOI: 10.4301/S1807-1775201815004.

Tobin, James. "Artificial intelligence: Development, risks and regulation", UK Parliament,

House of Lords Library, In Focus, 18 July, 2023.

Woodford, James. "Mind-reading AI can translate brainwaves into written text", New Scientist, 12 December, 2023.